NĀGĀRJUNIAN DISPUTATIONS

''I only wish *I* had such eyes,'' the King remarked in a fretful tone. ''To be able to see Nobody! And at that distance too! Why, it's as much as *I* can do to see real people, by this light!''

Lewis Carroll, *Through the Looking-glass*

NĀGĀRJUNIAN DISPUTATIONS

A PHILOSOPHICAL JOURNEY THROUGH AN INDIAN LOOKING-GLASS

Thomas E. Wood

MONOGRAPH NO. 11

SOCIETY FOR ASIAN AND COMPARATIVE PHILOSOPHY
University of Hawaii Press
Honolulu

Printed in the United States of America

94 95 96 97 98 99 5 4 3 2 1

Library of Congress Cataloging-in-Publication Data

Wood, Thomas E., 1946–
Nāgārjunian disputations : a philosophical journey through an Indian looking-glass / Thomas E. Wood.
p. cm. — (Monographs of the Society for Asian and Comparative philosophy ; no. 11)
Includes bibliographical references and index.
Contents: Madhyamakakārikā — Vigrahavyāvartanī.
ISBN 0-8248-1609-9
1. Mādhyamika (Buddhism) 2. Nāgārjuna, 2nd cent. I. Nagārjuna, 2nd cent.. Madhyamakakārikā. 1994. II. Nāgārjuna, 2nd cent. Vigrahavyāvartanī. 1994. III. Title. IV. Series: Monograph . . . of the Society for Asian and Comparative philosophy ; no. 11.
BQ7410.W66 1994
294.3'92—dc20 93-35686
CIP

Camera-ready copy was prepared by the author.

University of Hawaii Press books are printed on acid-free paper and meet the guidelines for permanence and durability of the Council on Library Resources

The Society for Asian and Comparative Philosophy Monograph Series was started in 1974. Works are published in the series that deal with any area of Asian philosophy, or in any other field of philosophy examined from a comparative perspective. The aim of the series is to make available scholarly works that exceed article length, but may be too specialized for the general reading public, and to make these works available in inexpensive editions without sacrificing the orthography of non-Western languages.

CONTENTS

value for the latter program. **11.** Relevant negation as a purely inferential or deduction-theoretic notion, as opposed to a semantic one. **12.** Even though no contradiction can be true, relevant logic may be useful for the study of inferences in natural language.

Speech act theory and the catuṣkoṭi
13-14. B. K. Matilal's appeal to speech act theories in defense of the claim that one can refute a proposition P without thereby committing oneself to the assertion of not-P. **15-16.** This claim fails to distinguish between asserting not-P (i.e., denial) and declining to assert P (i.e., illocutionary denegation). Since there are many passages in the Buddhist literature that do not fit the purely illocutionary analysis, speech act theory does not provide a solution to the "consistency problem" of the catuṣkoṭi. **17.** Sceptical negations as not falling neatly into either propositional or illocutionary negation. Although the Mādhyamikas used sceptical arguments for their own purposes, the Madhayamaka is not scepticism.

The Mādhyamikas' use of the catuṣkoṭi and the Liar Paradox
18-19. B. K. Matilal's interpretation of śūnyatā as logical indeterminability. The statement "All things are empty" as meaning that all statements are false (NS). **20.** NS, the liar paradox, and the Buridan-Prior theory of self-reference. Matilal's appeal to the Buridan-Prior theory in defense of NS. **21.** The difference between saying that things could be as NS says they are and asserting that it could be the case that things actually are as NS says they are. **22.** On Matilal's interpretation, the catuṣkoṭi would be falsified by any pair of contradictory assertions.

The Vigraha-vyāvartanī (VV) on the emptiness of statements
23-24. The NI and the NNI tested against Nāgārjuna's Vigraha-vyāvartanī (VV). Evidence against a purely linguistic or metalinguistic interpretation of emptiness in VV 1, 20. **25-27.** Nāgārjuna's statement that he has no

proposition to assert (nāsti ca mama pratijñā) is only a special instance of his nihilism. His assertion that there are no statements to be found either within or without the totality of causes and conditions (VV 1, 21). The parallel with the anattā doctrine of canonical Buddhism. Dependent existence = lack of self-nature = unorigination (VV 22). The assignment of the doctrine of dependent co-origination (pratītya-samutpāda), according to which dharmas actually arise, to the level of conventional truth (vyavahāra-satya). **28.** The connection between the VV's nihilism and its critique of the pramāṇa theory. **29.** The opponent's contention that something must exist in order to be negated, and Nāgārjuna's reply to it. **30-31.** The role of appearance statements ("It seems to me that ...") in Mādhyamika thought. **32.** The Mādhyamika dialectic involves abandoning the correspondence theory of truth.

III. A CRITIQUE OF THE NNI (II) *Page 119*

D. Seyfort Ruegg's non-nihilist interpretation of the Madhyamaka

33. Ruegg's interpretation of the Mādhyamikas' use of the catuṣkoṭi in "The Four Positions of the Catuṣkoṭi and the Problem of the Description of Reality in Mahāyāna Buddhism" (FPC). A summary of the major tenets of the FPC. **34.** A summary of the objections to them. **35.** The Mādhyamika doctrine of illusion (māyā) is a nihilistic doctrine. According to the Mādhyamika conception of śūnyatā, the equation between dependent co-origination and emptiness must be provisional (neyārtha), not final (nītārtha). **36.** The propositions of the catuṣkoṭi are not semantically or logically vague. **37.** It is true that the Mādhyamikas did not believe in entities that posssessed the property of non-existence, but this is not the special point of examples like the son of a barren woman (vandhyā-putra). **38.** Theories of non-existence and negative facts in India and the West. **39.** The Mādhyamikas were opposed to such theories, but the fact that they opposed the Naiyāyika doctrine of negative entities (abhāva-padārtha) only shows that they were consistent nihilists. "There are non-entities" is not the contradictory of "There are entities." **40.** Hence the Mādhyamikas' use of the catuṣkoṭi does not involve contradiction. The importance of the distinction between contraries and contradictories. **41.** The catuṣkoṭi presents a consistency problem precisely because the negation that is used in it is the prasajya negation. **42.** Ruegg's views on the catuṣkoṭi compared with those of B. K. Matilal and J. F. Staal. **43.** Objections to interpreting the Mādhyamikas as having made contradictory assertions or denials. **44-47.** MMK(V) 18.8. The use of "neither...nor" and "not: neither...nor" statements in the Mādhyamika texts. **48.** The Law of the Excluded Middle (LEM). **49.** Ruegg's claim that Mādhyamika reasoning is based on the principles of non-contradiction and the excluded middle is inconsistent with his claim that at least some of their assertions were contradictory. **50.** Ruegg's interpretation of Bodhicaryāvatāra 9.35. The Mādhyamikas probably did accept the LEM, but BCA 9.35 is a statement of psychology, not of logic. **51.** According to Ruegg's interpretation, the Madhyamaka is a form of psychologism. **52.** The views of J. Kristeva and L. Mäll. Ruegg's interpretation of the Madhyamaka is anti-rationalist.

IV. A DEFENSE OF THE NI *Page 157*

1. The logic and semantics of the catuṣkoṭi under the NI. **2.** The Prajñā-pāramitā sūtras and the Mādhyamika texts support this interpretation. This is true even of those passages which have been cited by proponents of the NNI in support of their interpretation. Examples of such passages are the Hṛdaya-sūtra, MMK(V) 13.7; MMK(V) 25.7-8; MMK(V) 25.9; MMK(V) 25.19-20; and MMK(V) 24.18. **3.** The historical connection between the Prajñā-pāramitā sūtras and the Mādhyamika school. **4.** In the Prajñā-pāramitā, dharmas are as unreal and non-existent as the self (ātman) was said to be in the other orthodox Buddhist

PREFACE AND ACKNOWLEDGEMENTS

I am indebted to Eli Franco and anonymous reviewers for comments and criticisms on earlier versions of this work. Whatever errors remain are my own.

Although the Mādhyamika works I cite have all been translated previously, I have provided in the Appendix translations of the ones that I cite the most frequently—the Vigraha-vyāvartanī (VV) and MMK 1, MMK 13, MMK 15, MMK 24 and MMK 25—for the benefit of readers who are not already familiar with these texts. Such readers may find it useful to have the VV and whole chapters of the Mūla-madhyamaka-kārikās to consult, rather than merely the isolated verses (kārikās) that come up in the course of my own discussion of the texts.

I have tried to stay as close as possible to the texts, but have made some concessions in the interests of readability. As a result of this compromise, the translations are not literal. For example, I have included words and even short phrases that are not in the original Sanskrit when I have felt that these were required to convey clearly the meaning of what are often very laconic verses.

ABBREVIATIONS OF SANSKRIT, PĀLI AND CHINESE TEXTS

AK(Bh)(SAV) = Abhidharma-kośa-(bhāṣya)-(sphuṭārthā vyākhyā)
AN = Aṅguttara-nikāya
ĀŚ = Āgama-śāstra
AŚP = Alāta-śānti-prakaraṇa
Aṣṭa. = Aṣṭa-sāhasrikā-prajñā-pāramitā-sūtra
AVGS = Aggi-vacchagotta-sutta
BĀU = Bṛhad-āraṇyaka Upaniṣad
BBh = Bodhisattva-bhūmi
BCA(P) = Bodhi-caryāvatāra-(pañjikā)
BSBh = Brahma-sūtra-bhāṣya (Śaṅkara)
Chānd. = Chāndogya Upaniṣad
ChWSL = Cheng wei shilun
GK = Gauḍapādīya-kārikās
Laṅk. = Sad-dharma-laṅkāvatāra-sūtra
MA(Bh) = Madhyamakāvatāra-(bhāṣya)
MAV = Madhyānta-vibhāga
MMK(V) = Mūla-madhyamaka-kārikā-(vṛtti)
MN = Majjhima-nikāya
MSA = Mahāyāna-sūtrālaṅkāra
MV = Mahā-vastu
NB = Nyāya-bindu
NS = Nyāya-sūtra
NVTṬ = Nyāya-vārttika-tātparya-ṭīkā
PVBh = Pramāṇa-vārttika-bhāṣya (Prajñākaragupta)
Sapta. = Sapta-śatikā-prajñā-pāramitā-sūtra
Śata. = Śata-sāhasrikā-prajñā-pāramitā-sūtra
Śikṣ. = Śikṣā-samuccaya
SN = Saṃyutta-nikāya
SSS = Sarva-siddhānta-saṅgraha
Tait. = Taittirīya Upaniṣad
Viṃś(V) = Viṃśatikā-(vṛtti)
VV(V) = Vigraha-vyāvartanī-(vṛtti)

ABBREVIATIONS OF CONTEMPORARY WORKS

AB75 = See Anderson, A. R. & N. D. Belnap, Jr. (1975).
BI = Buddhist irrationalism. See Staal (1975), ch. 2.
Bur. = Some problems of self-reference in John Buridan. See Prior (1976).
CBN = Conception of Buddhist nirvāṇa. See Stcherbatsky (1977).
CMP = Critique of the Mādhyamika position. See Matilal (1973).
CPhB = Central philosophy of Buddhism. See Murti (1955).
EBThK = Early Buddhist theory of knowledge. See Jayatilleke (1963).
Ep. = Epimenides the Cretan. See Prior (1976).
FIL = Foundations of illocutionary logic. See Searle & Vanderveken (1985).
FPC = Four positions of the catuṣkoṭi. See Ruegg (1977).
LI = Logical illumination. See Matilal (1977).
M79 = See Meyer, R. K. (1979).
MM86 = See Meyer, R. K. & E. P. Martin (1986).
MR73 = See Meyer, R.K. & R. Routley (1973).
NMD = Negation and the Mādhyamika dialectic. See Matilal (1971), ch. 5.
Perc. = Perception. See Matilal (1986).
RM73 = See Routley, R. & R. K. Meyer (1973).
RR72 = See Routley, R. & V. (1972).

NĀGĀRJUNIAN DISPUTATIONS

I: Introduction

1. For over fifteen hundred years, the prevailing view of the Mādhyamikas in India has been that they were absolute nihilists. According to the Mīmāṃsakas, the Vedāntins, the Naiyāyikas, the Jainas and even their fellow-Mahāyānists, the Vijñānavādins, the Mādhyamikas denied the reality of both nirvāṇa and saṃsāra.

In the first part of this century, St. Schayer (1931) and Th. Stcherbatsky (1927) rejected the nihilist interpretation of the Mādhyamikas, but at that time theirs was very much the minority view. It was not until the middle 1950s—about the time of T. R. V. Murti's influential book, *The Central Philosophy of Buddhism*—that non-nihilist interpretations of the Madhyamaka clearly became the dominant force in Mādhyamika studies.

Until that time, the prevailing view of Western scholarship had been represented by scholars like E. Burnouf, H. Jacobi, M. Walleser, I. Wach, A. B. Keith and L. de La Vallée Poussin. According to these scholars, the Madhyamaka was nihilism, pure and simple. Burnouf (1844: 560), the first Western scholar to publish translations and interpretations of the Mādhyamika writings, described the Madhyamaka as a "nihilisme scholastique." H. Jacobi saw the Madhyamaka as holding that "all our ideas are based upon a non-entity or upon the void." M. Walleser described it as "a negativism which radically empties existence up to the last consequences of negation," and as a philosophy of "absolute nothingness"; whereas there is a counterpart to the negations of the Vedānta, there is none in the Madhyamaka: negation in the latter is the "exclusive ultimate end" (Selbstzweck). I. Wach held that the Mādhyamikas were the most radical nihilists that ever lived. L. de La Vallée Poussin—"still the unsurpassed master of Buddhist studies," as Chr. Lindtner (1982: 7) has recently described him—saw the Mādhyamikas as describing things from two points of view, and therefore as "hesitating between two positions." From the point of view of worldly or relative reality, or the truth of experience, all things are empty (śūnya) because no substantial reality—no "being in itself"—can be attributed to them. However, from the point of view of reality or truth (tattva, paramārtha-satya), where one criticizes experience itself, one arrives at the conclusion that all those things that are said to be caused are not caused at all. One cannot attribute any manner of being to them whatever. Causal production is in fact a non-production, and even the so-called relativity does not exist. According to Poussin, therefore, the Mādhyamika analysis ultimately destroys the notion of causality just as effectively as it destroys all ideas of experience and religion. Not only do the dharmas of Buddhist philosophy not exist substantially: they do not exist at all, either in reality or appearance. "They are like the daughter of a barren woman, like the beauty of the daughter of a barren woman: this beauty evidently does not exist except in so far as it may be described; but, in reality, the object described, the description, and the person describing are all similarly non-existent."[1]

2. The present work is a defense of the earlier, nihilist interpretation (NI) of the Madhyamaka against some of the leading non-nihilist interpretations (NNI) that have arisen to challenge it in recent times. This defense is conducted on two fronts. First, as a purely exegetical matter, it will be argued that the NI fits the Mādhyamika writings better than the NNI. Second, it will be argued that the NNIs are not, as they are often claimed to be, more defensible on philosophical grounds.

Proponents of the NNI have often claimed, implicitly or explicitly, that the nihilist position is philosophically untenable and even manifestly foolish or absurd, and that it is therefore preposterous to suppose that the Mādhyamikas actually held it. I shall be arguing, however, that the NI is no more difficult to defend philosophically than the NNI, although in the case of the NI the problems are epistemological, whereas in the case of the NNI, they are primarily logical.

3. The dispute between the proponents of the NI and the NNI may seem complex, but this appearance is somewhat deceptive, for all the disputes basically come down to a disagreement over how the Mahāyānist conception of "śūnyatā" (emptiness, voidness) is to be interpreted.

According to the NI, the Mādhyamika doctrine that all dharmas are void (sarva-dharma-śūnyatā) is the logical culmination of the attack undertaken by early Buddhism against the doctrine of the self (P. attā; Skr. ātman). The arguments that were developed in early Buddhism against the ātman doctrine were of a quite general nature. For example, it was said that a self or ego would have to be unchanging; and it was held to be untenable (even absurd) to maintain that someone could remain the same from birth to death, since the mental and physical properties of a person undergo change all the time. This criticism is closely related to very general objections to the distinction between substances and properties—a distinction which has of course been attacked in the Western philosophical tradition by Hume and many others.

Early Buddhism analyzed a person reductively into five sets or heaps (skandhas) of constituent mental and physical elements called dharmas. A Hīnayānist text of the classical period called the Milinda-pañha employs the useful example of a chariot to explain this anattā/dhamma doctrine. Just as, it is said, it would be an error to think of a chariot as an entity apart from its constituent parts like the axle, the hub, the wheel etc., so it is an error to think that there is an entity or substance apart from the constituent elements of form, feeling, perception, impulses and consciousness. The ever-changing stream of constituent physical and psychophysical elements or dharmas is real, but the self is unreal.

Although the early Buddhist critique of the ātman doctrine appears to have been based on considerations which apply to the substance/property distinction generally, the attack on the ātman doctrine in *early* Buddhism appears to have been a rather limited one. Some of the early texts speak of all things (dharmas) as being empty or void (śūnya), but such passages in the early texts specify that all dharmas are empty (suñña) in the sense that they are devoid of a self (attā). (Cf. SN iv.54.) Thus, the doctrine of voidness (suññatā) in early Buddhism does not appear to have gone much beyond the anattā doctrine.

In the Mahāyāna, the same kinds of arguments that had been directed in early Buddhism against the ātman doctrine were directed against the dharmas themselves, i.e., against the postulated ultimate constituent elements of a personality. The earliest Mahāyāna sūtras, the Prajñā-pāramitā, assert that the dharmas are just as unreal or non-existent as the self had been declared to be in canonical Buddhism. Prima facie, then, the Mahāyāna doctrine that all dharmas are empty is simply a generalization of the Hīnayāna doctrine that the self is empty. Although both are in a sense nihilistic doctrines, there is an important difference between them, for the Hīnayāna is only a nihilistic doctrine with respect to the *self.* The Mahāyāna is more radical, because it denies the existence of both self and dharmas. This, in brief, is the nihilist interpretation (NI) of the Mahāyāna in general, and of the Madhyamaka in particular.

Although there is disagreement on points of detail, all the non-nihilist interpretations of the Madhyamaka reject this reading of the Mahāyāna doctrine of voidness. According to the NNI, "śūnya" in the Madhyamaka means, not empty or void per se, but indeterminate or "beyond all logical categories or linguistic description." Closely connected with this interpetation of the Mādhyamikas' use of the term "śūnya" is what might be called a linguistic turn in the analysis of the Madhyamaka. According to the NNI, the Mahāyānist critique of the dharma theory of the Hīnayāna was not intended to show that the dharmas were non-existent, but only that the dharma theory did not adequately express the way things really are. In other words, according to the NNI, it is not really entities (dharmas) that are void, but rather *theories* of dharmas that are void.

Both interpretations are in agreement that the Mādhyamikas believed that all putative entities, whether conditioned or unconditioned, saṃsāric or nirvāṇic, phenomenal or absolute, fail to withstand logical investigation. The difference between the interpretations lies in the conclusions that are drawn from this point of common agreement. According to the NNI, to say that an entity is logically indeterminable does not mean (or does not necessarily mean) that the entity in question is unreal or non-existent. According to the NI, a logically indeterminable object (i.e. a logically impossible one) is necessarily non-existent.

This is one of the points where the controversy between the NI and the NNI takes on a general philosophical interest that transcends purely historical concerns or the minutiae of what might be called Buddhist dogmatics. At issue is the old and very important question whether the fundamental laws of logic determine the bounds of sense. Any *non*-nihilistic attempt to interpret the Mādhyamika texts, I shall argue, is likely to lead to some violation of the rules of logic. I believe that this is a decisive point for interpreting the Mādhyamikas. Thus, I shall be arguing a) that nothing—not even an Absolute, if there is such a thing—can violate these fundamental logical laws, and b) that there is no evidence that the Mādhyamikas thought that these logical laws could be violated. If nothing withstands logical investigation, then what one must conclude is that nothing exists (sarvaṃ sarveṇa nāsti). According to the NI, this is what the Mādhyamikas did conclude.

4. Although scepticism is not an end in itself in Mādhyamika thought, it does have an important role to play there. What the Mādhyamikas did, essentially, was to join their arguments against substances and causality with a tradition of scepticism which was well-developed in India even before the time of the Buddha. Later, epistemological issues became the storm center of the controversies between the Mādhyamikas and the other schools. The metaphysical and ontological disputes over the notions of substance and causality never ceased to be important, of course, but these disputes were one-sided, because the onus was always on the non-Mādhyamika philosophers to present a philosophical doctrine of substances and causality that could withstand the Mādhyamikas' attacks. In the ontological and metaphysical disputes, therefore, the Mādhyamikas were always on the offense, their opponents always on the defense. The Mādhyamikas did not have the same advantage on the epistemological front, for here their opponents were in a position to argue that the *Mādhyamika* view was incoherent. The epistemological controversies that took place between the Mādhyamikas and their opponents were justly celebrated, and remain to this day among the most vivid and interesting in the entire history of Indian philosophy.

These epistemological issues emerged in their sharpest form in the disputes between the Mādhyamikas and their idealist opponents, the Vijñānavādins. The Mādhyamikas agreed with the idealists (at least at the absolute or pāramārthika level) that philosophical proofs of the reality of an external world fail to withstand examination. So far, this is just standard idealist doctrine. Nevertheless, it is misleading to think of the Mādhyamikas as idealists. They were *nihilists,* who maintained that nihilism is what pure phenomenology becomes when it is made absolutely consistent.

S. N. Dasgupta once called the Mādhyamika philosophy a nihilistic idealism.[2] This seems to me to be an accurate and illuminating characterization of it, but one that needs to be approached with some care. According to the prevailing interpretation (especially in the West), idealism is the philosophical view that everything is mind—i.e., either a mind (or minds), or things whose sole existence is to be perceived by minds. According to this standard definition, the Mādhyamikas could not have been idealists, for the Mādhyamikas did not believe in the existence of mind any more than they believed in the existence of matter (or anything else). If idealism is understood as the *ontological* view that mind and only mind exists, then Dasgupta's characterization of the Madhyamaka as a nihilistic idealism is a contradiction in terms. The Mādhyamikas, however, attempted to develop a *non-ontological* version of idealism, and their efforts in this direction are of considerable philosophical interest.

5. According to common sense, when we are in our ordinary state of waking consciousness we are in perceptual contact with a world of solid, substantial objects whose existence does not depend on their being perceived. Idealists of all persuasions deny this fundamental proposition of common sense, but idealists have had different ideas about just what what it was that they were doing when they did deny it. Some idealists have defended their views as being nothing more than the correct philosophical account of the solid world of our ordinary experience. (George Berkeley is a good example of this.) But a different interpretation holds that idealism really does deny that reality has the kind of hard, solid, substantial character which common sense instinctively believes. Idealists of the latter sort have wanted to stress how *unsubstantial* reality is on the idealist view. This tendency has been much more pronounced in India than in the West. There are exceptions to the rule (e.g., the idealism of the classic or Upaniṣadic idealism, or the Āgamic school of Kāśmīra Śaivism), but for the most part the Indian idealists emphasized the unsubstantiality of the world under the idealist interpretation. The Vijñānavādins and the Mādhyamikas held different positions on this end of the philosophical spectrum. The Vijñānavādins advocated an *ontological* version of idealism, and thereby stopped short of a position of complete nihilism. The Mādhyamikas were much more radical—and, they argued, much more consistent—in advocating a *non-ontological,* nihilist version of idealism.

There are Mahāyāna sūtras, like the Daśa-bhūmika, which assert that everything is mind-only (cittamātram idaṃ yad idaṃ traidhātukam), and even the Mādhyamikas themselves seem, at first sight, to have been implicated in some version of the mind-only doctrine by their own statements. [Cf. MMK 7.34, 17.33 and 23.8-9, where Nāgārjuna compares all the dharmas to a dream, an hallucination, an illusory city in the sky (gandharva-nagara) etc.] But there was controversy over the interpretation of such statements. According to the Mādhyamikas, such descriptions have no ontological implications, whereas according to the Vijñānavādins, they do. This disagreement entails two very different interpretations of the Mahāyāna doctrine that all dharmas are void (sarva-dharma-śūnyatā). According to the Mādhyamikas, the doctrine of universal voidness means that mind and matter are entirely unreal and non-existent. The Vijñānavādins rejected this interpretation of the doctrine, called it nihilism (which it clearly was), and interpreted the doctrine to mean that dharmas are devoid of the reality that the ordinary, deluded person *thinks* that they have. The ordinary, deluded person thinks that appearances (ābhāsa) or perceptions (vijñapti) are *of* something that exists apart from those appearances and perceptions. This doctrine of duality the Vijñānavādins denied. According to them, perceptions are non-dual, i.e. of themselves alone.[3] To say that all dharmas are void is to say that they have no existence outside the mind, like dreams and hallucinations, and not (as the Mādhyamikas claimed) that they have no existence even as mental phenomena or as *percepts*. The Vijñānavādin interpretation of emptiness (śūnyatā) was therefore a doctrine of other emptiness, for it held that minds and percepts are not śūnya (empty, void) in themselves. They are only void with respect to something else, i.e. material objects.

6. The other philosophers of India criticized the Mādhyamika nihilism even more severely than the ontological idealism of the Vijñānavāda. Vācaspati Miśra's judgement was probably typical: the Mādhyamikas, he declared, were fools (devānām-priya).[4] The attitude of the other Indian philosophers toward the Mādhyamikas seems to have been at least partially responsible for the hostility with which the NI is regarded by most modern-day interpreters. Today it seems to be taken for granted that to impute nihilism to the Mādhyamikas is to take them to have been fools. Consequently, the NNI is often presented by its proponents as a sympathetic interpretation of the Madhyamaka, and the NI as an unsympathetic one. But here, surely, the question of which interpretation is the more sympathetic one depends very much on what the available textual and historical evidence tells us about what the Mādhyamikas actually believed. If the evidence indicates that the Mādhyamikas were in fact nihilists, then the only way that one could defend the Mādhyamikas as philosophers would be to make a case for nihilism. In view of all the available historical and textual evidence, it seems to me that the advocates of the NNI have done a considerable disservice to the Mādhyamikas by simply conceding to their critics in advance that only a fool could be a nihilist. A case of sorts *can* be made for the nihilist position. It may not in the final analysis prove to be a defensible position, but that does not necessarily mean that the Mādhyamikas were fools to have advocated it.

The Mādhyamikas held that it is a mistake to try to impose a metaphysics or ontology on our descriptions of what we call our "experiences" (anubhava). We describe these by means of statements of the form "It seems that.." or "It appears that...". These do not permit us to infer that there is either mind or matter. Once the nature of empirical knowledge is correctly understood, the Mādhyamikas said, it can be seen that cognitions are appearances and *nothing but appearances*. There is nothing behind them, material or mental. They are not *of* anything, nor do they exist in anything or consist of anything. Even to call them appearances implies an ontological status for them, and this is misleading, because by their very nature they are false (mṛṣā) and non-existent (asat). Appearances are nothing but a pure void (śūnyam).

To the opponent, this claim was absurd. How, the Vācaspati Miśras of India exclaimed, could even *cognitions* be non-existent? If cognitions are also unreal, these philosophers asked, how could there be experience at all? How could it possibly be the case that *nothing* exists?

What the critic took to be nonsense the nihilist took to be self-evident. What the realist and even the idealist took to be self-evident the nihilist took to be quite unfounded—even absurd. The nihilist simply replied to his idealist opponent as follows:

> Where did you get this obsession that something has to *exist*? It is understandable why the materialist or dualist would wish to maintain that things exist, but it is absurd for you as an idealist to maintain that they do.
>
> You believe that an analysis of cognitions and their related judgements shows that nothing exists outside of or apart from consciousness. Although it is true, at least from the level of absolute truth (pāramārthika), that external objects do not exist, you have failed to note that to exist is to exist *objectively*, so mind cannot be real either. It is absurd to suggest that something can exist but not be seen or otherwise perceived (na vidyate, na dṛśyate). This violates what we mean by "existence."

You say that mind exists, but what are your grounds (pramāṇa) for asserting this? Has anyone ever *seen* one of the percepts that you are constantly talking about? Indeed not: only something objective, like a pot or a cow, *could* be seen. By your own admission, mind and cognitions cannot be seen, so you cannot base your existence-claim on perception.

If you say that one knows that cognitions exist because cognitions are grasped by other cognitions, the question then becomes: "How do you know that cognitions are grasped by other cognitions?" If at this point you appeal to other cognitions, you fall into an infinite regress (anavasthā). If you reply that such a regress does not occur because cognitions are self-cognizing, this too will not do. How could it be so? Can a knife cut itself or a fire burn itself? If you cannot cite anything in our objective experience with the peculiar property of acting on itself, what grounds do you have for asserting that something that we never *could* experience has this unthinkable property?

To be a consistent idealist, you must give up the notion of existence altogether. For what is it to *exist*? If you analyze this matter psychologically and philosophically, you will see that this notion of existence is inseparable from peoples' deluded notions of solid, enduring, substantial material objects existing apart from and independent of consciousness. As an idealist, you have seen that this view is nonsense, but you have not yet seen that it is absurd to continue to hold to the idea of *existence* after the notion of duality has been abandoned. Without duality, existence is a meaningless notion. The ordinary people (pṛthag-janāḥ) are deluded because they think that there are real material objects which we see, touch, hear, smell etc. But you—half-hearted and hesitant idealist that you are—have done something even more absurd. You have taken the concept of existence, which *might* be appropriately applied to an external, objective entity (if there were such a thing), and imposed this concept on the so-called cognitions themselves, and gone on philosophizing about real minds and existent cognitions. How confused can you get?

7. The controversy in India between the Mādhyamikas and their opponents led to a kind of stalemate. The school that was the least prepared to concede anything to them, the Nyāya-Vaiśeṣika, adhered to a view of what might be called extreme or naive realism. The Nyāya-Vaiśeṣikas attempted, with great ingenuity, to construct a metaphysical and ontological system that would justify common sense in the face of the Mādhyamikas' onslaught against it. Their attempts in this direction remain one of India's great contributions to philosophy, but the Mādhyamikas remained unmoved by them.

The outcome of the controversy between the Mādhyamikas and their idealist opponents in India was also inconclusive, and in some respects even less satisfying. The Vijñānavādins continued to maintain that cognitions are self-cognizing; the Vedāntins continued to maintain that the *self* (ātman) is self-cognizing; and the Mādhyamikas continued to deny both claims. Neither the Vijñānavādins nor the Advaitins seem to have made a direct assault on the Mādhyamika claim that the notion of existence becomes invalid as soon as duality (dvayatva) is denied, and that nihilistic idealism or non-ontological idealism is therefore the only consistent form of idealism.

Although I do not believe that the Mādhyamika arguments have demonstrated the impossibility of ontology and metaphysics, the Mādhyamikas may have succeeded in putting the burden of proof on the opponent to provide one. If so, the opponent must do one of two things, neither of which has been accomplished to date, and conceivably might never be accomplished.

First, the opponent of the Mādhyamikas might try to show that some version of materialism or dualism is true. Since the Madhyamaka is essentially a non-ontological or nihilistic idealism, idealist presuppositions are at the bottom of all of the

Mādhyamikas' attacks on other systems (at least at the pāramārthika level). If idealism is to be ruled out as a philosophical alternative, then some version of materialism or dualism must be established. Either 1) eliminative materialism must be shown to be tenable (i.e., mind and mental phenomena must be shown to be unreal and non-existent, like phlogiston or demons), whereas matter is not; or 2) it must be shown that matter is in some way the basis of mind, which has no existence apart from it (epiphenomenalism, non-reductive materialism), or 3) mind and matter must be shown to exist independently of each other, in which case it must also be explained how they interact (if indeed they do).

Second, the opponent of the Mādhyamikas might try to show that ontological *idealism* is true, i.e., that *only* mind and mental phenomena actually exist. Here the problem lies in showing how mind can be said to exist if it can never be perceived objectively. Since idealists have typically argued that imperceptibility is as much a part of the essence of the mind as the ability of the mind to perceive *other* things, it might be unreasonable to expect the idealist to establish the existence of mind on the basis of *perception.* But then the Mādhyamika is in a position to argue that the idealist must provide some *other* grounds for believing in the existence of mind.

The ontological idealist faces the problem of solipsism as well. If solipsism is to be rejected, then one must show how and why it is that the world does not disappear when one goes to sleep and how and why it is that there are (at least apparently) other minds than one's own. This would entail providing a theology or cosmology of idealism; but to date we have no viable philosophical or scientific theory of consciousness whatever, much less a theology or cosmology that is based on this notion.

The Mādhyamika is convinced that none of these projects will ever be accomplished, just as the circle will never be squared and the triangle will never be trisected. Anyone who believes that it must be possible to meet the Mādhyamika's challenge in one of the above ways has, in effect, not been convinced by the Mādhyamikas' point of view. It natural to feel, perhaps, as the present author does, that there *must* be something wrong with the

Mādhyamika dialectic, for it leads to a nihilistic conclusion that seems unacceptable. But it is one thing to dismiss the Madhyamaka, and quite another to mount a defense against it. The Mādhyamikas were interesting philosophers, and their arguments should be taken seriously. They were, perhaps, the most radical philosophers that have ever lived, but it was precisely for this reason that they made such an important and unique contribution to Indian philosophy. If nothing else, the Mādhyamikas continue to have an enduring value in philosophy because they challenge us to "modify, clarify, and reorganize our philosophical theories" (NMD 167). Few philosophers in the history of the world have done this as brilliantly or as effectively as the Mādhyamikas.

1. According to the NI, the Mādhyamikas did not believe in an Absolute—indeed, did not believe in the existence of anything whatever. According to most versions of the NNI, the Mādhyamikas did believe in an Absolute, which they took to be ineffable and logically indeterminable.

A related controversy has arisen over the interpretation of the early Buddhist teachings. Typically, the early texts represent the Buddha as having given negative responses to all four presented alternatives to certain questions. (There are also instances where only two alternatives are involved, and even some passages which leave the four alternatives unnegated, but the latter are very rare.) At a later point in time, the four alternatives (or their negations) were called the catuṣkoṭi. The negative form of the catuṣkoṭi, which is the standard one, has the following form:

(a) It is not the case that x is ϕ.
(b) It is not the case that x is not-ϕ.
(c) It is not the case that x is both ϕ and not-ϕ.
(d) It is not the case that x is neither ϕ nor not-ϕ.

The catuṣkoṭi is undoubtedly based on the following set of ten theses which the Buddha did not explain but simply set aside when questioned about them:

1. The world is eternal (sassato loko).
2. The world is not eternal (assasato loko).
3. The world is finite (antavā loko).
4. The world is infinite (anantavā loko).
5. The soul and the body are the same (taṃ jīvaṃ taṃ sarīraṃ).
6. The soul and the body are different (aññaṃ jīvaṃ aññaṃ sarīraṃ).
7. The Tathāgata (i.e., the Buddha) exists after death (hoti tathāgato param maraṇā).

8. The Tathāgata does not exist after death (na hoti tathāgato param maraṇā).
9. The Tathāgata does and does not exist after death (hoti ca na ca hoti tathāgato param maraṇā).
10. The Tathāgata neither does nor does not exist after death (n'eva hoti na na hoti tathāgato param maraṇā).[1]

The proponents of the NNI take the catuṣkoṭi to be fundamental to the Buddhist teachings—perhaps even as its most important and distinctive feature. They interpret it to mean that reality is in some sense logically indeterminable, and hence that no statement about the true nature of things (tattva, dharmatā) is really true. Hence the highest teaching of the Buddha is, paradoxically, a non-teaching, i.e., a dharma of silence, and as such a rejection (at least from the highest or pāramārthika point of view) of all the logical alternatives or possibilities to a given question.

In this and in succeeding chapters I shall argue for a very different approach to the catuṣkoṭi.

First, I shall argue that the claim that one can reject all the logical alternatives to a given question is untenable and in fact incoherent.

Second, I shall argue that no Buddhist school—including the Madhyamaka—maintained that it was possible to reject, negate or deny all the logical alternatives to a given question.

Third, I shall argue that the catuṣkoṭi, although it is a fairly prominent aspect of the Buddha's teachings, is not the most fundamental one. This is what one might expect on a priori grounds. If one wished to ascertain someone's views about a range of alternatives on a given question, and one's interlocutor gave consistently negative replies to all of them, as the Buddha is said to have done, one would naturally assume that one had not yet hit on what he *did* believe. It seems to me that the situation is essentially the same in the case of the Buddha, who rejected or negated all the standard alternatives to various religious and philosophical questions that were presented to him by his interlocutors. In the case of the Buddha, the correct answer to the questions lies outside the possibilities that the questioner has offered, and may conceivably lie outside the possibilities that the interlocutor is willing to *consider,* but that does not mean that the *Buddha* thought that reality was logically indeterminable.

2. Interpreting the catuṣkoṭi involves answering the following three questions. First, what does it mean that the Buddha set aside these questions? For example, does it mean that the Buddha denied them or negated them outright? Second, were (1)-(2), (3)-(4), (5)-(6) and (7)-(10) taken by the Buddha to be exhaustive of all the possible alternatives for each of the questions? Third, if the Buddha negated or rejected each of the possible alternatives, did he contradict himself in doing so?

K. N. Jayatilleke's *Early Buddhist Theory of Knowledge* (EBThK), which was published in 1963, remains the most important and impressive attempt to address these questions within the context of the Pāli canon. Since Jayatilleke's work represents a non-nihilist interpretation of the catuṣkoṭi, and one that seems to have had some influence on the non-nihilist interpretation of the Madhyamaka, it will be useful to consider his work in some detail.

3. According to the Pāli texts, the ten aforementioned questions were treated as "avyākata" and "ṭhapanīya" questions by the Buddha. The terms "avyākata" and "ṭhapanīya" are usually translated (as for example by I. B. Horner in her PTS translations) as "unanswered" and "ignored," respectively. (An equivalent translation of the term "ṭhapanīya," which has also been used, is "set aside.") With some minor qualifications, Jayatilleke accepts these translations.

Given the literal meaning of the terms "avyākata" (unanswered) and "ṭhapanīya" (set aside, ignored), it is not at all obvious that the Buddha actually denied or negated the ten questions, for one does not necessarily negate or deny a proposition when one chooses to leave it unanswered, ignores it, or sets it aside. Jayatilleke considers at some length the possibility that the avyākata questions are not actually denied or negated by the Buddha, but he eventually reaches the conclusion (correctly, I think) that this possibility must be rejected (EBThK §599-605; §810-817).[2, 3] Jayatilleke called this view the pragmatist view. It might also be called the purely soteriological view. Since the catuṣkoṭi is often presented by the texts in a soteriological context, there is some support for this interpretation in the canon.

A good example of this is the Cūḷa-māluṅkya-sutta (MN i.426-432). According to this sutta, the Buddhist monk Māluṅkyaputta became displeased one day that the Tathāgata had not explained, had set aside and had ignored the ten avyākata questions. Māluṅkyaputta went to the Buddha, and told him that if he did not explain to him whether the world was eternal etc. he would disavow the training for a monk (bhikku) and revert to secular life. The Buddha pointed out to Māluṅkyaputta that he had never told him (or any other monk) that he would explain whether the world was eternal etc. if he took up the religious life under his direction. The Buddha compared the person who seeks an answer to these questions to a man who has been pierced with a poisoned arrow. It would be quite unreasonable for such a person to insist on ascertaining the caste, name, or place of origin of the person who had shot him with the arrow, or the kind of bow that was used, or the kind of tree from which the bow and arrow were made etc. Then the Buddha says:

> The living of the Brahma-faring, Māluṅkyaputta, could not be said to depend on the view that the world is eternal. Nor could the living of the Brahma-faring, Māluṅkyaputta, be said to depend on the view that the world is not eternal. Whether there is the view that the world is eternal or whether there is the view that the world is not eternal, there is birth, there is ageing, there is dying, there are grief, sorrow, suffering, lamentation and despair, the suppression of which I lay down here and now. [Similarly for the other ten views.]

The Buddha says that he has not explained these views because they are "not connected with the goal, are not fundamental to the Brahma-faring, and do not conduce to turning away from, nor to dispassion, stopping, calming, super-knowledge, awakening nor to nibbāna." On the other hand, the

Buddha says, he *has* explained certain other things, i.e., "This is suffering," "This is the origin of suffering," "This is the course leading to the cessation of suffering," and "This is the cessation of suffering," and he has done so because these things are "connected with the goal, are fundamental to Brahma-faring" etc.

If this sutta's purely pragmatic or purely soteriological reasons for setting aside and ignoring the ten views were the only reasons given in the canon for setting aside or ignoring them, what many have regarded as an inconsistency problem would not even arise. This would be true even if one *were* to take the positions of the catuṣkoṭi as describing mutually exhaustive and exclusive logical alternatives, for one can set aside or ignore a proposition for purely soteriological or pragmatic reasons without in any way implying that that proposition is false. Pragmatic and soteriological reasons, in short, are orthogonal to reasons that touch the truth or falsity (or meaninglessness) of propositions, and therefore would not ordinarily raise problems of logical consistency at all.

Though the purely pragmatist interpretation of the catuṣkoṭi is an attractive one for this reason, Jayatilleke points out (EBThK §814) that it cannot be a sufficient explanation for the catuṣkoṭi because *other* reasons are given for setting aside, not explaining and ignoring the ten views which cannot be made to fit this interpretation.

An interesting example of this is SN ii.61, which says that living the religious life would be impossible if the soul were identical with the body, and that the religious life would also be impossible if the soul were not identical with the body. As Jayatilleke points out, "this implies that the theses 'the soul is the same as the body' and 'the soul is different from the body' were both in a sense known to be false" (EBThK §814). Since it was surely taken as a given in the Saṃyutta-nikāya that living the religious life was possible (the sutta was, after all, written by and largely for monks), the passage in question is an argument of the following form:

(1) If the soul were identical with the body, the living of the religious life would not be possible. The same is true if the soul were not identical with the body.
(2) But living the religious life is possible.
(3) Therefore the soul cannot be identical with the body or different from it.

The purely pragmatic interpetation finesses the whole question of the logical consistency of the catuṣkoṭi, because according to that interpretation one need not suppose that *any* of the alternatives in question were held to be false, or even neither true nor false. But since there are passages in the canon like SN ii.61, which do assert or imply that the ten views are false, the pragmatic interpretation cannot be the whole explanation of the catuṣkoṭi.

Another difficulty with the purely pragmatic or soteriological interpretation of the catuṣkoṭi is that there are passages in the canon which suggest that the ten views were set aside, ignored, and not explained on the grounds that they were only *partial* truths. Udāna 68-69 is an interesting example of this. In this passage, the Buddha uses the well-known parable of the blind men and the elephant to explain why he eschews the conflicting views of the samaṇas and brāhmaṇas of his day. A number of blind men are asked to feel an elephant, but are not told what it is. Later the men give very different accounts of what the object is, each of which is valid from one particular viewpoint. The Buddha compares these conflicting accounts by the blind men to the ten avyākata theses that were held by various recluses (samaṇas) and brāhmaṇas. The samanas and brāhmaṇas who hold these views, the Buddha says, get caught up in pernicious wranglings and controversies that are not only irrelevant to the spiritual life, but even quite antithetical to it. This attitude towards the debated philosophical positions of the day, which is reminiscent of the Jaina syādvāda, is found in other places in the Pāli canon as well (e.g. the Aggi-vacchagotta-sutta). Such passages provide further evidence against the adequacy of the pragmatist interpretation. Asserting that a proposition P is only a partial truth is of course *compatible* with purely pragmatic or soteriological reasons for rejecting P, but it is also a *different* kind of reason for doing so.

4. Although the pragmatic or soteriological explanation cannot be the whole truth of the matter, pragmatic considerations do figure prominently in the Buddhist texts. It is, therefore, necessary to explain how the purely pragmatic reasons fit into the larger picture.

The key, I think, lies in recognizing the complementary nature of the pragmatic reasons for rejecting the ten alternatives, on the one hand, and the anattā/dhamma teaching of Buddhism, on the other. Most of the philosophers of the Buddha's day believed in the existence of a self or soul (P. attā; Skr. ātman). The Buddha rejected this view in favor of the teaching that what people misleadingly or erroneously *call* a self is in fact just an ever-changing, impermanent flow of mental or physical elements called dhammas (Skr. dharmas), which arise and perish according to the principle of dependent co-origination (pratītya-samutpāda). The Buddha seems to have regarded his anattā/dhamma teaching and his praxis or soteriology as merely complementary aspects of one and the same teaching. A particularly interesting example of this is the Aggi-vacchagotta-sutta (AVGS) of the Majjhima-nikāya (§I.483-489). In this sutta the Buddha contrasts the pernicious spiritual effects of the speculative views (diṭṭhi) of the samaṇas and brāhmaṇas with the beneficial spiritual effects of his own teaching (which he refers to as a *dhamma*). The latter teaching, he says, replaces the ātman and substance theory of the heretical sects of the day with the teaching that there is no self but only the dhammas of form, feeling, willing, conception and consciousness. His teaching, he says, leads to destruction, dispassion, ceasing etc., whereas the heretical views involve the "holding of views, the wilds of views, the wriggling of views, the fetter of views." In the AVGS, then, the linkage of the pragmatic and soteriological concerns of the Buddha with the anattā/dhamma theory are made explicit.

When confronted with interlocutors who adhered to a line of thought that was antithetical to his anattā/dhamma doctrine, the Buddha appears to have been faced with two choices. He could either set the question aside and refuse to answer it, on the grounds that the questions and the assumptions they made did not conduce to the spiritual life or the attainment of nibbāna (a purely pragmatic reason), or he could attempt to reason with the interlocutor, show him the error of his thinking, and replace the interlocutor's way of looking at things with the correct view (i.e., the anattā/dhamma theory). These are not mutually exclusive approaches, as the AVGS shows. In most of the suttas, however, the dhamma theory is not fully developed. The extent to which the Buddha was prepared to discuss the more theoretical aspect of the teachings with his interlocutors must have depended very much on the interlocutors and the Buddha's judgement about the best way of dealing with them to help them spiritually (upāya-kauśālya). Presumably the monks and nuns of his own order were given more explicit and detailed explanations of the anattā/dhamma theory than those who were outside it.

5. Since Jayatilleke believed that the Buddha actually negated or denied the various positions represented in the avyākata questions, he had to face the question whether the Buddha believed that the various positions represented *all* the possible logical alternatives for those questions.

One of the central questions involved here is whether the alternatives that are involved in the catuṣkoṭi are genuinely contradictory (i.e., logically exclusive and exhaustive), or whether they are merely contraries—a question that had been raised some years before Jayatilleke wrote by P. T. Raju (1954: 710-711). Jayatilleke thought the Buddha did regard the alternatives as logically exclusive and exhaustive. He also argued that the catuṣkoṭi diverged from Western logic (which recognizes only one logical contradictory for any given proposition) because the Indian philosophers wanted a more detailed way of canvassing the logical alternatives to given questions than the one that considers only a thesis and its contradictory. The Indian philosophers, he claimed, considered *four* logical alternatives rather than two, i.e., P, Not-P, Both P and not-P, and Neither P nor not-P. Furthermore, he claimed, the catuṣkoṭi does not involve a rejection of the laws of non-contradiction and the excluded middle, for *within* the four propositions of the catuṣkoṭi, P, not-P are contraries rather than contradictories. Taken *collectively,* however, P, Not-P, Both P and not-P and Neither P nor not-P *do* exhaust all the possible *logical* alternatives. Take, for example, the pair hot/cold. Jayatilleke argued that the four possibilities hot, cold, both hot and cold (i.e., hot and cold in different parts) and neither hot nor cold (i.e., tepid) do cover all the possible *logical* alternatives to the question of the temperature of an object. According to Jayatilleke, therefore, the negations of the avyākata/ṭhapanīya questions must be taken collectively as denying all of the logical possibilities involved in a given question, regardless of whether the logical possibilities are stated in the binary form (1)-(6) or in the more detailed and informative quarternary form (7)-(10).

Having reached the conclusion that the alternatives presented in the catuṣkoṭi, when taken collectively, were *logically exclusive and exhaustive,* and that the Buddha *denied* or *negated* each of them, Jayatilleke had to face head on the criticism that the Buddha had contradicted himself, i.e., had committed himself to an inconsistent and hence logically incoherent and meaningless set of assertions. Jayatilleke maintained that the Buddha had not done so, however, on the grounds that each of the propositions (1)-(10) was a *meaningless* proposition.[4] It was therefore perfectly possible—indeed, appropriate—for the Buddha to have denied each and every one of the koṭis simultaneously. According to Jayatilleke, the putative propositions were not syntactically or semantically ill-formed, but they were meaningless because they transcended the limits of meaningful language and discourse. Jayatilleke frequently cited Wittgenstein in defense of this position, whose lectures at Cambridge in the years 1945-47 he had attended (EBThK 10, n. 4). Wittgenstein is referred to eleven times in the text itself. EBThK §800-817, which is concerned with the limits of empiricism and knowledge, is the capstone of the entire work. It ends with the following quotation from Wittgenstein's *Tractatus* (§7): "Whereof one cannot speak, thereof one must be silent."

6. Although Jayatilleke's account of the avyākata questions in early Buddhism contines to exert a considerable amount of influence on modern scholarship, there are problems with it.

First of all, where Jayatilleke does appeal to positivist or quasi-positivist principles about meaning and meaninglessness (e.g., EBThK §523-599) in interpreting the Pāli texts, those principles are applied to very different kinds of statements than the ones that figure in the catuṣkoṭi. Second, there is no evidence that the Buddha himself adhered to positivist tenets like the verificationist principle, or even a *Tractatus*-like picture theory of meaning. Had the Buddha appealed to such principles in rejecting, denying or otherwise setting aside the avyākata questions, one would naturally expect to find evidence for this in the texts themselves, and this evidence is lacking.

Third, the claim that the questions involved in the catuṣkoṭi are meaningless is prima facie implausible. It is conceivable that someone with positivist leanings might be tempted to make a case for this for the last six avyākata alternatives (i.e., the ones involving the notion of a soul), but the claim is quite implausible in the case of the first four alternatives. The first of these asserts that the world is eternal, the second asserts that it is not eternal, the third asserts that the world is finite, and the fourth asserts that the world is infinite. Is there any reason to think that these propositions are meaningless, even according to positivist principles? Presumably, no modern-day positivist would say so, since such questions are currently a matter of much discussion by contemporary mathematicians, physicists and cosmologists. It is now taken for granted by contemporary scientists that it is meaningful to ask whether the universe is finite or infinite, eternal or non-eternal; i.e., such questions are now thought to be empirically *decidable*. So far as I know, no positivist would have maintained that these contemporary cosmological theories are meaningless.

It is true, of course, that there have been some *non*-positivist philosophers (notably Kant) who have thought that propositions about the eternality or non-eternality, finitude or infinitude of the world are antinomic in nature, and therefore in some sense meaningless. It is also true that many interpretations of the catuṣkoṭi have appealed to Kant's theory of the antinomies of pure reason. I do not believe that the Kantian analogy is a useful one in connection with the catuṣkoṭi—in most respects it even seems dangerously misleading—but that is not a theme I shall pursue here. Here I shall only note that imposing a Kantian interpretation on propositions (1)-(4) of the catuṣkoṭi would have the untoward consequence of saddling the Buddha with a philosophical view which is now thought to be untenable.

According to Kant, the propositions that the world is finite, infinite, eternal and non-eternal lead to antinomies, i.e., inconsistencies and contradictions within reason itself. But in modern mathematics and physics, models embodying each of these propositions have been developed, and there is no reason to think that any of these models involves logical inconsistencies. One might be inclined to argue in defense of Kant that his claim only means, for example, that finite and infinite geometries are in some sense *unimaginable,* i.e., that they lead to antinomies within the sensory manifold or the domain of apperception. But even if this were true, it is doubtful that it could throw much light on the catuṣkoṭi, for there is no reason to think that the Buddha thought that a proposition had to be *imaginable* in order for it to be meaningful.

A fourth problem with Jayatilleke's interpretation of the avyākata questions is that, by his own admission, there is at least one sense in which the Buddha's views were non-positivistic, and even different from those of Wittgenstein in the *Tractatus*. According to Jayatilleke (EBThK §817), "The Buddhist while saying that it is meaningless to ask whether one exists in (hoti), does not exist in (na hoti), is born in (upapajjati), is not born in (na upapajjati) Nirvāṇa, still speaks of such a transcendent state as realizable," and a few lines later he says: "The transempirical [according to the Buddhist] cannot be empirically described or understood, but it can be realized and attained." As Jayatilleke seems prepared to concede, this is inconsistent with both a positivist and a Wittgensteinian philosophy.

This admission makes one wonder why Jayatilleke thought that positivism was relevant to the analysis of the catuṣkoṭi at all. Most of the positivists (and certainly the Wittgenstein of the *Tractatus*, who does not seem to have been a positivist) believed in the classical laws of non-contradiction and the excluded middle, so they of all people would have insisted that it makes no sense to speak of someone as neither existing, nor not existing, nor both existing and not existing, nor neither existing nor not existing—in this or in any other state; and they would have been (if anything) even less inclined to speak of such a state as *realizable* or *attainable*.

Furthermore, if there had been a transempirical or transcendental claim underlying the Buddha's rejection of the ten speculative views, one would expect the Buddha to have said (in regard to the last four theses, for example) that the Tathāgata *does* exist after his nibbāna, but that his state cannot be described in language (even though it might be attained). But the Buddha even denied that the Tathāgata *exists* after his parinibbāna (cf. the seventh of the avyākata/ṭhapanīya questions). Hence Jayatilleke's interpretation of the Buddhist catuṣkoṭi appears to be unfaithful to both positivism and the Pāli texts.[5]

The attempted marriage of positivist views about the limits of meaningfulness for propositions, on the one hand, and mystical views about a transcendent, transempirical reality which can be realized and attained on the other, is perhaps the strangest aspect of Jayatilleke's magnum opus. Not too surprisingly, most scholars have been more sympathetic with Jayatilleke's claim that the catuṣkoṭi involves an appeal to a transcendent, transempirical and translinguistic Absolute than with his appeal to positivist principles of meaningfulness. R. H. Robinson, for example, who gave Jayatilleke's book a generally favorable review, spoke with some scorn of those parts of the book where Jayatilleke "reveals the cloven hoof of the positivist" (1961: 81). However, Jayatilleke's positivist views about meaningfulness are not, as Robinson seems to have thought, a merely incidental feature of his interpretation of the catuṣkoṭi. Jayatilleke attempted to explain away the apparent inconsistency of the catuṣkoṭi or avyākata questions by appealing to the alleged positivist (or quasi-positivist) bounds of meaningfulness of human language. If one rejects these views, then one has eo ipso rejected Jayatilleke's explanation of the Buddha's interpretation of the avyākata questions, and one then finds oneself back at the original question: Why did the Buddha ignore these questions and set them aside? And did he contradict himself in setting all of them aside? That is, if Jayatilleke's appeal to positivist or quasi-positivist principles of meaningfulness is rejected, then Jayatilleke's explanation of the avyākata questions must be rejected as well. This means, in effect, that nearly everything goes, for the avyākata questions are clearly what Jayatilleke was primarily interested in explaining. He returns to the question repeatedly throughout his work, and ends it with a discussion of this very question as its high point (EBThK §800-817).

7. According to Jayatilleke's interpretation of the catuṣkoṭi, the Buddha regarded the catuṣkoṭi as exhausting all the possible logical alternatives to a given question. This, it seems to me, is the most objectionable feature of the interpretation, for the anattā/dhamma theory of Buddhism is *not* represented in any of the presented alternatives, and we *do* know that this theory (in some form or another) was taught by the Buddha.

The ātman theory was not negated or set aside by the Buddha on the grounds that all discourse about the ātman transcended the limits of linguistic, logical and empirical discourse: it was rejected on the grounds that it made certain empirical claims that were untenable, e.g., that a person could remain unchanging from birth to death in virtue of some essence (svabhāva) that remains unchanged while the properties inhering in, or manifested by, that essence do change. All reference to such a self or essence was to be replaced with the view that what people call a self is in fact just a stream of mental and physical properties or elements called *dharmas*. Just as, it might be argued, what the ancient Scandinavians called "Thor's hammer" turned out to be nothing but a discharge of electrons to the earth in the presence of certain atmospheric conditions, so what people call a "self" is in fact nothing but an ever-changing time-series of elementary mental and physical constituents. There was nothing about the description of these dharmas to suggest that they were regarded as in any way translogical or transempirical entities, much less that all talk about them was meaningless. On the contrary, the dharma theory was regarded as the correct view, at least in part, precisely because it *was* empirically verifiable, whereas the ātman doctrine was repudiated as an untenable metaphysical view (though not, apparently, a meaningless one).

Consequently, if the avyākata positions had been regarded as logically exhaustive alternatives, the anattā/dhamma theory of the Buddha would have had to be included among them. Since it was not, the Buddha could not have regarded these questions as having exhausted all the logical alternatives to the religious and philosophical views in question.

8. In order to put the avyākata and ṭhapanīya questions in perspective, it will be helpful to compare them with other philosophical or religious questions to which the Buddha responded differently. This is a matter that Jayatilleke (EBThK §452-458) investigated in some detail. According to Jayatilleke, the Buddha's responses to these questions can be categorized into the following four groups: a) the question that was answered categorically (ekaṃsa-vyākaraṇīya); b) the question that was met with a counter-question (paṭipucchā-vyākaraṇīya); c) the question that ought to be explained analytically (vibhajja-vyākaraṇīya); and d) the question that should be set aside (ṭhapanīya).

a) The categorical (ekaṃsa) teaching is straightforward. Jayatilleke (EBThK §449) cites as typical examples of these the four-fold noble truths (i.e., everything is suffering etc.), which were held to be categorically true. Other examples, which he took from the Milinda-pañha (EBThK §459), are the questions "Is form impermanent?" "Is sensation impermanent?" etc., to which one must answer categorically in the affirmative: "Yes, form is impermanent" etc. Another example that he cites (EBThK §461) is the question of the form "Does everyone die?", to which one should reply categorically: "Yes, they die."

b)-c) What the analytical questions (vibhajja) and the counter-questions (paṭipucchā) have in common is that no categorical answer to them is possible that would not be somehow misleading or false. These questions, therefore, need to be *reframed* or *clarified* or *restated* before a reply to them can be made. Since replying to the interlocutor with a counter-question would appear to be only one of the possible ways of doing this, there does not appear to be any clear distinction to be drawn between these two kinds of questions. They are also similar because clarifying them or restating them in a form that can be categorically answered is relatively simple and straightforward.

This, it seems to me, is the main thing that distinguishes them from the related ṭhapanīya questions.

One type of question that must be analyzed before being answered is of the form "Are all x ϕ?" The AK (cited in EBThK §463) gives as an example "Is everyone reborn?" According to Buddhism, the answer to this question is No, because, while those with defilements (kleśas) are reborn, those without defilements (i.e. the Arhats and the Buddhas) are not. According to the AK, however, a merely negative answer to this question would be insufficiently informative, since a merely negative answer (na sarve janiṣyantī ti) would leave it unclear whether the reply means that no one is reborn or that only some are reborn. According to the AK, therefore, the question "Is everyone reborn?" should be subjected to analysis and clarification (√vibhaj) before an answer to it is given.

A related example is the following one: "What does one experience after performing a volitional act with one's body, speech or mind?" (cited in EBThK §465). This example, which Jayatilleke cites from MN iii.208, needs to be analyzed because it cannot be properly answered in the form in which it is put. There is no one karmic consequence for actions, for the karmic consequences of an action depend on the context, the intention, the ethical quality of the action etc. The sutta says that a paribājjaka by the name of Potaliputta gave a categorical answer to this question, which was foolish of him, because it required analysis first (samiddhinā mogha-purisena Potaliputtassa paribbājakassa vibhajja-byākaraṇīyo pañho ekaṃsena byākato).

That the vibhajja questions are not different in kind from the counter-questions (paṭipucchā) is shown by the following example that Jayatilleke cites (EBThK §467) from the AK: "Is man superior or inferior?" As in the previous two cases, the question cannot be answered categorically because there are some beings (i.e. the gods or devas) who are superior to man and some beings (e.g. animals) that are inferior. Hence, as the Abhidharma-kośa says, one should reply to the question "Is man superior or inferior?" with a counter-question: "In relation to whom?" Once this ambiguity has been settled, the question can be answered categorically.

d) According to Jayatilleke, the ṭhapanīya questions were left unanswered or set aside by the Buddha on the grounds that the propositions figuring in them were held to be meaningless. This interpretation places these questions in a very different class from the questions that are to be analyzed or answered with a counter-question. But it seems to me that the ṭhapanīya questions are very much like the vibhajja and paṭipucchā questions, except that the ṭhapanīya questions cannot be reframed so *easily*. Reframing them was possible, according to the Buddha, only by providing *an alternative conceptual framework or paradigm*. Specifically, the ṭhapanīya questions required the abandonment of a metaphysics of substances and selves in favor of a metaphysics of primitive, unanalyzable ontological elements or dharmas that arise and perish according to verifiable norms or laws (pratītya-samutpāda). Analyzing and clarifying questions that presuppose the former paradigm is not a simple matter, for in their case a deeply rooted attachment (abhiniveśa) to false modes of thought has to be uprooted. The ṭhapanīya questions, therefore, are not different in *kind* from the vibhajja and paṭipucchā questions, but they do deserve a separate category because the amount of conceptual revision and clarification required by them is much greater.

9. The Aggi-vacchagotta-sutta (AVGS) of the Majjhima-nikāya (MN i.483-489) shows that there is a close affinity between the vibhajja and ṭhapanīya questions, as well as a close affinity between the avyākata/ṭhapanīya questions and the anattā/dhamma theory.

In this sutta, a wandering brāhmaṇa ascetic (parivrājaka) of the Vātsya gotra (Vaccha-gotta) asks the Buddha each of the ten avyākata/ṭhapanīya questions in succession. To each of them the Buddha replies: "I am not of this view, that the world is eternal; this indeed is the truth, all else is false" and so on, for each of the other nine questions. When Vacchagotta asks the Buddha why he does not assent to any of the alternatives, the Buddha criticizes them as speculative views (diṭṭhi) which only serve as fetters to people who hold them, and prevent them from turning away from misery and from attaining "dispassion, stopping, calming, super-knowledge, awakening, and nibbāna."

Vacchagotta then asks whether the *Buddha* has any speculative view (P. diṭṭhi, Skr. dṛṣṭi). The Buddha replies that he does not, and then proceeds to expound the *anattā/dhamma* theory.

Thus, the Buddha's denial that he has a "diṭṭhi" does not mean that he has no teaching whatever, for the Buddha *gives* Vacchagotta a teaching, which he calls a "dhamma." He claims, however, that his teaching differs from the teachings of others because his teaching is not a speculative or metaphysical view. Thus he says:

> Vaccha, going to 'speculative view'—this has been got rid of by the Tathāgata. But this, Vaccha has been seen by the Tathāgata: 'Such is material shape (rūpa), such is the arising of material shape, such is the going down of material shape ... ' [and so on, for each of the other four skandhas]. Therefore I say that by the destruction, dispassion, stopping, giving up, casting out of all imaginings, all supposings, all latent pride that 'I am the doer, mine is the doer,' a Tathāgata is freed without clinging.[6]

At this point, another "catuṣkoṭi" gets introduced. Vaccha asks the Buddha: "Where does a monk (bhikku) arise whose mind is freed thus?" The Buddha tells him: "Arises does not apply (na upeti)," and similarly for the other questions concerning not arising, both arising and not arising, and neither arising nor not arising. Vacchagotta tells the Buddha that he is bewildered by all of this. The Buddha tells him: "You ought to be at a loss, Vaccha, you ought to be bewildered. For, Vaccha, this dhamma is deep, difficult to see, difficult to understand, peaceful, excellent, beyond dialectic, subtle, intelligible to the wise." He also says that it is hard for Vacchagotta to grasp this teaching (dhamma) because Vacchagotta is of *another* view.[7]

The Buddha explains his own teaching (dhamma) with an analogy. He asks his interlocutor: "If someone were to quench a fire, and then ask you: To which direction has that fire gone from here, to the east or west or north or south, what would you reply?" Vacchagotta replies that each of these questions does not apply (na upeti) to the case. A fire, when it is burning, burns because of a supply of fuel, and when the fire is quenched for lack of fuel, it simply *goes out*. The Buddha then draws the following moral:

> Even so, Vaccha, that material shape by which one recognizing the Tathāgata might recognize him—that material shape has been got rid of by the Tathāgata, cut off at the root, made like a palm-tree stump that can come to no further existence and is not liable to arise again in the future. ... Freed from denotation by [material shape and the other skandhas] is the Tathāgata, Vaccha, he is deep, immeasurable, unfathomable as is the great ocean. 'Arises' does not apply, 'does not arise' does not apply, 'both arises and does not arise' does not apply, 'neither arises nor does not arise' does not apply.

In the sutta, each of the four alternatives is said to be inapplicable (na upeti) because each implies that there is a self or soul *now* (i.e., the Tathāgata) which is different from the skandhas of material form etc. This is declared to be a false doctrine. All of the alternatives in question are to be rejected *in favor* of another teaching in which Vacchagotta's way of thinking about the matter cannot even be stated.[8]

10. Jayatilleke, as might be expected, interprets the passage differently. He says (EBThK §474):

> If a categorical answer to the question as to whether the Tathāgata exists or is born (upapajjati) after death is possible, it should be possible to say according to the laws of logic that one of the four alternatives must be true. Now we observe that the Buddha takes the four (logically) possible answers and shows that none of them 'fit the case' (upeti), or adequately describe the situation...This means that no categorical answer [to these questions can be given].

And in §476 he says:

> The simile [of the fire] illustrates that the question, 'in which direction has the fire gone?' is one to which no categorical reply by means of any of the (logical) alternatives is possible by the very nature (logical) of the question....It therefore makes no sense to ask 'in which direction has the fire gone?' for we would be making a category mistake and thereby asking a nonsensical question, to which no meaningful answer can be given.

Part of what Jayatilleke says here seems to be right, and some of it seems to be wrong. The part that seems right is the claim that the question "In which direction has the fire gone?" shows that the questioner is confused about the nature of fire. The part that seems wrong is the claim that each of the four alternatives (i.e. gone to the east, gone to the west, gone to the south and gone to the north) exhausts all of the possible *logical alternatives* of the question. If there is such a thing as a category mistake, and if the question "In which direction has the fire gone?" is one of them, then the question has *no logical alternatives at all*, since it is a *nonsensical* question. To speak of the logical alternatives of a question that commits a category mistake is itself a mistake.[9]

Furthermore, the question "In what direction has the fire gone?" *does* have an exact and appropriate answer, which is this: "The fire has not gone anywhere. It has simply gone out (nibbāna), i.e., it has become extinct, non-existent." If, as Jayatilleke claims, the possibilities "to the north," "to the south," "to the east" and "to the west" were all of the *logically possible* alternatives to the question "In what direction has the fire gone?", what would one have to say about the answer "The fire has not gone anywhere—it has simply gone out?" That it is an *illogical* alternative? But this is the *correct* answer, and a quite straightforward one at that.

This kind of question differs from the vibhajja questions because in the case of the avyākata/ṭhapanīya questions the interlocutor expects an answer given in the same conceptual terms as the one in which he has phrased his question, and it is not possible to do this. But this does not mean that by denying the alternatives that are recognized by the *interlocutor* one denies all of the possible logical alternatives. Another logical alternative is that the *whole framework* in which the interlocutor is thinking of the matter is incorrect, and that it needs to be replaced with another one.

Questions typically have presuppositions, and these presuppositions should be considered part of the question. When we take certain views for granted we are apt to miss this point, and to be baffled when confronted with something that challenges these presuppositions, just as, for example, physicists were puzzled when the Michelson-Morley experiment failed to reveal any ether drift. This example from physics shows that one must not be too hasty to conclude that all of the logical possibilities of a given question have actually been considered. Very often all that has happened is that one has limited oneself to the alternatives *defined by a certain theory or framework.* And if one fails to note this, one will be likely to overlook the fact (as I think Jayatilleke did) that the correct answer to a certain question (especially a phoney question) is *another theory* (dhamma).[10]

If one does overlook this point, one will be tempted to jump to the conclusion (as Jayatilleke apparently did) that since none of the logical alternatives of a given question fits the case, what one must be dealing with is something mystical that transcends the bounds of human knowledge and language. But there is very little in the Aggi-vacchagotta-sutta to justify this interpretation. In the AVGS, the Buddha clearly refers to his own teaching (dhamma), i.e., the anattā/dhamma teaching. This theory is explicit in the passage that refers to "material shape (rūpa), the arising of material shape, and the going down of material shape etc." It is also implicit in the fire analogy, for this analogy was frequently used by the Buddhists to explain their doctrine that there is no permanent self, but only an ever-changing time series of constituent physical and psycho-physical elements called dharmas (dhammas).

11. Once the Buddha's negative response to the ten questions is placed in the context of the anattā/dhamma theory, it becomes clear that his teachings in the AVGS do not require an appeal to a transempirical, translogical or translinguistic reality or Absolute. The point of the sutta might be paraphrased as follows:

> You, Vacchagotta, hold a speculative view (diṭṭhi) which I have rejected in favor of a different teaching (dhamma). You believe in the existence of substances and selves. From this point of view and this point of view only, it makes sense to ask whether or not the world is finite or eternal, whether the soul is or is not identical with the body, whether the Tathāgata exists after death, or not, or both or neither. Since I do not adhere to concepts like "world" (loka) and "self" (attā) as you do, I must simply set your questions aside. There is no way to answer your questions categorically in the form in which you state them, for your views are all based on the idea of a subsisting entity, whether it be a physical thing, a whole universe, or a self or soul.[11]
>
> The dhamma that I teach is profound, subtle and only to be comprehended by the wise, but perhaps the example of a fire will serve to bring home to you the general point that lies behind it in a vivid and intuitive way. To suppose that there is a thing or entity, whether it be a world or a physical object or a self is incorrect, and will prove on examination to be just as untenable as supposing that there is an entity Fire. If there were such a substance or entity as Fire, it might make sense to ask questions like "Where does the fire go when it is quenched?" But this kind of question clearly does not make any sense. On examination, it will prove to be the same for questions like "Where does the Tathāgata go after his parinirvāṇa?" What people call the Tathāgata is just a process like a flame

rather than a real entity, so it makes no sense to ask where the Tathāgata has gone once his parinirvāṇa has occurred and "he" has terminated the cycle of births and deaths forever. "Arises" does not apply, for "he" is not reborn anywhere. "Not arises" does not apply, for this suggests that "he" exists now and perishes later. Similarly for the other possibilities, i.e. "both arises and does not arise" and "neither arises nor does not arise." None of these possibilities apply because, like the fire, the Tathāgata at his parinirvāṇa has simply *gone out* (nibbāna, nirodha).

This teaching is profound and difficult, because it entails the overthrow of your whole, presently ingrained world-view. At your present stage you cannot possibly grasp it fully. This dhamma can only be fully grasped by those who have adopted a different view and the way I have laid down for its realization. You will by degrees be able to grasp this teaching if you commit yourself to the life prescribed by me for the monk (bhikku), and if you meditate constantly on the fundamental truths of this dhamma, e.g., that everything is suffering, that there is no enduring entity but only a continuous chain of dependent co-origination, that there is no self but only a physical and psychophysical aggregate of dhammas etc.

12. According to Jayatilleke's mystico-positivist interpretation of early Buddhism, the Buddha believed in a transempirical, mystical reality that transcends all the possible logical categories with which one might try to conceive it. Significantly, however, there seems to be no evidence in the early texts that the Buddha's contemporaries attributed this position to him. Jayatilleke himself gives a very detailed analysis of the historical and philosophical milieu in which Buddhism arose (EBThK, chs. I-III), but even he does not cite any instances from the Pāli texts in which the interlocutor takes the Buddha to have been teaching an absolutist doctrine, and I am not aware that there are any such passages. This counts rather strongly against any absolutist interpretation of the Buddha's teaching. Several centuries before the lifetime of the Buddha, the Upaniṣadic thinkers had developed a philosophy of an Absolute, which they held to be unthinkable and inexpressible, beyond thought and words. If the Buddha had believed in something similar, one might reasonably expect his interlocutors to have examined him on this point, attempting to ascertain how his views of the Absolute differed from those of the Vedic teachers, or criticizing him for holding absolutist views.

To judge from the Buddhist and non-Buddhist texts, however, the views that were attributed to the Buddha by the other philosophers and religious thinkers of the day had nothing to do with a doctrine of an Absolute. Basically, the views that were imputed to him were of two kinds. The first included a number of related charges, e.g., that the Buddha was an "eel-wriggler" (amarā-vikkhepa-vādin); a casuist or sophist (vitaṇḍā-vādin); or a sceptic. The second view was that the Buddha was a materialist (uccheda-vādin) in disguise, who believed that the self or person was identical with the body and that at the time of one's physical death one simply ceased to be.[12]

It is not surprising that the philosophers of the day were inclined to regard the Buddha as an eel-wriggler, casuist, sophist or sceptic, for when presented with a list of alternatives that seemed to them to be logically exhaustive and exclusive, the Buddha set aside, did not answer and ignored all of them. But the fact that such views were imputed to the Buddha, *and* that the Buddha *denied* them, is perfectly understandable in the light of the anattā/dhamma theory. The Buddha *did* have an answer to these questions, but it was a very radical answer that undermined many of the presuppositions in terms of which the other philosophers had framed their questions.

The anattā/dhamma theory also explains why the Buddha was often thought to be an annihilationist, even though the Buddha disavowed this charge. The ucchedavādins held that the soul was identical with the body—or at any rate they denied that it was capable of surviving the death of the physical body. The Buddha repudiated much of this view. He accepted the prevailing view of the religious thinkers of the day, according to which individuals continue to experience the karmic consequences of their actions in later lifetimes. However, the Buddha reinterpreted this doctrine in a very significant way. Whereas the other religious thinkers of India regarded the agent of action and retribution as an enduring self or soul, the Buddha taught that what continued was not an unchanging entity, but only a process, like the flame of a lamp. The process that we call an individual is undoubtedly connected with the process that we call a physical body in a very complicated way, but the Buddha held that the process we call an individual is not *dependent* on the body, and in the normal case continues on without it when the physical body dies. Thus the Buddha was not a materialist or annihilationist (ucchedavādin). He openly repudiated this view as an erroneous one that was incompatible with the living of the religious life.

13. Although the Buddha taught that the psychophysical process that we call an individual *usually* continues after death, he also taught that this was *not* true of the Buddha and the Arhat. Like the rest of the religious thinkers of India, the Buddha regarded rebirth as *undesirable*—even if one were to be reborn as one of the gods (something that he thought could and did happen). According to the Buddha, all states of existence without exception are impermanent and in the final analysis states of suffering (duḥkha). The aim of the religious life is to put an end to this cycle of birth and death (saṃsāra). This hard-won goal the Buddha and the Arhat have achieved by diligently pursuing the eight-fold path to liberation. To all appearances, the Buddhas continue to experience karmic consequences in their present lives even after they have achieved the state of Buddhahood, but at the time of their physical deaths (parinirvāṇa), the whole saṃsāric process is terminated for them forever.

This teaching raises the question whether the Buddha taught what might be called a doctrine of *eventual* annihilation. Significantly, there is evidence within the early texts that some of the Buddha's *followers* interpreted the teaching in this way. An interesting example is provided by the Yamaka-sutta (SN xxii.85). In this sutta, the bhikku Yamaka comes to the conclusion one day (apparently after the parinirvāṇa of the

Buddha) that what the Buddhist doctrine finally amounts to is that the person who has attained the religious goal simply ceases to exist at the time of his physical death. The other monks find this view heretical and pernicious, and Sāriputta, one of the Buddha's earliest and most important disciples, is informed of it.

Prima facie, the fact that the other monks find this view heretical and pernicious counts against the annihilationist interpretation, but as the sutta proceeds the evidence on this point becomes much more equivocal. After hearing Yamaka's opinions on the question in his own words, Sāriputta begins instructing him in the right view. He begins by getting Yamaka to admit that the five skandhas of form, sensation, willing, conception and consciousness are transitory, that whatever is transitory is evil and liable to change, and that it is not possible to say of anything that is transitory and evil and subject to change: "This is mine; this am I; this my self." Yamaka is instructed that when the learned and noble disciple conceives an aversion to these five skandhas he becomes free from passion, and knows that his rebirths have been exhausted, that he has lived the holy life, and that he is "no more for this world."

At this point, one begins to wonder why the other bhikkus had been so scandalized to find Yamaka attributing a doctrine of (eventual) annihilation to the Buddha. This puzzlement deepens at the next stage of the argument.

Sāriputta asks Yamaka whether he thinks that the saint is identical with the skandhas, is different from them, or if he is simply devoid of form, sensation, perception etc. Yamaka replies that he does not think of the saint in any of these ways. Then Sāriputta says:

> Considering now, brother Yamaka, that you fail to make out and establish the existence of the saint in the present life, is it reasonable for you to say: 'Thus do I understand the doctrine taught by the Blessed One, that on the dissolution of the body the priest who has lost all depravity is annihilated, perishes, and does not exist after death?'

This, it is said, makes Yamaka see the error in his previously held view of the Buddha's teaching. When Sāriputta then asks him, "Brother Yamaka, the priest who is a saint and has lost all depravity, what becomes of him on the dissolution of the body, after death?" Yamaka says:

> I would reply, brother, as follows, if I were asked that question: 'Brethren, the form was transitory, and that which was transitory was evil, and that which was evil has ceased and disappeared. The sensation ... perception ... predispositions ... consciousness was transitory, and that which was transitory was evil, and that which was evil has ceased and disappeared.' Thus would I reply, brother, if I were asked that question.[13]

The sutta, therefore, seems to end on a decidedly nihilistic note, for the Buddhist doctrine is surely a nihilistic one if this is the *whole* answer to the given question.

14. The doctrine contained in Sāriputta's catechism to Yamaka is implicit in the AVGS's analogy of the extinction of a fire. As the Buddha points out in the AVGS, it would be a sign of confusion to ask where the fire has gone after it has been quenched. Although the point is not explicitly made in the AVGS, there is a sense in which it would *also* be a mistake to say that the fire *does not exist* or *ceases to exist* when it is extinguished—at least in so far as a fire is conceived as some kind of *entity*. We use this loose way of speaking in ordinary speech, but according to Buddhism it is not strictly correct. The problem with it emerges as soon as one tries to specify what this fire is. The whole point of the fire analogy in the AVGS is that there is no entity (vastu, svabhāva) called "fire," but only a process or set of inter-related conditions and events that are constantly undergoing change from moment to moment. It is impossible, on examination, to identify an entity Fire either within or without the totality of conditions and occurrences that are called "fire." Hence, to say something like "The fire does not exist after it is quenched" or "The fire goes out" only means that at one moment a certain kind of process or inter-related set of occurrences and conditions is taking place, and that at another moment it isn't. But there is no entity that at one point exists and then *ceases* to exist.

This point is made explicitly in an untraced sutta which is cited in the Kathā-vatthu.[14] In this teaching the Buddha distinguishes between three kinds of teachers: the eternalist, who maintains that there is a self now and that there will be one in the future; the *nihilist,* who maintains that there is a self now which will cease to exist in the future; and the fully realized one, who maintains that there will be no self in the future and that there is no self *now.* That is, according to this sutta the difference between the Buddhist teaching and the ucchedavāda is that the ucchedavādin believes that there is a self that *perishes,* whereas the Buddhist teaching is that there is no self that perishes, but only a physical and psychophysical series of everchanging elements that gets extinguished (nirodha, nibbāna).

Thus, the early Buddhist teaching was neither an eternalist nor an annihilationist view, at least as these terms were understood by the debating samaṇas and brāhmaṇas of the day. The Buddhist teaching was neither the one nor the other, since it was a no-self and no-substance view which denied the very thing that was presupposed by both the annihilationists and the eternalists.

In one respect, the early Buddhist teaching was less nihilistic than the ucchedavāda, for the Buddhist teaching maintained that there was karmic retribution for one's actions, even after the death of the physical body. In another respect, however, the Buddhist teaching appears to have been even *more* nihilistic than the ucchedavāda, for the ucchedavādins, typically, believed that there was at least a self *now,* even though it would cease to exist after the death of the body. The Buddhists, however, denied the existence of the self (attā, ātman) at any time.

This suggests that early Buddhism reinterpreted the concept of extinction (nirodha, nirvāṇa), but by no means denied it or rejected it outright they way the eternalists did. To judge from the AVGS, the Yamaka-sutta, the unknown sutta cited by the Kathā-vatthu et alia, the Buddha's teaching differed from the ucchedavāda in only two respects: 1) the extinction in question was held to be the extinction of a process rather than of an entity or substance, and 2) the extinction in question was not something that happened inevitably in the ordinary course of events, but was regarded instead as something to be achieved. This nirodha or nibbāna was regarded as the highest good because all states of existence were held to be states of impermanence and suffering (dukkha).

15. The early Buddhist doctrine claimed to offer an alternative or middle path between the extremes of eternalism and nihilism by replacing the concept of a self or soul with the anattā/dhamma theory. The claim that the Buddha-dharma was a genuine alternative to the prevailing views was based on the claim that what had previously been conceived as permanent substances or entities should be analyzed instead as processes or series of impermanent entities. But could the analysis actually be carried out? In particular, what was the ontological and epistemological status of the dharmas themselves? This was a matter of concern, for prima facie, many of the destructive arguments that early Buddhism had directed against the soul-doctrine were of a quite general nature, and would appear to apply with equal force against any putative entity *whatever*—including the putative dhammas or dharmas. Thus, early Buddhist doctrine appears to have gone only half way towards a *thorough* rejection of an ontology of entities, for while the existence of a self was denied, it was replaced with the notion of the dharmas, which were also regarded as entities (albeit of a more impermanent and impersonal kind). A more radical—and perhaps more consistent—attack on the notion of substances, essences, entities, ontologies etc. would have subjected these putative dharmas to the same kind of criticism that the early Buddhists had applied to the notion of the self.

Thus, the seeds of the nihilist interpretation of the Buddha's teachings were clearly present even in early Buddhism, though they did not come to fruition there. The nihilist interpretation was repudiated in the early canon, but it was one thing to repudiate nihilism, and quite another to show that the dharma theory occupied a viable middle ground between nihilism, on the one hand, and the ontological views of the non-Buddhist schools on the other. In fact, there is evidence within the Pāli canon itself that nihilism was regarded as more than a merely academic possibility even at a very early stage. Two passages that are noteworthy in this connection are the Kaccāyana-sutta (SN ii.17) and Saṃyutta-nikāya ii.76.

The former sutta begins when Kaccāyana asks the Buddha to define what is meant by "right view." The Buddha replies that the world usually bases its views on two things: existence and non-existence. But, the Buddha says, he who with right insight sees the uprising of the world as it really is does not adhere to the view that the world is *non-existent*. Similarly, he who with right insight sees the passing away of the world as it really is, *does not adhere to the existence of the world.* He then criticizes those philosophers who imprison themselves in dogmas and go in for system-building, all of which is based on the delusion of a self. The wise man, the Buddha says, does not grasp at things or at a self; he simply thinks: "What arises is suffering; what passes away is suffering." Then he says:

> Everything exists: this is one extreme. Nothing exists: this is the other extreme. Not approaching either extreme the Tathāgata teaches you a doctrine of the middle way: Conditioned by ignorance activities come to pass, conditioned by activities consciousness; thus conditioned [arises] name-and-shape; and sense arises, contact, feeling, craving, grasping, becoming, birth, decay-and-death, grief, suffering, ... even such is the uprising of this entire mass of ill. But from the utter fading away and ceasing of ignorance [arises] ceasing of activities, and thus comes ceasing of this entire mass of ill.

Note that this characterization of Buddhism as a middle path between eternalism and nihilism differs from the usual one, where eternalism is taken to be the view that the soul is eternal, and annihilationism is taken to be the view that the soul perishes at the death of the physical body. In the Kaccāyana-sutta, the teaching of a middle path between 1) existence and 2) non-existence is interpreted instead as a teaching 1) that things are impermanent (rather than eternal) and 2) that the world is not *non-existent*.

In other words, in the Kaccāyana-sutta the middle path is said to be between the extremes of *eternalism* (the view that things exist now and never perish) and *nihilism* (the view that nothing ever exists). The sutta implies that there were philosophers in the Buddha's time who maintained these views, and it therefore provides important evidence that nihilism was an established philosophical position even in the time of the Buddha. Further evidence for this historical claim can be found in the Saṃyutta-nikāya (ii.76), which mentions the doctrine that everything is entirely non-existent (sabbaṃ natthī ti).[15] Nihilism, therefore, is probably a *very* old doctrine in India—even approaching, perhaps, the antiquity of the Upaniṣadic idealism (ca. 8th century BCE).

As the Kaccāyana-sutta shows, the early Buddhists repudiated nihilism. This is exactly what one would expect, given that nihilism is incompatible with the dharma theory. Nevertheless, it was probably not an easy matter to keep nihilism at bay, for a very good case could be made that the dharma theory, and the doctrine of dependent co-origination with which it was closely connected, were only half-hearted attempts to overthrow the non-Buddhist ideologies and cosmologies of substances and entities. Thus, despite the strictures against nihilism that were present in the canonical texts themselves, the possibility always lay open of claiming that nihilism was the *purest,* most *rigorous* and most *consistent* form of the Buddhist teachings, while the dharma theory was an inferior and provisional one. This abstract possibility began to take on historical significance when the old exegetical distinction between the direct (nītārtha) and indirect (neyārtha) meaning of the Buddha's teachings began to take shape as the distinction between the concealed (saṃvṛti) truth and the ultimate truth (paramārtha), and when the Mahāyāna introduced the notion of a secret teaching which was revealed by the Buddha only to his closest and most advanced disciples.

The earliest Mahāyānist literature, the Prajñā-pāramitā, shows that these doctrinal developments and the critique of the dharma theory and the doctrine of dependent co-origination were simply different aspects of one and the same movement of thought within Buddhism. The Mādhyamika school represents the culmination and the purest example of all of these tendencies. Of all the Buddhist schools, only the Mādhyamikas were bold enough to take the early Buddhist critique of the ātman doctrine and carry it through to what may be its logical conclusion with an uncompromising and even ruthless consistency.

Negation in the Madhyamaka

1. Jayatilleke defended the logical consistency of the catuṣkoṭi on the grounds that it is not inconsistent to reject P, Not-P, Both P and not-P and Neither P nor not-P when the propositions in question are meaningless ones. Jayatilleke's suggestion was an interesting one, for if it were true that the propositions figuring in the catuṣkoṭi were meaningless, the purely logical problem of the catuṣkoṭi would be solved, for it is possible—indeed obligatory—to in some sense reject both P and not-P when P is a meaningless proposition. Despite its prima facie attractiveness, however, Jayatilleke's interpretation must be rejected, for there is no reason to think that the propositions figuring in the catuṣkoṭi are meaningless, or even that the Buddhists thought that they were.

The fact that a strict verificationist or positivist criterion of meaningfulness is no longer in favor in philosophical circles may have something to do with the fact that Jayatilleke's suggestion has not been pursued by most of the recent work on the problem of the catuṣkoṭi. Typically, more recent work on the catuṣkoṭi has attempted a purely linguistic solution to the problem. According to these interpretations, the Buddhist catuṣkoṭi is logically consistent because the kind of *negation* that figures in the catuṣkoṭi is not the standard negation of classical logic.

The first to argue in this way was apparently Y. Kajiyama (1973) in his influential article "Three Kinds of Affirmation and Two Kinds of Negation in Buddhist Philosophy." Kajiyama's paper was not specifically intended as an attack on the problem of the catuṣkoṭi, but was instead an attempt to describe and contrast the various uses of affirmation and negation in some of the Buddhist schools, and to compare these with their use by the grammarians (Vaiyākaraṇas) and the non-Buddhist philosophers. Nevertheless, Kajiyama's characterization of the Mādhyamikas' use of negation in this paper has been cited by other writers (e.g.

B. K. Matilal) as providing a way of viewing the catuṣkoṭi that exempts it from the charge of logical inconsistency.[1]

Kajiyama based his analysis of the Mādhyamikas' use of negation on Bhāvaviveka's commentary on MMK 1.3 in his Prajñā-pradīpa. The first four verses of the MMK (if one counts the two introductory verses) run as follows:

> No cessation, no origination, no destruction, no permanence, no identity, no difference, no coming and no going:
>
> anirodham-anutpādam anucchedam-aśāśvatam /
> anekārtham-anānārtham anāgamam-anirgamam //1//
>
> I pay homage to the Fully Awakened One, the best of teachers, who has taught dependent co-origination, the quiescence of all phenomena, the auspicious.
>
> yaḥ pratītya-samutpādaṃ prapañcopaśamaṃ śivam /
> deśayāmāsa saṃbuddhas taṃ vande vadatāṃ varam //2//
>
> Entities never originate, at any time or at any place, either from self, from others, from both, or from no cause.
>
> na svato nāpi parato na dvābhyāṃ nāpy ahetutaḥ /
> utpannā jātu vidyante bhāvāḥ kvacana kecana //3//
>
> There are only four causal conditions: the primary, the objective/supporting, the proximate and the superordinate. There is no fifth.
>
> catvāraḥ pratyayā hetur ārambaṇam anantaram /
> tathaivādhipateyaṃ ca pratyayo nāsti pañcamaḥ //4//

The remaining twelve verses of MMK 1 complete the line of thought by denying that things arise from any of the four conditions mentioned in MMK 1.4.

Prima facie, then, the meaning of these verses is as follows:

1. There are four and only four ways in which things might arise (MMK 1.4).
2. Things do not arise in any of these four ways (MMK 1.1a, 1.5-1.15).
3. Therefore, things do not arise at all (anutpādam).

Note that Nāgārjuna does not directly attack the view that things perish in MMK 1, but only the view that things *arise,* and this despite the fact that the introductory verse begins with "does not perish" (anirodham) rather than "does not originate" (anutpādam). This is easily explained, however, since if things do not arise, the question of whether things perish does not arise. In principle, of course, someone might maintain that there are things which, though they have never originated, will cease to exist at some time in the future, but this is not a view which any Buddhist would have taken seriously, and Nāgārjuna does not bother to mention it.[2] Once this recherché possibility is dismissed, one is left with an unmistakably nihilistic view, according to which 1) nothing exists without having originated, and 2) nothing does originate. From 11) and 2) it follows that nothing exists at all. As a corollary, nothing perishes either.[3]

What I have called the "prima facie" interpretation treats the negations in MMK 1.3 as propositional negations (prasajya-pratiṣedha) rather than exclusion- or term-negations (paryudāsa-pratiṣedha). That is, on the prima facie interpretation, MMK 1.3 is a conjunction of the following four negations: 1) it is not the case that things arise from themselves, 2) it is not the case that things arise from others, 3) it is not the case that things arise from self and others, and 4) it is not the case that things arise from no cause. If it were interpreted as containing paryudāsa negations, on the other hand, MMK 1.3 would mean the following:

> Not from self, not from others, not from both, not from no cause: [thus it is that] bhāvas arise and are born, everywhere and at all times.

Interpreted in this way, the sentence would imply that there is some *other* way that things arise, and it is clear that this is not what Nāgārjuna meant. The two most important commentaries on the MMK agree on this point. One of these, which is extant in Sanskrit, is Candrakīrti's Vṛtti (Prasannapadā). The other, which exists only in Tibetan and Chinese, is the Prajñā-pradīpa of Bhāvaviveka.[4]

These commentaries state that the verse is to be taken prasajya-pratiṣedhavat rather than paryudāsa-pratiṣedhavat. Candrakīrti points out that "not from self" (na svataḥ) etc. cannot be taken as implying that things arise from others because the thesis that things arise from others etc. will also be negated, and so on. Bhāvaviveka, to judge from two translations from the Tibetan that I have been able to consult (Galloway 1989: 26, n. 4, and Kajiyama 1973: 168), insists on the same thing.

Kajiyama's translation goes as follows:

> This negation 'not from themselves' (na svataḥ) must be understood in the sense of prasajyapratiṣedha (med par dgag pa), because [here] negation [and not affirmation] is primarily meant and because [the author] intends to destroy the net of all concepts and to establish non-conceptual intuition which [at the same time] is endowed with all knowable objects. If you grasp it as paryudāsa (ma yin par dgag pa), [the phrase will] affirm that [there are] things [which] are not produced, since it [paryudāsa] has affirmation as its primary objective. Teaching the non-production [of things positively], it will differ from the traditional doctrine [of the Madhyamaka]. For a sūtra says that if you practise the non-production of matter, you deviate from practising the perfect wisdom (prajñāpāramitā). In the present case, we have to impose a restriction (avadhāraṇa) [on the sentence by means of the particle eva] so that it may mean "Things are never produced from themselves." If you restrict it in a different way, it may mean "Things are produced not from themselves." What follows then? It will be concluded

> that "Things are produced from others." Similarly, when it is restricted so as to mean "Things are not produced from themselves alone," what results from it is "Things are produced from themselves and others." However, this [meaning] is not intended either because it deviates from the traditional doctrine.

To judge from Kajiyama's translation, what Bhāvaviveka says in his commentary on MMK 1.3 is this:

> "Na svataḥ" etc. must be understood as prasajya negations, because the meaning of a paryudāsa negation is primarily affirmative, whereas Nāgārjuna's meaning is primarily negative. What Nāgārjuna would have meant taken paryudāsa is: "Things are as follows: not arisen from self, not arisen from others, not arisen from both, not arisen from no cause." But this is clearly not Nāgārjuna's meaning. In the present case, we have to impose a restriction (avadhāraṇa), and say "It is false that things are produced from themselves."[5] Note, however, that if you restrict it in any other way, you will fall into other errors. For example, if you restrict it by saying "Things are produced not from themselves alone," this will suggest (as a paryudāsa negation) that things are produced from others, which is not correct.[6] Likewise, if you restrict it by saying "Things are not produced from themselves alone," the implication would be (à la paryudāsa) that "Things are produced from themselves and others," and this is not correct either.[7]

What is a little less clear are the conclusions that Kajiyama wished to draw from Bhāvaviveka. In this connection he says (ibid., p. 172-173):

> In the Mādhyamika philosophy, the theory of two kinds of negation has much bearing upon the interpretation of the doctrine of "emptiness" (śūnyatā). Bhāvaviveka,

> the founder of the Svātantrika school, asserts that negation used by a Mādhyamika must be always prasajyapratiṣedha. As can be seen from the above cited passage of his, the Mādhyamika proposition that things are not produced from themselves must not be understood to mean that they are produced from others, both, or without a cause. A Mādhyamika, when he negates one concept, actually intends to negate all the human concepts together with it; something other than the concept negated is not to be affirmed either. For Bhāvaviveka, to negate the essential nature (svabhāva) in everything is the only way to establish nirvikalpajñāna as the highest truth or non-conceptual wisdom, in which neither an entity nor a non-entity is grasped. Here, the theory of two kinds of negation is enhanced almost to a soteriological interpretation.

Part of what Kajiyama says here is perfectly straightforward, i.e., that Nāgārjuna and Bhāvaviveka do not take the assertion that things are not produced from themselves (na svataḥ etc.) as implying that they are produced from others, both, or without a cause. According to Kajiyama, however, this is not a purely linguistic point, but has implications for the interpretation of śūnyatā, for the *ultimate* implication is, he says, that when the Mādhyamika negates a concept, he means to negate "all the human concepts together with it." According to Kajiyama, therefore, the Mādhyamikas' use of the prasajya negation is connected with the notion of a non-conceptual wisdom, in which neither an entity nor a non-entity is grasped.

I do not wish to enter at this point into the question whether the Mādhyamikas believed in a "non-conceptual wisdom, in which neither an entity nor a non-entity is grasped." [This particular question will be taken up in some detail later, however (v. infra, pp. 246-252)]. Here I shall only raise the question whether this view, even assuming that it is true, can be justified by the Mādhyamikas' use of the prasajya negation in passages like MMK 1.3.

All that *can* be inferred from MMK 1.3, together with the fundamental principles of Buddhist philosophy, is that one cannot infer from the negations "not from self" (na svataḥ), "not from others" (na parataḥ), "not from both" (na dvābhyām) and "not from no cause" (na *ahetutaḥ) either of the following two things: 1) that things exist, but without originating and 2) that things originate, but in some other way than the four ways that are mentioned in the verse. Note, in particular, that it certainly does not follow from 1) and 2) that Nāgārjuna believed that nothing could be inferred *at all* from the negation that things do *not* originate from self, from others, from both or from no cause. For it is clear that Nāgārjuna did accept and indeed very much wanted to prove at least one proposition, i.e., that things do *not* originate (na *utpādaḥ) at all. Indeed, all of the verses of MMK 1 are intended to demonstrate this very proposition, which is also explicitly asserted in the first of the two introductory verses (anirodham-*anutpādam* etc.).

It is, it seems to me, not entirely clear what Kajiyama means by a "non-conceptual wisdom, in which neither an entity nor a non-entity is grasped." However, it is reasonably clear that he counts as conceptual the propositions "is produced from self," is "produced from others," etc. But if these are conceptual, it is hard to see why the propositions "It is *false* that things are produced from themselves" (bhāvāḥ svata utpannā naiva vidyante) etc.—which Kajiyama regards as propositions that a Mādhyamika *would* accept—aren't conceptual propositions as well.

This is a quite general point about propositions and their negations. Take any other proposition, e.g., *John smokes*. Surely, if the assertion *John smokes* is conceptual, then the assertion that John does not smoke is also conceptual. Similarly, if the proposition *Things are produced from themselves* is conceptual (and Kajiyama, presumably, would agree that it is conceptual) then the proposition *Things are not produced from themselves* is conceptual as well. Kajiyama has given us no reason to think that the proposition *Things are not produced from themselves* is any less conceptual than any other negative proposition (e.g., *John does not smoke*). Nor has he given us any reason to think that the point could be established by appealing to what might be called the logic of propositional negation (prasajya-pratiṣedha).

There is very little in Kajiyama's paper about the more general proposition "It is false that things arise, period," which is unfortunate, because if there had been, more light might have been thrown on the notion of a "non-conceptual wisdom, in which neither an entity nor a non-entity is grasped." But in any case this proposition, when it is taken in conjunction with the proposition that nothing exists without originating, would seem to lead to nihilism.

B. Galloway (1989), who has also translated part of the Prajñā-pradīpa's commentary on MMK 1.3, is specifically concerned with the more general proposition. He is also concerned to avoid the nihilistic interpretation of the passage. It is therefore of some interest to see how Galloway translates and handles the Prajñā-pradīpa's commentary on this verse.

The part of Bhāvaviveka's commentary on MMK 1.3 that Galloway has translated I reproduce below (ibid, p. 26, n.4):

> Taken as a paryudāsa negation, affirmation would be primary: thus (1) "dharma do not arise" (dharmā utpannā na), showing [affirmative] nonarising, without an instrumental case (karaṇa-kāraka); but according to tradition those who practice in the nonarising of form are not those who practice in the prajñāpāramitā. We must take [as prasajya negation] "existents from themselves just do not arise" (bhāvāḥ svata utpannā na *eva). Otherwise we would have to accept [the paryudāsa negations] (2) "arise, just not from themselves" (svata na *eva *utpannā), meaning "arise from other things": or (3) "arise not just from themselves" (svata eva na *utpannā), meaning "arise from self and other things": these are not acceptable, because of the separation [of the predicate] from the instrumental.

This is rather similar to Kajiyama's translation and my paraphrase of that translation; the main difference is that Galloway has "without an instrumental case" (Tib. byed) and Kajiyama does not. As a non-Tibetanist I cannot assess the relative merits of the two translations on this particular point, but the differences in translation do not appear to me to make any significant difference to the interpretation of the passage. According to Kajiyama's translation, Bhāvaviveka argues at this point that "na svataḥ" etc. must be taken as prasajya rather than paryudāsa negations because, if they were taken paryudāsa, affirmation would be primary, and the result would be that there are things which are not produced. Galloway's translation "without an instrumental case" does seem to fit this sense, because in MMK 1 all the possible ways in which or by means of which (cf. the instrumental case) an entity arises are refuted. Taken paryudāsa, MMK 1.3 might be taken to mean that things exist without any means (i.e. of causality) at all; but this was clearly not Nāgārjuna's intention.

Although Galloway's translation comes close to Kajiyama's, his interpretation of the passage is somewhat different. Thus he says, "We must take [as prasajya negation] 'existents from themselves just do not arise (bhāvaḥ svata utpannā na *eva)'" etc., and the latter (or at least something that is virtually impossible to distinguish from it) is rejected on the grounds that it is an *annihilationist* view.[8]

According to Galloway, one thing that is at issue is whether nihilism can be excluded as an interpretation of MMK 1 and Bhāvaviveka's interpretation of it. Galloway's main argument against the nihilist interpretation is contained in the following passage (ibid., p. 7):

> Bhāvaviveka in his Prajñāpradīpa considers possible negations of the affirmative proposition 'things arise from themselves' and objects to the negative version 'things do not arise' on the ground that it implies an annihilationist 'nonarising,' that is, there is a 'positive' implication of an annihilationist kind. He objects too to 'things arise, just not from themselves' on the ground

> that it implies that they arise from other things. He further objects to 'things arise, not just from themselves' on the ground that it implies that they arise from both self and other things; and all these he characterizes as paryudāsa. But he does not object to 'things just do not arise from themselves,' and this is the formulation from which he draws no implication and which he calls prasajya. He does not want us to conclude that things do not arise at all, nor does he want us to conclude that they arise in a particular way. He simply rejects 'things arise from themselves' and proposes no alternative theory of arising (any such theory would be wrong from the Mādhyamika point of view because it would presuppose a real 'thing' of which arising could validly be predicated). Things do not arise from themselves, but no statement is made about how they do arise.

One of the merits of Galloway's paper is that it focuses attention on the issue of nihilism. This question needs to be addressed, since this is the prima facie reading of MMK 1 (v. supra, pp. 48-49). Galloway contends that MMK 1.3 (and its Prajñā-pradīpa commentary) are not nihilistic, but there a number of problems with his attempt to avoid the prima facie interpretation of this verse.

First, there is a grammatical point. Galloway interprets the nihilist position as a kind of affirmative view. (Cf. the statement, ibid., p. 7, about Bhāvaviveka's rejection of a "'positive' implication of an annihilationist kind.") But for purely grammatical reasons, if nothing else, it is hard to see how the implication of nihilism is an implication of a positive kind.

Second, Galloway holds that the argument of MMK 1.3 and Bhāvaviveka's commentary on it is that things arise somehow, but that nothing is said about *how* they arise. This possibility seems to me to be unequivocally excluded by the fact that MMK 1.4 excludes four possibilities for the arising of things, and then declares that there is no fifth way in which they could arise. Here, clearly, it is not just a matter of not being *told* what the fifth way is, for we are explicitly told that there is no other way. The conclusion, surely, is that things do not arise at all. Indeed, it is all the more surprising that Galloway should have denied *this*, since the whole chapter seems to be a commentary on the term "anutpāda" (non-origination) of the first verse.[9]

Third, Galloway's interpretation of MMK 1.3 is based on the claim (which he attributes to Bhāvaviveka) that there is a kind of negation which has no implication to any other statement. This is perhaps the central claim of Galloway's non-nihilist interpretation of the Madhyamaka, as it is of many of the most recent versions of the NNI generally. Thus Galloway says: "[Bhāvaviveka] does not object to 'things just do not arise from themselves,' and this is the formulation from which he draws no implication and which he calls prasajya" (ibid., p. 7); and elsewhere he says that "the [Mādhyamika] prasajya negation is a nonimplicative one" (ibid., p. 26, n. 4). He even suggests introducing the symbol **0** into our logical notation for a statement with "no content" which "leads nowhere," which he calls a "zero statement."

Despite the importance which this kind of claim has in many of the non-nihilist interpretations of the Madhyamaka, it seems to me that it goes far beyond what the Indian grammarians (Vaiyākaraṇas) actually said about the prasajya negation, which they discussed in considerable detail. The point is easy to miss, perhaps, since it is true that the Vaiyākaraṇas held that the paryudāsa negation was implicative in a way that the prasajya negation was not. But it seems to me that on examination the implication (arthāpatti) that is involved in the Indian grammarians' treatment of paryudāsa negation is of a quite specific and even trivial kind. No sweeping philosophical conclusions can be drawn from the fact that the prasajya negation was not thought to be implicative in the way that paryudāsa negations were thought to be.

2. So far as I can tell, this is true even of the grammarians that Kajiyama cited in his 1973 paper. After reaching the conclusion that Nāgārjuna's thesis in MMK 1.3 must be understood in the sense of the prasajya kind of negation, Kajiyama turned to a brief discussion of the views of four

Buddhist grammarians and philosophers (Avalokitavrata, Arcaṭa, Durveka Miśra and Jinendrabuddhi) on the differences between prasajya and paryudāsa negation. For our purposes, it is sufficient to note Kajiyama's Tibetan-to-English translation of the following passage from Avalokitavrata's commentary on Bhāvaviveka's Prajñā-pradīpa. This begins by citing the following verse from an unknown grammarian:

> Negation which is stated through implication, affirms a positive idea [too] by a single sentence (ekavākya), and, besides having these (characteristics), does not use the [affirmed] term itself, is paryudāsa; what is different [from this] is the other [or prasajyapratiṣedha].

Avalokitavrata's commentary on this verse is as follows:

> ...The following is meant. Negation having the following characteristics must be regarded as paryudāsa: (1) it states implication (arthāpatti); (2) by a single sentence (3) affirms a positive entity [too]; [4] having [the characteristics of] implication and the affirmation of a positive entity, does not use the very word [of the entity], as when one, meaning a kṣatriya, uses not the word kṣatriya but the word abrāhmaṇa. "What is different is the other" means that negation which is different from this, i.e. which is different from paryudāsa, is prasajyapratiṣedha ... This [prasajyapratiṣedha] has the following characteristics: (1) it does not show the sign of arthāpatti; (2) is devoted to negation, aims only at negation, i.e., simply negates what is asserted by the other party; (3) does not affirm the existence of an entity or a non-entity; (4) having [the characteristic of] negation and without having [those of] implication and the affirmation of an entity, expresses [the object of negation] by its own word, as when one, meaning 'not a Brahman' says 'not a Brahman' by which he simply makes negation.

These rather cryptic descriptions of the prasajya/paryudāsa distinction can be made clearer by a couple of examples.

It is appropriate to begin with an example from the Vedic ritual, since the distinction in question was probably first drawn in this early literature (cf. Edgerton 1929: §341-§350). Take the phrase "nā 'nuyājeṣu." "Na" is a negative particle; "anuyāja," which means "after-offering," is the name of an oblation which is offered in some of the Vedic sacrifices (yajña); and "anuyājeṣu" is the locative plural of "anuyāja." When "na" and "anuyājeṣu" are combined, the "a" of "anuyājeṣu" is dropped and the "a" of "na" is lengthened, giving "nā 'nuyājeṣu."

In Sanskrit syntax, occurrences of strings like "nā 'nuyājeṣu" can be ambiguous. Take the sentence "nā 'nuyājeṣu yeyajāmahaṃ karoti" (i.e., not at the anuyājas does one say *ye-yajāmahe*). This can mean either:

Paryudāsa:

(1) One says *ye-yajāmahe* at the sacrifices—except the anuyājas.

or

Prasajya:

(2) One does not say *ye-yajāmahe* at the anuyājas.

That is, the distinction between the paryudāsa and prasajya negations is a distinction between the scope of the negative particle (nañ), for the paryudāsa is a term-bound negation, whereas the prasajya is a verbally-bound negation. Both negations state or imply that the *ye-yajāmahe* formula is not uttered on the occasion of the anuyāja oblations, but the prasajya negation is limited to this exclusion, whereas the main point of the paryudāsa negation is that one *does* utter *ye-yajāmahe* at the *other* kinds of sacrifices.

This example illustrates the distinctions that Avalokitavrata mentions in his commentary on the Prajñā-pradīpa. Thus, the paryudāsa negation is essentially an *affirmative* rather than a negative statement, for what it really says is that one *does* utter *ye-yajāmahe* at the time of the *non*-anuyāja oblations (i.e., prayājya, ājyabhāga, āvāpa etc.). Here the prayāja etc. are not specifically mentioned by their own names, but are instead designated simply (and in a single sentence) as all sacrifices *except for* the anuyāja ones (anuyāja-vyatirikteṣu yeyajāmahaṃ karoti).

The prasajya has none of these characteristics. Its meaning is primarily negative, for rather than restricting the class of sacrifices at which one *does* say *ye-yajāmahe,* it simply says that at the anuyājas one does not utter this formula. Since the meaning of the prasajya is primarily negative rather than affirmative, there is no implication (arthāpatti) in the prasajya to the kinds of sacrifices at which one does say *ye-yajāmahe.* And since the "na" of "nā 'nuyājeṣu" is actually bound with the verb "do" (karoti) in the prasajya-pratiṣedha, the reference of the sentence is to the anuyāja oblations (or their ritual formulae) themselves. In the paryudāsa negations, on the other hand, where the "na" is bound with "anuyāja" rather than with the verb, what the sentence is primarily about are the non-anuyāja offerings.

Let us consider one more example—one that involves the term "brāhmaṇa" that is mentioned by Avalokitavrata. Take the sentence "na brāhmaṇāya rājā pāpaṃ karoti." "Na" is the negative particle; "brāhmaṇāya is the dative singular of "brāhmaṇa" (used in the example below as a singular class noun); and "rājā pāpaṃ karoti" means "the king does evil." In Sanskrit, the sentence "na brāhmaṇāya rājā pāpaṃ karoti" (i.e., not to the brāhmaṇas is the king an evil-doer) is ambiguous between the paryudāsa and prasajya negations. It can mean either:

Paryudāsa:

(1′) The king is an evil-doer—except to brāhmaṇas.

Or

Prasajya:

(2′) The king is not an evil-doer to brāhmaṇas.

All the distinctions that were mentioned previously in connection with "nā 'nuyājeṣu" apply to this one. Since the meaning of the paryudāsa negation, where the negative particle (nañ) is bound with the noun, is essentially affirmative, the sentence "na brāhmaṇāya rājā pāpaṃ karoti" means, when taken as a paryudāsa negation: "An exception to the rule that the king is an evil-doer is that he does not do evil to the brāhmaṇas." In the prasajya negation, on the other hand, where the negative particle is bound with the verb, the negation is a propositional one—i.e., taken as a prasajya negation, the sentence simply means: "It is not the case that the king is an evil-doer to brāhmaṇas," and this carries no implication as to whether he is, or is not, an evil-doer to any of the other castes.

There is one point to be noted about the prasajya negation that will become important later in the discussion of the Mādhyamikas' use of the catuṣkoṭi. In the above example, the prasajya negation is limited to the denial that the king harms brāhmaṇas, i.e., there is no implication to an affirmative assertion that the king harms non-brāhmaṇas (kṣatriyas, vaiśyas, śūdras etc.), as there is in the paryudāsa negation. However, it does not follow from this that the prasajya negation has no implications *at all,* for if it is *true* that the king is *not* an evil-doer to brāhmaṇas, then it is obviously *false* that he *is* an evil-doer to brāhmaṇas. In other words, if the following sentence is true

The king does not harm brāhmaṇas,

then the following sentence is *false*:

The king *does* harm brāhmaṇas.

3. In the light of the foregoing examples, it is clear why the commentators felt obliged to discuss the paryudāsa/prasajya distinction in connection with MMK 1.3. Take the sentence "na svata utpannā jātu vidyante bhāvāḥ" (i.e., no entities arise from self). This sentence is ambiguous in Sanskrit (just as, to some extent, its translation is in English). It can mean either:

Paryudāsa:

1″. Things arise—but they do not arise from self.

Or

Prasajya:

2″. Things do not arise from self—simpliciter.

If Nāgārjuna had meant "na bhāvāḥ svata utpannā jātu vidyante" to be taken paryudāsa, he would have meant that things arise *in some other way than from themselves.* He would thereby have been committed to the view that things do originate, even though they do not originate in this particular way. But, as all the commentators point out, this is not what he meant—i.e., the negations in MMK 1.3 are to be taken as prasajya rather than paryudāsa negations.[10]

Nevertheless, proponents of the NNI have wished to avoid interpreting Nāgārjuna to mean that things do not originate *at all*, for, given a couple of other assertions that were fundamental to all the Buddhist schools, the assertion that things do not originate at all leads directly to the conclusion that nothing whatever exists, and this is the nihilist position that most of the present-day interpreters of the Madhyamaka wish to avoid at all costs. According to the prevailing interpretation of the Madhyamaka, the term "emptiness" (śūnyatā) does not mean non-existence, but rather dependence in co-origination (pratītya-samutpāda). According to the NNI, therefore, the prasajya negations in MMK 1.3 consist entirely in the denial that things arise in *those specified ways,* i.e., there is no implication in MMK 1.3 to *either* the statement that things arise in some *other* way, *or* to the statement that things do not arise at all.

What the NNI's interpetation of MMK 1.3 amounts to, then, is that Nāgārjuna denied simpliciter (i.e., prasajyavat) that things arise from self (and similarly for the claim that things arise from others, from both, and from no cause), but did not assert simpliciter that things do not arise at all. But I do not believe that this interpretation is tenable. Nāgārjuna could have avoided committing himself to the assertion that things do not arise at all only if he had held that there was some *other* way that things do arise (even if he thought that we could not know what that was), and this is the very possibility that is excluded when (as the commentators insist) "na svataḥ" etc. are *not* taken as paryudāsa negations.

If Nāgārjuna had wished to avoid the nihilistic conclusion that things do not originate *period,* he would not have said in MMK 1.1a that things do not arise (anutpāda). Furthermore, he would either have had to specify the way that things *do* arise, or he would have had to state explicitly that things arise, but in some *miraculous* or *inexplicable* way (āścaryavat). But, as the commentators point out, he does not mean by "not from self" (na svataḥ), "not from others" (na parataḥ), "not from both" (na dvābhyām) and "not from no cause" (na *ahetutaḥ) either that things exist without having been originated, or that things arise even though we are not supposed to ask *how* they do arise, for as they point out, the negations in MMK 1.3 are *prasajya negations.* The view that things arise (though we are not supposed to ask how), which is the one that Galloway attributes to Nāgārjuna (ibid., p. 7), is pretty clearly the view that Nāgārjuna is concerned to argue *against,* for in MMK 1 he says explicitly 1) that things do not arise from the four causal conditions hetu, ārambaṇa, anantara and adhipateya, and 2) *that there are no other causal conditions.* It seems to me, therefore, that in his attempt to avoid the nihilist implications of MMK 1, Galloway has attributed to Nāgārjuna the very proposition that he denied (i.e., that things arise, though we are not told how), and has denied the very proposition that he clearly did affirm (i.e., that things do not originate at all).

If all the possible ways in which things *could* arise can be shown to be impossible (as MMK 1 asserts), then the obvious conclusion to draw (given the fundamental Buddhist principle that nothing exists that is unoriginated) is that nothing whatever exists. And this, as we shall see, is exactly what the Mādhyamikas did assert—sarvaṃ sarveṇa nāsti.

Relevant logic and negation

4. According to at least some of the proponents of the NNI, there is a kind of negation which has the following property:

> N1 One can negate, reject or deny a proposition P in such a way that no conclusions can be drawn from this negation, rejection or denial to the truth or falsity of any other statement.

Here we shall be concerned only with the relation between a proposition P and its negation, i.e., with N2, which at least some proponents of the NNI have endorsed:

> N2 One can negate, reject or deny a proposition P without committing oneself to the affirmation of not-P.

B. K. Matilal, in particular, claimed that some philosophers and grammarians in India accepted N1 and N2. When N1 and N2 are examined in detail, this turns out to be a rather startling claim.[11]

Consider a trivial (though perfectly relevant) hypothetical example. Suppose someone tells you one day that he had gone to the movies the previous night. Later in the same day he tells you that he had not gone to the movies the previous night. This is a contradiction: it *cannot* be the case that he both went to the movies and did not go to the movies on a certain day. Faced with this contradiction, you might want to search for an explanation. For example, you might try to determine if your friend had unaccountably lied or suffered a lapse of memory in asserting either that he did or didn't go to the movies. Another possibility is that your friend is just playing on words or making a bad joke. (Did he mean that he watched a movie at home on his VCR rather than in the movie theater—so that in a sense he went to the movies and in a sense he didn't—or does he mean that he did go to the movie theater but was present only in body and not in spirit?) The point is that one of his statements *must* be in error if he is using words (including the term "not") correctly and with the meanings that they have in ordinary language. If he is not using those terms in the way that they are used in ordinary language and in logical theory, he needs to explain himself.

If one cannot infer from A's assertion that he did not go to the movies that the proposition that A *did* go to the movies is false, how is A's use of the term "not" a negation at all? Note that we learn the meaning of expressions like "not" and "if..then" in ordinary language by learning which inferences are allowed from statements involving these expressions and which are not. This is also true of logical systems, where expressions like " $\wedge$ " and " $\supset$ " are given partial meaning by the axioms and the rules of inference.[12] Thus, one cannot separate the question of what a logical term means from the question of how the logical relations between propositions are changed when these terms are used in them. A statement from which no inferences could be drawn would be a *meaningless* statement, and a meaningless statement cannot be an affirmation or a negation.

Note also that the meaning of logical terms in a system is determined, not only syntactically by the axioms and the rules of inference and the set of theorems derivable from the axioms, but also directly, by the explicit provision of a semantics in the form of truth conditions. If someone sees me writing expressions like "A $\supset$ B," "P $\supset$ Q," "X $\supset$ Y" etc. on a piece of paper, and wants to know what the symbol " $\supset$ " means, I can give him an explanation by saying: any statement which is formed by putting any statement A before this sign and any statement B after this sign is true if and only if it is not the case that A is true and B is false. In a similar way, the semantics for the negation sign in the propositional calculus is given by the following truth condition: not-P is true iff P is false. This is entirely different from the situation we would be in if there were in fact a negation as described in N1 and N2 above. What could the truth conditions be for a negation from which no conclusions could be drawn to any other statement? More specifically, how would one give the truth conditions of a negation P which did not entail the affirmation of *not-P?* Allowing such "statements" into a logical system would be innocuous in one sense, perhaps, provided their introduction left the set of axioms and the set of theorems derivable from the axioms by the rules of inference entirely unchanged—i.e., provided they could be kept from infecting any of the rest of the system. But such a negation would be innocuous precisely because it was entirely *meaningless,* and as such had no place in the logical system at all.

5. If I understand him correctly (NMD 162-165; Perc. 65-66), B. K. Matilal claimed that there is a kind of negation as described in N1 and N2 above, at least in part, in order to exonerate Nāgārjuna of the charge of having contradicted himself, i.e., from having committed himself to a set of assertions that is meaningless or at least analytically false. If Nāgārjuna had been using negation in the ordinary way, where denying P entails the assertion of not-P, then Nāgārjuna would have contradicted himself in the catuṣkoṭi, and this would be a fatal objection to his philosophy. According to Matilal's suggestion, however, Nāgārjuna used negation in a non-standard way; i.e., his negations should be interpreted according to N1 and N2 above. Thus, Nāgārjuna did not say anything meaningless or absurd.

What this defense of the catuṣkoṭi suggests is that a formally precise language should have two quite different symbols corresponding to two quite different kinds of negation in natural language, i.e., one symbol to designate the negation which does entail the affirmation of not-P, and another to designate the kind of negation which doesn't. Prima facie, this would appear to be rather implausible, since it implies that someone who negates P consistently (i.e., without *also* asserting P, or not-not-P) is using negation in a *different* sense from the person who negates P inconsistently (i.e., who *also* asserts P or not-not-P). If there were such a negation, someone who asserted both that he went to the movies on a certain day and that he did not go to the movies on that day could extricate himself from the charge of inconsistency simply by claiming that he was using "not" in some special, non-standard or non-classical sense. But we clearly do not treat contradictions in this insouciant way.

6. Intuitively, our problem with the assertion that John both did and did not go to the movies on a certain day, or that a certain chair both weighs and does not weigh fifty pounds, is that we are at a complete loss to know how those assertions, taken jointly, could possibly be true; and since the notion of truth is very closely connected with the notion of meaning, it is hard to see what a speaker could *mean* by jointly asserting these things. The ordinary, instinctive belief that contradictions could not possibly be true or even meaningful is enshrined in the definition of negation that is found in standard, classical logic, i.e.:

DN: $\neg$A is true iff A is false.

Attempts, however, have been made by a group of relevant logicians in Australia (Canberra) to provide a truth-functional semantics for negation that does *not* exlude the possibility of true contradictions. Any logic that attempts to achieve this goal falls within the class of what has been called inconsistency-tolerant or contradiction-tolerant logic—a rubric that relevant logic (RL) shares with paraconsistent logic, with which it is related. Since Matilal (Perc. 66) appealed to R. Routley (now known as R. Sylvan), one of the leading exponents of Australian relevant logic (AuRL), in defense of N1 and N2, it will not be out of place to consider the views of the relevant logicians here.[13]

7. In the early 1970s, R. and V. Routley (RR72) claimed that one could obtain a recursive, semantic definition for inconsistency-tolerant negation in the following way.

First, one introduces the notion of a *set up* (designated by H, H′, H″; a*, a**, a*** etc.), which is defined as a class of propositions or sentences or well-formed formulas (wffs). These set ups play a role in their semantics similar to the one played by the notion of a possible world in Kripke's extension of Tarskian semantics to modal logic. Set ups differ from these possible worlds, however, for set ups can contain, for any proposition P, both P and its negation not-P.

One then proceeds to apply the notion of a set up to the truth-definition of negation in the expected Kripkean manner, except that one relaxes the constraint that the set up in which not-A is defined must be the *same* set up as the one for which A is defined. That is, the expected Kripkean extension of DN:

DN(K) $\neg$A is true in W iff A is false in W, for all W

is changed to the following:

DN(RL) ~A is in H iff A is not in H′,

where H′ is taken to be the image of H under a one-one function (RR72: 338). According to AuRL, DN(RL) gives the needed recursive characterization of negation while remaining free of the classical constraint that W must be consistent.

It is natural, of course, to ask how one is to understand H′, which is described as the image of H under a one-one function. Routley and Meyer (RM73: 202) attempted to put some more flesh on these bare bones in the following way:

> Negation...requires...the admission of theories that are inconsistent, incomplete, or both...We save nevertheless something like the familiar recursive treatment of negation by distinguishing a strong and a weak way of affirming a sentence A in a given set-up. The strong way is to assert A; the weak way is to omit the assertion of $\bar{A}$. This yields for each set-up a the complementary set-up a*, where what is strongly affirmed in a is weakly affirmed in a* and vice versa. The wanted recursive clause then says that $\bar{A}$ holds in a just when A doesn't hold in a*; the reader will have noted that under normal circumstances, when we affirm just what we don't deny, a and a* coincide, whence the account of negation reduces to the usual one.

This account applies the *-operation to a set up, but it is more typical for accounts of AuRL (e.g., MR73) to introduce this operation directly into the object language, as in the following definitional scheme:

DN(RL′) $\bar{A}$ = df. ¬A*.

It was said, in the context of set ups, that $\bar{A}$ holds in a just when A doesn't hold in a*. When the *-operation is introduced into the object language, A* (or a*) becomes simply the *denial* of A. Thus, Meyer and Martin (MM86: 306) describe a* in the following way:

> The Australian plan now lays it down that to each proposition a there is a corresponding proposition a*...The intuitive content of a* is that it is the proposition to which one is committed if one does not deny a.

And somewhat later in the same paper (p. 312), they explain A* as simply ¬~A (where ¬ is Boolean negation and ~ is De Morgan negation), or equivalently, as ~¬A.

According to the proponents of AuRL, it is easy to see how contradictions like *A* ∧ *not-A* can be true once we have these concepts in our grasp. *A* ∧ *not-A* will be true, they say, just in case A is weakly affirmed, for it is not at all problematic to "undeny" A and to deny one's "undenial" at one and the same time. As Meyer and Martin put it [MM86: 309]: "Double negation doesn't work on 'not denying'; we may simply be suspending judgment."[14]

8. If these proposals were tenable, AuRL would have provided us with a semantic definition of negation that allows that a contradiction could actually be true. Since this directly contradicts our deeply rooted intuition that chairs cannot both weigh and not weigh fifty pounds, and that John cannot both go and not go to the movies on a certain day, these proposals are suspect on prima facie grounds. In fact, I do not think that these proposals can withstand examination—and if they can't, then they cannot be used to justify the NNI's interpretation of the catuṣkoṭi, as Matilal claimed (at least by implication).

Some of the problems with DN(RL′) begin to emerge as soon as one asks: "What *is* the proposition to which one is committed when one does *not* deny A?"

a) Let us first consider a deductive system **S** comprising axioms, rules of inference, and theorems that are closed under a set of inference rules.

For **S** there are two possibilities to consider: either **S** is complete with respect to A or it is incomplete. In the latter case (i.e., incompleteness), neither $\vdash$A nor $\vdash \neg$A $\in$ **S**. In the former case (i.e., completeness), at least one of $\vdash$A, $\vdash \neg$A $\in$ in **S** (though of course we may not know which). If at least one, but not more than one, of $\vdash$A, $\vdash \neg$A is contained in **S**, then **S** is both consistent and complete with respect to A.[15]

On the assumption that **S** is consistent and complete with respect to A, ¬A, the notion $\bar{\text{A}}$ proves to be ill-defined. For in this case someone who asserts $\bar{\text{A}}$ says, in effect: "I take no position on either A or ¬A," which amounts to: "Either A $\in$ **S** or ¬A $\in$ **S**, though I don't know which." In this case, clearly, $\bar{\text{A}}$ cannot express a *single* proposition, for here the assertion of $\bar{\text{A}}$ is compatible with either A or ¬A, and while relevant and paraconsistent logicians have held that A and not-A can both be true, no one has ever suggested that they can have the same *meaning*. It is equally clear that there is no such thing as the proposition $\bar{\text{A}}$ when **S** is inconsistent with respect to A, ¬A, for the contradiction $A \wedge \neg A$ doesn't exclude any possibility, and is therefore contentless or meaningless.[16]

There are also objections to DN(RL′) on the assumption that **S** is *incomplete* with respect to A, ¬A, for in this case, $\bar{\text{A}}$ becomes unassertable (i.e., meaningless) in **S**.

There will, of course, always be such statements for any formal system of interest. This is shown in Gödel's incompleteness theorem of 1931. Gödel showed that no formalized, recursively enumerable set of propositions **S** containing elementary arithmetic will be be able to capture the notion of truth-in-S: i.e., there will always be sentences which are intuitively true but which are not provable in **S**. Let us say that U(**S**) is one of these formally undecidable propositions. Then the *fact* that U(**S**) is not provable (i.e., assertable) in **S** cannot be stated by U(**S**) or by any other sentence of **S**. It can only be stated in a higher or more powerful language than **S** itself (i.e., a metalanguage).

b) This remains true when the point is generalized to a theory **T** which includes the non-deductive truths of a language **L**. Suppose that a theory **T** is incomplete with respect to the non-deductive statements A, ¬A. What one must suppose in this case is that the non-denial of A in **T** entails something like: A, ¬A are in some sense *unassertable* in **T**. But the problem is that **T** cannot include a sentence that says of itself or some other sentence of **T** that it is unassertable in **T**. Intuitively, it is easy to see why. Let U(**T**) = the statement: "A, ¬A are unassertable in **T**." If A, ¬A are *used* in U(**T**), then they must have a meaning in U(**T**), for if they are used in U(**T**), the meaning of A, ¬A must contribute to the meaning of the larger expression U(**T**). And if A, ¬A have a meaning in U(**T**), then a fortiori they have a meaning in **T**. And if A, ¬A have a meaning in **T**, then they must be *assertable* in **T**.[17]

One can, of course, *name* a sentence, and then state that the sentence so named is meaningless or unassertable in one's own language. Barnie, for example, can quite sensibly say that the sentences "Schnee ist weiss," "Schnee is nicht weiss" are not assertable by him in his language. (He may, for example, be a speaker of English who does not know German and who therefore does not understand these sentences.) But here it is essential to be clear about just what it is that Barnie has asserted. He has said that he cannot assert (now) "Schnee ist weiss," "Schnee is nicht weiss" in his own language, but he has *not* said that he cannot assert that Schnee ist weiss, Schnee is nicht weiss, nor has he asserted that he cannot assert that snow is white, snow is not white.

Negations or denials of a sentence P are not the same thing as assertions, like Barnie's, of the non-assertability of "P." Negating or denying a proposition P is very different from saying that P is meaningless. When a speaker negates P by uttering "¬P", the proposition P is actually *used* in that utterance, for the negation "¬P" asserts that the world is *not* the way that P says that it is.

Therefore, if $\bar{A}$ is a negation at all, A must be used in $\bar{A}$ rather than mentioned—i.e., the operators ¬ and ~, however else they are interpreted, must operate on A itself, and not on a *name* of A. But if A is used and not just mentioned in sentences like "I deny A" or "I negate A," then not-A cannot be the same thing as asserting that A is unassertable, for this would be a contradiction.

Hence it would get us nowhere to suggest that $\bar{A}$ be taken to mean that **T** is incomplete with respect to A, ¬A. But as I have previously argued, $\bar{A}$ has no meaning if **T** is *complete* with respect to A, ¬A. Hence there is no such thing as the proposition $\bar{A}$. And this is a serious matter, for if DN(RL′) is required in order to provide a semantics for RL (and no one has suggested a better way to do it), then RL has not been provided with a semantics.[18, 19]

9. Logicians recognize, of course, that theories run the *risk* of inconsistency. The disagreement is over what it to be concluded from this fact. According to at least some of the relevantists and those sympathetic to them (e.g., R. and V. Routley, R. K. Meyer, G. Priest, et. al.), what we should conclude from this fact is that consistency or non-contradiction is not a necessary criterion of meaningfulness and truth. The critics of relevantism maintain that this could not possibly be the right conclusion to draw, because the suggestion that contradictions can be true (or even meaningful) makes no sense. I do not see how the relevantist could be said to have met this criticism without producing a definition of negation which did make sense and which did permit inconsistency and contradiction.

Indeed, the claim that DN(RL′) makes no sense, and the claim that contradictions make no sense, are probably just two different facets of the same thing. As D. K. Lewis (1982: 434) has put it:

> No truth does have, and no truth could have, a true negation. Nothing is, and nothing could be, literally both true and false. This we know for certain, and *a*

> *priori,* and without any exception for especially perplexing subject matters. The radical case for relevance should be dismissed just because the hypothesis it requires us to entertain is inconsistent.

Relevantists, who find such statements dogmatic, have cited in their defense a number of philosophers (e.g., G. W. F. Hegel, J. Łukasiewicz, et. al.) who have held that it might be the case that at least some contradictions are true. But while such examples are not entirely irrelevant (no pun intended), they cannot be taken as decisive either. Intelligent people have supposed that it was possible to square the circle, trisect an angle, and prove that the Fifth Postulate of Euclid is not an independent axiom. We now know that these things are in fact impossible. Similarly, the fact that intelligent people have thought it possible that at least some contradictions are true does not mean that it *is* possible that at least some contradictions are true. Furthermore, the overwhelming weight of philosophical opinion, then and now, has been that contradictions cannot be true. Intuitively and a priori, the case for the classical position seems strong enough to demand of the relevantist a semantic definition of negation that clearly does allow for the possibility of true contradictions. As I have just argued, this has not been done, and I do not believe that it can be done.

10. However, this does not necessarily mean that there is nothing of value in relevant logic. As the relevantists are quite right to point out, the undeniable fact of life is that our theories often turn out to be inconsistent (cf. all those disturbing paradoxes that are still with us), and classical logic does lead us from any inconsistency whatever to complete triviality through the dreaded *ex falso quodlibet* (i.e., $\vdash A$, $\vdash \neg A \vDash \vdash B$).[20]

Relevant logic may prove to be of some value in showing how, despite the quodlibet, we are able to navigate in the world even though our heads are filled with inconsistent theories. But this does not mean that there must be some classical rules of logical inference that are invalid *as rules of logic.* Some relevantists have made this claim even about the disjunctive syllogism (D.S.), but as J. P. Burgess has pointed out (1981,

1983), the D.S. is a common-sensical inference that is used in quite ordinary—even trivial—kinds of argumentation. Since the quodlibet (i.e., $\vdash A,\ \vdash \neg A \models \vdash B$) tends to spread the infection of a contradiction everywhere in a system, the claim can certainly be made that as a rule of inference it is oblivious to the issue of relevance, but it is unlikely that even the quodlibet is a *logically* invalid rule of inference.[21]

It may be that we escape the full rigors of classical rules of inference like the quodlibet by invoking *non-logical* principles (perhaps heuristic ones) that tend to counteract logical rules for the purposes of everyday life. Thus, even though it is true, on well-established classical principles, that anything whatever does follow from a logical contradiction, we may simply be disinclined to infer B from A, ¬A unless (as the relevantists have insisted) there is some relation of *relevance* between A and B—and this for reasons that have nothing to do with the pure *logic* of the matter.

It was common in the 1950s and 1960s for Oxford philosophers to claim, on a variety of grounds, that the truth-functional operators of modern day logical theory distort the logic of terms like "and," "not," "if..then," "neither..nor" etc. in ordinary language. But as Burgess has pointed out (1981: 99), such claims are heard much less frequently nowadays, partly because H. P. Grice (v. Grice 1989) argued convincingly that the divergences in question are not divergences in logic at all, but simply arise from the fact that in natural language certain conversational rules of implicature are superimposed over the logic that is common to both formal and informal language. The same may be true of the condition that inferences from A to B in ordinary language be relevant ones. Considerations of this kind would themselves tend to rule out the quodlibet.

11. Recent work in the axiomatics of RL seem to be moving at least some of the relevantists in the direction of thinking of RL in this way—i.e., away from the highly controversial claim that classical logic is in some sense invalid, whereas RL is not, to the much more modest view that RL might be useful, as a restricted subset of classical logic, for certain limited purposes.

In the middle 1970s, for example, R. K. Meyer and R. Routley showed that one can obtain virtually all of the distinctive features of RL by simply taking classical logic and adding certain special constraints to it. (These constraints are called fusion constraints in the axiomatics, but the details of this need not concern us.) What this work indicated was that RL is not, as it is sometimes claimed to be, a radically different kind of logic from classical logic, but rather a modification of it, in much the same way that modal logic has now come to be seen as merely an extension of classical logic. As Meyer and Routley have put it (MR73: 183):

> It now turns out... that *not only* can classical negation be added to R+, producing the system CR..., but also that the original relevant negation ¯ of R can be explicated *directly* as a certain kind of classical negation. That is to say, from a certain viewpoint classical negation is a *more general* kind of negation than is relevant negation, the latter being subsumed under the former.

The finding of Meyer and Routley that relevant negation is epiphenomenal to the fusion constraints that are present in relevant logic but absent in classical logic has led to a kind of schism in RL (Dunn 1983: 214). Hard-liners have argued that there is no such thing as classical or Boolean negation—or at any rate that classical negation cannot, or should not, be introduced into RL.[22] Meyer, who was principally responsible for the discoveries that led to the crisis in RL, at first found the results disappointing (MR74: 183), but seems now to have taken the line that RL should be viewed as a special case of classical logic (Meyer 1978).

Though the hard-liners seem to regard the more conservative and irenic of these two approaches as a kind of heresy, the more irenic approach would seem to be perfectly consistent with the basic intuitions that inspired relevantism in the first place (cf. AB75). As Burgess (1983: 42) has pointed out, Anderson and Belnap's work in the late 1950s and early 1960s on the notion of entailment never involved the claim that contradictions could be true, nor the equivalent claim that the quodlibet, the D.S. etc., are *semantically* invalid rules of inference. The attempt by relevantists like the Routleys and R. K. Meyer to provide a semantic definition of negation which would *replace* the "not-P is true if and only if P is false" principle was in fact a later development. What the Meyer-Routley work in the 1970s seems to show is that this very radical attempt to *overthrow* classical logic was also a deviation from the earlier, more conservative program.

In view of the Meyer and Routley findings in MR73, there is much to be said for Meyer's contention (1974) that relevant negation is not the same *kind* of thing as semantic negation, but rather a purely inferential or deduction-theoretic one, of the kind that had been studied earlier by H. B. Curry (v. Curry 1976). Inferential negation is primarily a syntactic or deductive notion, in which negation is relativized to a given deductive system **S**, and not-P is then given the meaning "P leads to an assertion that is refutable or absurd"—i.e., $\vdash \neg A$ = df. $A \rightarrow f$, where *f* is taken to be a disjunction of assertions that are either refutable or absurd in the system **S**. If any contradiction whatever is taken as "absurd" (and therefore as falling within *f*), then the system **S** will be no more tolerant of contradiction than classical logic. But what has interested relevantists, paraconsistent logicians, dialetheists etc., is the possibility that *f* could be defined more weakly, i.e., that the system **S** could include *some* contradictions, but avoid complete triviality by restrictions on the classical rules of inference.[23]

12. Systems which try to quarantine the quodlibet in this way are certainly worth investigating, since complete triviality (i.e., P and not-P, for any P) must be avoided at all costs. Nevertheless, it is essential, in order to put the investigation of purely inferential notions of negation into proper perspective, to note that even *one* contradiction is unacceptable. There is no reason to think that a purely inferential negation in the above sense could be anything more than a special case of classical negation, and certainly no reason to think that the concept of a purely inferential or deduction-theoretic negation could be used to justify the claim that a contradiction could be true. It seems to me that there is nothing in RL, as it stands today, that could justify these stronger claims, and therefore nothing in RL that could be used to justify N1 and N2.

We simply cannot be insouciant (or even resigned or fatalistic) when we find contradictions in our theories. Unfortunately, this seems to have been the counsel of some, at least, of the later relevantists. (Sometimes the more radical relevantists give the impression that if one lives with contradictions long enough, one can even grow to like them.) But nothing is, and nothing could be, both true and false. No truth does have, and no truth could have, a true negation. It is absurd to suggest that the chair that I am sitting on weighs fifty pounds and that it does not weigh fifty pounds—and this for the very same reason that makes it absurd to suggest that there could be a set that is both a member and not a member of itself. When such contradictions arise, things really do crash and burn, and we have no choice but to set about locating the cause of the disaster.

Speech act theory and the catuṣkoṭi

13. In order to negate or refute an utterance U, one must negate or refute what U asserts, i.e., the propositional content P of that utterance. Any negation which does this is at one and the same time an assertion of the truth of not-P and an assertion of the falsehood of P (v. supra, pp. 64-66). Thus, any negation of a statement P from which no conclusion could be drawn to any other statement (including not-P or the falsity of P) would fail to be a negation of the statement at all.

Prof. Matilal, of course, never denied that there are *some* uses of negation which fit what he called the standard, classical or logical definition of negation, according to which the assertion of $\neg$P entails the falsity of P. He acknowledged this in his early paper "Negation and the Mādhyamika Dialectic" (p. 164), and he continued to acknowledge it in some of his later writings on the subject, e.g., *The Logical Illumination of Indian Mysticism* (LI) and *Perception* (Perc.).[24] Even in these later writings, however, Matilal maintained that it is *possible* to negate or refute a proposition without committing oneself to the standard or classical two-valued logic of affirmation and negation. With increasing frequency, his later writings presented this claim in terms of the illocutionary or speech-act theories of contemporary philosophers of language like J. L. Austin and J. R. Searle. Matilal (Perc. 66-67) argued that, just as one can perfectly well say: "I do not promise to come, nor do I promise to not come," so one can deny both P and ¬P. Accordingly, the Buddha could deny that the Tathāgata exists after his parinirvāṇa and also deny that he doesn't exist after his parinirvāṇa, and Nāgārjuna could deny that nirvāṇa exists and also deny that it doesn't exist.

It seems to me, however, that the assertion that one can *refute* or *negate* a proposition P without committing oneself to the falsity of P and the truth of not-P is neither entailed nor permitted by the speech act theories, because the negation of the *illocutionary force* of an utterance *does not touch the propositional content of that utterance at all.* One may, of course, decline to negate a proposition, and one may even explicitly *say* that one declines to negate a proposition. But if one does either of these things one has not negated the proposition, and hence one has not refuted it.

Speech act theories of language draw a distinction between a proposition P and the assertion of P. Take the proposition *John smokes.* I can do many things with this proposition. I can, for example, assert it. I can also deny it or negate it. I can also ask if John smokes, or insist that John smoke etc. But whether I assert, deny, ask or insist that John smoke(s), the proposition *John smokes* remains the same, whereas what I *do* with that proposition—what J. L. Austin (1962a) called the illocutionary act of the utterance—varies. Anyone who has seen that the proposition P, the assertion of the proposition P, the negation of the proposition P, and the assertion of the negation of the proposition P are very different things, will see at once the desirability of having a notation that distinguishes between them. Here Frege's assertion sign ($\vdash$) comes in handy. With it, one can easily distinguish between P, $\vdash$P, ¬P, and $\vdash$¬P. Furthermore (and this is what is particularly important for Matilal's analysis of the catuṣkoṭi), one can easily distinguish between 1) asserting P, 2) asserting ¬P, 3) not asserting P, and

4) not asserting $\neg$P. Using Frege's assertion sign, the first is represented as $\vdash$P, the second as $\vdash\neg$P, the third as not-$\vdash$P, and the fourth as: not-$\vdash\neg$P.

14. The most detailed application of the speech act theory to the catuṣkoṭi in Matilal's writings is Perc. 65-67.[25] In this passage, Matilal began by asserting that Nāgārjuna (whom he described as a sceptic) wishes to refute all the possible logical alternatives to a given question. This raises an obvious logical difficulty. Matilal noted that according to "the standard notion of logic," refutation of a proposition P involves the negation of P, and that the negation of P is logically equivalent to the assertion of not-P. According to standard logic, therefore, the sceptic cannot refute without thereby committing himself to something. At this point Matilal said (Perc. 65-66):

> I think the radical sceptic has an easy answer to this problem. He may say that his refutation should not, and need not, be equated with the negation as it is understood in standard logic (where to negate p means to assert not-p). His refutation is a strong refutation of a possibility (cf. Indian notion of prasajya-pratiṣedha) but without any implication for the contrary or contradictory possibilities. This notion of refutation is more or less prominent in our question-and-answer activity. It is a non-committal act of refutation or what I once called the commitment-less denial of the Mādhyamikas.[26]
>
> ...The sceptic may or may not find his position paradoxical, but what we should not do is to attack or threaten the sceptic with the two very sharp horns of a dilemma, or a paradox which has been generated in the first place by our own standard classical logical definition of negation. The standard classical theory of negation in a two-valued system does capture, we must admit, a very pervasive sense of negation. But it is also a fact that some important uses of negation are left out in the account that we get from standard logic. The

> sceptic's use of negation, perhaps, can be better understood as an act of refutation, an illocutionary act where one negates some illocutionary force rather than a proposition.
>
> I wish to refer here to J. R. Searle's distinction between a propositional negation and an illocutionary negation to explain the sceptic's point. This is, I think, quite suitable to explain the Sañjaya-type or the Nāgārjuna-type negation. Such negations were obviously formulated in the context of speech-acts. For example, Sañjaya said, 'I do not say it is so. Nor do I say it is otherwise...' and so on. If we construe assertion as an illocutionary act and the proposition is represented by p, then we can write, 'I assert that p.' By illocutionary negation, we can then write for the sceptic's utterance, 'I do not assert that p.'... Here the sceptic does not make another assertion such as 'not-p,' for illocutionary negation usually negates the act or the illocutionary force. A propositional negation would leave the illocutionary force unchanged, for the result would be another proposition, a negative one, similarly asserted as the affirmative one.
>
> The sceptic's attitude of non-assertion is therefore a possible one, and this does not force him into a contradiction. He can very well say, 'I do not say that it is p. Nor do I say that it is not-p,' just as I can say, 'I do not promise to come, nor do I promise not to come.' I think the Buddhist dilemma or tetralemma could be better explained in the context of such illocutionary acts.

Later in the same work (pp. 88-90), this point is filled out with some logical notation. The sentence "I do not say that there is an after-life" is represented by

(1) $\neg \vdash (\exists x)(x \text{ is } F)$.

This, Matilal pointed out, is an illocutionary negation, and as such needs to be distinguished from the following propositional denial:

(2) (I say): "There is no after-life," which is symbolized by

$\vdash \neg(\exists x)(x \text{ is } F)$

Matilal also noted that (1) needs to be distinguished from another illocutionary negation:

(3) "I do not say that there is not an after-life," which is symbolized by

$\neg \vdash \neg(\exists x)(x \text{ is } F)$.

15. There is obviously an important distinction to be drawn between not asserting that P and asserting not-P. But this distinction cannot be used to dispel the apparent inconsistency of the catuṣkoṭi for precisely the reason that Matilal himself mentions, i.e., that in an illocutionary act "one negates some illocutionary force rather than a proposition" (Perc. 66). The problem is that if one negates only the illocutionary force of an utterance, one does not touch the propositional content of the utterance at all—and one cannot negate or refute an utterance without negating or refuting the *proposition* asserted by that utterance.

That the distinction in question cannot be used in the way that Matilal wished to use it would, I think, be self-evident were it not for the fact that there are some passages which—at least if they are taken alone or out of context—*do* fit the illocutionary analysis. For example, in the Aggi-vacchagotta-sutta (AVGS), the Buddha is said to have responded to each of the ten avyākata questions by saying: "I am not of this view..this is indeed the truth, and all else is falsehood," and when Vaccha asks why the Buddha perceives a peril in approaching any of the ten views (diṭṭhi, dṛṣṭi), the Buddha replies that such views lead to wrangling, anguish, and the fettering of views, and do not conduce to "turning away from, nor to dispassion, stopping, calming, super-knowledge, awakening, nor to nibbāna." There is a very similar passage in the Cūḷa-māluṅkya-sutta (MN i.483-489). In this sutta the Buddha says that he does not explain, sets aside and ignores these questions because living the brahma-faring does not depend on any of these views. He then says (after giving the parable of the man dying from an arrow wound): "Whether there is the view that the world is eternal, is not eternal etc., there is birth, old age and death, the suppression of which I lay down here and now." At the end of the sutta, he also repeats what is said in the AVGS, i.e., that these views are not explained by him because they are not connected with the goal, are not fundamental to brahma-faring, and do not conduce to turning away from, nor to dispassion, stopping, calming, super-knowledge, awakening nor to nibbāna. Yet another passage which fits this pattern of denial is Udāna 66-70. Here the samaṇas and brāhmaṇas who held and debated speculative views are criticized for being quarrelsome, wrangling and disputatious, and for wounding one another with the weapons of the tongue, saying: "Dhamma is such and such, dhamma is not such and such; it is, it is not."

If these passages were the only ones to be considered, one could conclude that the Buddha's negations were illocutionary rather than propositional negations, for none of the reasons given by the Buddha in these passages are reasons for thinking that any one of the ten views is actually *false* (or at least, false simpliciter). For the most part, the reasons given are normative, evaluative or pragmatic—even better, *soteriological.* As such, the reasons given do not provide a rational basis for *negating* any of the ten propositions. What they offer instead is a rational basis for not thinking them of any use or importance, and therefore for *not asserting* any of them.

It is passages like these that suggested to Jayatilleke the possibility that the Buddha's reasons for not answering (avyākata) and setting aside (ṭhapanīya) the ten questions were purely *pragmatic.* As was noted in the previous chapter, however, Jayatilleke rejected this as the explanation (or at least as the whole explanation) of the catuṣkoṭi, and, I think, with good reason. The problem is that there are also instances where the Buddha rejected the ten theses for reasons that entail that the ten views are actually false. One example that Jayatilleke mentions (EBThK §814) is SN ii.61, which says that the religious life would be impossible if the soul were identical with the body, and that it would also be impossible if the soul were not identical with the body. As Jayatilleke notes, this implies that "the theses 'the soul is the same as the body' and 'the soul is different from the body' were both in a sense known to be false."[27] Another objection to the purely pragmatic or illocutionary interpretation is that it fails to do justice to the *positive* teachings of the Buddhist religion, e.g. the anattā/dhamma teaching. As I have argued in the previous chapter, it is clear from the suttas of the Pāli canon that at least one of the reasons why the Buddha set aside and did not answer the ten views is that their very formulation was incompatible with his own teaching (dhamma), according to which there is no self or person (puggala, attā), but only an everchanging flow of dhammas belonging to the five categories (P. khanda, Skr. skandha) of form, feeling, willing, conception and consciousness.

In the suttas, therefore, there are at least two things that must be kept in mind. On the one hand, there are soteriological or pragmatic reasons for setting aside the ten views. These reasons fit the illocutionary paradigm. On the other hand, there is the anattā/dhamma teaching, which as a dhamma (teaching) is held to be incompatible with the ten views of the other schools. This kind of reason for rejecting the ten views does *not* fit the illocutionary paradigm, for if the truth of the anattā/dhamma theory is incompatible with the truth of any of the ten theses, then the rejection of the latter in favor of the anattā/dhamma theory is a *propositional* negation, not an illocutionary one. In the suttas these two kinds of reasons for rejecting the ten views are regarded as complementary ones. Nevertheless, from a logical point of view they *are* essentially different kinds of reasons. Since the Buddha taught that the anattā/dhamma teaching, and only this teaching, led to release from suffering, he could set aside the ten questions both for soteriological reasons (which do not necessarily imply that any of the ten theses are actually false) as well as for reasons which imply that the given views *are* false. Although the former reasons fit the illocutionary paradigm, the latter do not. Hence a purely pragmatic or purely illocutionary explanation of the catuṣkoṭi proves to be inadequate even for the Pāli texts.

The problems with a purely pragmatic or purely illocutionary explanation of the catuṣkoṭi are, if anything, even clearer in the case of the Mādhyamika texts. Take as an example the twenty-fifth (i.e. nirvāṇa) chapter of the MMK. In MMK 25.4-6 Nāgārjuna argues that it is *not the case* that nirvāṇa exists (na bhāvaḥ), in MMK 25.7-8 he argues that nirvāṇa is *not* non-existent (na: abhāvaḥ), in MMK 25.11-14 he argues that nirvāṇa is *not* both existent and non-existent (na: abhāvo bhāvaś-ca), and in MMK 25.15-16 he argues that it is not the case that nirvāṇa is neither existent nor non-existent (naivābhāvo naiva bhāvaḥ). These verses cannot be interpreted as purely illocutionary negations, for if Nāgārjuna had only meant to negate the illocutionary force, he would have had to say "I do not *say* that ..." rather than "It is not the case that ...". This point is confirmed by the kinds of reasons that Nāgārjuna gives for rejecting each of the four positions. These reasons are incompatible with the *truth* of the respective propositions, and are therefore propositional negations rather than illocutionary ones. In MMK 25.4, for example, he says that nirvāṇa is not a bhāva because if it were it would have the characteristics of old age and death; in MMK 25.5 he says that it is not a bhāva because if it were it would be a conditioned thing; and in MMK 25.6 he argues that it is not a bhāva because if it were it would not be non-appropriating (anupādāya). These kinds of reasons do not fit the criteria for the negation of illocutionary force, because one cannot argue that nirvāṇa is not a bhāva *on the grounds that* nirvāṇa is not subject to birth and death etc. without negating the *proposition* that nirvāṇa is a bhāva.

The reasons given by Nāgārjuna in MMK 25.4-16 are very different from the kinds of reasons given in some (but not all) of the passages in the Pāli canon. In at least some of the passages of the Pāli canon, the Buddha simply says: "I do not say that x is true, and I do not say that x is false," and none of the reasons he gives call into question the actual truth of any of the given alternatives. For example, the contention that taking a stand on the avyākata questions does not lead to the peace of nirvāṇa does not necessarily mean that none of these positions is true, for it is at least arguable that a proposition can be true even though holding it or being attached to it leads to undesirable consequences. On the other hand, Nāgārjuna (and the Buddha) frequently argue that each of the alternatives is inadmissible, and this means that these negations must be directed primarily against the propositional *content* rather than the illocutionary *force* of the sentences in question.[28]

This does not mean, of course, that Nāgārjuna's negations in MMK 25.4-16 etc. do not have an illocutionary force at all. Obviously, if I know that X thinks that something that is not subject to birth and death is not a bhāva, and if I also know that X thinks that nirvāṇa is not subject to birth and death, then I will be able to conclude that X does not *assert* or *believe* that nirvāṇa is a bhāva. But I can conclude this because I know other things that X does believe or assert, and because these things *contradict* the view (or at least are taken by X to contradict the view) that nirvāṇa is a bhāva. Unless the reason given is intended to negate the propositional content, there would be no point in giving it as a reason, and if the reason negates the propositional content, the negation is not a mere illocutionary negation.

The point is an important one because it bears directly on the question whether the Mādhyamika can deny or negate a proposition P without asserting not-P. What the foregoing considerations show is that, while one can certainly *decline to assert* P without asserting not-P, one cannot give reasons which imply that P is *false* without implying not-P; and these kinds of reasons do figure in at least some of the passages where the catuṣkoṭi appears. If Nāgārjuna (or the Buddha) had simply remained silent, or had confined himself to pure monosyllabic negations, saying "No, no" etc. (neti, neti) to any proposition, then one might have been able to characterize him as merely refusing or declining to assert P, i.e., as engaging only in illocutionary negation. However, both Nāgārjuna and the Buddha sometimes give reasons for not accepting certain propositions which are incompatible with the *truth* of those propositions. In these cases, at least, they have thereby entered the fray, and committed themselves to the truth of the *negations* of those propositions. Nāgārjuna, for example, has clearly committed himself in MMK 25 to the propositions that nirvāṇa is not a bhāva, that nirvāṇa is not an abhāva, that nirvāṇa is not both a bhāva and an abhāva, and that it is not the case that nirvāṇa is neither a bhāva nor an abhāva, just as he has committed himself in MMK 1 to the proposition that things do not arise (anutpāda).

16. Matilal cited Searle (1969: 32-33) in defense of his analysis of Nāgārjuna, but I do not think that Searle would agree that speech act theory either implies or allows that the purely illocutionary negation of a proposition P is compatible with giving reasons that count against the truth of P. This seems clear from what Searle says about the distinction between illocutionary and propositional negation in *Speech Acts* (the work that Matilal cited in Perc.), but it emerges even more clearly in a more recent work that Searle has co-authored (Searle and Vanderveken 1985, henceforth referred to as FIL).

What was called illocutionary negation in *Speech Acts* is called illocutionary *de*negation in FIL (at least when the illocutionary force is made explicit). The point of an illocutionary denegation of the form ¬F(P), where F is an illocutionary force, is to make it explicit that a speaker does not perform F(P) [FIL 26]. For example, the illocutionary denegation of asking someone to leave the room is "I am not asking you to leave the room." The same definition applies to what Searle and Vanderveken call "English assertive illocutionary verbs" like *assert, claim, affirm, suggest, state, deny, disclaim, assure, accuse, blame* etc. (FIL 18-183). For example, the illocutionary denegation of asserting that John smokes would be "I do not assert that John smokes," and the illocutionary denegation of denying that John smokes would be "I do not deny that John smokes."

This account of illocutionary denegation gives the expected result: it excludes the possibility that one could illocutionarily denegate a proposition P by giving reasons that count against the truth of P. For example, if I respond to the claim that John smokes by saying "But that's impossible: he had a blood test yesterday and the nicotine level in his blood was zero," I would be doing more than merely making it explicit that I was not asserting that John smokes. I would be *denying* that John smokes, or at least calling the truth of *John smokes* into question. Both of these speech acts touch the *proposition* that John smokes. In general, denying that P or questioning that P is not a matter of *not* doing something (which is what is involved in illocutionary denegation); it is a matter of engaging in what Searle and Vanderveken call an assertoric illocutionary act, e.g., denying that P, affirming that not-P, suggesting that not-P, etc.

In fact, Searle and Vanderveken state explicitly that denying that P is *equivalent to affirming not-P* (FIL 162, 183). This, too, shows that what Matilal called refutation (FPC 65-66) corresponds to what *Speech Acts* calls *propositional* negation rather than illocutionary negation. This point finds further confirmation in some of the rules for illocutionary acts, which FIL calls "laws for illocutionary forces" (ibid., chapter 8). One of these laws is that all (non-expressive) illocutionary acts of the form $F(P \mathbin{\&} \neg P)$ are self-defeating (FIL 169). Another law is that an elementary illocutionary act (that is not expressive) is relatively incompatible with any illocution with the same illocutionary point whose propositional content is the truth functional negation of its propositional content (FIL 161). Examples of illocutionary acts that are relatively incompatible in this sense are "I urge you to do this and I request that you do not do it," "I promise you to come and I vow not to come," "I assure you that she is here and she is not here."

Thus, Searle's theory of speech acts provides no solution to the consistency problem that is presented by the catuṣkoṭi, for the catuṣkoṭi apparently denies P, denies not-P, denies both P and not-P and denies neither P nor not-P. Denial is an assertoric illocutionary act (FIL 183). As such, the law just mentioned applies to it, and what that law says is that one cannot both assert P and assert not-P, or deny P and deny not-P.[29]

17. Note also that asserting not-P must be distinguished from scepticism about P. Assimilating Nāgārjuna's philosophy of śūnyatā to scepticism is, perhaps, a fairly natural thing to try to do, since propositions like *Things do not arise at all* and *Things are entirely non-existent* (sarvaṃ sarveṇa nāsti) fly in the face of common sense; and it is fairly natural to interpret anyone who repudiates common sense as a sceptic. Nevertheless, this identification is a mistake, as a couple of comparisons will make clear. In recent times, some philosophers (e.g., P. Feyerabend and R. Rorty) have maintained that there is no such thing as consciousness. This surely flies in the face of common sense—as the proponents of this position (called eliminative materialism) are the first to admit. Nevertheless, the proponents of eliminative materialism are not sceptics—they are simply proponents of a very radical branch of materialism. Another example is provided by idealism. Idealists (pace the good Bishop Berkeley) also deny some of the fundamental principles of common sense. But idealists are not really sceptics, for they wish to replace common sense with *another theory*. The same point applies to the Mādhyamikas. If, as the NI holds, the Mādhyamikas believed that nothing arises and nothing perishes, and that nothing exists, whether it be saṃsāric or nirvāṇic, mental or physical, then they were nihilists, and not sceptics. Materialism, idealism and nihilism are primarily ontological and metaphysical views, and not epistemological ones (though they may have epistemological implications or presuppositions), whereas scepticism is *by definition* an epistemological position. In general, anyone who believes that materialism, idealism, nihilism etc. are true is no more a sceptic than a person who holds the view of common sense.

Sceptics like Sañjaya maintain that, for any proposition P, we are never in a position to know P, and therefore that we are never in a position to assert P. Such sceptics take this line either because they think that there are never any good reasons for thinking that P, or because there are, for any proposition P, equally good reasons for thinking that P and for thinking that not-P. Consequently, the sceptic is not prepared (at least as a philosopher) to *assert* either P or not-P.

Let us formalize this. Let $\vdash \Diamond_K P$ stand for the assertion that it is epistemically possible (i.e., possible for all we know) that P. Now at least one kind of sceptic *asserts,* for any empirical proposition P, both

(1) $\vdash \Diamond_K P$

and

(2) $\vdash \Diamond_K \neg P.$

Accordingly, this kind of sceptic *denies* that one can assert P and also denies that one can assert not-P. Thus for any proposition P the sceptic is led to the position expressed by the following conjunction:

(3) $\neg \vdash P \; \& \; \neg \vdash \neg P.$

[Note that the conjuncts of (3) are illocutionary negations rather than propositional negations.]

It is true that the sceptic presents arguments which, *if decisive,* would be incompatible with the truth of each of the "refuted" propositions, but according to the sceptic, such arguments cannot be decisive. One is therefore never in a position to assert either P or not-P, and must rest content with the two-fold abstention of *not* asserting P and *not* asserting not-P.

According to Prof. Matilal, Nāgārjuna was a sceptic in this sense. This interpretation of Nāgārjuna appeared most prominently in his latest work on the topic, *Perception.* Thus, he spoke there of the "mystical scepticism of Nāgārjuna and Śrīharṣa" (Perc. 26). On page 67 he referred to the "sceptic in the Sañjaya-Nāgārjuna tradition," and said in this connection: "the sceptic's argumentation, through constant practice, is supposed to lead one to an insight into the nature of what is ultimately real (prajñā)," and added that in the case of these philosophers there is a "transition from radical scepticism to some sort of mysticism."

The sceptical interpretation of Nāgārjuna is no doubt a tempting one for anyone who wants to advocate an illocutionary analysis of the catuṣkoṭi *and* the view that Nāgārjuna has aimed at a *refutation* of the propositions that figure in the catuṣkoṭi. There are, however, a number of problems with interpreting Nāgārjuna as a sceptic.

1) It is, of course, perfectly consistent to assert both $\Diamond_K$ P and $\Diamond_K \neg P$, but is this what Nāgārjuna *meant*? Take MMK 25.4-6 and 25.7-8. Surely Nāgārjuna was not arguing that it is possible (for all we know) that nirvāṇa is not a bhāva, and also possible (for all we know) that nirvāṇa is not an abhāva.

This becomes even clearer when one looks at the *reasons* Nāgārjuna gives for negating the propositions that figure in the catuṣkoṭi. These are invariably reasons for thinking that the propositions in question are *false*, rather than reasons for thinking that they *might* be false. Take MMK 25.4, for example, which asserts that nirvāṇa is not a bhāva on the grounds that nirvāṇa does not belong to the realm of birth and death (i.e., is not impermanent). If Nāgārjuna's argumentation were sceptical in nature, one would have to read MMK 25.4 as follows: "It is possible, for all we know, that nirvāṇa is not a bhāva, because it is possible, for all we know, that nirvāṇa is not subject to birth and death." But this reading is surely absurd, for in Buddhism it is true *by definition* that nirvāṇa is not impermanent. Thus, what is in question here is not scepticism, but a simple question of semantics, or, if one prefers, a simple matter of Buddhist dogmatics. To suppose that it is a matter of scepticism would imply that Nāgārjuna held, on sceptical grounds, that the four-fold noble truths of Buddhism were no more true than the denials of those truths. This, I take it, would be patently absurd.[30]

2) It also seems implausible to suggest, as the purely sceptical-illocutionary analysis of the Madhyamaka does, that the *Buddha* was a sceptic. I shall not attempt to prove this here, since I believe that it has been already been well-established by Jayatilleke, who had also noted the similarity between the Buddha's response to the avyākata questions in some of the passages of the Pāli canon and the response to the same or very

similar questions by the sceptic Sañjaya (see EBThK §175-182, §808-813). Eventually, however, Jayatilleke rejected the thesis that the Buddha was a sceptic who belonged to this tradition, and did so on the grounds that there is no evidence that the Buddha ever rejected or declined to assert any of the ten views on the grounds that he did not know whether they were true or false. Furthermore, as Jayatilleke pointed out, it is unlikely that this is the correct explanation for the Buddha's handling of the ten questions in view of Buddhism's emphasis on the Buddha's claim to *knowledge* and *insight* (ñāṇa-dassana).

Thus, a purely sceptical-illocutionary analysis of the catuṣkoṭi appears to be untenable for two reasons. First, refutation is connected with asserting a proposition P or with asserting not-P, and not with *not* asserting that P or *not* asserting that not-P. In invoking speech act theories of language to justify the assertion that one can *refute* a proposition P without committing oneself to the assertion of not-P, therefore, Prof. Matilal appears to have equated illocutionary negation with propositional negation, despite his insistence that these two things must be distinguished. Second, one must take into account the kinds of reasons that are given for rejecting or setting aside a proposition in order to decide whether or not the rejection of that proposition is made for sceptical reasons. As I have argued, neither the Buddha's nor Nāgārjuna's *reasons* justify the claim that either one was a sceptic.

The Mādhyamikas' use of the catuṣkoṭi and the Liar Paradox

18. Typically, the Pāli texts depict the Buddha as having denied that there is a self or soul, and as having wanted to replace talk about such a putative entity with statements about physical and psychophysical entities called dhammas. The Mādhyamikas declared that even these dhammas were empty or void (śūnya). The NI takes this to mean that the putative dharmas were held to be as non-existent as the self was said to be in the early Buddhist teachings and the Abhidharma.

According to Prof. Matilal (v. infra, p. 236), this is an unsympathetic interpretation that misrepresents the Mādhyamikas' meaning. On his view, the Mādhyamikas did not interpret the doctrine that all things are void to mean that all things are non-existent or unreal, but instead took it to mean that things are empty in the sense of being logically indeterminable. On this interpretation, the Mādhyamikas held that no predicate or description can truly be applied to reality; and in particular, none of the four positions of the catuṣkoṭi applies to it.

According to the NI, this linguistic turn in the interpretation of the Madhyamaka is unhistorical. The dharma theory of early Buddhism was a theory of reality, i.e., an ontology and metaphysics. In particular, it was a theory about the ultimate constituents of reality, in much the same way that the atomic theory of modern science (which is, of course, a very different theory) is a theory of the ultimate constituents of matter. According to the NI, the Mādhyamikas held that even these putative ultimate constituents of reality were unreal. Since the Mādhyamikas were, if anything, even less sympathetic to any other theory of reality, the NI concludes that the Mādhyamikas were nihilists.

19. According to Matilal, the Mādhyamikas did not reject the dharma theory completely, but maintained only that it was not a completely adequate *description* of reality.[31] On this view, one might say, it is really theories or concepts about dharmas that are empty rather than the dharmas themselves. This line of interpretation apparently reached its culmination in Matilal's *The Logical Illumination of Indian Mysticism* (LI), where the Mahāyānist doctrine that all things are empty was taken to be equivalent to the proposition that no statement is true.

Although this appears to have been his final (and most succinct) formulation of the doctrine of śūnyatā, it is also useful to look at some earlier formulations of the doctrine in his writings, for these serve to clarily some of the implications of the theory.

Matilal's linguistic interpretation of the doctrine of śūnyatā appeared in his earliest writing on the subject, "Negation and the

Mādhyamika Dialectic" (NMD). The following is a sample of his views about śūnyatā at that time:

(1) The doctrine of śūnyatā 'emptiness' is, in fact, the critique of all views, all philosophical systems. But it is my contention that this doctrine may be dangerously misinterpreted not only by its opponents but also by its so-called proponents to the effect that it actually DISPROVES all views, all philosophy. If anything, this doctrine simply shows that it is neither proper nor is it logically (or, dialectically) justifiable to regard any particular metaphysical system as absolutely valid. (NMD 147-48)

(2) The general pattern of [Nāgārjuna's] argument can be summed up as follows. If we assume any object x to be independently existent, then either we cannot give any consistent (rational) account of that object, by which we can avoid logical contradiction (cf. na yujyate) or our assumption of its independent existence will lead to some absurd consequence which will run counter to our experience (cf. nopapadyate). (NMD 148)

(3) As far as I can see, dependent origination and dependent designation are but two different ways of referring to the same notion—emptiness...The first eliminates the metaphysics of causality and replaces it by the theory of origination through dependence only. The second exposes the futility of linguistic designation and thereby denies the possibility of any conceptual knowledge of reality and replaces it by the notion of designation through dependence only. (NMD 150)

(4) [Nāgārjuna] does not intend to REJECT one position in the sense that he would be willing to accept the contradictory position. (NMD 151)

(5) Emptiness...transpires into the theory of indeterminableness of saṃvṛti (the phenomenal world). But this theory of

> indeterminableness of the phenomenal world is not a theory in itself. This remark should not be treated as mere verbal jugglery for it is possible to give a coherent sense to the claim just made. The theory of emptiness is itself not a theory simply because it cannot be successfully negated...
>
> The notion of the indeterminable is such that it is possible for one to assert the apparently self-defeating proposition: What is indeterminable is NOT and, at the same time, IS indeterminable. Thus, the negation of the indeterminable will also be indeterminable...
>
> Suppose I maintain that x is indeterminate. This means that either no predicate can be SUCCESSFULLY applied to x or all predicates, including the contradictories, are AT ONCE applicable to x. In order to negate the proposition "x is indeterminate" successfully, one has to show that a particular predicate 'P,' and not its contradictory 'not P,' will be applicable to x... But the whole point of Nāgārjuna's dialectic reasoning is to argue that no such predicate 'P' can be found to be applied to x without involving us eventually into some kind of commitment to also apply 'not P' to x. (NMD 158)

(6) The purported Mādhyamika thesis is: The phenomenal world is indeterminate, i.e., is such that no predicate is applicable to it. (NMD 160)

(7) Śūnyatā is itself not a theory of the phenomenal world; the assertion that we cannot assert any predicate of some subject x, is not itself an assertion asserting any predicate of that x. It would, perhaps, be in order for the Mādhyamika to say that the property indeterminacy is itself indeterminate because he would agree that the indeterminate is and is not indeterminate at once. (NMD 161)

(8) When [all logical alternatives, as e.g. in the catuṣkoṭi] are denied, 'emptiness' prevails. (NMD 164)

As was previously noted, this interpretation of śūnyatā as a doctrine of the indeterminableness of reality finally crystalized in 1977 (LI 9) as the formula "No statement is true":

> To simplify matters for our discussion, let me substitute for the statement of Nāgārjuna, 'Nothing has its own-nature' the statement 'No statement is true' or 'All statements are false.' Instead of talking about *things* we talk about statements. As far as I can see, this does not misinterpret his philosophical motivation, for instead of referring to the 'world of things' we are referring to the 'world of statements.' Thus, the 'own-nature' of a thing is represented here by the *truth* of a statement, and the lack of 'own-nature' by the *falsity* (lack of truth) of the statement. In fact, a Nāgārjunian might happily agree to translate 'Everything is empty' as 'Every statement is false,' for all statements may be viewed as prapañca and therefore as belonging to the saṃvṛti level, which will imply that they are false from the point of view of the paramārtha or Ultimate reality.

As Matilal pointed out, however, there is the following objection to this position. If the Mahāyānist doctrine that all dharmas are void (which I shall abbreviate as SDŚ, for sarva-dharma-śūnyatā) is equivalent to the statement

NS: No statement is true.

then the truth of the Madhyamaka reduces to the question: Is *NS* true? The problem here is that NS asserts that no statement is true, and if it is true that no statement is true, then NS must itself be false, for NS is itself a statement. Therefore NS is self-defeating. The doctrine of śūnyatā, interpreted as a doctrine of the "logical indeterminableness" of reality, must therefore be deemed incoherent.

According to Matilal (NMD 158-59), this is the way that most of the critics of the Mādhyamikas in India (e.g., the Naiyāyikas) attempted to refute the Mādhyamika philosophy.

Matilal claimed, however, that this was not a valid refutation. In defense of the Mādhyamikas on this point, he appealed to some of A. N. Prior's views on the paradoxes of self-reference.

Matilal's suggestion for dealing with the foregoing objection to the doctrine of logical indeterminableness was as follows (the reference to Prior is contained in a footnote to this passage):

> To assist Nāgārjuna, we may note that he has a very easy way out. For he can consistently hold that no statement is true without ever asserting NS[32]... If NS is claimed to be a thesis, it can be either proved or disproved, be either accepted or rejected. But since Nāgārjuna does not make such a claim, the attack of the opponent would be wide of the mark... Only a proposition can be true or false. But since NS is not claimed as a proposition, we cannot even begin to think of its contradictory, viz., 'some statement is true.' (LI 12-13)

20. The critic's objection to NS, as we have seen, is that NS could not possibly be true, for it implies its own falsity. This feature of the logic of NS is due, at least in part, to the fact that NS is a self-referring statement—i.e., it says something about all statements, and since it is (or purports to be) a statement itself, it says something about itself. Paradoxes and antinomies arising from self-referring statements have been a matter of considerable interest to philosophers in India and in the West. One proposed solution to these paradoxes and antinomies, which was reached independently by philosophers in India (e.g. Udayana) and the West (e.g. Russell and Tarski), is to distinguish between different levels of language or discourse.[33] According to these hierarchical theories, statements like NS cannot be taken to be self-referring. The assertion that no statement is true (NS), for example, can be regarded as meaningful only if NS itself is not regarded as part of the assertion. If one wants to include NS in an assertion that no statement is true, one can only do this by means of a statement in a different and more comprehensive language, which is called in Western logic a metalanguage. According to these hierarchical theories, NS as a *self-referring* statement—and Matilal did take it as a self-referring statement—is meaningless.[34]

The Udayana-Russell-Tarski approach to the semantic paradoxes and antinomies does appear to avoid logical inconsistencies, but it has not appealed to everyone. Some have argued that the hierarchical theories are ad hoc, i.e., that they fail to provide an intuitively satisfying solution to the problem of the paradoxes and antinomies. The logician A. N. Prior was one of these. Prior advocated a different line of attack on these problems, because he wanted to avoid what he called "the Babylonish captivity of a hierarchy of languages" (Bur. 145). It would not be possible to discuss here all of the details of Prior's interesting views on these matters. However, some of his views must be mentioned, however briefly, in order to properly evaluate Prof. Matilal's claim that Prior's theories can be used to justify the doctrine that reality is empty in the sense of being logically indeterminable.

Take the paradox of the Cretan. A Cretan says:

C: Nothing asserted by a Cretan is true.

Here we run into the same phenomenon that we observed in the case of NS, i.e., C seems to imply its own falsity. This is a rather odd and untoward consequence, for C appears to be a purely empirical proposition, and it has been a fairly universal dogma in the empiricist tradition in Western philosophy that descriptive sentences which are not sentences of logic or mathematics are either contingently true or contingently false. As we have just seen, this is not the case with C (as uttered by a Cretan), for C, even though it is an empirical proposition, could not possibly be true.

What about the possibility that C is false? If C is taken as self-referring, and if C is false, then, Prior argues, there must be at least one other utterance made by a Cretan which is true. According to C, nothing asserted by a Cretan is true; and if this is itself false, then at least one thing asserted by a Cretan must be true. However, we have just seen that C itself cannot be true in any case, so C cannot be that utterance. It follows, then, that if

C is false there must be at least one *other* utterance made by a Cretan which is true. This, too, is an odd consequence, though Prior finds the "Babylonish captivity of a hierarchy of languages" so unattractive as an alternative that he urges us to swallow this consequence as well.[35]

Suppose the Cretan asserts C, and that no Cretan says anything else. Then, Prior argues, it is indeed true that nothing asserted by a Cretan is true. But it cannot follow from this that C is true, for as we have already seen, C can *never* be true. What we must say, therefore, according to Prior, is that in the circumstance just described, nothing asserted by a Cretan is true, but only because the Cretan who utters C has not said anything at all, *i.e., in these circumstances C is meaningless.* Furthermore, if other things are asserted by Cretans, but only false ones, then it is still the case that in uttering C the Cretan has not asserted anything, because C can only be meaningful if there is at least one other assertion made by a Cretan which is actually *true*. Finally, if there is at least one other utterance made by a Cretan which is true, then it is not the case that everything asserted by a Cretan is false, and therefore the Cretan who utters C has actually asserted (though falsely) that nothing asserted by a Cretan is the case. "And all of this," as Prior says, "regardless of whether or not Epimenides [the Cretan] *knows* that he is a Cretan, or knows what other Cretans are saying" (Ep. 76).

Although he conceded that these implications were odd, Prior did not think that they made his approach to these matters untenable, for the implications are not contradictory ones. C would be a logically inconsistent assertion only if it were also true on the assumption that it was false. But as A. Church (1946) was apparently the first to point out, there is no way of *deducing* that C is true from the assumption that it is false. Therefore, as Prior says (Ep. 71), "we can consistently suppose [C] to be false, and this is all that we can consistently suppose." Prior argued on this basis that it is unnecessary to invoke a hierarchy of languages à la Russell and Tarski in order to avoid the logical inconsistencies that seem to threaten self-referring propositions. Provided that one is prepared to make the proper distinctions and to swallow some odd but logically harmless consequences of such self-referring propositions, one need not invoke more than one language to give a consistent semantics for statements like C.

This may be one of the reasons why Matilal found the Church-Prior theory attractive. Since the theory permits self-referring expressions, it recognizes NS (taken as self-referring) as a well-formed expression, whereas the Udayana-Russell-Tarski approach does not. What I have called Matilal's linguistic interpretation of the doctrine of emptiness would be declared meaningless by the hierarchical theories. Matilal, therefore, needed to show that a consistent semantics for self-referring propositions can be provided without invoking more than one language. According to Prior, this could actually be done.

21. Before turning to a more detailed examination of NS in connection with Nāgārjuna's Vigraha-vyāvartanī, it will be helpful to consider one of the consequences of the Church-Prior theory. According to this theory, there are sentences which truly state the ways that things *could be*, but which are nevertheless unassertable as statements about the way things *actually* are—or which are at least unassertable by certain persons at certain times. This was implicit in our description of Prior's analysis of C, the utterance of the Cretan or Liar. It is also true of the following sentence or utterance NP, which Prior took from the medieval theologian and logician J. Buridan:

NP: There are no negative propositions.

According to Prior, NP is a self-referring sentence. Prior maintained that if one thinks about what NP actually means as a self-referring sentence, one is forced to conclude that it could never be true, because in order to be asserted it must exist, and whenever it exists it will be false. Thus he says (Bur. 144):

> Buridan insists that the proposition 'No proposition is negative' must be classified as a 'possible' one because things could be as it signifies, even though it could not

> possibly be true. It cannot possibly be true, because it will only be true if it exists, and if it exists there will be at least one negative proposition, namely itself. But if God were to annihilate all negative propositions there would in fact be no negative propositions, even if this were not then being *asserted* in any proposition at all. In short, *it can be that no proposition is negative,* though it cannot be that 'No proposition is negative' is true.

Prior's claim that "things could be as NP signifies, even though it could not possibly be true" assumes that it makes sense to speak of propositions (or sentences) as coming into and going out of existence. Consider a world W that is rather like our own world, except that at time t the only *propositions* it contains are the following ones:

(1) Snow is black.
(2) Ravens are white.
(3) $2 + 2 = 5$.
(4) Grass is green.

Suppose now that someone in W utters NS: "No statement is true." This statement is false in W, because "Grass is green" is true in W. But Prior assumes that it makes sense to speak of propositions or sentences going out of existence.[36] If so, what happens if the proposition "Grass is green" vanishes from W? Prior maintains that in that case NS in W becomes *meaningless.* Yet according to Prior it *would* be the case in W that no statement is true if (1)-(3) were the only sentences in W. In other words, in this case no statement would be true in W even though this fact was not assertable in W, for to assert this in W one would have to assert the proposition "No statement is true," and one could not assert this proposition unless it existed, and if it existed it would be false.

It is important to be clear about what Prior is claiming here. What he is saying is:

> It could be the case that no statement is true, because there is a possible world W which *we* could describe correctly by saying "No statement in W is true."

But of course this is different from arguing: In *this* world (i.e., the actual world) it is possible that no statement is true.

Buridan and Prior only argue that things *could* be as NP says they are. This is very different from arguing that it could be the case that things *actually* are as NP says that they are; and of course Buridan and Prior do not maintain this, but explicitly repudiate it. Consider, for example, what Buridan says about his tenth sophism (Hughes 1982: 85):

> 10.0 There are the same number of true and false propositions.

Buridan asks whether this sophism is "possible" (i.e., whether it could be the case that the number of true and false propositions were equal), and also whether the sophism itself could be true. About this he says:

> We can say at once that it is possible, since it could be the case that there were just the same number of true and false propositions. This would be so, for instance, if there were only these four: 'God exists,' 'God is good,' 'A man is a donkey' and 'God does not exist.'
>
> I also maintain that it could be *true,* provided we have a case in which we are taking the time to which the verb refers, not as the actual time when the sophism was formulated, but as the time when there were only the four propositions just listed. In fact, even 'Every proposition is negative' could be true in that way; but it cannot be true if the time referred to by the verb is taken to be the time at which it was being stated, nor can the present sophism be either. Nevertheless, even assuming that the case posited in the sophism is exactly as we stated it, some other person arriving on the scene

> can quite truly say, speaking of the time of the case itself, 'There *were* exactly the same number of true and false propositions.' But if the verb is in the present tense no one can say it truly, except in the way just explained, i.e. by using the tense of the verb to refer to a different time from the precise time of utterance of his propositions.

So far as NS is concerned, then, the result is this: either NS is the only proposition that is asserted, or it isn't. If there is at least one other proposition that is asserted, and if at least one of these is true, then NS is false. On the other hand, if NS is the only sentence that is uttered, or if all other sentences that are asserted are false, then NS is meaningless. In other words, *if* NS is meaningful, it is false.

If it makes sense to speak of propositions appearing and disappearing, then one could argue (as Prior and Buridan did) that we can envision a possible world in which all true propositions have been eliminated. *We* can of course say truly about that possible world that no propositions in *that* world are true, because we are at a semantic distance from that world. In a very similar way, we non-Cretans are at a semantic distance from the Cretan's assertion that no statement made by a Cretan is true, and can therefore meaningfully say that things are as *our* proposition C (i.e., "Nothing asserted by a Cretan is true") says they are, even when the *Cretan* utters C and no other Cretan says anything that is true. But we cannot be at a semantic distance from NP or NS—not, at least, if NP and NS are asserted about the actual world. Here we are in exactly the same position with respect to NP or NS that the Cretan is in with respect to C. This is why, according to Prior and Buridan, NP and NS could not possibly be true as asserted of the actual world. As statements of the way things *actually* are, NP and NS are either false or meaningless.[37]

According to Prior and Buridan, therefore, one cannot, as Prof. Matilal claimed (LI 12-13), "consistently hold that no statement is true without asserting NS." Perhaps Prof. Matilal succumbed here to the same temptation that we noted earlier (v. supra, pp. 81-91), i.e., that of identifying *not asserting* that p with asserting that not-p. It would of course be perfectly possible for someone *not to* assert that no statement is true; and someone who did this would not be implicated in any way with the statement or proposition *No statement is true*. But one cannot actually *assert* that no statement is true without implicating oneself in the *statement* or *proposition* that no statement is true.

As Matilal described the situation, NS is the sentence "No statement is true." What one must conclude from this, surely, is that what NS *asserts* (i.e., the propositional content of NS) is that no statement is true. But if this is the case, then it apparently makes no sense to claim that Nāgārjuna can maintain that no statement is true without asserting NS, because "maintaining that no statement is true" and "asserting NS" actually *come to* the same thing.[38]

22. There is yet another objection to interpreting the catuṣkoṭi to mean that no statement is true. If the catuṣkoṭi were logically equivalent to NS, then the catuṣkoṭi would be falsified by any set of statements which contained at least one sentence which was true. This condition will be satisfied by any set of *contradictory* statements, e.g.:

1) $2 + 2 = 5$.
2) It is not the case that $2 + 2 = 5$.

or

1) $2 + 2 = 4$.
2) It is not the case that $2 + 2 = 4$.

This counter-example might be thought to beg the question, since contradictions cannot arise if negation is used in such a way that no implications can be drawn from not-P to any other statement. But I have already given my reasons for thinking that there is no such negation. Furthermore, evading the objection in this way would require the much *stronger* claim that there is no classical negation at all. This is a claim that even Matilal was not prepared to make (see, e.g., NMD 164 and Perc. 65-66).

The Vigraha-vyāvartanī on the emptiness of statements

23. Prof. Matilal's interpretation of the doctrine of emptiness, according to which "x is empty" means "x is false," entangles that doctrine in all the problems connected with the paradox of the liar. But did the Mādhyamikas take "x is empty" to mean "x is false," in the sense in which a statement is false? Perhaps the best place to look for an answer to this question is the Vigraha-vyāvartanī (VV) and its commentary (vṛtti), for the statement (vacana) that all things are empty is the principal topic of this work.[39]

The opponent in the VV begins by asking whether the statement that things are without self-nature (svabhāva) is itself without self-nature (asvabhāva). According to the opponent, the Mādhyamika position can be shown to be untenable whether Nāgārjuna gives an affirmative or a negative answer to this question. This objection is stated clearly in the first verse (VV 1), which says:

> If the self-nature (svabhāva) of all things is not to be found anywhere, your statement (vacana) must be without self-nature (asvabhāva). It is therefore unable to negate self-nature.
>
> sarveṣāṃ bhāvānāṃ sarvatra na vidyate svabhāvaś-cet /
> tvad-vacanam-asvabhāvaṃ na nivartayituṃ svabhāvam-alam //1//

The opponent's objections continue through VV 20. Nāgārjuna begins his reply to the opponent with the following verse (VV 21):

> If my statement (vacas) exists neither within nor without the combination of causes and conditions, then the emptiness (śūnyatva) of things is established, because in that case things would lack a self-nature (bhāvānām-asvabhāvatvāt).

hetu-pratyaya-sāmagryāṃ ca pṛthak cāpi mad-vaco na yadi/
nanu śūnyatvaṃ siddhaṃ bhāvānāmasvabhāvatvāt //21//

24. VV 1 and VV 21, it seems to me, present difficulties for Prof. Matilal's interpretation of the doctrine of emptiness, for these verses suggest that the assertion that all *sentences* or *statements* are empty is merely a special instance of the more general assertion that *everything* is empty.

Matilal argued that in Mādhyamika works the expressions "x is śūnya" (empty) or "x is niḥsvabhāva" (devoid of self-nature) mean that *statements about* x are empty or devoid of self-nature. At least one of the reasons for making this metalinguistic move is to suggest that the Mādhyamikas were principally interested in showing that all statements and theories about things are inadequate, and that things are therefore logically indeterminate rather than non-existent. Thus, all the statements in the Mādhyamika writings which apply, prima facie, to things (e.g., "mind is void," "all things are void," "form is void," "self is void," etc.) have to be taken as abbreviated assertions of the voidness of statements *about* mind, dharmas, form, self etc., rather than as assertions of the emptiness of those things directly.

But if "x is śūnya" and "x is niḥsvabhāva" were meant to apply primarily to statements or sentences (vacas), why didn't the Mahāyānists actually *say* this? Why didn't they say, for example, that all *statements* about things are empty rather than saying that all *things* are void (sarva-*dharmāḥ* śūnyāḥ)? Furthermore, if the Mādhyamikas did attack the dharma theory because they thought that there were no dharmas, as the *NI* holds, then one would expect to find passages in the Mādhyamika writings where it is stated or implied that the voidness of statements about dharmas is only a *special case* of the more general rule that all things are void. VV 1 and VV 21 seem to me to instances of this. VV 1 argues that if all *things* (bhāvas) are without self-nature, then it will follow that Nāgārjuna's own *statement,* since it is a thing (bhāva), will also be without self-nature. Here, the conclusion that the opponent takes to be the absurdum of Nāgārjuna's position is clearly regarded as the corollary of the more general proposition that all *things* are empty. There can be little doubt that Nāgārjuna views the matter in the same way, for in VV 21 he says that if his statement (vacas) cannot be found within the combination of causes and conditions, this will only confirm the statement that all *things* (bhāvas) are devoid of self-nature. Here, too, the metalinguistic statement is regarded as a mere corollary or special case of the *non*-metalinguistic assertion that all *things* are void.[40]

25. Once it is acknowledged that Nāgārjuna takes the statement that all statements are void to be a mere corollary of the more general statement that all things are void, it becomes much more difficult to avoid the conclusion that the VV advocates a doctrine of nihilism. Interpreted in this way, it seems unlikely that Nāgārjuna intended the assertion that even his own statements were empty to mean that they were "indeterminate": what he seems to have meant is that, like any other putative entity (bhāva), all statements (vacana) are actually non-existent. This is, I think, the most natural interpretation of VV 29, for example, where Nāgārjuna says that he asserts no proposition or statement:

> If I had any proposition (pratijñā), this defect (doṣa) would attach to me. But I have no proposition. Therefore I am not at fault (naivāsti me doṣaḥ).
>
> yadi kācana pratijñā syān-me tata eṣa me bhaved-doṣaḥ /
> nāsti ca mama pratijñā tasmān-naivāsti me doṣaḥ //29//

Another example is VV 63, where Nāgārjuna says that he does not negate anything:

> I do not negate anything (kiṃcit), nor is there anything (kiṃcit) to be negated. Hence you malign me and misrepresent me when you say that I negate anything.
>
> pratiṣedhayāmi nāhaṃ kiṃcit pratiṣedhyam-asti na ca kiṃcit /
> tasmāt-pratiṣedhayasīty-adhilaya eṣa tvayā kriyate //63//

Proponents of the NNI have interpreted VV 63, not as a nihilistic statement, but as meaning that Nāgārjuna does not engage in negation. But this is prima facie implausible, for there are many negative sentences in his writings, including VV 29 and VV 63 themselves. (Cf. also VV 23.) Furthermore, Nāgārjuna's two principal commentators, Bhāvaviveka and Candrakīrti, state explicitly that Nāgārjuna engages in negation. (V. supra pp. 49-64, and the discussion there on the prasajya-*pratiṣedha*.) It seems to me, therefore, that it is more natural to interpret the verse as follows: "There is nothing to be asserted or negated; everything is completely non-existent and void; I do not negate *anything*." In short, Nāgārjuna's negations really amount to the negation of existence, or equivalently, to the *assertion that nothing exists* (sarvaṃ sarveṇa nāsti).[41]

The nihilism of Nāgārjuna's position also emerges clearly when one compares VV 21 with VV 1, to which it is a reply. VV 21 asserts that if a statement is not found either within or without the combination of causes and conditions, then the emptiness (śūnyatva) of things is thereby established, since that in itself would show that things lack a self-nature. One of the striking things about this verse is its similarity to what the Buddhist texts say about the self or ātman. The orthodox Buddhists had argued that no self could be found either within or without the aggregates of physical and psychophysical constituents (skandhas), and they concluded from this that the self must be non-existent. As an orthodox Buddhist, Nāgārjuna adhered to this anātman doctrine. If this fact is not kept in mind, much of the point of VV 21 will be lost. What Nāgārjuna says in VV 21 about the statement SDŚ (and the equivalent statement SDN = sarva-dharma-niḥsvabhāvatā) is exactly what the other orthodox Buddhist schools said about the ātman or self. Since his statement (vacas) cannot be found either within or without the totality of causal conditions, it is non-existent, just as he later asserts (in VV 29 and 63) that he has no proposition and that he does not negate anything (kiṃcit). According to Nāgārjuna, this is what exempts him from the fault that the opponent wishes to pin on him. It is quite true, he says to the opponent, that the statement that all things are without self-nature cannot be found either within or without the combination of conditions, but this is not a fault (doṣa) for me, as you think, because this is precisely what one would expect *if all things are empty*.[42]

26. K. Bhattacharya (1978) holds that Nāgārjuna's opponent in the VV is a Naiyāyika, but it is more likely, I think, that his opponent is a Buddhist Ābhidhārmika who uses the logic and debate strategies of the Naiyāyikas to attack the Mādhyamika position. [Cf. Lindtner (1982: 71, n. 241).] This is a point of some importance for the interpretation of the VV, for if Nāgārjuna's opponent was a Hīnayānist rather than a Naiyāyika, the exchange between Nāgārjuna and his opponent on the particular question under discussion is more likely to throw light on Nāgārjuna's views about some of the fundamental principles and doctrines of Buddhism, including the fundamental doctrine of dependent co-origination.

The Hīnayānists held that, even though the dharmas are impermanent, they do arise and perish as part of the causal process, and hence that they *do* exist within the totality of their causes and conditions; as such, they may even be said to possess the property of being dependent (niḥsvabhāva=pratītya-bhāva). Nāgārjuna's position in the VV is as incompatible with this Hīnayānist view as it is with the Naiyāyika view.

Consider VV 22:

> The dependent existence (pratītya-bhāva) of things is what is called emptiness (śūnyatā). This dependent existence (pratītya-bhāva) is, indeed, the same thing as its lack of self-nature (asvabhāva).
>
> yaś-ca pratītya-bhāvo bhāvānāṃ śūnyateti sā proktā /
> yaś-ca pratītya-bhāvo bhavati hi tasyāsvabhāvatvam //22//

When this verse and VV 21 are combined with other fundamental principles of Buddhism, one immediately gets the result that even dependent entities are non-existent, as follows:

(1) VV 22 asserts that dependent existence (pratītya-bhāva) is the same thing as the lack of self nature (asvabhāva) and emptiness (śūnyatā).

(2) VV 21 asserts, in effect, that the statement that things lack a self-nature (bhāvānām-asvabhāvatva) is equivalent to the statement that things exist neither within nor without the combination of causes and conditions.

(3) According to fundamental Buddhist principles, something that cannot be found within the totality of causes and conditions (e.g., the ātman) is non-existent (asat, abhāva).

From (1)-(3), then, we get the consequence that even dependent entities (pratītya-bhāvas) are non-existent.

Hence, it is clear that Nāgārjuna does *not* dispute the charge of nihilism that the opponent levels against him. What he does instead is to argue that his doctrine of nihilism, precisely because it is all-embracing and therefore consistent, is immune to the defect (doṣa) that the opponent wishes to pin on him. The opponent argues that if SDŚ is true, then SDŚ is itself empty, and that if SDŚ is itself empty, it cannot refute self-nature. The flaw in this argument, as Nāgārjuna points out in VV 21, is that it presupposes that there is a self-nature to be negated. Since Nāgārjuna denies this, the objection has no force against him. That is, Nāgārjuna agrees that it follows from SDŚ that SDŚ is itself empty, but the opponent has apparently failed to note that this is no objection against a consistent nihilism, for if all things are empty there is no self-nature to be negated.

27. The nihilism of Nāgārjuna's position is also evident from the next verse, which says:

> Just as an artificially created person (nirmitaka) might negate (pratiṣedhayeta) another artificially created person, or a magical person might negate another magical person created by his own magic, so it is in the case of my negation (pratiṣedha).

nirmitako nirmitakaṃ māyā-puruṣaḥ svamāyayā sṛṣṭam /
pratiṣedhayeta yadvat pratiṣedho 'yaṃ tathaiva syāt //23//

According to Nāgārjuna, the statement that things have a self-nature and the statement that there is no such self-nature are equally void. They are like things of magic. Furthermore, since the thing that is negated is unreal, there is no need for the negation itself to be real. Hence his own statement is not defective. In particular, there is no special difference between SDŚ and any other statement to be accounted for, for SDŚ is just as void as all other statements and all other things.

In VV 27, Nāgārjuna says that his statement (SDŚ/SDN) can be compared to a phantom which destroys a man's false belief in a phantom woman. This, he says, is entirely different from the situation as it is conceived by the opponent, who compares Nāgārjuna's negation to a real utterance like "Do not make a sound," which prevents (vāraṇa) a *future* utterance (cf. VV 3). According to Nāgārjuna, SDŚ does not prevent self-nature. If lack of self nature could be prevented, then by failing to prevent it there could be a cessation of the lack of self-nature, and thereby self-nature could be established. But it is not so, Nāgārjuna says (VV 28), and it is precisely for this reason that there is no inconsistency in his position. If, for example, Nāgārjuna were using real sound, then he could not consistently assert SDŚ, according to which things do not really exist. But, Nāgārjuna says, sound does not exist (na hi vidyate dhvaneḥ sattā). Hence there is no contradiction.

Here it will also be useful to look at VV 28 and VV 29 together. They are as follows:

> Now this reason (hetu) is similar to the thing that is to be proved (sādhya), for indeed sound does not exist (na hi vidyate sattā). But we do not speak without accepting the conventional truth (saṃvyavahāra).

atha-vā sādhya-samo 'yaṃ hetur-na hi vidyate dhvaneḥ
sattā /

> saṃvyavahāraṃ ca vayaṃ nānabhyupagamya kathayāmaḥ //28//
>
> If I had any proposition (pratijñā), this defect (doṣa) would attach to me. But I have no proposition. Therefore I am not at fault (naivāsti me doṣaḥ).
>
> yadi kācana pratijñā syān-me tata eṣa me bhaved-doṣaḥ /
> nāsti ca mama pratijñā tasmān-naivāsti me doṣaḥ //29//

In the light of the foregoing considerations, it seems to me that what Nāgārjuna is saying in these verses may be put this way:

> My statements may seem odd and even contradictory according to the standards of ordinary speech (vyavahāra), since the latter is deeply implicated in a obstinate attachment (abhiniveśa) to the concept of existence (sattā). However, the fault is not with us: it is with language itself. We have no choice but to resort to the conventions of ordinary speech when we debate these points with you. We do not have the luxury of inventing our own language, and in any case the highest truth is not expressible in words (prapañca). But there is no contradiction in reality, for even language and words are unreal (asat). It would, of course, be inconsistent for a nihilist to maintain that there are real propositions or sentences or words to be asserted. This is as true of the proposition or sentence SDŚ as it is for any other proposition. But unfortunately for you, I am a thoroughly consistent nihilist. I hold that it is in fact true that all things are void (śūnya, niḥsvabhāva) and non-existent (asat), but I deny that the truth of this assertion implies that there is a *proposition* to this effect (conceived either as a physical or abstract entity) which *is* true.[43]

28. At this point, the argument of the VV takes an epistemological turn. In VV 5-6, the opponent argues that

Nāgārjuna is in no position to assert SDŚ, for he has no grounds for doing so. The opponent takes the position that it is only by appealing to one of the established and recognized instruments or means of knowledge, called pramāṇas, that one can establish anything. The opponent contends that Nāgārjuna cannot satisfy this canon of debate on pain of inconsistency. Perception, the opponent says, perceives real things (bhāvas); furthermore, the perception itself must necessarily be a real thing. The same is true of all the other recognized modes of knowledge, e.g., inference, verbal testimony and comparison or analogical reasoning. But Nāgārjuna cannot establish his thesis through perception or any of the other pramāṇas, for Nāgārjuna believes that both the objects of knowledge (prameyas) and the means of knowledge (pramāṇas) are unreal. Hence SDŚ is shown to be groundless.

Nāgārjuna's reply to VV 5-6 shows once again that he is committed to the nihilist position. If it had been Nāgārjuna's view that at least some things exist, one would have expected him to have criticized the opponent on the grounds that he has misunderstood or misinterpreted the Mādhyamika position. Instead, we find Nāgārjuna arguing that there is no perception etc. Thus he says (VV 30):

> If I apprehended anything through perception (pratyakṣa), then I would either affirm or deny. But there is no such thing. Hence there is no fault (upālambha).
>
> yadi kiṃcid-upalabheyaṃ pravartayeyaṃ nivartayeyaṃ vā /
> pratyakṣādibhir-arthais-tad-abhāvān-me'nupālambhaḥ //30//

He then proceeds in VV 31-51 to deliver a lengthy (and very interesting) critique of the pramāṇa theory, which is intended to show that that theory is incoherent.[44]

29. In VV 57-69, Nāgārjuna responds to a number of interrelated objections which have been raised by the opponent in VV 9-20. The opponent has argued as follows:

Your position as a Mādhyamika is untenable, for if there were no self-nature of things, one would have to say that there was a non-self-nature (niḥsvabhāva) of things. But if there were no self-nature, then even the name "non-self-nature" (niḥsvabhāva) would not exist, for there is no name without an object (VV 9). A similar problem arises for you in connection with negation. There can be a negation (pratiṣedha) only of something that exists, and hence your negation must be the negation of an existent self-nature (VV 11). If that self-nature does not exist, what do you negate by your statement that there is no self-nature? For the negation of a non-existent entity is established without words (VV 12). Nor can you extricate yourself from the difficulty by comparing SDŚ to a statement which dispels another person's perception of a mirage, for if SDŚ were like this, you would inevitably be committed to a realist view, according to which there is perception, an object perceived and a perceiver of that object, as well as the negation, the thing that is negated, and the one who negates (VV 13-14), because even mirages are real in some sense.

On the other hand, if you say that there is no perception etc., then there can be no negation; and if there is no negation, then the existence of things cannot be negated either, in which case the existence of things is established, including the existence of self-nature (VV 15-16). Furthermore, if there is no perception etc., you cannot provide a reason for your statement, and hence you cannot establish or prove (siddhi) your statement (VV 17). And if you take the line that SDŚ can be established in the absence of a reason, then you will have to say that my statement, which asserts that there is a self-nature, can be established in the same way (VV 18).

According to Nāgārjuna, all these criticisms are based on simple misunderstandings. For example, Nāgārjuna points out in VV 58 that, although the expression "non-existent" (asat) can be taken as a name in a figurative sense (nāmāsad-iti), it is absurd to suppose, as the opponent does, that it must actually designate something. This would be a contradiction, for the term "non-existent" literally implies that there is no designatum. What we must conclude from this, Nāgārjuna says, is not that *he* is caught in a contradiction, but rather that the opponent, who apparently takes all uses of language at face-value, is simply confused. No such problems arise for Nāgārjuna, who upholds the doctrine of the emptiness of all things, according to which neither names nor their supposed designata are real.

The opponent, Nāgārjuna says, is confused about negation as well. The opponent argues that in order to negate an entity x, one must suppose that x exists. But here it is the opponent who is entangled in difficulties, for if x does exist, then it cannot truly be said of x that it is not existent. Therefore, it is the opponent's position that is absurd, not the śūnyatāvādin's. Furthermore, the opponent cannot take the line that emptiness does *not* exist without abandoning the principle that negation is only of an existent, for the opponent wishes to *negate* the doctrine of emptiness, and yet he does not want to say that emptiness exists, either.

Furthermore, Nāgārjuna says, the negation of a non-existent entity does not *establish* the non-existence of that entity, but simply makes its non-existence known (jñāpayate). This is how one must understand the negation of a mirage (VV 65-66). Nāgārjuna points out (VV 66) that the opponent's mistake lies in the assumption that one can only negate something that is real. But a mirage is *un*real. It exists dependently (pratītya-saṃbhūtaḥ, as VV 66 says), and to say that an entity x exists dependently is equivalent to the claim that it cannot be found within the totality of causes and conditions. According to fundamental Buddhist principles, this means that the mirage does not exist. Accordingly, Nāgārjuna maintains that it is this *non*-existence of the mirage that is made known (jñāpayate) by the statement that the mirage does not exist.

30. The last verse of the Vigraha-vyāvartanī says:

> All things prevail for the one for whom this śūnyatā prevails. Nothing prevails for the one for whom śūnyatā does not prevail.

prabhavati ca śūnyateyaṃ yasya prabhavanti tasya sarvārthāḥ /
prabhavati na tasya kiṃcin-na prabhavati śūnyatā yasya //70//[45]

In interpreting this verse, it is important to note that the Mādhyamika expects to find insoluble philosophical problems everywhere, not because he thinks that there is a reality that is indeterminable and inexpressible, but because he thinks that nothing exists. According to the Mādhyamika, everything can be shown to be impossible or untenable (na yujyate) in exactly the same sense in which the son of a barren woman is impossible or untenable—i.e., such things "make no sense" and therefore could not possibly exist. Paradoxically, one might say, one cannot explain things by supposing that they are real—one can only explain them by supposing that they are *un*real.

According to the Mādhyamikas, the world is a phantasmagoria, so any attempt to explain it realistically as philosophers are inclined to do is doomed to failure. Someone who set out to make an ethological study of pink elephants would not succeed, for there are no pink elephants—it is just that some deluded people have hallucinated them. According to the Mādhyamikas, it is the same in the case of what are called real elephants. We are inclined to think that the two cases are different because the behavior of real elephants is less chaotic and erratic than the behavior of hallucinatory pink elephants. According to the Mādhyamikas, however, regularity or consistency of appearances is not a sufficient criterion of *existence.* As soon as we get into the deepest level of scientific and philosophical questions, we find insoluble problems everywhere. Our situation with regard to the mind-body problem, causality, atoms, motion, time or any other ultimate scientific and philosophical category, is exactly like that of a man trying to pin down the nature of pink elephants. Both efforts are doomed to failure, for ultimately there is no motion, no mind, no matter etc., any more than there are pink elephants. To think otherwise is an illusion. Thus, all things shine or make sense for the Mādhyamika because he understands that the world is a phantasmagoria and because he does not expect it to be anything else. He is therefore in accord with the true nature of things (yathā-bhūtam), and is not subject to the confusions of the ordinary person.

31. Nāgārjuna's position in the VV on the emptiness of statements might be summarized as follows:

(1) SDŚ and SDN are true.

(2) However, SDŚ and SDN have no *ontological* presuppositions. In particular, they are not true in virtue of something that makes them true.

(3) According to the absolute truth, there is nothing but *unreal* appearances.

If Nāgārjuna is right about all of this, then, among other things, the correspondence theory of truth must be abandoned.[46]

Here the opponent is likely to protest that Nāgārjuna has undercut his whole philosophy, or at least his basis for asserting it. For what sense could it make to say that something is true unless there is something real (sat) that *makes* it true? As the opponent objects in VV 18, if there is nothing that makes SDŚ true, why isn't the statement that things are *a*śūnya just as true as the statement that they are śūnya?

I believe Nāgārjuna's answer would be: because the view that things are aśūnya doesn't work. If you proceed on the assumption that things are aśūnya, you will soon be disappointed, for two reasons. The first (a soteriological reason) is that the view that things are real lies at the very root of one's suffering in saṃsāra. The other reason is more strictly philosophical: things are unreal because on examination they prove to make no sense, like the sons of barren women. But this does not mean that the truth of SDŚ/SDN is established by the *non*-existence of things, or that the lack of self-nature of things is established by something that could be called the non-self-nature of things. This would be as absurd as taking the non-existence of the Emperor's clothes to be a kind of thing (padārtha). Things are empty (śūnya) because one finds on examination that the hypothesis that things are non-empty is untenable. Thus, while other statements can seem to be true, only SDŚ (and its logical equivalents) actually *are* true. For Nāgārjuna and the Mādhyamikas, seeming comes to end with emptiness (śūnyatā), which is the absolutely true nature of things (yathā-bhūtam, paramārtha).

32. Prof. Matilal argued that SDŚ can be translated without loss of meaning into the assertion that no statement is true (NS). He also maintained that things could be the way that SDŚ/NS says they are. I have previously raised a number of objections to this interpretation of the Mādhyamika doctrine of emptiness (v. supra, pp. 99-103). To these previous objections I believe it is necessary to add another one, i.e., that Matilal's interpretation is too realist in its orientation to be consistent with Nāgārjuna's point of view. To say that things are (or could be) the way that SDŚ says they are (i.e., indeterminable, according to Matilal's interpretation) is still to accept a realist (i.e., correspondence) theory of truth. But Nāgārjuna seems to have been as opposed to the correspondence theory of truth as he was to any other form of realism. For Nāgārjuna, there is, in an ontological (but not syntactic) sense, no negation, no negator, nothing to be negated etc. Consequently, it cannot be said that things are the way that SDŚ says they are, precisely because SDŚ asserts that there are no things (sarvaṃ sarveṇa nāsti). Hence there is nothing that *makes* SDŚ true. This involves abandoning the correspondence theory of truth altogether, and with it every last bit of clinging to the viewpoint of realism—including the claim that reality is in some sense logically indeterminable.[47, 48]

D. Seyfort Ruegg's interpretation of the Madhyamaka

33. In 1969 D. Seyfort Ruegg published a major study of the Tathāgata-garbha school of Buddhism. In that work he briefly discussed (1969: 383 sq.) the Madhyamaka school's treatment of the catuṣkoṭi. The ideas that he presented there on the Madhyamaka received a more detailed treatment in his 1977 article, "The Uses of the Four Positions of the Catuṣkoṭi and the Problem of the Description of Reality in Mahāyāna Buddhism" (henceforth abbreviated as FPC). The FPC also includes a discussion of the views of the Vijñānavāda and the Ratna-gotra-vibhāga, a Mahāyānist text belonging to the Tathāgata-garbha school which, in Ruegg's words, "deals especially with the positive characterization of reality." Here I shall be concerned only with Ruegg's description of the Mādhyamikas' use of the catuṣkoṭi in his influential and frequently cited paper.[49]

The FPC can, I think, be summarized under the following eight points:

1. The Mahāyānist doctrine of māyā (illusion) means only that things are *like* a magical projection. Therefore, the doctrine should not be taken in a nihilistic sense. It only means that things are falsely *imagined* to be otherwise than they are in their "true nature of dependent origination and emptiness" (FPC 51).[50]

2. The avyākṛta/sthāpanīya questions were set aside by the Buddha and the Mādhyamikas because of a "certain logical and semantic vagueness in their terms," as a result of which they could not be "meaningfully decided" (FPC 2).

3. The Mādhyamikas also repudiated the four propositions of the catuṣkoṭi because they believed that the subject terms figuring in those propositions were non-referring—or as Ruegg puts it, because of the "empty (null, nirvastuka) nature of the subject term and its relation to a predicate" (FPC 58-59, n. 4).

4. Although the Mādhyamika texts frequently compare all putative entities and dharmas to nonsensical entities like the sons of barren women (vandhyā-putra), these comparisons (dṛṣṭānta)

should not be taken in a nihilistic sense either. Something that is contingently non-existent, like a hare's horn, could be said, perhaps, to be either a *non*-entity that possesses the property of existence or an *entity* that possesses the property of *non*-existence, but the son of a barren woman cannot be said to be an entity or a non-entity, i.e., it cannot be said to either exist or non-exist. Existence/non-existence, ātman/anātman etc. represent conceptual dichotomies and extreme views deriving from "discursive development (prapañca) and [are] related to either eternalism or nihilism, the twin extreme positions." As such they are repudiated by the Mādhyamikas. (FPC 68, n. 137; 8-9; 18; 63, n. 66; 63, n. 55; 61, n. 34.)

5. Many modern interpreters of the Madhyamaka have addressed the question whether the Buddhists, and the Mādhyamikas in particular, took the positions of the catuṣkoṭi to represent contraries or contradictories. According to Ruegg, this kind of question reflects our logical concerns rather than those of the Mādhyamikas. Sometimes the positions of the catuṣkoṭi represent contraries and sometimes they represent logical contradictories. In both cases, the positions were negated by the Mādhyamikas with a view to breaking down the "dichotimizing universe of conceptualization and discourse." It is particularly important to realize, however, that the Mādhyamikas negated the four positions even when they *were* contradictories, i.e., that they did in fact contradict themselves. As Ruegg puts it, "contradiction must not disappear; and all the four koṭis are to be negated or rejected" (FPC 46-47).

6. Despite the fact that the Mādhyamikas were prepared to countenance logical contradictions, they were not irrationalists. "Madhyamaka reasoning (yukti) is based on the twin pillars of the principles of non-contradiction and excluded middle" (FPC 54).

7. It is important to distinguish the Mādhyamika position from that of the Vedānta, which Ruegg characterizes as a belief in an indeterminate Absolute to which no predicates apply. In particular, one of Ruegg's major concerns in his paper is to show that the "Neither P nor not-P" form of statement [$\neg(P \vee \neg P)$], which is frequently found in connection with the vandhyā-putra kinds of analogy in the Mādhyamika texts, does not imply that

the Mādhyamikas believed in any kind of Vedāntist Absolute. According to Ruegg, the "neither...nor" type of statement represents only a provisional truth, which is explicitly negated by the fourth position of the catuṣkoṭi [i.e., $\neg\neg(P \vee \neg P)$]. This *negated* form of the "neither...nor" statement represents the Mādhyamika's pāramārthika or final position—at least in so far as the paramārtha can be expressed within language at all.

8. The whole purpose of the Mādhyamika dialectic is to bring the mind to a stop. This is accomplished by putting an end to all discursive thinking consisting of conceptual development (prapañca) and dichotimizing conceptualization (vikalpa) involving the complementary opposites of affirmation and negation. When the four positions, which are exhaustive of all the "imaginable positive and negative positions within discursive thought" have been exhausted or "zeroed," there remains no third, indeterminate position for the mind to seize on and cling to; and the mind therefore becomes still (FPC 54).

34. In my critique of the FPC, I shall be principally concerned to establish the following eleven points:

1′. Emptiness (śūnyatā) cannot be *literally* identified with dependent co-origination (pratītya-samutpāda). At any rate, it cannot be so identified in those passages where śūnyatā is said to be free from dependency and relativity, i.e., as having the soteriological value of being *free from* the phenomenal process of cause and effect.

2′. The avyākṛta/sthāpanīya questions are not logically or semantically vague, and one must therefore look elsewhere for a solution to the consistency problem of the catuṣkoṭi.

3′. It is true that the Mādhyamikas believed that the subject terms of propositions are null or non-referring, but this fact tends to support the NI, not the NNI. Furthermore, there is no logical connection between the claim that the subject terms of the avyākṛta/sthāpanīya questions are non-referring or null and the claim that the terms figuring in the catuṣkoṭi are logically or semantically vague.

4′. Although it is true that the Mādhyamikas rejected both entities and non-entities, this is not the particular point of the son-of-a-barren-woman (vandhyā-putra) analogy, for the

Mādhyamikas would have been equally opposed to the idea that a *contingently* non-existent entity was a real entity or a real non-entity. Furthermore, the vandhyā-putra analogy is consistent with the NI but not with the NNI.

5′. In rejecting all four positions of the catuṣkoṭi, the Mādhyamikas were not rejecting all the possible logical alternatives to a given question. Since the Mādhyamikas maintained that nothing exists, and since this alternative is not denied in the catuṣkoṭi, the Mādhyamikas did not contradict themselves.

6′. The passages where the Mādhyamikas *seem* to deny that nothing exists are passages where terms like "abhāva" must be taken as the contrary rather than the contradictory of "existence" (bhāva). In these passages, "abhāva" *does* mean (as Ruegg indeed suggests) something like non-existent entity (abhāva-padārtha). But taken in this way, the assertion that things are not "abhāva" does not contradict the claim that things are not "bhāva."

7′. Ruegg's claim that "contradiction must not disappear" from our interpretation of the Mādhyamikas, if true, would be fatal to the philosophy he is interpreting, as well as to his claim that "Madhyamaka reasoning (yukti) is based on the twin pillars of the principles of non-contradiction and excluded middle." If the Mādhyamikas *had* countenanced contradictions, their philosophy could not have been based on the law of non-contradiction. Furthermore, if the Mādhyamikas had countenanced contradictions, the Mādhyamikas would have been irrationalists.

8′. It is true that the Mādhyamikas did not believe in a Vedāntist type of Absolute, but this is because they did not believe in *any* kind of Absolute—determinate, indeterminate, or neither. The Mādhyamikas were nihilists, and therefore did not believe in the existence of anything at all (sarvaṃ sarveṇa nāsti). Furthermore, in the Madhyamaka the negated and unnegated "neither...nor" statements are not (as they appear to be) contradictory statements. In the negated "neither...nor" statement the negation "not-P" is an internal negation, whereas in the *un*negated "neither...nor" statement "not-P" is an external or propositional negation.

9′. To say, as Ruegg does, that the Mādhyamika dialectic repudiates all "conceptually imaginable positions within the domain of discursive thought" implies that the Mādhyamikas might have believed in a real, existent, *non*-conceptually imaginable domain. But if this is all that the Mādhyamikas had meant, their position would be consistent with the Kantian philosophy of a Ding an sich.

It is true, of course, that (unlike Kant) the Mādhyamikas did not believe in entities of any kind, but what the Kantian example shows is that the claim that reality is conceptually unimaginable does not necessarily entail the Mādhyamika view that there are no entities (or non-entities). Nor does conceptually unimaginability have anything to do with logical or semantical vagueness of terms, or with the claim that the subject terms of the catuṣkoṭi are null or non-referring.

10′. It is true that the Mādhyamikas held that the highest reality (paramārtha) is ineffable (*niṣ*prapañca) and beyond conceptualization, but this point does not present a difficulty for the NI. Nihilism is also in some sense conceptually unimaginable (v. infra, pp. 247-252). It is, furthermore, the only form that conceptual unimaginability can take that is consistent with all the other things that the Mādhyamikas said about the true nature of things (paramārtha).

11′. Ruegg claims that Mādhyamika reasoning was based on the logical principle of non-contradiction etc., and also insists that logical laws do not apply to the paramārtha. It seems to me that in taking this position Ruegg is endorsing the view of psychologism, according to which logical laws are valid *within* the domain of thought, but may or may not be valid outside of thought. There is confirmation for this in the fact that when Ruegg suggests possible affinities between the Madhyamaka and contemporary Western philosophy, the comparisons are between the Madhyamaka and continental semioticians like J. Kristeva and L. Mäll. This suggests that the interpretation that Ruegg attributes to the Mādhyamikas is an irrationalist one, for deconstructionist semiotics is irrationalist.

35. One of Ruegg's most explicit references to the NI occurs at FPC 51, where he says that the Mahāyānist doctrine of māyā means only that things are *like* a magical projection, and that this view should not be taken in a nihilistic sense, but only in the sense that things are falsely imagined to be otherwise than they are in their "true nature of dependent origination and emptiness." The admonition that the māyā doctrine should not be taken in a nihilistic sense means, presumably, that one should not infer from that doctrine that things do not exist in any fashion whatsoever. This interpretation is confirmed by what Ruegg says about the true nature of things, which he describes as "*dependent origination* and emptiness."

The attempt to avoid the nihilist interpretation of the Madhyamaka by identifying the true nature of things (tattva) and emptiness (śūnyatā) *with* dependent origination has been made by many proponents of the NNI, beginning, I believe, with Th. Stcherbatsky (1927). Stcherbatsky's attempt to identify dependent co-origination (pratītya-samutpāda) with emptiness (śūnyatā) will be examined critically in some detail later (v. infra, pp. 194-199) in connection with the discussion of MMK 24.18, but since this equation obviously plays an important role in Ruegg's interpretation of the catuṣkoṭi, I shall say something about it here.

Prima facie, the pratītya-samutpāda = śūnyatā equation is not an implausible one, at least from a purely exegetical point of view. There is a considerable amount of textual evidence from the Mādhyamika writings to support it, if for no other reason than that it forms the point of *departure* for the Mādhyamika dialectic. But it is unlikely that this equation can be taken literally, for if it could, the whole difference between the Hīnayānist view of causation and the Mahāyānist view would vanish.

The Hīnayānist view of dependent origination can be set out as follows:

(1) There are entities that really *do* originate and perish depending on their causes and conditions.

(2) As such, they are impermanent and involved in suffering.

(3) Nirvāṇa is the extinction of all suffering.

From (1)-(3) it follows that:

(4) Nirvāṇa entails the extinction (nirodha) of things that originate and perish depending on their causes and conditions.[51]

The Mādhyamikas did not accept this view. They held that things do *not* originate (anutpatti-vāda, ajāta-vāda) and that the dharmas are unreal (asat, śūnya), whereas the Hīnayānists thought they were real (sat, aśūnya). Furthermore, the Hīnayānists held that those things that do originate also perish; whereas the Mahāyānists condemned this view as a typical annihilationist doctrine (uccheda-vāda). It is very hard to believe that these were not substantive disputes. To suppose that they were not is to suggest that the Hīnayānists and the Mahāyānists argued for centuries over nothing.

The doctrine of dependent co-origination (pratītya-samutpāda) clearly implies that things *do* arise, and this is contradicted by the plain meaning of the doctrine that things do *not* arise (anutpatti). There is simply no way that the rules of Sanskrit grammar can be twisted in order to yield a *reversal* of the meaning of "pratītya-samutpāda," i.e., so that it can be interpreted to mean "does *not* arise." The qualification "dependent" (pratītya) does not *negate* the assertion that things arise (utpāda)—it merely *specifies* that things arise in a particular way, i.e., as depending on their causes and conditions.[52] Moreover, when the claim that nothing arises is conjoined with the principle that nothing can exist which is *un*originated—a proposition that the Mādhyamikas also accepted—one immediately gets the proposition that nothing exists at all (asat, abhāva), which, as we shall see, was also a fundamental Mādhyamika doctrine.

Controversy over the interpretation of the doctrine of dependent co-origination in the Mahāyāna is made possible by the fact that the meaning of the terms "śūnya" and "śūnyatā" (empty/emptiness) in Sanskrit can be made to fit both the

Hīnayānist and the Mahāyānist conceptions. The adjective "śūnya" means 1) empty, void; 2) vacant; 3) non-existent; 4) lonely, desolate, deserted; 5) utterly devoid or deprived of; 6) bare or naked. The corresponding nominatives "śūnyam" and "śūnyatā" mean 1) vacuum, void, blank; 2) sky, space, atmosphere; 3) non-entity or absolute non-existence. (It is also relevant here that the Indian mathematicians who discovered the number zero called it "śūnyam.") Although all these meanings are closely related, there is an important distinction to be drawn in connection with some of them. According to one meaning, "śūnya" is a relation or two-place predicate; according to another meaning, it is a one-place predicate. Thus, one could say that a purported entity (e.g., a married bachelor or the son of a barren woman or the horn of a hare) is entirely non-existent and void. In this use, "x is śūnya" is a one-place predicate. On the other hand, one could say that a jar is śūnya, in the sense that the jar is empty of water. This kind of expression uses "x is śūnya" as a two-place predicate.

The second use corresponds to what might be called a notion of "other emptiness" or "relational emptiness," whereas the first corresponds to what might be called a non-relational notion of emptiness. Rather roughly, one might say that the former corresponds to the Hīnayānist conception of emptiness, and that the latter corresponds to the Mahāyānist conception. In the Hīnayāna, dharmas are not held to be unreal or non-existent (i.e., are not empty in the non-relational sense). However, they were held to be empty in the *relational* sense for two reasons. First, dharmas were held to be empty on the grounds that they do not comprise or constitute a self (attā; ātman); i.e., they are empty of self or devoid of a self. Second, dharmas were held to be empty on the grounds that they do not *self*-exist or have *self*-nature (svabhāva), since they were held to arise and perish depending on their causes and conditions. In the Madhyamaka, on the other hand, things were held to be empty in the non-relational sense, because the Mādhyamikas claimed that things never arise or exist at all (ajāta, anutpatti).

Philosophical confusion will inevitably arise if one fails to distinguish between these two different conceptions of emptiness.

On the Sautrāntika view, for example, nirvāṇa or non-existence (abhāva) is something that is achieved or brought about by the *realization* that things are empty in the sense that they are *dependently originated*; once this realization arises, complete dispassion arises, and with it nirvāṇa and liberation. In the Sautrāntika-vāda, therefore, the equation between pratītya-samutpādaḥ and śūnyatā can be valid without qualification, because śūnyatā is understood in the *relational* sense. But in the Mahāyāna, the equation cannot be valid without qualification, for the cardinal Mahāyānist doctrine is that the dharmas are already extinct, non-existent (abhāva), quiescent (śānta) etc. In *this* context, śūnyatā must be identified, not with dependent co-*origination,* but with the notion that things are *already*, by their very nature, quiescent, non-existent, extinct and unoriginated.

According to the Hīnayānists, dharmas are devoid of independent (svātantrika) existence, since they arise and perish depending on their causal conditions. They are, therefore, empty (śūnya) in a purely relational sense. Confusion arises, however, because there are some passages in the Mahāyānist texts that express the Hīnayānist view of emptiness and others that express the Mahāyānist view.[53] In one respect, this is not very surprising, since the Mahāyānists regarded the Hīnayānist doctrine as a provisional one that was useful for *introducing* the pāramārthika view of the Mahāyāna, which superseded it. Nevertheless, the result can be confusing, and some care needs to be taken to place any given passage that involves the concept of śūnyatā or dependent co-origination in the context of the sytem as a whole.

The passages in the Mahāyānist texts that *identify* pratītya-samutpādaḥ with śūnyatā would seem to justify Poussin's claim (ERE, "Madhyamaka, Mādhyamikas," pp. 236-237) that the Mādhyamikas hesitated between two positions. On the one hand, they maintained that things were composed of dharmas which arise and perish according to the law or principle of dependent co-origination. On this view, śūnyatā is neither nothingness nor a transcendent-immanent principle: it is simply the very nature of what exists; i.e., things are void because they are *produced by causes*. As Poussin observes, all this is "quite within the logic of Buddhism and not unreasonable." But Poussin also pointed out that "our teachers often go much further," arguing that the notion of causality itself will not bear examination. On this view, "not only do the dharmas not exist substantially; they do not exist at all, either in reality or apparently. They are like the daughter of a barren woman, like the beauty of the daughter of a barren woman:...in reality, the object described, the description, and the person describing are all similarly non-existent."

The possibility cannot be completely dismissed, of course, that the Mādhyamikas were simply inconsistent on this fundamental point, sometimes endorsing the view that things arise and perish, and at other times criticizing that view as a false or inferior doctrine. But it seems to me that one need not assume that the Mādhyamikas *were* inconsistent on this point, for it may be possible to reconcile the apparent inconsistencies by appealing to the purely *exegetical* distinction between the concealing truth (saṃvṛti) and the ultimate truth (paramārtha). I am unable to think of a plausible way in which this distinction can be invoked if the less radical view is taken as the ultimate truth and the more radical teaching is taken as the provisional one, but I think it is possible to reconcile the two teachings if the Hīnayānist view is taken as the provisional teaching and the more radical view is taken as the final teaching.

This is what one might have predicted, of course, for when the Mahāyānist texts invoke the two truths distinction, they invariably describe the Hīnayānist view (according to which causation is real, and real entities arise and perish according to causal laws and conditions) as the inferior doctrine. Here, too, the historical evidence provided by the Mādhyamikas' contemporaries must be taken into consideration. It is surely significant that the Mādhyamikas' contemporaries took them to be out-and-out nihilists, who endorsed the very radical doctrines described by Poussin under his second formulation. The opponents of the Mādhyamikas (including their fellow-Mahāyānists, the Vijñānavādins) could not have failed to notice the ambivalence in Mādhyamika thought over the interpretation of the doctrine of dependent co-origination, and would surely have made an issue of it in their discussions and debates with them. This indicates, it seems to me, that when push came to shove, the Mādhyamikas did come down, in the final analysis, on the more radical side of the fence, for the radical side of the fence was taken by their opponents as the *definitive Mādhyamika position.* The opponents of the Mādhyamikas would not and could not have done so if the Mādhyamikas themselves had not, in the final analysis, accepted this as their final position or pratijñā (at least in so far as the paramārtha can be expressed in language at all). If this is the case, then we should expect to find evidence here and there within the texts that the Mādhyamikas themselves believed that the traditional pratītya-samutpādaḥ = śūnyatā equation could not be taken *au pied de la lettre.* When MMK 24.18 comes up for discussion later, I shall argue that this is indeed the case (v. infra, pp. 192-199).

36. Prof. Ruegg mentions at least three reasons why the Mādhyamikas rejected the four positions of the catuṣkoṭi: 1) the propositions that are negated in the catuṣkoṭi suffer from a certain semantical and logical vagueness of their terms; 2) the subject terms of the propositions are empty or null (nirvastuka); and 3) the rejected propositions are (or were thought to be) conceptualizable, whereas the true nature of reality (paramārtha) is non-conceptualizable. Proposition 3) I shall take up in due course. Here I wish to consider only 1) and 2).

Proposition 1) seems to me to be an implausible claim, since questions about the spatial and temporal finiteness of the world, or about the relationship between the soul and the body, or about the existence of the soul after death, do not seem to be semantically and logically vague; hence it is unlikely, in the absence of any evidence to the contrary, that the Mādhyamikas rejected the positions of the catuṣkoṭi for this reason. Furthermore, it is important to note that 1) and 2) do not come to the same thing. For example, the sentences "The present king of France is bald" (as uttered in 1994) and "Pegasus is a winged horse" suffer from radical reference failure, but no one, presumably, would maintain that this is due to any logical or semantical vagueness of their terms. The same is true of sentences containing expressions like "the son of a barren woman." Such expressions are nonsensical, but this does not mean that they are vague. Since there is nothing logically or semantically vague about the terms "round," "square," "married," "is a bachelor," "son," "barren" or "woman," there would appear to be no reason to hold that there is something logically or semantically vague about "round square," "married bachelor" or "the son of a barren woman" either. Such expressions are meaningless, but vagueness is a property that belongs to *meaningful* propositions, not meaningless ones.

37. Nonsensical expressions like "the son of a barren woman" (vandhyā-putra) play an important role in Ruegg's analysis of the Madhyamaka. It seems to me that Ruegg feels that such expressions are important for the following reason. There is no winged horse and there is no king of France (in 1994), but there could be, whereas there could not possibly be the son of a barren woman. Ruegg, I think, has felt that the vandhyā-putra analogy is particularly suitable for explicating the Mādhyamika philosophy for this reason. The point of the Mādhyamika dialectic, he says, is to show that the true nature of things is dependent and relative (pratītya). As he interprets this doctrine, it entails that there are no entities, but it also entails that there are no *non*-entities, either. Thus, śūnyatā, as the true nature of dependent co-origination, is equally opposed to existence and non-existence, which Ruegg interprets as opposition to entities and non-entities.[54] The present king of France, or Pegasus, or donkeys' horns, are examples of things that might be regarded as non-entities (or perhaps as entities that possess the property of *non*-existence). But vandhyā-putras are not even non-entities, for "vandhyā-putraḥ" is a meaningless expression. There is no way of getting a handle on this kind of expression, because one cannot even imagine the thing it purports to denote. And since one cannot think it or imagine it, one cannot grasp it in order to apply the property of existence (or non-existence) to it. I think that this is perhaps what Ruegg means when he speaks of the vandhyā-putras as entities to which "no qualification can be applied meaningfully."[55]

If this is in fact what Ruegg is arguing, then part of it seems right, but another part of it seems wrong. It is true that there is an important distinction to be drawn between a) talking about a non-existent thing that could exist, and b) talking about a non-existent thing that couldn't possibly exist because the referring expression involved is a meaningless one. However, the difference between these two things is not the difference between something that is an existent non-entity (or, perhaps, an entity that has the property of non-existence) and one that is not, for it is a mistake to speak of even the present king of France or Pegasus as entities possessing the property of non-existence, or as non-entities possessing the property of existence. Therefore, one cannot account for the difference between something that couldn't possibly exist, and one that could exist but doesn't exist, in this way.

Since I believe that the foregoing account of the distinction in question is mistaken, I hesitate to ascribe it to Prof. Ruegg. However, there is a considerable amount of textual evidence in its favor in the FPC.

(a) For example, at FPC 34-35 he says:

> ...Vasubandhu has also alluded to the question of the jīva, one of the factors contained in the list of avyākṛtavastus ... Vasubandhu explains that the Blessed One has not spoken of a jīva in terms of either identity or difference (tattvānyatva) since it does not exist. Nor has he ascribed non-existence to it lest a nominal (prājñaptika) or fictitious entity possess the property of even non-existence.

And in a footnote to this passage (n. 137, p. 68) Ruegg says:

> Yaśomitra remarks [AK(Bh)(SAV) 9, p. 470] that the pudgala is not even existent on the surface level (saṃvṛtisat); and as an empty term it cannot therefore even be said to have the property of non-existence.

(b) FPC 8-9 is even more apposite, for it contains an explicit association between the distinction in question and the issue of nihilism:

> ...Just as the view of the existence of an ātman does not correspond to reality, so also its opposite, the view of the existence of non-self, would not do so. Hence the teaching that there exists neither self nor non-self is appropriate because it alone allows one to avoid positing a speculative entity—be it a positive ātman or a negative anātman—as the propositional subject of the substantive verb *asti* 'exists.' ...

> ... Either term of the conceptual dichotomy (vikalpa) ātman/anātman is an extreme deriving from discursive development (prapañca) and related to either eternalism or nihilism, the twin extreme positions that the Middle Way eschews by its very definition. To say that these two doctrinal extremes are nothing but polarizations of discursive and dichotomizing conceptualization no doubt amounts to saying that they relate in the final analysis to empty (null) subjects.

(c) At FPC 63, n. 66, Ruegg cites the following sentence from MMKV 25.15-16: tasmān naiva bhāvo naivābhāvo nirvāṇam iti yā kalpanā sāpi nopapadyate eveti na yuktam etat, i.e., "Therefore even the idea that nirvāṇa is neither being nor non-being is not correct...". Ruegg's gloss on this sentence runs as follows (I use his translation):

> This supposition is also not possible because it still presupposes that bhāva and abhāva are real (siddha), and that nirvāṇa is some sort of entity that consists in the bi-negation of these two reals.

(d) At FPC 18 he says that the Madhyamaka does not "postulate the existence of any entity of which something might then be predicated in positive or negative terms."

38. At this juncture it might be helpful to place Ruegg's interpretation of the Madhyamaka on this particular point in philosophical and historical perspective.

There have been philosophers, both in India and the West, who have claimed that besides existent entities and positive facts there are also non-existent entities and negative facts. Perhaps the most famous advocate of this kind of view in Western philosophy was Meinong. Take the sentence "Mt. Everest has snow on its peak." Many philosophers have claimed that the meaning of this sentence is given (at least in part) by the following analysis: The thing denoted by the expression "Mt. Everest" (i.e., Mt. Everest) has snow on its peak. But if this is at least a partially correct analysis of the meaning of the sentence "Mt. Everest has snow on its peak," what are we to say about the sentence "The golden mountain has a castle on its peak?" Presumably we cannot say that this sentence means that the thing denoted by the phrase "the golden mountain" has a castle on its peak unless that expression has a denotation, and this is a problem, for there is no golden mountain. Meinong had a theory about such sentences which he thought could handle this difficulty. Meinong held that the sentence about the golden mountain is *about* a concept or some similarly ideal entity. The golden mountain, he said, does not exist as an actual entity, but it does *subsist* as an ideal entity. This explains why the sentence in question is a meaningful one. It *is* about something, though it does not make a statement about an actual or physical golden mountain.

Like Meinong, the Naiyāyikas of India also believed in the reality of what might be called ideal entities (e.g., universals or concepts). They also believed in what might be called negative facts (abhāvas). Take the sentence "The cat is on the mat." What makes this sentence true when it is true? The obvious reply is: the cat's *being* on the mat, or the *fact* that the cat is on the mat. But if this is what makes the sentence true, what is it that makes the sentence *false* when the cat is *not* on the mat? According to the Naiyāyikas, the correct answer is: the cat's *not* being on the mat. And according to the Naiyāyikas, a cat's *not* being on a mat is just as real (i.e., just as much a padārtha) as a cat's *being* on a mat.[56]

Now it seems to me that Ruegg's interpretation of the Madhyamaka on the point about non-existent entities (abhāvas) is right about two things. First, I think it is true that in at least many cases the Mādhyamikas took the *claim* that something was abhāva or non-existent to mean that it was non-existent in the sense that the Naiyāyikas would have said that it was non-existent. Second, I think it is true that the Mādhyamikas did not believe that anything was non-existent in this sense. But Ruegg also suggests that to deny abhāvas in this sense amounts to repudiating nihilism (v. supra pp. 131-132, esp. the citation of FPC 8-9), and this seems to me to be mistaken. The denial of abhāvas does not imply this, nor is there any reason to think that the Mādhyamikas thought that it did.

39. Let us begin by noting that the assertion that there are non-entities (e.g., negative reals or abhāva-padārthas) is not the contradictory of the assertion that there are entities. The contradictory of "There are entities" (and there is only one such contradictory) is: "It is not the case that there are entities." Furthermore, the assertion that there are entities is logically compatible with the assertion that there are *non*-entities.

This point can be made more clearly, perhaps, by devising some logical notation. (I do not, however, wish to attach much importance to the notation I am suggesting.) Let us assume for the sake of argument that the concepts "entity" and "non-entity" can be treated as predicates. Let E be the predicate "is an entity" and N-E be the predicate "is a non-entity." Then the claim that there are entities gets symbolized as $\exists x(Ex)$ and the claim that there are non-entities gets symbolized as $\exists x(N\text{-}Ex)$. These clearly do not contradict each other. Both could be true.

The same is true of their negations, as will perhaps become clearer by applying the suggested notation to them. For "It is not the case that there are entities" we get $\neg\exists x(Ex)$ and for "It is not the case that there are non-entities" we get $\neg\exists x(N\text{-}Ex)$. These are not inconsistent assertions, either.

Hence, in asserting $\neg\exists x(N\text{-}Ex)$, the Mādhyamikas did not *contradict* the assertion $\neg\exists x(Ex)$. Furthermore, in making the former assertion the Mādhyamikas did not in any fashion repudiate, undermine or qualify their nihilistic stance, as Ruegg seems to suggest. What the Mādhyamikas did, essentially, was to say: "There are no entities," and then to add (as a corollary, as it were): "And do not go on to make the further, egregious mistake of construing even non-existence as a kind of thing or reality (padārtha)."[57]

40. Once this point has been grasped, it can be seen, I think, that Ruegg's claim that contradiction must not disappear from our interpretation of the Madhyamaka (FPC 47) can and should be rejected. It also shows, it seems to me, why we must reject his suggestion that the Mādhyamikas did not regard the distinction between contraries and contradictories as an important or relevant one (FPC 47).

According to Ruegg, some of the propositions that were negated by the Mādhyamikas are contraries and some of them are contradictories (FPC 22; FPC 40; FPC 45-46.) Both were negated by the Mādhyamikas toward the end of zeroing, nullifying or breaking down the dichotimizing universe of conceptualization and discourse. According to Ruegg, the Mādhyamikas often *did* negate contradictory pairs (or quadruples) of propositions rather than mere contraries, for if they had not, there would have been a position to which the mind could cling which escaped rejection or negation. As Ruegg puts it (FPC 47), "Contradiction must not disappear; and all the four koṭis are to be negated or rejected."

This seems to me to be unacceptable for two reasons.

First, Ruegg does not cite any examples in the FPC where the Mādhyamikas did contradict themselves. The cases of "bipolar concepts" which he does cite are, as I have just argued, examples of *contraries* rather than contradictories. This is clear for the pair "bhāva/abhāva," for as Ruegg himself interprets this "dichotomy," the one term means that there are entities, and the other means that there are non-entities, and these are not contradictory opposites; nor are the negations of these two bipolar concepts contradictories.

Second, it cannot be an indifferent or irrelevant matter *philosophically* whether the Mādhyamikas negated contrary propositions as opposed to contradictory ones. On the assumption that a statement S makes a significant statement about the world at all (e.g., does not suffer from reference failure), S has one and only one contradictory, and S will be true if and only if its contradictory is false. On the other hand, a sentence can have any number of opposites or alternatives. That is why, for example, one can deny that x is cold without thereby committing oneself to the proposition that x is hot. But the logical relation between "x is hot" and "x is cold" is very different from the relation between "x is hot" and "it is not the case that x is hot," or between "x is cold" and "it is not the case that x is cold." The latter two pairs of sentences are logical contradictories: when one is true, the other *must* be false. The assertions "x is hot" and "it is not the case that x is hot," or "x is cold" and "it is not the case that x is cold" are logically inconsistent, i.e., the conjunction formed by them is meaningless. The distinction between contraries and logical contradictories is therefore a crucial one, and it is essential, in order to maintain even a minimal amount of sense in interpreting the catuṣkoṭi, not to overlook it or disregard it.[58]

41. Once one has gotten clear about the contrary vs. contradictory distinction, one is in a better position to evaluate the use of negation in the catuṣkoṭi.

The paryudāsa negation can be ruled out at once. This is not primarily a negation at all, but an affirmation where the thing in question is referred to as an entity that is not something else (v. supra, pp. 92-64). One example that I have previously used is the sentence "Not to the brāhmaṇas is the king an evil-doer" (na brāhmaṇāya rājā pāpaṃ karoti), which in the paryudāsa sense means that the king is an evil-doer—except to brāhmaṇas.

I am, therefore, in agreement with the prevailing scholarly view that the kind of negation used in the catuṣkoṭi is the prasajya negation. However, I cannot agree with a proposition that has frequently been inferred from this claim. It is now usually assumed (since Kajiyama 1973) that since the kind of negation that figures in the catuṣkoṭi is the prasajya-pratiṣedha, the negations in the catuṣkoṭi have no implications to any other statement. But as I have already argued, this is surely not what the prasajya-pratiṣedha means. It *is* true that the prasajya negation of *John smokes* has no implication about the truth or falsity of statements about the sun, moon or stars, or even about Sue's smoking or Ralph's or Devadatta's. But the prasajya negation of *John smokes* does undoubtedly imply something about the truth or falsity of at least *one* proposition—i.e., the proposition that *John* smokes, and what it obviously implies about *this* proposition is that it is *false*. This simple fact (i.e., the law of non-contradiction) was well-recognized in the Indian tradition. One interesting passage (out of a very large number that could be cited) is mentioned by Jayatilleke (EBThK §562). The passage in question occurs in SN iv.298,299, where Nigaṇṭha Nātaputta is charged with inconsistency for asserting that his interlocutor is upright, honest and sincere and also asserting that his interlocutor is not upright, honest and sincere. His interlocutor points out to him that Nigaṇṭha has contradicted himself, or as he puts it, "If your former statement [P] is true, your latter statement [¬P] is false, and if your latter statement [¬P] is true, your former statement [P] is false" (sace purimaṃ saccaṃ pacchimaṃ te micchā, sace pacchimaṃ saccaṃ purimaṃ te micchā). This seems to me to have been the view of all the Indian philosophers and grammarians, as well as the ordinary man and woman on the street. If they had held any other view, speakers of Sanskrit could have defended themselves against the charge of inconsistency simply by maintaining that they were using negation in such a way that no implications followed from their negation to any other statement. But there is no such negation, nor do I think that there is any evidence that the Indian grammarians (Vaiyākaraṇas) and philosophers thought that there was.

42. At this point it might be useful to compare Ruegg's views about the contrary/contradictory and paryudāsa/prasajya distinctions with the views of two other writers on the subject who are criticized (at least implicitly) in the FPC, i.e., B. K. Matilal and J. F. Staal.

(a) According to Matilal, the catuṣkoṭi's negations are prasajya negations, and as such have no implications to any other statement. The Mādhyamikas, therefore, were not guilty of violating the law of non-contradiction (and thereby of having uttered nonsense) in affirming the catuṣkoṭi.[59]

(b) According to Staal (BI 38), prasajya negations *do* have implicitions to other statements (i.e., $\vdash \neg P$ implies the falsity of P). Indeed, the possibility of contradiction arises *only* for such negations. Hence, unless the Mādhyamikas were uttering gibberish, it must be possible to explain the fact that the Mādhyamikas negated all four positions of the catuṣkoṭi in a way that is consistent with logical principles like the law of non-contradiction.[60]

(c) Prof. Ruegg agrees with Matilal and Staal that the negations in question are prasajya negations, but he sides with Staal in maintaining that prasajya negations do involve at least the possibility of contradiction. According to Ruegg, however, the fact that the Mādhyamikas contradicted themselves is *not* something that has to be justified or explained away, as Staal has claimed. The Mādhyamikas did contradict themselves (at least sometimes), but this does not mean that what they said was incoherent or meaningless.[61]

43. Thus, Ruegg's position on the catuṣkoṭi would appear to be even more explicitly anti-logical than Matilal's. Matilal argued that there is a kind of negation which is such that the negation of P does not involve the assertion of not-P. At least one of his motivations was to find an interpretation of the catuṣkoṭi that does not involve a violation of the law of non-contradiction (LNC). Ruegg, on the other hand, insists that the negations in question *are* logical negations. His principal reason for insisting on this point seems to lie in the contention that the Mādhyamikas regarded the four positions as exhausting all the logically possible and conceptually imaginable positions on a given question, and that all these had to be negated in order to bring the mind to a stop. According to Ruegg, therefore, anyone who fails to see that the Mādhyamikas *did* contradict themselves in negating all four positions of the catuṣkoṭi has failed to understand the Mādhyamikas correctly.

However, it is hard to see how logical contradictions and logical inconsistency *could* fail to be a fault. The gravamen of the charge that a person has contradicted himself has always been that he has uttered something *meaningless.* If I say that John smokes and also that he does not smoke, then I have made (ignoring irrelevant questions of vagueness) joint assertions that cancel each other out, and which therefore assert absolutely nothing. Contradictions are therefore meaningless, just as "The son of a barren woman sang the round square" is meaningless: it is merely a sound-blast (śabda-mātra, flatus voci), a mere string of lexical items from the English language which, taken as a whole, have no meaning whatever. What Ruegg is obliged to show, therefore, is that the Mādhyamikas could have asserted P & ¬P, ¬P & ¬¬P, etc., where the negations are logical negations and P and ¬P are logical contradictories, without having uttered complete nonsense.[62]

44. Although Ruegg is not averse to contradictions per se, there are some apparent contradictions in the Mādhyamika texts that even he wants to explain away. One of the apparent contradictions that concerns him is the occurrence in Mādhyamika texts of propositions of the form "Neither P nor not-P" as well as their denials, "*Not*: neither P nor not-P." Propositions of the latter kind (i.e., the standard, *negated* form of the fourth koṭi) are very common in the Buddhist and Mādhyamika texts, but propositions of the former kind are also found, often in connection with the analogies (dṛṣṭānta) of non-existent entities like hares' horns and the sons of barren women.

Ruegg devotes a considerable amount of attention in the FPC to this feature of the Mādhyamika texts. It should be emphasized, however, that Ruegg does *not* find this apparent contradiction problematic as such, for unlike most other writers on the catuṣkoṭi, Ruegg does not, in principle, find contradictions meaningless or otherwise objectionable. What does concern Ruegg is that the Mādhyamikas might be thought to have regarded these two kinds of statement as having equal value. According to Ruegg, this is not the case, for in the Mādhyamika philosophy the unnegated "neither...nor" kind of statement represents an inferior or provisional view, whereas the fourth koṭi represents the final or pāramārthika view (at least in so far as the paramārtha can be represented within language at all).

Ruegg's reason for thinking that the "neither...nor" statements are provisional is that they imply a Vedāntist or quasi-Vedāntist view that there is some kind of entity, however hard to define (FPC 36), which is indeterminable as either P or not-P. According to Ruegg, this could not represent the highest view of the Madhyamaka, for this would still be a position to which the mind could cling, and the ultimate object of the Buddhist catuṣkoṭi and Buddhist practice is to avoid clinging to any position. Thus, the "neither...nor" statements, even though they might be found here and there in the Mādhyamika texts as provisional statements, are ultimately negated, voided or zeroed.

45. One passage that receives a considerable amount of attention from Ruegg in this connection is MMK(V) 18.8. The kārikā itself runs as follows:

> The Buddha's teaching is: everything is true, [or not true], also true and not true, neither true nor not true.

> sarvaṃ tathyaṃ [na vā tathyaṃ] tathyaṃ cātathyam-eva ca/
> naivātathyaṃ naiva tathyam-etad-buddhānuśāsanam //8//

What Ruegg says about this verse (which gives, rather anomalously, the *un*negated form of the catuṣkoṭi) is that the last koṭi of the verse (i.e., "neither true nor not true") does not represent the pāramārthika viewpoint of the Mādhyamikas, because it would be consistent with or even imply a Vedāntist or quasi-Vedāntist view, according to which there is an indeterminate reality to which no predicate or its negation could be applied.

One of the problems with Ruegg's interpretation is that there does not seem to be anything in MMK 18 to suggest that Nāgārjuna intended "neither true nor not true" to be taken as anything less than final or pāramārthika. The main problem for Ruegg, however, lies in reconciling his interpretation of the fourth koṭi of MMK 18.8 with MMK*V* 18.8. Candrakīrti's commentary on the fourth koṭi of this verse, which immediately follows his commentary on the *third* one, runs as follows:

> However, to those who have practiced for a long time (aticirābhyasta) insight into the true nature of things (tattva-darśana), [but] who have not completely uprooted the roots of the tree of obstructions (āvaraṇa), the teaching is: "neither not-true nor true." In order to remove the last vestiges of confusion, both alternatives

> [i.e., "true" and "not-true"] are rejected, as when one says that the son of a barren woman is neither dark in color nor white.[63]

About this passage Ruegg says (FPC 6):

> It is furthermore important to observe that the context clearly shows that such a method of teaching that takes 'all' to be just so, etc., according to the situation, does not represent an attempt to define ultimate and ineffable reality ... Candrakīrti accordingly observes that, when teaching in this manner that 'all' is just so, etc., the Buddha has ordinary unintelligent folk in mind in the first statement, and the Āryas in the statement to the effect that all is false (mṛṣā: atathya). As for the teaching that 'all' is neither tathya nor atathya, it is intended for persons who have for a long time cultivated insight into reality but have not yet totally eradicated the obstacles (avāraṇa); such a use of the 'neither...nor' type of statement is held to be appropriate because it is applied when speaking of a subject that is empty (null) like the son of a barren woman (vandhyāsuta), so long as the particular disciples addressed have only partially understood the non-substantiality of all dharmas. (We would say that such a sentence containing such an empty subject is not well-formed semantically, and that any qualification is therefore inapplicable.) Such a method of progressive and accommodated teaching is, then, considered to be simply a useful device (upāya) employed by the compassionate Buddha to introduce people in a preliminary manner to the quintessence of reality (tattvāmṛtāvatāra).

And in a footnote to this passage (FPC 6) he says:

> Similarly, we might say of something that it is roughly so, i.e. neither just so nor quite the opposite, although

> if analysed it would require further qualification. It is to be noted that the 'neither...nor' form of statement is here intended for a category of persons inferior to those in question under MMK 18.6; for here this formulation does not refer to the highest level of understanding of reality.

46. There are, I think, a number of problems with Ruegg's interpretation of MMK and MMKV 18.8.

First, Candrakīrti says explicitly that the teaching "neither not-true nor true" is intended to *remove the last vestige of confusion,* and it is very hard to see how it could do this if it didn't truly state the way things are when all vestige of confusion has been removed. Nor could one evade this objection by arguing that statements like "neither not-true nor true" still lie within the domain of language (prapañca), for of course the *negated* "neither...nor" statement also lies within the domain of language, and even Ruegg takes the latter kind of statement pāramārthika.[64]

Another problem with his interpretation, it seems to me, is that it seriously compromises what Ruegg says about the vandhyā-putra analogy (dṛṣṭānta). If I understand Ruegg correctly, he maintains that the vandhyā-putra kind of analogy is apposite for the Mādhyamikas precisely because, as a meaningless expression, a vandhyā-putra cannot be conceived as either an entity or a non-entity. According to Ruegg, the Mādhyamikas thought that ultimate reality (i.e., the paramārtha) was also free from concepts like "entity" and "non-entity." It is therefore a bit suprising to find Ruegg insisting that the vandhyā-putra analogy in MMKV 18.8 does *not* refer to the highest reality.

An interesting example of this apparent discrepancy occurs at FPC 9, where, after claiming that the conceptual dichotomy between ātman and anātman represents "polarizations of discursive and dichotimizing conceptualizations," Ruegg specifically mentions the vandhyā-putra analogy (FPC 62, n. 38). The most natural way of interpreting this passage, it seems to me, is to suppose that Ruegg cites the analogy of the son of a barren woman (who is neither light nor dark) as an example of something that is *free from such discursive and dichotimizing conceptualizations*, for if the vandhyā-putra analogy were to be taken merely as an example of a *non*-entity, it would itself be an example of something that fell into one of the two bipolar opposites, e.g., ātman/*anātman*, entity/*non-entity*, existence/*non-existence* etc.

Furthermore, Ruegg himself seems to have doubts about his interpretation of MMKV 18.8. At FPC 17 Ruegg repeats the claim that the Mādhyamikas rejected the "neither...nor" kind of statement on the grounds that it presupposes a Vedānta-like indeterminate entity. But he then goes on to say in a footnote (FPC 63-64, n. 71):

> Still, Candrakīrti's explanation of MMK 18.8, which compares the case to the negation of the qualifications 'pale' and 'dark' with respect to the son of a barren woman (vandhyāsuta, i.e. an empty subject), does not seem to have made this point absolutely clear. For the bi-negation of these qualifications in the case of the vandhyāsuta would apparently correspond to the fourth koṭi *before* its negation, whereas (as seen above) it too has to be, and in fact is, negated by the Mādhyamikas. The discrepancy is puzzling, and may be due to an oversight or to inaccurate composition on Candrakīrti's part; or the point may have seemed to him so obvious in view of what is said elsewhere that he did not feel it necessary to dwell on it. Again, it might be that Candrakīrti switched just here from thinking of the 'neither...nor' form of statement represented by the fourth position of the catuṣkoṭi to the 'neither...nor' type of statement to be found for example in MMK 25.10cd.

These remarks are puzzling. The claim that the "bi-negation of [paleness and darkness] ... would apparently correspond to the fourth koṭi *before* its negation," and that this bi-negation is negated by the fourth koṭi, seems to me to contradict the passages

I have cited previously, where Ruegg seems to me to commit himself quite unmistakably to the view that the vandhyā-putra analogy and the "neither...nor" statements describe the *ultimate* reality (i.e., non-conceptualizability, freedom from bipolar opposites, etc.). Furthermore, it is hard to accept his proposed interpretation of MMK(V) 18.8 when we are also told that it may require us to suppose either that Candrakīrti contradicted himself (cf. "through oversight"); did not express himself properly (cf. "inaccurate composition"); assumed that the reader could figure out for himself why he had apparently contradicted himself (because the solution would be apparent to the reader "in view of what he said elsewhere," so that he did not feel "it necessary to dwell on it"); or that in MMKV 18.8 Candrakīrti switched ("just here," and here only) from thinking of the "neither...nor" form of statement represented by the *fourth* position of the catuṣkoṭi to the "neither...nor" type of statement to be found for example in MMK 25.10cd.

Furthermore, I am not sure that the passage that Ruegg cites in defense of his interpretation (i.e., MMK 25.10cd) is apposite. MMK 25.10cd, which reads "na bhāvo nābhāvaḥ," comes after MMK 25.4-6 and 25.7-8, which argue, respectively, that nirvāṇa is not a bhāva and not an abhāva. It seems to me, therefore, that MMK 25.10cd is most naturally read as *summarizing* what has been established in these verses, i.e., that it means "not a bhāva, not an abhāva," where the two terms are simply concatenated. Further support for this interpretation can be found in the fact that MMK 25.10 is then *followed* by MMK 25.11-14, which argue that nirvāṇa is not *both* a bhāva and an abhāva (abhāvo bhāvaś-ca) and by MMK 25.15-16, which argue that it is not the case that nirvāṇa is neither existence nor non-existence (na: naivābhāvo naiva bhāvaḥ). Thus, if MMK 25.10 did anything more than merely recapitulate the preceding six verses, MMK 25 would mention five verbal formulations for the koṭis rather than four.

47. Ruegg's attempts to explain away MMKV 18.8 seem so forced and unnatural that one suspects that his explanation must have run off the rails somewhere. But where?

I suggest that we begin by questioning the assumption that the Mādhyamikas regarded the negated and the unnegated forms of the "neither...nor" statement as contradictory ones. Of course, such statements *are* contradictory on one reading [i.e., $\neg(P \vee \neg P)$ and $\neg\neg(P \vee \neg P)$]. But I do not think that we have to take the Mādhyamikas' use of "neither...nor" and "not: neither...nor" as contradictory, provided that we interpret them in the light of the distinction between internal and external negation.

Take the proposition "John smokes." If one negates the *predicate* "smokes" in this sentence, one gets the statement "John is a non-smoker," where the negation is internal; whereas if one negates the sentence externally or propositionally, one gets the statement "It is not the case that John smokes." Usually, the availability of these two different kinds of negation in natural language does not lead to confusion, but there are cases where it can. Negations of subject-predicate statements that suffer radical reference failure fall into this category.

Take the sentence, "Santa Claus neither smokes nor does not smoke." It can be argued that the sentence in question is ambiguous. On the one hand, it can mean that it is not the case that Santa Claus smokes and that it is also *not* the case that Santa Claus does not smoke. But the negation can also be taken as an *internal* negation, in which case the sentence means: "Santa Claus is such that he possesses the property of being-neither-a-smoker-nor-a-non-smoker." It is arguable that these two interpretations of the sentence do not mean the same thing, for the second interpretation seems more explicitly committed to a number of ontological and metaphysical assumptions than does the first one, e.g., that Santa Claus exists, that he possesses a property, and that the property of neither smoking nor not smoking is one of these properties.

The suggestion, then, is that the negated and unnegated "neither...nor" statements do not have to be regarded as contradictory ones once the distinction between internal and external negation is taken into account. Indeed, in the light of this distinction the negated and unnegated statements simply represent two different aspects of the same teaching. "Santa

Claus neither smokes nor does not smoke" (where "neither...nor" is to be taken externally) negates the two propositions "Santa Claus smokes" and "Santa Claus does not smoke," presumably on the grounds that there is no Santa Claus. On the other hand, the sentence "It is not the case that Santa Claus neither smokes nor does not smoke" (where "neither...nor" is to be taken as an internal negation) is most naturally interpreted as negating the claim that there is an entity Santa Claus that has the peculiar property of being neither a smoker nor a non-smoker. Thus, the "not: neither...nor" statement need not be taken as contradicting the "neither...nor" statement if the bi-negation "neither...nor" is taken as an external negation in the first case and as an internal negation in the second case.

48. The distinction between internal and external negation, and the question of the logical form of the propositions of ordinary language, also needs to be taken into account when one addresses the question whether the Mādhyamikas accepted the law of the excluded middle (LEM). This is a question that has been discussed by many writers on the Madhyamaka, including Ruegg.

Here it will be useful to introduce the notion of a *significant* statement. We might think of a significant statement as one that hooks on to the world in the expected and required way and succeeds in saying something about it. This way of formulating the question seems to me to have the advantage of helping to sideline the Russellian vs. Strawsonian question of the logical form of subject-predicate sentences—a question which seems to me to be largely irrelevant to the question of whether the LEM is a universally valid law of logic.

Taken à la Russell (1905), sentences of the subject-predicate form—provided that they are not semantically meaningless like "The son of the barren woman sang the round square"—are always significant as I have defined "significant," i.e., they always succeed in hooking on to the world and saying something about it. Take the sentence "The present king of France is bald," as uttered in 1994. There is no king of France in 1994. Nevertheless, according to Russell's analysis, this sentence is a significant one (as I have defined the word "significant") because it *asserts* that there is a king of France, and this assertion is false.

Taken à la Strawson (1950), sentences that suffer radical reference failure are not significant in the above sense, since they do not succeed in saying anything about the world either truly or falsely. Strawson insists, however, that such sentences are still *meaningful,* at least in the very weak sense that, unlike "The son of the barren woman sang the round square," they are bona fide sentences which *could* be used (if the facts were different) to say something informative about the world truly or falsely.

I am not at all sure that the LEM was ever meant to apply to all meaningful sentences in the very weak sense in which Strawson uses the term "meaningful sentence." *If* one uses the term "meaningful" to mean what Strawson means by it, then it seems to me that the LEM is more properly understood as a law about what I have called significant statements, i.e., statements that do succeed in hooking on to the world and saying something about it. Taken in *this* way, a very strong case can be made that the LEM is universally valid, and that the Mādhyamikas accepted it as such.[65, 66]

49. Although Ruegg claims that the Mādhyamikas upheld the universal validity of logical laws like the LEM, it it seems to me that this claim means very little in his case, because he also maintains, on psychologistic grounds, that the laws of logic are valid only as laws of thought.

One passage where Ruegg *seems* to endorse the universal validity of the laws of logic occurs at FPC 54:

> Madhyamaka reasoning (yukti) is based on the twin pillars of the principles of non-contradiction and excluded middle; and the negation of the four koṭis then serves to bring to a stop all discursive thinking consisting of conceptual development (prapañca) and dichotimizing conceptualization (vikalpa) involving the solidarity of complementary opposites expressed as affirmation (vidhi) and negation (pratiṣedha). When the four koṭis—taken as being exhaustive of all imaginable positive and negative positions within discursive

> thought—have been used up, there remains no 'third' (indeterminate or putatively dialectical) position between the positive and negative which discursive thought could then seize on and cling to; and the mind therefore becomes still. This exhaustion—and 'zeroing'—of all the discursively conceivable extreme positions by means of the negation of all four koṭis corresponds to the Middle Way, and to reality as understood by the Mādhyamika as emptiness of own being and non-substantiality of all factors of existence.

Since Ruegg does not consider logical contradictions to be meaningless or even objectionable per se, it seems at first sight rather strange to find him arguing in this passage that "Madhyamaka reasoning (yukti) is based on the twin pillars of the principles of non-contradiction and excluded middle." I shall return to this puzzle shortly, but first I would like to note some possible connections between Ruegg's remarks in this passage and his views about nihilism.

One way of reading the above passage is to take it as specifying the sense in which the Mādhyamikas were not nihilists. According to this reading, the Mādhyamikas did not deny reality altogether, but merely repudiated all *conceptualizations* of reality or all conceptually possible positions, where "conceptually possible" is defined as the "frame of dichotimizing conceptualization (vikalpa) which involves pairs of binary concepts" (FPC 63, n. 55). Thus, the catuṣkoṭi denies the validity of all things within the domain of conceptualization, but does not deny the reality of a domain that transcends the laws of logic. Anything that is not conceptually possible in the defined sense is then to be regarded as *either* non-existent (like the sons of barren women) *or* as belonging to this transcendental realm.

This, I think, would be a fairly natural way of interpreting the passage I have cited. However, there are problems with this reading. For one thing, what it suggests is that although all conceptually *imaginable* positions are negated or rejected, there are some *un*imaginable positions which are not. If this is in fact what the passage means, then it seems to me that it is incompatible with Ruegg's other claim that the Mādhyamikas rejected all indeterminate third values to which the mind could cling—for I imagine that even Ruegg would insist that the mind can cling to a position even when it is thought to be *un*imaginable.

If Nāgārjuna had only rejected all *conceptually imaginable* positions, his philosophy would be compatible with the Kantian doctrine of a Ding an sich! But Nāgārjuna rejected the notion of ineffable *dharmas* as much as he rejected the notion of an ineffable ātman. This kind of move had been tried even before Nāgārjuna's time by the Pudgalavādins, who had maintained that there was an indeterminable, ineffable self or person (pudgala, ātman) which was neither the same as nor different from the skandhas. This quasi-self was rejected with abhorrence by all the orthodox schools of Buddhism (including the Mādhyamikas)—and there is no reason to think that the Mādhyamikas would have been any more sympathetic to the claim that there were ineffable, non-conceptualizable *dharmas*.[67]

Nāgārjuna rejected the dharma theory because he thought that there *were* no dharmas, not because he thought that the dharmas were transcendental and ineffable. The very fact that the Mādhyamikas spoke of illusions and of non-existent and even nonsensical entities in connection with the dharmas is sufficient evidence that they had in mind something different, and much stronger, than the Kantian idea that material objects have a true nature and reality but one that is not imaginable or perceptible (cf. the Ding an sich). Kant would never have dreamed of speaking of the ordinary objects of our experience as dreams, illusions, sky-flowers, cities in the sky, the sons of barren women etc., as Nāgārjuna and the other Mādhyamikas did. What this shows, it seems to me, is that Nāgārjuna was not a Kantian or even a precursor of Kant. Nāgārjuna was denying outright the *reality* of all things or dharmas, and not just their conceptualizability. In insisting on this point I am not suggesting that Ruegg himself regards Nāgārjuna as a Kantian. I am only pointing out that to speak of the rejection of all conceptually *imaginable* positions, as Ruegg does in FPC 54, does not differentiate the Mādhyamika position from the Kantian one, which Nāgārjuna would undoubtedly have rejected.[68, 69]

50. Ruegg says that the paramārtha is, by definition, non-conceptualizable, i.e., beyond the domain of language, logic and thought. He also maintains that the paramārtha is the level of reality that is described by the fourth koṭi, i.e., "not: neither...nor," at least in so far as the paramārtha can be described within the limitations of language at all. But this, too, raises a problem, for the fourth koṭi is equivalent (at least classically) to the LEM, i.e., "Either P or not-P." This makes it very hard to see how the two claims just mentioned can be reconciled. That is, how can the paramārtha be non-conceptualizable if the paramārtha is also describable (at least within the limits of language) by the LEM? Although there has been a great deal of philosophical discussion about the LEM, no one has ever suggested that it is in any way associated with the view that reality is *non*-conceptualizable. On the contrary: the LEM seems, if anything, to have quite the opposite implication.

This problem suggests that we should take a closer look at Ruegg's claim that "Madhyamaka reasoning (yukti) is based on the twin pillars of the principles of non-contradiction and excluded middle" (FPC 54). It seems to me that when Ruegg ascribes to the Mādhyamikas the view that there is no indeterminate third position, he is not really interested in upholding the LEM at all: he is only insisting on the point because he believes that the Mādhyamikas wanted to push the mind to a reality that is beyond all *thought*. If I am right about this, then Ruegg's statement that the Mādhyamikas based their philosophy on the laws of non-contradiction etc. is a misleading one, for what he seems to mean is simply that we must abandon the realm of thought altogether, and this seems to be a psychological point (or perhaps a soteriological one) and not a point about logic.

There is confirmation for this interpretation of the FPC at FPC 48-49, where Ruegg attributes to J. F. Staal the view that the Mādhyamikas rejected the law of the excluded middle. This does not seem quite accurate, incidentally, since what Staal actually argued was that they would not have been irrational if they *had* denied the validity of the LEM; but this point is less important for our present purposes than the fact that Ruegg criticizes Staal for claiming that the Mādhyamikas did reject the LEM, and that he does so on the grounds that this claim is "tantamount to affirming that, for the Mādhyamikas, there exists some third position or value between the affirmation and the negation of a predicate (or proposition)."

The particular passage that Ruegg cites to refute this interpretation of the Madhyamaka is BCA 9.35, where Śāntideva says:

> When neither the thought of existence nor the thought of non-existence stands forth before the mind, then, being deprived of support due to the absence of any place of resort, the mind becomes still (praśāmyati).
>
> yadā na bhāvo nābhāvo mateḥ saṃtiṣṭhate puraḥ /
> tadānyagaty-abhāvena nirālambā praśāmyati //9.35//

After citing this passage, Ruegg proceeds to criticize Staal for failing to draw the conclusion from this verse that for Śāntideva, at least, "the principle of the excluded third is not only valid but altogether fundamental in the philosophical thought of his school."

But what is surprising, it seems to me, is not that Staal failed to draw this conclusion from BCA 9.35, but that Ruegg *does* draw it, for what BCA 9.35 says is that one should not think of either existence or non-existence, and that when neither the thought of existence nor the thought of non-existence stands before the mind, the mind has no support and becomes quiet. As such, BCA 9.35 does not rule out *any* of the relevant logical possibilities, for it would be perfectly consistent for someone to maintain any one of the following four alternatives: 1) reject LEM and assert BCA 9.35; 2) reject LEM and reject BCA 9.35; 3) assert LEM and assert BCA 9.35; and 4) assert LEM and reject BCA 9.35. In short, BCA 9.35 is a statement of *psychology*—or, if you will, of soteriology—and not a statement of logic at all.[70]

51. Why does Ruegg think that it is consistent to maintain both that the laws of logic are valid and that ultimate reality is beyond the laws of logic? It seems to me that Ruegg believes that he can have it both ways because he adheres to the doctrine of psychologism. (Unfortunately, there is no convenient term for designating someone who holds this philosophical position, but perhaps such a philosopher can be referred to as a psychologician.) It is Ruegg's adherence to psychologism, it seems to me, that explains why he feels on the one hand that he can deny that logical laws apply to the domain that is perceived by the ineffable knowledge of the Buddhas, and yet at the same time insist on the validity of logical laws as governing all thought and all objects of thought.

According to psychologism, the laws of logic are restricted in their validity. They do not apply to reality itself (or at least not to higher reality), or at any rate we cannot *know* whether they do so. Laws of logic are nothing more than laws of thought. They *describe* the way the mind behaves or thinks, just as physical laws describe the way physical objects and sub-atomic particles behave. But logical laws are not valid (or may not be valid) for the reality that exists outside of human thought. For example, psychologism seems to be committed to the view that a chair could in fact both weigh and not weigh forty pounds. It may be true, according to the psychologician, that we cannot help *thinking* that it is impossible for a chair to do this, but according to psychologism we cannot dismiss the possibility that reality itself does not conform to the law of non-contradiction, the law of the excluded middle etc., which only describe the way that *we* think about the world.

Quite apart from its prima facie implausibility, there is the following objection to psychologism. While physical laws do presumably describe the behavior of physical objects and sub-atomic particles, it is patently untrue that all thoughts obey the laws of logic. (Human beings are, notoriously, quite capable of thinking illogically.) So we must rephrase the definition to somehow read: logic describes the way the mind *should* work. But the problem with this formulation is that it is *normative* rather than descriptive, and the analogy with scientific laws therefore breaks down, for physical laws are not thought to describe the way that objects and particles *should* behave.

Can one account for the normative character of the laws of logic without abandoning the psychologistic claim that they are valid only for human thought, and not for reality itself? One possible approach is to try to justify logic *empirically*. This approach, which was actually advocated by J. S. Mill in the 19th century, has been overwhelmingly rejected in the analytic tradition of contemporary Western philosophy.[71] For one thing, only a desperate person would try to maintain that "2 + 2 = 4" is true because we have learned from experience that every time we add two things and two things we come up with four things. It would appear to be equally absurd to suggest that these are the grounds that we have for *asserting* that 2 + 2 = 4. The problem with this inductive view, and with the psychologistic view as well, is that we seem to know *in advance* that reality will conform to our logic and our mathematics. When we use mathematics and logic in science, and construct hypotheses, and test them, and find that the hypotheses are not verified, we change our physical hypotheses, not our logic and our mathematics.[72, 73]

52. Taken (as I think it must be) as a defense of psychologism, Ruegg's paper provides a good example of the difference between the mode of analytic philosophy that still prevails in the U.S., the U.K., Australia and New Zealand, and a mode of philosophy that is widespread on the continent of Europe. In the Western analytic tradition, psychologism has been in disrepute since at least the time of Frege. It is not surprising, therefore, that when Ruegg does find affinities between the Madhyamaka and modern Western philosophy, those affinities often lie with continental semioticians like J. Kristeva and L. Mäll.

These semioticians can, I think, be usefully compared with the German, English and American psychologicians of the 19th and early 20th centuries. According to continental semiotics, logic as it has developed in the West from Aristotle to the present day is not totally invalid, but its validity is a highly restricted one. It applies to the domain of scientific discourse as well as some ordinary discourse, but the semioticians believe that there is a domain to which it does not apply. This domain is investigated by "trans-linguistic" or "trans-logical philosophy" and "metapoetics" (FPC, n. 154); "Mäll's theory of 'post-logical' thought" (FPC 53), where A is A because it is Ā; by "Oriental pragmatics" (FPC 53); by "zerology" (FPC 53); and by J. Kristeva's theory of paragrammatism, which is based on the notion of "orthocomplementary" structures, which are said to describe the relations of elements in the "paragrammatic space of poetic language" (FPC 53-54). According to Ruegg, such semiotic theories promise to throw more light on the Madhyamaka than the prevailing "ethnocentric" approaches, which, he thinks, have gotten unnecessarily bogged down over questions concerning the logical structure of the catuṣkoṭi to the exclusion of other philosophical aspects (FPC 52).

I have my doubts that the Indian philosophers (who seem to me, on the whole, to have been a rather analytically minded group of people) would have had any interest in zerology or paragrammatic poetic spaces in their own philosophizing, even if they had been acquainted with them. It also seems to me that a strong case for the universality of classical logic can be made, and if it can be made, then it cannot be said that logic is ethnocentric. But these issues cannot be addressed here with the care and the detail that they obviously deserve.

One question that I do want to raise, however, is whether the Mādhyamikas were irrationalists, and also whether it is possible for *Ruegg* to dismiss the charge that they were irrationalists as nonsense (FPC 48).

There has been a considerable amount of discussion in the literature about the alleged irrationalism of the Madhyamaka. One of the difficulties involved in addressing this question is that there does not seem to be a consensus about how rationality and irrationality are to be defined. However, it seems to me that even the weakest definition of rationality would have to exclude the view that there is a trans-linguistic reality which is beyond even the law of non-contradiction. If the term "rationality" cannot exclude even *this,* it is hard to see how it could exclude anything at all. Judged by this very weak criterion, Ruegg's version of the Madhyamaka counts as an irrational philosophy, despite his insistence that the notion that the Mādhyamikas were irrationalists is nonsense (FPC 48), and despite his claim that "Madhyamaka reasoning (yukti) is based on the twin pillars of the principles of non-contradiction and excluded middle" (FPC 54). I do not believe that these claims of Ruegg's can be credited simply because he *also* claims that the Mādhyamikas did contradict themselves, and furthermore that they were quite justified in doing so (FPC 47). If the Mādhyamikas did believe in a trans-logical and trans-linguistic realm of orthocomplementary structures which describe the relations of elements in the paragrammatic spaces of poetic language, where A is A because it is $\bar{A}$, then the claim that they were also logicians and rationalists must surely be dismissed.

1. I doubt that the logical consistency of the catuṣkoṭi can be defended if the negations that figure in the propositions that are rejected are taken as external negations. However, the problems become much more tractable if they are taken as internal negations.

Typically, as we have seen, the catuṣkoṭi appears in the negated form. When the negations of the rejected propositions in the second, third and fourth koṭis are taken as internal negations, the general form of the catuṣkoṭi is given by 1)-4) below:

(1) It is not the case that x is ϕ.
(2) It is not the case that x is not-ϕ.
(3) It is not the case that x is both ϕ and not-ϕ.
(4) It is not the case that x is neither ϕ nor not-ϕ.

According to the NI, all four of these positions are rejected on the grounds that there is no entity x that has any of the four properties ϕ, not-ϕ, both ϕ and not-ϕ, and neither ϕ nor not-ϕ.

According to the NI, the Mādhyamikas did not believe that anything existed at all, so for them there were no x's, and 1)-4) could therefore be asserted of every conceivable putative entity, whether phenomenal or non-phenomenal (e.g., nirvāṇa). The non-Madhyamaka schools of Buddhist philosophy, on the other hand, did believe in the reality of certain kinds of entities which were called dharmas (though the lists of these dharmas tended to vary from school to school). Only these dharmas were thought to be exempt from negations or rejections of the form 1)-4). For the Mādhyamikas, however, 1)-4) applied to every putative entity, because when all things are held to be strictly non-existent, all *four* positions of the catuṣkoṭi will apply simultaneously to absolutely everything. This can be seen most clearly, perhaps, in the case of a clearly fictitious entity like Santa Claus, for we do not want to say that Santa Claus smokes, that he does not smoke, or that he both smokes and does not smoke; and as I shall argue momentarily, there is even a sense in which we do not want to say that he neither smokes nor does not smoke.

According to the NI, the same analysis will hold for the catuṣkoṭi when the properties in question are existence and non-existence. Here it is important to note that it is very natural in Sanskrit to assert that something exists by saying that x is an existent thing (bhāvaḥ), and to deny that x exists by saying that it is a non-existent thing (abhāvaḥ), for Sanskrit—especially philosophical Sanskrit—has a very marked preference for nouns and adjectives over verbs. But by the same token, it is more natural in Sanskrit than it is in English to deny *both* that Santa Claus exists (i.e., is a bhāvaḥ) *and* to deny that he does not exist (i.e., to deny that he is an abhāvaḥ, or non-existent *entity*).

It might be objected that the foregoing analysis of the catuṣkoṭi fails to give a plausible analysis of 4) in the case where x is a non-existent or fictitious entity, since our linguistic intuitions seem to tell us that it is true rather than false that Santa Claus neither smokes nor does not smoke. Indeed, as we have already seen (v. supra, p. 140), there are passages in the Mādhyamika texts that assert that the son of a barren woman, for example, is neither light nor dark. However, such passages do not present any substantive problems for the foregoing nihilist interpretation, for such cases are easily accounted for on the grounds that Sanskrit, like the other Indo-European languages, employs both internal and external negation.

When Candrakīrti asserts that the son of a barren woman is neither light nor dark (i.e, not-light), the negation in question is probably an external negation. Even in this example, however, it is *possible* to interpret the negation in question as an internal negation. When the negation is understood in this way, one will want to *deny* that the son of a barren woman is neither light nor dark—for one would not want to be committed to the existence of a son of a barren woman who has the property of being-neither-light-nor-dark, and this is the sort of thing that linguistic expressions of the form "neither P nor not-P" imply when they are taken as internal negations.

It is also important to note that when one does take the negations of the rejected second, third and fourth koṭis as internal negations, and the x's as non-referring, one cannot regard the four positions as truth-functionally related. This result is exactly what a solution to the consistency problem of the catuṣkoṭi requires, but it is a feature that has certain disadvantages, for it is usually convenient to infer from the negation of P that P is false, or from the negation of the negation of P that P is true—i.e. to use a propositional negation. Such inferences do seem to hold for negations even in ordinary language when the entities in question are held to exist. For example, when the referring expressions in P are taken to be non-null, one can infer from not-P is true that not-not-P is false. But in the case of the catuṣkoṭi, both not-(P) and not-(not-P) are True. The non-truth-functionality of the catuṣkoṭi can be justified, however, for the purpose of the catuṣkoṭi is simply to throw into the sharpest possible relief the nihilist position, i.e., the view that there are no entities with the property of existence, non-existence, both existence and non-existence, neither non-existence nor non-existence, etc.

2. In the remainder of this chapter, my task will be to apply the foregoing interpretation of the catuṣkoṭi, and the interpretation of the Mādhyamika philosophy that is implied in it, to a number of passages from the Prajñā-pāramitā and Mādhyamika texts. So far as the Madhyamaka is concerned, I shall be concentrating mostly on Nāgārjuna's MMK, since this is undoubtedly the single most important text of the Madhyamaka school.[1]

Some of the passages in this chapter will be cited as lending prima facie support to the NI. (This is particularly true of most of the passages from the Prajñā-pāramitā.) However, the Prajñā-pāramitā-hṛdaya-sūtra and the passages that I have selected from the MMK have been chosen precisely because they might appear to present problems for the NI—indeed, they have even been cited by proponents of the NNI as providing important evidence for *their* interpretation. It will be my aim to show that the NI can explain these supposedly hard cases, and that, on examination, they actually support the NI rather than the NNI.

3. The historical connection between the Madhyamaka and the Prajñā-pāramitā sūtras is not fully understood, but it was undoubtedly very close. In the Mahāyāna there were even legends that asserted that the Prajñā-pāramitā represented an esoteric teaching that had been imparted by the Buddha only to his most advanced disciples; that these had been kept in custody in the underworld by the nāgas (supernatural serpent beings); and that Nāgārjuna, who has often been compared in the Mahāyāna to a second Buddha, revealed the Prajñā-pāramitā once again to the world after he had recovered them from the nāgas during a journey to the underworld.[2]

The persistent theme of these sūtras is that all things (dharmas) are void (śūnya). The Mahāyānists themselves insisted that this doctrine set their own views apart from the teachings of the schools that belonged to what they called the Lesser Vehicle (Hīnayāna). The prevailing view of the canonical texts of early Buddhism, as represented by the Pāli canon of the Theravāda school and a few surviving texts and fragments from other schools that are extant in Tibetan and Chinese, is that there is no self or soul (attā, ātman), but only a stream of impermanent, impersonal entities called dharmas. This was perhaps the fundamental doctrine of all the orthodox Hīnayānist schools. What the Prajñā-pāramitā sūtras did, essentially, was to extend this teaching to the point where everything, including the dharmas themselves, were declared to be non-existent and unreal (asat, śūnya).

4. Proponents of the NNI have wanted to read another meaning into the doctrine that all dharmas are void. According to the NNI, it is not that the dharmas themselves are unreal or non-existent, but only that all statements or theories about the dharmas are inadequate, on the grounds that reality (and therefore the dharmas) are beyond linguistic description and logically indeterminable (v. supra, pp. 92-95).

It seems to me that this interpretation must surely be unhistorical, because the Prajñā-pāramitā texts state explicitly that *the dharmas are to be thought of as no more real than the ātman,* and according to orthodox Buddhism, the ātman was simply *non-existent.* In this respect, the following passage from the Aṣṭa-sāhasrikā (p. 29) is typical:

> A Bodhisattva should produce the thought that 'as in each and every way a self does not exist (sarveṇa sarvaṃ sarvathā sarvātmā na vidyate), and is not perceived (nopalabhyate), so in each and every way all dharmas do not exist, and are not perceived.' He should apply this notion to all dharmas, inside and outside.

Note that the above passage states quite explicitly that just as *in each and every way the dharmas do not exist,* so in each and every way the self does not exist. Since no entities were recognized in orthodox Buddhism apart from the dharmas, this is a very explicit statement of *nihilism.*

Note also that it would not do to argue that "does not exist" (ṅa vidyate) should not be taken in a nihilistic sense. First of all, I do not think that there is a non-nihilistic sense of the expression "does not exist" (na vidyate). Even if there were, however, it would be of no use to the NNI so far as this passage is concerned, for the passage in question puts the dharmas and the self (ātman) on the same footing, and the orthodox Buddhist view was that there was no self *in the nihilistic sense.* The only way that the nihilist interpretation of the foregoing passage could be avoided, therefore, would be to maintain that the Mahāyānists did not believe that the *ātman* was non-existent (at least not paramārthataḥ). So far as I know, there isn't a shred of evidence to support such a contention. Furthermore, if this *had* been the Mādhyamika view, that view would have been either identical with, or very similar to, the views of the Vatsīputrīyas or Pudgalavādins, who maintained that there was a self which was logically indeterminable. But surely the Mādhyamikas were not crypto-Pudgalavādins!

5. There are, of course, passages in the Mādhyamika writings where it is said that the dharmas are *not* non-existent (na: abhāvaḥ). As I have previously argued, however, these passages do not deny that the dharmas are *absolutely* non-existent (atyantābhāva); they only mean that they are not non-existent in the sense in which, e.g., the Naiyāyikas held that things are non-existent (v. supra, pp. 132-135).

This interpretation of the "na *abhāvaḥ" passages is confirmed by all those passages in the Mahāyānist texts which *do* assert that all the dharmas are non-existent—for otherwise the Mādhyamikas would have *contradicted* themselves. Consider the following passages from the Prajñā-pāramitā:

> All dharmas are empty (śūnya), signless, wishless, unproduced (anutpanna), not-extinguished and non-existent (abhāva). [Aṣṭa. 482][3]

*

> Neither of these dharmas,—he who would go forth, and that by which he would go forth—exist (na vidyate), nor can they be perceived (nopalabhyate). Since all dharmas do not exist (avidyamāna), what dharma could go forth by what dharma? [Aṣṭa. 24]

*

> Śāriputra: If, venerable Subhūti, the Bodhisattva is a non-production (anutpāda), and also the dharmas which constitute him, and also the state of all-knowledge, and also the dharmas which constitute it, and also the common people, and also the dharmas which constitute them,—then, surely, the state of all-knowledge is reached by a Bodhisattva without any exertion? [A discussion ensues on this point, in which Śāriputra attempts to convince Subhūti that it makes no sense to speak of the attainment of something which is neither eternal nor produced. Śāriputra ends by saying:] Non-production (anutpāda) is just talk. Non-production just appears before the mind's eye. Non-production is just a flash in the mind. Absolutely it is nothing more than that. [Aṣṭa. 30]

*

Perfect wisdom does not cling to any dharma, nor defile any dharma, nor take hold of any dharma. For all these dharmas neither exist (na saṃvidyante) nor are they got at (nopalabhyante). [Aṣṭa. 203]

*

All dharmas are situated in space, they have not come, they have not gone, they are the same as space. Space has not come, nor gone, nor is it made, nor unmade, nor effected; it has not stood up, does not last, nor endure; it is neither produced nor stopped. The same is true of all dharmas which are, after the fashion of space, undiscriminate. Because the emptiness of form etc., neither comes nor goes. Nor does the emptiness of all dharmas. For all dharmas are situate in emptiness, and from that situation they do not depart. They are situated in the signless, the wishless, the ineffective, in non-production (anutpāda), no-birth (ajāti), in non-existence (abhāva), in dream and self (ātman), in the boundless, in the calm quiet, in nirvāṇa, in the unrecoverable; they have not come, nor gone. [Aṣṭa 297-298][4]

*

The development of perfect wisdom is like the development of space, or of all dharmas, or of non-attachment, of the infinite, of what is not (asad-bhāva), of not-taking-hold-of. [Aṣṭa. 301]

The most natural way of taking the assertion that something is non-existent is to suppose that it asserts that the thing in question is *absolutely* non-existent or non-existent simpliciter. (This was called atyantābhāva by the Indian philosophers.) Were it not for the fact that some philosophers (both Indian and

Western) have maintained that non-existence is itself a kind of thing, one could say that something is non-existent and assume that one would be understood to have meant that the thing in question is non-existent simpliciter. For example, if one were to assert in 1994 that the present king of France does not exist, one could ordinarily expect to be taken to mean, roughly, that there is no x such that x has the property of being the sole, supreme ruler of France. It is only because some philosophers have insisted that non-existence is itself a kind of thing (padārtha) that there is a danger of being misunderstood, particularly when addressing a philosophical audience. In this context, one might very well have to supplement the assertion that the king of France is non-existent by adding that *he is not a non-existent either.* This, I think, is the only reason why the Mādhyamikas sometimes asserted that things are not non-existent (na *abhāva).

6. The Prajñā-pāramitā sūtras and the Mādhyamika śāstras maintain that things seem to exist, but do not. This is the celebrated doctrine of illusion (māyā, avidyā), which makes its first unequivocal appearance on the stage of Indian history and philosophy in these texts.[5] The following passages from the Prajñā-pāramitā are typical.

> The Lord: The dharmas do not exist in such a way as the foolish, untaught common people are accustomed to suppose. Śāriputra: How then do they exist? The Lord: As they do not exist, so they exist. And so, since they do not exist (avidyamāna), they are called [the result of ignorance] avidyā. [Aṣṭa. 15][6]

*

> Pūrṇa: But what then is that form of which you say that it is neither bound nor freed, and what is that Suchness of form etc.? Subhūti: The form of an illusory man (māyā-puruṣa) is neither bound nor freed. The Suchness of the form of an illusory man is neither bound nor freed. Because in reality it is not there at all

(asad-bhūtatvāt), because it is not isolated, because it is not produced (anutpannatvāt). [Aṣṭa. 22-23]

*

The deity Śakra then conjured up flowers and scattered them over the venerable Subhūti. The venerable Subhūti thought to himself by way of reply: These flowers which [now] appear among the Gods of the Thirty-three are magical creations. They have not issued from trees, shrubs or creepers. These flowers which Śakra has scattered are mind-made. Śakra replied: These flowers did not issue forth at all. For there are really no flowers, whether they issue forth from mind (na hi manonir-jātāni kānicit-puṣpāṇi) or from trees, shrubs or creepers. [Aṣṭa. 41]

*

Subhūti: Like a magical illusion are those beings, like a dream. For beings and magical illusions or dreams are not two different things. All objective facts are also like a magical illusion, like a dream. The various classes of saints, from Streamwinner to Buddhahood, also are like a magical illusion, like a dream. Devas: A fully enlightened Buddha also, you say, is like a magical illusion, is like a dream? Buddhahood also, you say, is like a magical illusion, is like a dream? Subhūti: Even nirvāṇa, I say, is like a magical illusion, is like a dream. How much more so anything else! Gods: Even nirvāṇa, holy Subhūti, you say, is like an illusion, is like a dream? Subhūti: Even if perchance there could be anything more distinguished, of that too I would say that it is like an illusion, like a dream. For illusion and nirvāṇa, illusion and dreams, are not two different things. [Aṣṭa. 39-40]

Note that passages like the last one make the non-nihilist interpretation of the Mādhyamika doctrine of nirvāṇa, universal emptiness, perfect wisdom etc. appear rather implausible. It is true, of course, that the Mahāyānists personified perfect wisdom etc. for the purpose of meditation and religious practices. It is also true that much of the religious poetry that gives expression to these personifications (e.g., Rāhulabhadra's Prajñā-pāramitā-stotra) are beautiful and infused with great feeling. Nevertheless, all such personfications are, in the final analysis, personifications of emptiness or non-existence, as the following passages will show:

> [The Bodhisattva] should meditate on prajñā-pāramitā (the perfection of wisdom) as a dharma which does not exist (na vidyate), cannot be apprehended (nopalabhyate). [Aṣṭa. 10]

*

> Thereupon a certain monk saluted the Lord with folded hands and said to the Lord: I pay homage, O Lord, to the perfection of wisdom! For it neither produces nor stops any dharma. Śakra: If someone, holy Subhūti, would make efforts about this perfection of wisdom, what would his efforts be about? Subhūti: He would make efforts about space. And he would make his efforts about a mere vacuity if he would decide to train in perfect wisdom or to work on it. [Aṣṭa. 197]

*

> Subhūti: This is a perfection of what is not (asat-pāramiteyam), because space is not something that is. This is a perfection which equals the unequalled, because all dharmas are not apprehended. This is an isolated perfection, on account of absolute emptiness. This perfection cannot be crushed, because all dharmas are not apprehended. This is a trackless perfection,

because both body and mind are absent ... This perfection has had no genesis, because no dharma has really come about (anutpatti). This is a perfection which does nothing, because no doer can be apprehended. This perfection does not generate [cognize] anything, because all dharmas are without self ... This is a perfection of a dream, an echo, a reflected image, a mirage, or an illusion, because it informs about non-production (anutpāda)... This perfection knows no purification, because no possible receptacle [which might have to be purified] can be apprehended. [Aṣṭa. 205]

*

Mañjuśrī: What are the qualities and what the advantages of a perfection of wisdom which is without qualities? How can one speak of the qualities or advantages of a perfect wisdom which is incapable of doing anything, neither raises up nor destroys anything, neither accepts nor rejects any dharma, is powerless to act and not at all busy, if its own-being cannot be cognized, if its own-being cannot be seen ... if it neither produces nor stops any dharmas, neither annihilates them nor makes them eternal, if it neither causes to come nor to go, brings about neither detachment nor non-detachment, neither duality nor non-duality, and if, finally, it is non-existent (abhāva)? The Lord: Well have you, Mañjuśrī, described the qualities of perfect wisdom .. It is called "perfect wisdom" because it is neither produced nor stopped. And it is so because it is calmly quiet from the very beginning, because there is escape, because there is nothing to be accomplished, and, finally, because of its non-existence (abhāvatvāt). For what is non-existence, that is perfect wisdom (yaś cābhāvaḥ sā prajñāpāramitā). [Sapta./Tucci 32b-34a]

7. If everything is entirely void, then the Buddha could not have been real either. The authors of the Prajñā-pāramitā sūtras did not hesitate to accept this conclusion, which was the inevitable consequence of their extension of the arguments against the self to the dharmas.

The early Buddhists had held that there is no soul, self or person (attā, ātman, pudgala). The Buddha was of course no exception to the rule that there is no self. The only thing (or at least one of things) that made the Buddha different was that he had *realized* that there was no self. But if there is no self, what is it that we *call* a person, and what is the Buddha really? The answer given by the canonical writings is that what we call a person is just an ever-changing stream of impersonal physical and psycho-physical elements or dhammas.

By generalizing and extending the arguments against the self that had been developed and accepted by all of the other orthodox Buddhist schools, the Mahāyānists arrived at the view that even the dharmas are unreal. It is a corollary of this rejection of the dharma theory that the Buddha himself could not have been any more real than a dream or a mirage. This is the view of the Prajñā-pāramitā:

> Tathāgatas certainly do not come from anywhere, nor do they go anywhere. Because suchness (tathatā) does not move, and the Tathāgata is suchness. Non-production does not come nor go, and the Tathāgata is non-production. One cannot conceive of the coming or going of the reality-limit, and the Tathāgata is the reality-limit. The same can be said of emptiness, of what exists in accordance with fact, of dispassion, of stopping, of the element of space. For the Tathāgata is not outside these dharmas. The suchness of these dharmas and the suchness of all dharmas and the suchness of the Tathāgata are simply this one single suchness. There is no division within suchness. Just simply one single thing is this suchness, not two, nor three. Suchness has passed beyond counting, because it is not (asattvāt). [Aṣṭa. 512]

*

Dharmodgata: Equally foolish are all those who adhere to the Tathāgata through form and sound, and who in consequence imagine the coming or going of a Tathāgata. For a Tathāgata cannot be seen from his form-body. The dharma-kāyas are the Tathāgatas and the real nature of dharmas does not come or go. There is no coming or going of the body of an elephant, horse, chariot or foot-soldier which has been conjured up by a magician. Just so there is neither coming nor going of the Tathāgatas. A sleeping man might in his dreams see one Tathāgata, or two, or three, or up to one thousand, or still more. On waking he would, however, no longer see even one single Tathāgata. What do you think, son of good family, have these Tathāgatas come from anywhere, or gone to anywhere? [Sadāprarudita:] One cannot conceive that in that dream any dharma at all had the status of a full and perfect reality, for the dream was deceptive. [Dharmodgata]: Just so the Tathāgata has taught that all dharmas are like a dream. [Aṣṭa. 513-514]

*

The Lord: How, Mañjuśrī, should the Tathāgata be seen and honoured? Mañjuśrī: Through the mode of suchness (tathatākāreṇa) do I see the Tathāgata, through the mode of non-discrimination (avikalpākāreṇa), in the manner of non-observation (anupalaṃbha-yogena). I see him through the mode of non-production (anutpādākāreṇa) and non-existence (abhāvākāreṇa). [Sapta./Masuda 195]

8. There have been proponents of the NNI who have maintained that in the Madhyamaka "śūnyatā" is a name for the Buddhist Absolute; that it is another name for dependent co-origination; and that śūnyatā and pratītya-samutpādaḥ, emptiness and relativity, nirvāṇa and saṃsāra, the absolute and the phenomenal, are simply two different names for the same thing. According to the NI, however, "śūnyatā" in the Madhyamaka simply means emptiness in the sense of non-existence. According to the proponents of this interpretation, it is unlikely that the Mādhyamikas believed that emptiness and dependent co-origination could be identified (except as a conventional designation, i.e., one that may be unavoidable for teaching an inferior type of disciple or student), for the meanings of "sūnyatā" and "pratītya-samutpādaḥ" in Sanskrit, and their use in Buddhist philosophy, would seem to preclude any such literal identification.

Similar controversies arise over the interpretation of some of the passages in the Prajñā-pāramitā sūtras. The Hṛdaya-sūtra provides a good example of this. After a brief homage to the perfection of wisdom (prajñā-pāramitā), the sūtra says:

> Avalokita, the holy Lord and Bodhisattva, was moving in the deep course of the wisdom which has gone beyond. He looked down from on high; he beheld but five heaps (skandhas); and he saw that in their own being they were empty (svabhāva-śūnya). Here, O Śāriputra, form (rūpa) is emptiness (śūnyatā) and the very emptiness is form; emptiness does not differ from form, nor does form differ from emptiness; whatever is form, that is emptiness, whatever is emptiness, that is form. The same is true of feelings, perceptions, impulses and consciousness.

There is nothing in the sūtra up to this point that conflicts with the NNI. Indeed, it might even be argued that up to this point the Hṛdaya supports the NNI rather than the NI, for the sūtra appears to place an equal amount of emphasis on form and emptiness, whereas according to the NI form is reduced to emptiness, but not vice versa. This in turn might be taken to support the contention that the Mādhyamikas believed in an Absolute, which they called by various names, e.g., nirvāṇa, suchness (tathatā), the reality limit (bhūta-koṭi) etc. On this view, form, feeling, perceptions, impulses and consciousness *are* the Absolute seen from the phenomenal point of view.

But the next section of the sūtra shows that this interpretation must be mistaken, for it specifies that what makes emptiness and form identical is the fact that there is no form etc. This passage—which seems to be cited much less frequently these days than the beginning of the sūtra—goes as follows:

> Here, O Śāriputra, all dharmas are marked with emptiness (śūnyatā-lakṣaṇa); they are neither produced (anutpanna) nor stopped, neither defiled nor immaculate, neither deficient nor complete. Therefore, O Śāriputra, where there is emptiness there is no form (na rūpam), no feeling, no perception, no impulse, no consciousness; no eye, no ear, no nose, no tongue, no body, no mind; no sight-organ element etc., until we come to: no mind-consciousness element; no ignorance, no extinction of ignorance etc., until we come to: there is no decay and death, no extinction of decay and death; there is no suffering, no origination, no stopping, no path; there is no cognition, no attainment and no non-attainment.

In this passage, the sūtra-kāra (or sūtra-kāras) argue that form etc. is the same as emptiness on the grounds that there is no form etc. There is no corresponding claim that emptiness is the same as form etc. on the grounds that things are not really *empty*. In fact, the Hṛdaya-sūtra's equation between emptiness and form etc. makes sense only because the relation between form and emptiness is regarded as asymmetrical in this way. Thus, the Prajñā-pāramitā sūtras, like the Mādhyamika philosophy that arose concomitantly with them, appear to teach a doctrine of pure, absolute nihilism.

9. Like the opening section of the Hṛdaya-sūtra, MMK 13.7 might appear, prima facie, to support the claim that the Mādhyamikas believed that reality is indeterminable and non-conceptualizable, and that, as such, it is beyond the categories of existence and non-existence, voidness and non-voidness.

Interpreted in this way, MMK 13.7 would provide a counterexample to the NI, according to which the Mādhyamikas believed that things are entirely void (śūnya) and entirely non-existent (sarvaṃ sarveṇa nāsti, atyantābhāva). A close analysis of MMK 13.7 shows, however, that it actually supports the NI rather than the NNI.

The line of argumentation in MMK 13 that leads up to this verse may be summarized as follows. The chapter begins with the assertion that all the mental formations (saṃskāras) are delusive by nature and that they are therefore untrue (13.1). The Buddha pointed out, by way of expounding the doctrine of śūnyatā, that if every delusive element is untrue, then there cannot be anything that deludes either (13.2). Nor can the opponent deny this, and maintain that there must be some real thing (svabhāva) at the bottom of everything, for the lack-of-self-nature (niḥsvabhāvatva) of things is clearly seen by the fact that they change their nature (13.3ab). Nor is niḥsvabhāvatva itself a thing: there is no self-nature (bhāva) even of non-self-nature (asvabhāva), and it is precisely in this sense that there is the śūnyatā of all entities (13.3cd). This is true regardless of how one conceives self-nature, for change (anyathā-bhāva) cannot exist either on the supposition that there is, or is not, self-nature (13.4). Change is not possible either for the same thing or for another thing; and neither the youth nor the old man can age (13.5). If one and the same thing could be said to change its nature then milk would become curds. It is also illogical to maintain that curds arise from anything other than milk.

MMK 13.7 and 13.8, which conclude the chapter, run as follows:

> If non-emptiness (aśūnyam) were anything at all (kiṃcit), then emptiness (śūnyam) could also be something (api kiṃcana). But since non-emptiness (aśūnyam) is nothing at all (na kiṃcid asti), how could emptiness be something?
>
> yady aśūnyaṃ bhavet kiṃcit syāc chūnyam api kiṃcana /
> na kiṃcid asty aśūnyaṃ ca kutaḥ śūnyaṃ bhaviṣyati //13.7//

> The Conquerors have declared emptiness to be the cessation of all speculative views (dṛṣṭi). Those who hold a speculative view of emptiness are declared to be incorrigible.
>
> śūnyatā sarva-dṛṣṭīnāṃ proktā niḥsaraṇaṃ jinaiḥ /
> yeṣāṃ tu śūnyatā-dṛṣṭis tān asādhyān babhāṣire //13.8//

10. As R. H. Robinson was apparently the first to point out (1957:297; 1967: 43, 130), Nāgārjuna might be thought to have committed the fallacy of negating the antecedent in this verse, for the argument of MMK 13.7 seems to have the following form:

$P \supset Q$
$\neg P$
Therefore, $\neg Q$.

This form of argument is frequently confused with the following argument (modus tollendo tollens), which is a valid argument:

$P \supset Q$
$\neg Q$
Therefore, $\neg P$.

Two proponents of the NNI, D. Seyfort Ruegg and B. Galloway, have argued that, properly interpreted, MMK 13.7 does not commit the fallacy of negating the antecedent.[7] According to these authors, Nāgārjuna asserts in MMK 13.7 that the doctrine that things are empty (śūnya) is on exactly the same footing as the doctrine that things are non-empty (aśūnya), i.e., that the view that things are void is no more true than the view that things are not void. For example, Ruegg says (FPC 55-56):

> If we apply here the well-known Mādhyamika principle of the complementarity of binary concepts and terms, what Nāgārjuna is saying becomes clear and, in terms of his system, valid: if two opposite concepts or terms stand in a relation of complementary correlation in the

> framework of dichotomous conceptualization—that is, if there are pratidvandvins (Tib. 'gran zla or 'gal zla)—the negation of one necessarily involves the negation of the other, without the problem of the antecedent and the consequent in a hypothetical syllogism ever arising.

Galloway takes a similar line, even arguing that all the difficulties in the verse should be resolved by simply taking the "if" (yadi) of the verse to read "if and only if" rather than "if" (1989: 24).

There are a number of problems with this kind of interpretation. First, Galloway's suggestion that the "if" of MMK 13.a should be read as "if and only if," rather than "if" alone, is not supported by what Nāgārjuna actually says.[8] Second, there is an enormous amount of evidence in the Mādhyamika texts against the claim that śūnya and aśūnya stand in a "relation of complementary correlation." The claim that they do stand in this relation would seem to imply that the Hīnayānist belief in the reality of the dharmas is just as true as the Mahāyānist assertion that the dharmas are utterly void (sarva-dharma-śūnyatā), and similarly that the statement that all things arise and perish is just as true (even at the level of absolute truth) as the assertion that things do not arise and perish there. But what the Mādhyamika texts assert, typically, is that the claim that dharmas exist and arise and perish in the causal process is true only from the standpoint of phenomenal truth, and it is hard to see how the foregoing interpretation of MMK 13.7 can be reconciled with such statements.

11. It seems to me that a much more natural interpretation of MMK 13.7 can be given along the lines of the NI, and, furthermore, that the nihilist line of interpretation provides a more promising way of absolving Nāgārjuna of the charge of having committed a logical fallacy. Note that as I have translated the verse, the conclusion of Nāgārjuna's argument is simply that emptiness (śūnyam) is not a thing. (Cf. also Ruegg's translation: "How will there [then] exist something empty?") This claim is quite consistent with the NI, for what MMK 13.7d denies is not the truth of the doctrine of emptiness, but only the claim that this emptiness is actually something (śūnyam api kiṃcana, kutaḥ śūnyaṃ bhaviṣyati).

Whether Nāgārjuna can be defended against the charge of having committed a crude logical error in MMK 13.7 is another question that depends in turn on whether the truth functional connective " $\supset$ " adequately captures the meaning of the ordinary language *if...then* construction. It has frequently been maintained that it cannot, particularly when the context is manifestly modal, causal etc. (cf. the "bhavet...syāt" of MMK 13.7ab). In particular, it has been argued that there are some ordinary language contexts where *If P then Q* means *Q only if P* rather than *P only if Q*. If this is indeed the case, then negating the protasis of an ordinary language *If...then* construction need not always be a fallacy.

Thus, if MMK 13.7ab actually means "Emptiness (śūnyam) could be something only if non-emptiness (aśūnyam) were something," rather than "Non-emptiness could be something only if emptiness were something," then Nāgārjuna has negated the consequent rather than the antecedent in MMK 13.7. I believe that this may very well be what Nāgārjuna was saying. In (1)-(6) below I have tried to set out in slightly more detail what the logic of the argument is. Steps (1), (4) and (5) are given explicitly in MMK 13.7. Steps (2) and (3) are not given explicitly in the verse, but it seems to me that they are implicit in it. In particular, it seems to me that (3) is equivalent to (1) via (2), and if this is indeed the case, then (4) operates on (3) to yield (5) via the valid inference modus tollendo tollens:

(1) ***IF*** non-emptiness were anything at all, then emptiness ***MIGHT*** be something.

(2) Emptiness could be something [only] on the condition that non-emptiness were something.

(3) Emptiness is something (kiṃcana) only if non-emptiness is something.

(4) But there is nothing to non-emptiness.

(5) Therefore there is nothing to emptiness, either.

In advocating this interpretation of MMK 13.7, I do not mean to suggest that this way of using the *If...then* conditional is the best way, or even a proper way, of using it. The logicians seem to me to have good reasons for stigmatizing this way of using the conditional. However, the conditional is often used (or misused) in this way, and as I shall presently argue, there are specific reasons for thinking that Nāgārjuna did use it in this way in MMK 13. Recognizing this fact is essential to properly interpreting MMK 13.7.

The foregoing point about the *If...then* construction can be generalized to other cases. In ordinary language, for example, the statement "***IF*** unicorns existed, they might be swifter than horses" would seem to be an acceptable way of saying that unicorns could be swifter than horses only if unicorns existed; and if this claim is true, then the inference from the added premise "Unicorns do not exist" to "Therefore, unicorns are not swifter than horses" is perfectly valid, even though, prima facie, it might appear to have the structure of the fallacy of negating the antecedent. Similarly, it could be argued that the statement "***IF*** there were real money, then there might be counterfeit money," said about a primitive society S in which all goods are bartered, would ordinarily be taken to mean that there can be counterfeit money only if there is real money; and if this is so, then deriving "Therefore, there is no counterfeit money in S" may be a perfectly valid inference to draw from the additional premise, "There is no real money in S." In short, it can and has been argued that in ordinary language the *If P...then Q* construction can mean either *P only if Q* or *Q only if P*. Which one is actually meant must often be determined by the context, although in actual speech vocal stress can help to remove the ambiguity (cf. the difference between "***IF P***, then Q" and "If P, ***THEN Q***").

12. To apply the foregoing points to MMK 13.7, we may begin by noting that, for the Mādhyamikas, śūnya (empty) = niḥsvabhāva (without a self-nature, not a real entity). Similarly, aśūnya (non-empty) = svabhāva (self-nature, real entity).

Furthermore, it is natural to take the indefinite pronouns *kiṃcit* and *kiṃcana* in MMK 13.7 to convey the meaning: "is a real entity," "has a self-nature," "is non-empty" etc. Thus one could also translate MMK 13.7 as follows:

> If non-emptiness (aśūnyam) were a real entity, then emptiness (śūnyam) might be a real entity. But non-emptiness is not a real entity (na kiṃcid asti). Therefore, how can emptiness be (bhaviṣyati) a real entity?

or

> If there were anything real, then emptiness might be real. But there is nothing real. Therefore how could emptiness be real?

In other words, Nāgārjuna says, if you cannot say that anything *real* exists, what sense does it make to say that *emptiness* exists?

This interpretation of MMK 13.7, it seems to me, is the one that is suggested by the argument of MMK 13 taken as whole. In each of the preceding verses, Nāgārjuna is principally concerned to show that śūnyatā (emptiness) or no-self-naturedness (niḥsvabhāvatā) is not itself a *thing* (bhāva). Everything is delusive, he argues, but we cannot even say that there is anything that does the deluding. Things lack self-nature because they are subject to change, but even this lack of self-nature is not itself a thing, for there is no being or nature (bhāva) even of non-self-nature (asvabhāva), and it is precisely in this sense that there is the śūnyatā of all things.

Right up to MMK 13.7, therefore, Nāgārjuna argues that there is no real entity anywhere, i.e., he argues only for śūnyatā, not aśūnyatā. There is nothing in MMK 13.1-6 that suggests that Nāgārjuna believed that for things to be śūnya there must be something else that is aśūnya; indeed, MMK 13.1-6 is directed specifically against this view. The non-nihilist interpretation, therefore, would require us to suppose that there is a radical break in the line of argument of MMK 13 at MMK 13.7, i.e., that the chapter first argues that there is nothing aśūnya in the first six verses, and then abruptly argues (without presenting any reasons or arguments) that nothing is śūnya either. On the nihilist interpretation, on the other hand, there is a consistent line of thought throughout the eight verses of MMK 13.

The nihilist interpretation of MMK 13.7 is supported by Candrakirti's commentary on the verse (note particularly the beginning and ending sentences of the passage):

> If śūnyatā were anything at all (yadi śūnyatā nāma kācit syāt), then it would have as its basis some real, existent thing (bhāva-svabhāva). But it is not so, for the following reason. If you were to take the view that śūnyatā is the universal characteristic (sāmānya-lakṣaṇa) of all dharmas, then the non-existence of any aśūnya dharmas would be the consequence, and there would be no aśūnyatā either. But when there are no aśūnya entities (padārtha), and no aśūnyatā either, then it follows that śūnyatā itself must be non-existent in the sense that a flower-garland in the sky is non-existent, for in that case there would be nothing for it to be related to (pratipakṣa-nirapekṣatvāt). And if śūnyatā is not (nāsti) in this sense, then it is certainly not dependent on any real entity (padārtha).

Candrakīrti's main concern, like Nāgārjuna's, is not to deny non-existence, but to avoid commitment to *existence* in any fashion. Śūnyatā is not a *thing,* in the sense in which, for example, the Naiyāyikas thought of non-existence (abhāva) as a thing (padārtha). Like a flower-garland in the sky or the son of a barren woman, śūnyatā is absolute non-existence (atyantābhāva), and as such is not dependent on any real entity.

Further evidence for this interpretation of MMK and MMKV 13.7 can be found in MMK(V) 13.8. MMK 13.8 says: "The Conquerors have declared emptiness to be the relinquishing of all speculative views (dṛṣṭi). Those who hold a speculative view of emptiness are declared to be incorrigible." In view of everything that precedes this verse, MMK 13.8 appears to have the following meaning:

> In order to teach the śūnyatā of all dharmas, the Buddha had to use the misleading concepts of ordinary discourse. When dealing with people who believed in existence, he had no choice but to use the term "non-existence," which ignorant people might take to refer to some peculiar entity, i.e., non-existence, in the same way that the term "cow" refers to a cow or the name "Devadatta" refers to Devadatta. But the Buddha's teachings about śūnyatā were just a provisional teaching (neyārtha), a mere figure of speech or façon de parler (upacāra, prajñapti). It would be as foolish to conclude from the Buddha's unavoidable use of ordinary discourse that śūnyatā is a thing as it would be to conclude from the expression "the non-existence of x" that the non-existence of x is itself a thing.

This is the very point that Candrakīrti makes in his commentary on MMK 13.8:

> The cessation of views is not itself a thing (na ca dṛṣṭi-kṛtānāṃ nivṛttimātraṃ bhāvaḥ). We will not even speak with those who have such an obstinate attachment to being as to make śūnyatā itself a thing (ye tu tasyām-api śūnyatāyāṃ bhāvābhiniveśinaḥ, tān prati avacācakā vayam-iti)...It is as if one were to say to someone, 'I have no wares to sell you' (na kiñcitnāma paṇyam) and the other were to reply, 'Give me those non-existent wares.' How would such a one be able to grasp that non-existence (paṇyābhāva)?

13. It seems to me that Nāgārjuna makes a very similar point in MMK 25.7-8:

> If nirvāṇa is not an existent thing (bhāva), how could it be a non-existent thing (abhāva)? Wherever there is

no existence (bhāva), there is no non-existence (abhāva) either.

bhāvo yadi na nirvāṇam abhāvaḥ kiṃ bhaviṣyati /
nirvāṇaṃ yatra bhāvo na nābhāvas tatra vidyate //25.7//

If nirvāṇa were a non-existent (abhāva), how could it be non-dependent? For indeed there is no non-existent thing that is not dependent.

yady abhāvaś ca nirvāṇam anupādāya tat katham /
nirvāṇaṃ na hy abhāvo 'sti yo 'nupādāya vidyate //25.8//

These are extremely important verses, since they are perhaps the clearest instances in the MMK where Nāgārjuna directly addresses the concept of non-existence and its logical relationship to the concept of existence. Prima facie, MMK 25.4-6 deny that nirvāṇa exists and MMK 25.7-8 deny that nirvāṇa does not exist—a joint denial that would appear to have the logical form of $\neg A \wedge \neg\neg A$, which is a contradiction. Nevertheless, it turns out that in these verses Nāgārjuna treats existence (bhāva) and non-existence (abhāva) as contraries rather than contradictories. In short, at the very point in the work where (according to the NNI) one might expect Nāgārjuna to embrace a contradiction, he declines to do so. By treating "bhāva" and "abhāva" as contraries in MMK 25.4-6 and 7-8 (and thereby avoiding direct contradiction), Nāgārjuna implied that at least one member of the dichotomy "existence"/"non-existence" must be true *when these terms are treated as contradictory ones.* An inspection of the passage shows, I believe, that the fundamental concept for Nāgārjuna is that of non-existence (abhāva), for in MMK 25.4-6 he categorically repudiates the concept of existence, but in MMK 25.7-8 only repudiates the concept of non-existence when it is taken in a special sense.

At first sight, the reasons given by Nāgārjuna in support of the assertion that nirvāṇa is not an abhāva are puzzling. Why would anyone hold that there can be no non-existence without existence? Take the sentence (as uttered in 1994): "The king of

France does not exist." What MMK 25.7-8 seem to imply is that the king of France cannot be non-existent unless there is something else that does exist. But this is odd, for at least two reasons. First, one would think that there would be no king of France even if nothing else existed. Second, if the non-existence of the king of France is dependent on the existence of some other thing, what *is* the other thing on which it is dependent?

Despite these obvious objections, I think that it may be possible to make sense of MMK 25.7-8, provided that we take these verses to be directed against the view that nirvāṇa is to be conceived (as the Sautrāntikas conceived it) as the *cessation* of something that previously existed.[9, 10] Nāgārjuna argues that if nirvāṇa is conceived in this way, it will be brought down to the level of the relational, causal nexus of birth and death. To speak of the cessation of something is, unavoidably, to speak of the non-existence of *something* that previously existed. Defining nirvāṇa as the cessation of the saṃsāric process, therefore, implies that nirvāṇa is something that emerges at some point in time when something else ceases to be.

The nihilistic interpretation of MMK 25.7-8 is supported by Candrakīrti's commentary on these two verses. In MMKV 25.7, Candrakīrti argues that nirvāṇa is not the mere impermanence (anityatā) of the defilements, birth-and-death etc., on the grounds that "abhāva" and "anityatā" are grasped (prajñapyate) as dependent on being [MMKV 25.8]. This, he says, is shown by the fact that the impermanence of donkey's horns etc. are never perceived. How, he asks, could impermanence exist without some entity (bhāva) as the subject of predication (kuto lakṣyaṃ bhāvam-apekṣya anityatā bhaviṣyati)?

To this position the opponent raises a very natural objection. If you define non-existence (abhāvatva) in that way, he says, it becomes impossible to say that the son of a barren woman is non-existent. Candrakīrti's response to this objection is illuminating. He *denies* that the son of a barren woman (vandhyā-putra) is a non-existent (abhāva), and he does so on the grounds that a vandhyā-putra is *never* existent. This is important for two reasons. First, it confirms that what Nāgārjuna meant by abhāvaḥ in MMK 25.7-8 was what other Indian philosophers (either then or at a later date) called dhvaṃsābhāvaḥ (i.e., non-existence after having previously existed). Second, it shows that the Mādhyamikas were not opposed to regarding nirvāṇa or śūnyatā as non-existence per se, but only to specific formulations or conceptualizations of nirvāṇa or śūnyatā as non-existence, particularly those that identified nirvāṇa or śūnyatā with non-existence in such a way that this non-existence was itself a thing, or which made it conceptually or causally dependent on some *other* thing. Śūnyatā as absolute, non-dependent (apratītya) non-existence (i.e., atyantābhāva) was never repudiated.

14. In his commentary on MMK 25.8, Candrakīrti cites in support of his interpretation MMK 15.5, which says:

> If existence (bhāva) cannot be established, then non-existence (abhāva) cannot be established either. For people declare non-existence to be the becoming-other (anyathā-bhāva) of existence.
>
> bhāvasya ced aprasiddhir abhāvo naiva sidhyati /
> bhāvasya hy anyathābhāvam abhāvaṃ bruvate janāḥ //15.5//

Although Candrakīrti does not cite them in this connection, two other verses in MMK 15 are equally apposite:

> The assertion of existence (astīti) is the grasping of permanency (śāśvata), and the assertion of non-existence (nāstīti) is the viewpoint of annihilationism (uccheda). Therefore the wise do not base themselves on existence and non-existence.
>
> astīti śāśvata-grāho nāstīty uccheda-darśanam /
> tasmād astitva-nāstitve nāśrīyeta vicakṣaṇaḥ //15.10//
>
> According to permanency (śāśvata), that which exists of its own self-nature (svabhāvena) never becomes non-existent. It follows from this that annihilation (uccheda) is the non-existence of that which was previously existent.

asti yad dhi svabhāvena na tan nāstīti śāśvatam /
nāstīdānīm abhūt pūrvam ity ucchedaḥ prasajyate //15.11//

These are important passages also. MMK 15.5 is particularly important, for it is the only place in the MMK where Nāgārjuna specifies how he is *using* the term "abhāva." Nāgārjuna does not necessarily *endorse* this definition: he merely says that this is how "people" (janāḥ) use or have used the term, and he implies that he is prepared to go along with it. Nāgārjuna does not specify who these people were, but it is likely that they were Buddhist philosophers, like the Sautrāntikas, who maintained that nirvāṇa was just an abhāva, i.e., the mere cessation of the saṃsāric process. Nāgārjuna's objection to this view is that it presupposes that there is something that exists first and then ceases to be. But since existence cannot be established (bhāvasya ced aprasiddhiḥ), non-existence cannot be established either (abhāvo naiva sidhyati).

Thus, MMK 15.5 and MMK 15.10-11 add further support to the nihilist interpretation of MMK 25.7-8. According to Nāgārjuna, things are totally unreal, like the sons of barren women. Nirvāṇa is not the cessation of something that arises in the causal process, for nothing ever did or will exist in the first place. Since there are no bhāvas, there are no dhvaṃsābhāvas, either. All things are completely void. Sarva-dharma-śūnyatā![11]

15. Early Buddhism did not extend its reductivist and phenomenalistic attack on the ātman doctrine to the dharmas themselves, but the Mahāyāna did. The emergence of the Mahāyānist doctrine of universal voidness (sarva-dharma-śūnyatā) marks a major watershed in the development of Buddhist thought. It led to the abandonment of old ways of thinking and viewing things, new openings and new departures, new puzzles and new solutions to old problems.

One of the things that was subjected to re-examination was the concept of nirvāṇa. In early Buddhism, nirvāṇa was simply the extinction of the suffering (duḥkha) inherent in the cycle of rebirth, i.e., a mere cessation of the flow of real but impermanent dharmas.[12] But if the dharmas are themselves unreal, what sense could it possibly make to speak of the extinction or nullification (nirodha, nivṛtti) of saṃsāra? If saṃsāra is no more real than a round square or the son of a barren woman, how can there be nirvāṇa?

The NI and the NNI approach this question very differently. According to the NI, what makes nirvāṇa and saṃsāra identical is that neither is real, just as in mathematics the arithmetical expressions $x = 5 - 5$ and $y = 10 - (4 + 6)$ designate the same thing, i.e., the null set. This is the nihilist interpretation of the Mādhyamika doctrine that there is no difference between saṃsāra and nirvāṇa.

The proponents of the NNI, on the other hand, have rejected the nihilistic interpretation of śūnyatā, and have interpreted the equation in question to mean that the Mādhyamikas believed in an Absolute which they regarded as identical with the phenomenal world (saṃsāra). This leads to a very different interpretation of the saṃsāra = nirvāṇa equation in the Mādhyamika texts. The nihilist interpretation holds that there is no distinction between saṃsāra and nirvāṇa because, on examination, both prove to be unreal. According to the NNI, both nirvāṇa and saṃsāra are real, but they are simply different aspects of one and the same thing.

16. MMK 25.9, MMK 25.19 and MMK 25.20 have frequently been cited by proponents of the NNI in support of their interpretation of the saṃsāra = nirvāṇa equation. The first to do so was probably Th. Stcherbatsky.

The Sanskrit of MMK 25.9 and Stcherbatsky's translation of it (CBN 206) are given below:

> Coordinated here or caused are separate things,
> We call this world phenomenal.
> But just the same is called Nirvāṇa,
> When viewed without Causality, without Coordination.

> ya ājavaṃjavībhāva upādāya pratītya vā /
> so 'pratītyānupādāya nirvāṇam upadiśyate //25.9//

Stcherbatsky's discussion of 25.9 in the introduction to his *Conception of Buddhist Nirvāṇa* (CBN 56) supplements his translation of the verse. After asserting that Nāgārjuna held that the "universe as a whole is the Absolute, viewed as a process it is the phenomenal," Stcherbatksy cited MMK 25.9, and then proceeded to say about it:

> Having regard to causes and conditions (constituting all phenomena) we call this world a phenomenal world. This same world, when causes or conditions are disregarded, (i.e., the world as a whole, *sub specie aeternitatis*) is called the Absolute.

In this context he also cited MMK 25.20. MMK 25.19-20 are as follows (I use here Stcherbatsky's translation, CBN 83):

> There is no difference at all / Between Nirvāṇa and Saṃsāra, // There is no difference at all between Saṃsāra and Nirvāṇa.
>
> na saṃsārasya nirvāṇāt kiṃcid asti viśeṣaṇam /
> na nirvāṇasya saṃsārāt kiṃcid asti viśeṣaṇam //25.19//
>
> What makes the limit of Nirvāṇa / Is also then the limit of Saṃsāra. // Between the two we cannot find / The slightest shade of difference.
>
> nirvāṇasya ca yā koṭiḥ koṭiḥ saṃsāraṇasya ca /
> na tayor antaraṃ kiṃcit susūkṣmam api vidyate //25.20//

About MMK 25.19-20 Stcherbatsky said (CBN 56): "In full accordance with the idea of a monistic universe, it is now asserted that there is not a shade of difference between the Absolute and the phenomenal, between saṃsāra and nirvāṇa."[13]

Although the Stcherbatskian interpretation of these verses is now the prevailing one, there is a very simple—and I believe decisive—philosophical and doctrinal objection to it. The problem is that in Buddhism saṃsāra is *defined* as what is relative (pratītya) and dependent (upādāya), and nirvāṇa is *defined* as what is *not* relative and dependent. Therefore, because

A cannot be identical with B if A has a property that B does not have, we must give up at least one of the following assertions:

(a) Nirvāṇa and saṃsāra are both real.
(b) Saṃsāra is dependent and relative.
(c) Nirvāṇa is non-dependent and non-relative.
(d) Nirvāṇa is the same thing as saṃsāra.

On the nihilist interpretation, the meaning of d) is given by the *denial* of a). But this solution to the difficulty is not available to the NNI, for the NNI holds that nirvāṇa and saṃsāra are real (i.e., different aspects of the same real thing).

17. There is further evidence against Stcherbatsky's interpretation of MMK 25.9 in Candrakīrti's commentary on that verse. MMKV 25.9 says (my translation):

> Whether it [i.e., the cycle of birth and death] be understood as entirely relative, or whether it be regarded as born dependent on causes and conditions, nirvāṇa is to be understood as the non-dependent, non-relative cessation (apravṛtti) of the incessant cycle of birth and death. Now a mere cessation (apravṛtti-mātra) cannot be conceived as either a bhāva or an abhāva. Thus: "Nirvāṇa is not a bhāva; nirvāṇa is not an abhāva."[14]

MMKV 25.9 raises some obvious problems for Stcherbatsky's interpretation of MMK 25.9. According to Stcherbatsky, 1) nirvāṇa is an Absolute, 2) saṃsāra is what is relative, and 3) nirvāṇa and saṃsāra are the same thing as seen from two different points of view. But Candrakīrti clearly stresses the *difference* between saṃsāra and nirvāṇa. Saṃsāra, he says, is what is dependent (upādāya) and relative (pratītya), whereas nirvāṇa is non-dependent (anupādāya) and non-relative (apratītya); furthermore, nirvāṇa is the mere cessation (apravṛtti-mātra) of what is dependent and relative. This is simply the orthodox way of describing nirvāṇa and saṃsāra. But it does not identify them—it draws the strongest possible *contrast* between them.

Stcherbatsky's attempt to accommodate MMKV 25.9 within his interpretation of MMK 25.9 is instructive. Stcherbatsky's translation of the passage from MMKV 25.9 that I have translated above goes as follows (CBN 206):

> But in any case, whether it be only imagined as relatively coordinated, or whether they be considered as produced by causes, when the continuity of birth and death has ceased, when there are neither relations nor causality, this same world as motionless and eternal is then called nirvāṇa. Now, the mere cessation of aspect can neither be considered as an Ens, nor as a non-Ens. Thus it is that Nirvāṇa is neither an Ens, nor a non-Ens.

There are a number of problems with this translation. First, the suggestion that nirvāṇa is something motionless and eternal that remains when what is dependent and relative has vanished is surely an eternalist (śāśvata) and heretical view, and one that Candrakīrti of all people would have strenuously repudiated. Furthermore, Stcherbatsky has, I think, misconstrued the meaning of "apravṛtti(-mātra)" in Sanskrit. Stcherbatsky's translation implies that a mere cessation (apravṛtti-mātra) means: "what is left after the cessation has occurred," but there is nothing in MMKV 25.9 (nor in Sanskrit grammar, so far as I know) to justify this translation. In Sanskrit, as in English, it is much more natural to construe cessation (apravṛtti) as the process of cessation than it is to construe it as the residue or substratum, if any, that is left *after* the cessation has occurred, just as the Sarvāstivādin definition of nirvāṇa as that *in which* extinction (nirodha) occurs is less natural than the Sautrāntika definition, which holds that nirvāṇa just *is* that cessation.

Stcherbatsky seems to have been aware of this objection to his translation of the passage in question, for in a footnote to it he gives an alternative translation/exegesis that drops the residue or substratum interpretation of apravṛtti in favor of a translation/exegesis that places more weight on the notion of a change of *aspect*. Thus he says (CBN 206):

> 'In any case whether it be established that it is imagined (prajñapyate) as coordinated (upādāya) or produced as caused (pratītya), in any case the non-operation (apravṛtti) of this duration of a lineage of births and deaths, whether as non-caused or as non-coordinated, is established as the nirvāṇa.' The non-operation or cessation of an imagined construction (prajñapti=kalpanā) is nothing but a change of aspect. Nirvāṇa is thus the Universe sub specie aeternitatis.

It seems to me that this does not meet the objection either. First, the alternative translation/exegesis is rather arbitrary, for in Sanskrit "apravṛtti" does not really mean change of *aspect*: its primary (mukhya) meaning is that of extinction pure and simple, as when a fire goes out, or of not undertaking any activity or not setting in motion. If the more specific meaning is what Candrakīrti had intended, presumably he would have *said* that the cessation in question was the cessation of an aspect (ākāra). But he does not say this.

Stcherbatsky's alternative translation/exegesis is also subject to the objection that it imputes to MMK(V) 25.9 an eternalist view that Candrakīrti and the other Mādhyamikas explicitly repudiated. The view that there must be a basis (āspada) even for illusion was a Vedāntist view, and one that the Mādhyamikas regarded as heretical (v. infra, pp. 232-235). For the Mādhyamikas, the world is wholly illusory, like an hallucination. The cessation of an hallucination (e.g., of a pink elephant) can hardly be called a change of aspect, because there is nothing which can be identified as the thing (or aspect) that the vanished elephant changes into. The appearance of the elephant simply vanishes.[15, 16]

18. Since there is nothing in MMK(V) 25.9 that corresponds to Stcherbatsky's notion of "seeing as," there is nothing in these passages to suggest that either Nāgārjuna or Candrakīrti thought that nirvāṇa and saṃsāra were simply the same thing seen from two different points of view, or that they identified them. On the contrary, the plain, unadorned Sanskrit of the verse draws an unmistakable *contrast* between the concepts of saṃsāra and nirvāṇa. I offer the following, therefore, as a much more literal translation of MMK 25.9:

> The cycle of birth and death is dependent (upādāya) and relative (pratītya). That which is non-dependent and non-relative is said to be nirvāṇa.
>
> ya ājavaṃjavībhāva upādāya pratītya vā /
> so 'pratītyānupādāya nirvāṇam upadiśyate //25.9//

That this is in fact the meaning of MMK 25.9 becomes clear as soon as the verse is placed in the context of the chapter as a whole.

MMK 25.9-10 summarize the preceding five verses. In MMK 25.4-6, Nāgārjuna argues that nirvāṇa cannot be an existent thing (bhāva), because all existent things are conditioned, subject to old age and death, and dependent (upādāya). In MMK 25.7-8, Nāgārjuna then argues that nirvāṇa cannot be an abhāva, because if nothing exists then it makes no sense to say that something ceases to exist (abhāva), and because an abhāva would have to be dependent. MMK 25.9-10 then serve to recapitulate the argument up to that point. MMK 25.10 says that the Buddha enjoined the abandonment of both being (bhāva) and non-being (vibhāva); hence the saying "Nirvāṇa is not being (bhāva), not non-being (abhāva)." MMK 25.9 prefaces this contention by summarizing the arguments of MMK 24.4-6 and 24.7-8. It says that nirvāṇa is not being, also not non-being, because both of these are dependent and relative and belong to the realm of birth and death, whereas nirvāṇa by definition is none of these. Hence nirvāṇa and saṃsāra are *contrasted* in MMK 25.9.[17]

19. Since one cannot equate two things A and B when A has properties that B does not have, the entire history of Buddhist philosophy and dogmatics is against the non-nihilist interpretation of the nirvāṇa = saṃsāra equation. One way out (which of course fits the NI) is to deny that either saṃsāra or nirvāṇa is real, but Stcherbatsky could not take this line, for all his energies were bent (at least at this period of his life) on repudiating the NI. He was therefore forced to interpret MMK 25.20 to mean that saṃsāra is the same thing as nirvāṇa when causes and conditions are disregarded (CBN 56). But this does not really deal with the problem, for one cannot assert that there is no difference between nirvāṇa and saṃsāra if a) the former is *defined* as devoid of causes and conditions, 2) the latter is *defined* as being dependent on causes and conditions, and 3) one has to disregard causes and conditions in order to see the latter as the former.

The following analogy may serve to make this point more clearly. Compare Stcherbatsky's interpretation of MMK 25.20 with the following hypothetical argument:

> Mind is that which is essentially conscious and can think. Matter is essentially that which is is unconscious and does not think. Nevertheless, mind and matter are identical. This can be seen when (and only when) the properties that distinguish matter from mind are disregarded. Mind is seen to be matter when we disregard its properties of thinking and being conscious; and conversely matter is seen to be mind when we disregard its properties of being unconscious and incapable of thinking.

This, clearly, would make no sense. Of course, some philosophers *have* wanted to identify matter and mind, but these philosophers have been aware, as Stcherbatsky seems not to have been aware, that such identifications cannot be hand-waved into existence, and that they have *consequences*. No materialist or idealist has ever held that mind can be identified with matter on the grounds that one can simply choose to disregard the properties that *seem* to distinguish the two of them. Such a method of reasoning would amount to a procedure for identifying any two things whatsoever, e.g., the moon and the sun, this chair and that elephant, my mind and your mind, etc. All one would have to do to achieve such identifications would be to disregard all the properties that differentiate thing A from thing B! Nor is there anything in the text of MMK(V) 25 to suggest that Nāgārjuna or Candrakīrti thought that nirvāṇa and saṃsāra could be identified in this cavalier fashion.

20. Stcherbatsky not only identified nirvāṇa and saṃsāra (where both were taken as real); he also identified dependent co-origination (pratītya-samutpāda) and emptiness (śūnyatā).[18]

Stcherbatsky's non-nihilistic interpretation of this equation (which he presents at CBN 47) quickly leads to the appearance of śūnyatā in some rather startling guises and incarnations. The line of reasoning that led Stcherbatsky from the non-nihilistic interpretation of the pratītya-samutpāda = śūnyatā equation to his pantheistic and cosmo-theistic interpretation of the Madhyamaka can be outlined as follows:

> The term "śūnya" is synonymous with "relative," and "śūnyatā" is synonymous with "relativity or contingency" (CBN 48). Since nothing in the Mahāyāna is held to have self-existence (svabhāva), the Buddha, even when he is in nirvāṇa, cannot have self-existence either. But this does not mean that there is no Buddha at all after his parinirvāṇa; it simply means that the Buddha exists beyond all logical determination (CBN 52). As such, he can be cognized only in a direct, mystic intuition (CBN 51, 52). The Buddha is in fact the cosmical order (dharmataḥ); his body is the cosmos (CBN 53). All the millions of existences (bhūta-koṭi) must be regarded as the body of the Buddha who is manifested in them. This is Relativity, the climax of wisdom (prajñā-pāramitā).
>
> The Mahāyānists believed in an Absolute, which they named the element of the elements (dharmāṇāṃ dharmatā; dharma-dhātu); relativity (śūnyatā); thisness (idaṃtā); suchness (tathatā); and the suchness of existence (bhūta-tathatā). In the Mahāyāna these were regarded as the same as the cosmical body of the Buddha (dharma-kāya) and the matrix of the Lord

> (tathāgata-garbha). In this last attribution, the unique essence of the universe becomes personified and worshipped under the names of Vairocana, Amitābha (the Buddha of the Pure Land and Infinite Light), the Goddess Tārā and others, and as a supreme God. Buddhism, therefore, is at once pantheistic and theistic, or cosmotheistic (CBN 55). The Absolute of the Mahāyāna is therefore nothing but the full blown Brahman of the brāhmaṇical systems (CBN 70).

This would appear to place an enormous amount of ontological and even cosmological weight on the concept of śūnyatā, which (as Stcherbatsky himself acknowledges on p. 50 of his work) simply meant in ordinary Sanskrit empty or void. Furthermore, the interpretation of śūnyatā with which the line of reasoning begins is prima facie suspect. If śūnyatā is taken as one of the Mahāyānists' designations of the Absolute (CBN 54-55), and if śūnyatā is taken to be, by definition, uncompounded and beyond relativity and dependence (CBN 47), then it seems quite impossible to argue (CBN 50, 52) that śūnyatā *means* dependently-coordinated existence (pratītya-samutpāda), for then the equation in question becomes a contradictio in adiecto. That is, it seems plainly inconsistent to assert a) that the Absolute is *beyond* dependence and relativity, b) that śūnyatā is *identical* with that Absolute, c) that pratītya-samutpādaḥ is relativity, and then d) to assert that śūnyatā and pratītya-samutpādaḥ are the same thing.

21. The main verse that proponents of the NNI have cited in support of a literal equation between emptiness (śūnyatā) and dependent co-origination (pratītya-samutpāda) is MMK 24.18, which says:

> We say that dependent co-origination (pratītya-samutpāda) is emptiness (śūnyatā). That (sā) is a conventional, dependent designation. That (sā) alone is the middle path.

> yaḥ pratītya-samutpādaḥ śūnyatāṃ tāṃ pracakṣmahe /
> sā prajñaptir upādāya pratipat saiva madhyamā
> //24.18//

Clearly, the phrase "conventional, dependent designation" (prajñaptir upādāya) is intended to tell us that the pratītya-samutpāda = śūnyatā equation has a spin on it. But what exactly does the expression mean?

It seems to me that the employment of this expression in this context provides clear evidence that Nāgārjuna took the emptiness = dependent co-origination equation to be untenable *in any literal sense.* "Pratītya" and "pratītya-samutpāda" were key concepts in the account that the earlier Buddhist schools had used to describe the nature of reality. According to that description, nothing is permanent or eternal; everything arises and perishes depending on its causes and conditions. Since Nāgārjuna believed that things are *un*originated (cf. MMK 1; v. supra, pp. 48-49), he was clearly committed to the view that the doctrine that things are *dependently* originated was a provisional teaching. Hence Nāgārjuna calls it a conventional designation (prajñaptir upādāya).

Given this context, MMK 24.18 might be paraphrased as follows:

> The śūnyatā = pratītya-samutpāda equation is only provisional. The highest truth (paramārtha-satya), according to which all dharmas are void, is unthinkable and cannot be put into words. However, the *entrance* to the paramārtha in the domain of everyday words and concepts is the doctrine of the emptiness of dependent co-origination. If one were to follow the logic of the matter to its ultimate conclusion, one would see that to say that all things are dependent and relative really amounts to saying that they do not originate at all. The doctrine of relativity (pratītya-samutpāda), therefore, *eventuates* in the doctrine of absolute voidness (śūnyatā). Thus, while "śūnyatā" certainly cannot be identified with dependent co-origination or relativity in

the final sense, the śūnyatā = pratītya-samutpāda equation, taken as a conventional or dependent one, can be efficacious in leading the individual to the highest truth of universal voidness (sarva-dharma-śūnyatā).

22. This is the reading of MMK 24.18 that is suggested by the NI. It is not how the verse is usually read, however, for most modern interpretations have followed Stcherbatsky in *literally* equating dependent co-origination with emptiness.[19] As in Stcherbatsky's case, the literal identification is justified on the grounds that the doctrine of dependent co-origination implies that things are empty in the sense that they have no *self*-existence (niḥsvabhāva) and do not *self*-originate (na svataḥ *utpādaḥ). Since the origination of things depends on their causes and conditions, it is said, things do not originate by or through their self-nature (svabhāvena). This non-origination by *self-nature* (svabhāvenānutpāda) is what is called emptiness (śūnyatā).[20]

It cannot be denied that all this is *part* of what is involved in MMK(V) 24.18, but it is doubtful that it can be the whole truth of the matter.

Note, first of all, that it is one of the fundamental principles of Buddhism that whatever is dependent and relative (pratītya) is implicated in suffering. There is no evidence that the Mādhyamikas ever questioned this principle; nor is there any reason to think that they could have rejected it without stepping outside the pale of orthodoxy altogether. There is, of course, evidence that the Mādhyamikas denied that anything originated at all (anutpatti-vāda), and on this view there is nothing relative and dependent (pratītya), and hence, on this view, the whole issue of suffering as it was conceived in the earlier schools does not arise (or at least gets transmogrified as the view that there is only the *appearance* of suffering). But as orthodox Buddhists the Mādhyamikas must have at least accepted the principle that if there were in actual fact anything dependent and relative, it would necessarily be implicated in suffering. According to the Hīnayānist view, anything that dependently co-originates (*pratītya*-samutpāda) is implicated in suffering, and will cease to exist (nirodha) in nirvāṇa. But the view that things do originate in a causal process and do get extinguished in nirvāṇa is a Hīnayānist view that the Mahāyānists rejected, for according to the Mahāyānists, nothing originates at all.[21]

If Nāgārjuna believed that, in the final analysis, things were unoriginated, then he could not have taken the teaching that things are empty in the sense of being *dependently* originated as the final teaching of the Buddha. This is surely why, after saying that dependent origination is the same thing as emptiness (MMK 24.18ab), Nāgārjuna adds that this is a conventional designation (MMK 24.18c), or as J. W. de Jong and J. May have translated the term, a "désignation métaphorique" (prajñaptir upādāya).

Some of the listings for the term "prajñapti" which Edgerton has given in his *Buddhist Hybrid Sanskrit Dictionary* help to throw some light on the meaning of MMK 24.18: (**1**) AKBh ii.214, where prajñapti-dharma is contrasted with dravya-dharma (**2**) MSA xix.43 (S. Lévi): "the word designates a notion which is purely verbal, as a means of making something known" (**3**) BBh 44.14, 49.4, 50.10 and Śikṣ. 257.8, where the term is associated with the "false" or the "covered" (saṃvṛti), as in nāmadheyamātraṃ saṃketamātraṃ saṃvṛtimātraṃ prajñaptimātraṃ (**4**) MV i.176.18, where the term has the meaning of mere convention, which the Buddhas have transcended (prajñapti-samatikrāntā[ḥ]) (**5**) Laṅk. 153.10, 11 (vs), where it is said that an ātman exists prajñapti-satyato, *by (exoteric) verbal convention,* but is not dravya-sat, i.e., *real in itself* (skandhānāṃ skandhatā tadvat prajnaptyā na tu dravyataḥ).

All these usages suggest that an upādāya-prajñapti is an expression or proposition that does not express or state the way that things really are. The term "prajñapti" was first used by the Buddhists in connection with the concept of the self, which they declared to be *non-existent.* What really existed, they said, was an ever-changing stream of impersonal and highly impermanent physical and psycho-physical entities called dharmas. The term "self" (P. attā; Skr. ātman) was held to be a mere "upādāya-prajñapti." Since the self was a mere prajñapti (verbal concept with no corresponding reality), the term "attā/ātman" (self) had no meaning or reference in itself. It was nothing more than a term of convenience.

One of the standard illustrations (dṛṣṭānta) for this anattā/anātman doctrine in early Buddhism was that of the chariot. Strictly speaking, the Buddhists said, there is no chariot, for a chariot is nothing but the assemblage of certain constituent parts (rathāṅgāni), e.g., the axle, wheel, hub, reins etc. We use the term "chariot" as a term of convenience for the purposes of ordinary life (saṃvṛti-satya, vyavahārya-satya), but that does not mean that there is such a thing. The early Buddhists produced categorized lists of all the possible things that they thought could exist (i.e., the dharmas), and since things like chariots and selves were not among them, chariots and selves were held to be unreal. Whatever meaning the terms "chariot" and "self" have as terms of convenience was held to be entirely derivative on terms that referred directly to the real, constituent components (dharmas) of those things. A precise and rigorous language for expressing the Buddhist world view (which, in part, the dharma theory actually was) would not include terms like "chariot" or "self" at all. The Buddhas and Arhats see a world of impermanent dharmas, and only them. Deluded people, on the other hand, superimpose on these real constituent elements of things false concepts like "chariot" and "self" (pudgala, ātman).

There seems to be a consensus among scholars that the term "prajñaptir upādāya" in MMK 24.18a is to be understood within the context of these traditional Buddhist teachings. That is, according to what seems to be the prevailing view, MMK 24.18c asserts that the concept of dependent origination, the concept of emptiness, and the equation between the two fail to describe the ultimate reality. As J. W. de Jong has put it (1949: xiv): "One will find in Nāgārjuna and Candrakīrti many designations for this [ineffable] reality (śūnyatā, tathatā, pratītyasamutpāda, etc.). But Candrakīrti insists on the fact that these designations are only indirect and metaphorical (upādāyaprajñapti) and that the reality (tattva) cannot be designated by words (prapañcaiḥ aprapañcitam), cannot be taught by others (paropadeśa—āgamyam)."

So much about the verse is relatively uncontroversial. The more controversial aspect of MMK 24.18, however, is how

Nāgārjuna and the other Mādhyamikas conceived of this ultimate reality.[22]

It is possible, I think, to give an intuitively satisfying explanation of MMK(V) 24.18, and of the term "prajñaptir upādāya," if and only if we take Nāgārjuna as having held that at the level of ultimate reality things are *un*originated and non-existent, as the NI holds. According to this interpretation, the argument of MMK(V) 24.18 against the opponent goes as follows:

> At the level of ultimate truth, things are in fact completely void and unoriginated (śūnyam idaṃ sarvam, anutpanna). However, only the most advanced aspirants are capable of grasping this truth directly. In dealing with people who are incapable of grasping this truth, the Buddhas have to resort to the usages of ordinary speech, for they have no other way of pointing to the ultimate truth (MMK 24.10). In dealing with such people, it is sometimes useful to say that things are empty in the sense that they are *dependently* originated, for this tends to counteract the truly pernicious belief in self-originated and eternal entities. But this way of conceiving of the emptiness of things is only a half-truth. According to this way of thinking of the matter, things are unoriginated *only* in the sense that they arise depending on their causes and conditions (svabhāvenānutpāda). Speaking of dependent origination and of emptiness in *this* superficial, exoteric sense is a "désignation métaphorique" (prajñaptir upādāya), just as the term "self" or "soul" is an upādāya-prajñapti.
>
> You have failed to see this for two reasons. First, you have taken the dharmas to be real, whereas they are unreal. Without real dharmas, there can be no real origination. (Think of the law of dependent origination, if you like, as a function that maps dharmas onto other dharmas.) Second, you have failed to see that the

statement that things are unoriginated according to self-nature is at best a partial truth, because you have not pursued the matter to its logical conclusion. The *whole* truth is that things are unoriginated *simpliciter*.

In itself, the view that things are unoriginated according to self-nature (svabhāvenānutpāda) makes a very conservative and limited claim, i.e., that things are not originated from *self* (svataḥ). But to say that things are unoriginated from self implies that that they are originated from *others* (parataḥ), i.e., from other dharmas that comprise their causes and conditions. But things do not originate in this way, either—nor do they originate from both self and others, nor do they originate from no cause. In fact, things cannot originate from any of the four causes and conditions that you have enumerated, nor is there any other way that they can arise [MMK(V) 1].

The statement that things are empty in the sense that they are dependently co-originated; the statement that they are not *self*-originated; the statement that they are not originated according to *self*-nature, are all provisional teachings—désignations métaphoriques. If you take such statements as the final teaching of the Buddha, you will have overlooked the crucial distinction between the two truths that is implicit in those teachings. As a result, you will have failed to understand the deeper truth of the Buddha's teaching, and will bring great harm to yourself.

Take the example of a chariot. The term "chariot" is an upādāya-prajñapti, for what we call a chariot is known as such in virtue of its component parts (cakrādiny-upādāya rathāṅgāni rathaḥ prajñapyate). Since the chariot has no existence apart from its component parts, one can say that it is unoriginated by self-nature. But beware: this does not mean that it is originated in *some other way*. In truth, the chariot is simply non-existent (astitvābhāva)—and since it is non-existent, it cannot cease to exist either. As the Buddha has said: "That which is born depending on causes and conditions is really unborn" (yaḥ pratyayair-jayati sa hy-ajātaḥ).

If you could only grasp the fact that *everything* is non-existent in this sense, you would grasp the true śūnyatā—the one that is not a mere dependent designation. According to the final meaning of the doctrine of voidness, everything is a mere prajñapti *without a basis*, because, in the final analysis, there is really nothing for any term to refer to at all. What prevents you from seeing this is your mistaken belief that the so-called *parts* of the chariot—the axles, reins, wheels, chassis etc.—are real, even though the chariot is not. But in fact the very same arguments that go to show the unreality (astitvābhāva) of the chariot apply with equal force to the parts of the chariot—and ultimately even to the atoms themselves, should you wish to push the argument that far.

In the *final* analysis, therefore, dependent co-origination, non-origination, absence of existence (astitvābhāva), emptiness, dependent designation etc. all mean the same thing (paryāyāḥ; viśeṣa-saṃjñāḥ). But the person who believes that things exist on the grounds that things really do originate depending on their causes and conditions has not seen things the way they really are. When the doctrine of pratītya-samutpāda is taken as a doctrine of origination (i.e., as a teaching that merely specifies *how* things arise), rather than as a doctrine of non-origination, it belongs to the realm of falsehood, to the realm of mere designation. It is an upādāya-prajñapti.[23]

23. MMK 24.18 has frequently been cited by proponents of the NNI in defense of their own interpretation of the Madhyamaka, but as I have just argued, MMK 24.18 turns out, on examination, to support the NI rather than the NNI. I think that the same is true of MMK 24 (ārya-satya-parīkṣā) when taken as a whole.

MMK 24 contains Nāgārjuna's reply to a Buddhist critic who accuses Nāgārjuna of nihilism (śūnyam idaṃ sarvam). The critic opposes this view on the grounds that it undermines all the revered Buddhist teachings about suffering, the origin of suffering, the extinction of suffering and the path that leads to the extinction of suffering. If all dharmas are unreal (śūnya), the opponent says, then production and destruction must be unreal. Without real production and real destruction, the four-fold Āryan truths of Buddhism become baseless. These being baseless, the Buddhist order of monks and nuns (saṃgha) and the Buddhist teaching itself become baseless. Ultimately, the view that everything is void renders all our everyday, mundane practices nugatory.

So much about the chapter is uncontroversial. What is not uncontroversial is how Nāgārjuna's reply to the traditionalist critic is to be interpreted. According to the NNI, Nāgārjuna claims that the critic has *misinterpreted* him in claiming that his view is a nihilistic one. It is true, Nāgārjuna says, that all things are void (śūnya), but this is not nihilism. The critic has misunderstood the meaning of śūnyatā and the role that the distinction between the two truths plays in the Buddha's teachings. Once śūnyatā and the two truths doctrine have been properly understood, it will be seen that the doctrine that everything is void (śūnyam idaṃ sarvam) is not a nihilistic view and does not undermine the Buddhist teachings.

This is now the prevailing interpretation of MMK 24. But is it what Nāgārjuna actually says?

After presenting the critic's objections to the doctrine of universal voidness (śūnyam idaṃ sarvam) in the first six verses, Nāgārjuna launches his counter-attack against the critic in the following verse:

> In reply we have to say that you do not understand the purpose of the doctrine of emptiness (śūnyatā), śūnyatā itself or the meaning of śūnyatā. You thereby bring harm to yourself.
>
> atra brūmaḥ śūnyatāyāṃ na tvaṃ vetsi prayojanam /
> śūnyatāṃ śūnyatārthaṃ ca tata evaṃ vihanyase //24.7//

In the next three verses (MMK 24.8-10), Nāgārjuna argues that the teaching of the Buddhas is based on the doctrine of the two truths; that those who do not know the distinction of the two truths do not understand the profundity of the Buddha's teaching; and that without relying on the mundane truth (vyavahāra) the highest truth cannot be expressed. He then says:

> Emptiness (śūnyatā), when it is misconceived, will destroy a dull-witted person, like a snake that has been seized improperly or magic (vidyā) that has been employed incorrectly.
>
> vināśayati durdṛṣṭā śūnyatā manda-medhasam /
> sarpo yathā durgṛhīto vidyā vā duṣprasādhitā //24.11//

Proponents of the NNI seem to take it as obvious that MMK 24.7-11 are directed against the charge of nihilism. Stcherbatsky, for example, cited MMKV 24.7 in support of the following contentions (CBN 50):

> The term śūnya ... does not mean something void ... That this term never meant a mathematical void or simple non-existence is most emphatically insisted upon. Those who suppose that śūnya means void are declared to have misunderstood the term, they have not understood the purpose for which the term has been introduced.

T. R. V. Murti, whose interpretation of the Madhyamaka usually followed Stcherbatksy's very closely, cited the same verse (MMK 24.7) in connection with the following claim (1955: 234):

> Not only affirmative predicates (bhāva, sat) but also negative predicates (abhāva, asat) are denied of the real. The Mādhyamika does not specially favour the negative view. We are on the contrary expressly warned against taking śūnyatā as abhāva (non-existence).

I have to say that I am unable to find anything in MMK 24 to support this interpretation of MMK 24.7-11. Again, it is essential to place these verses within the context of the chapter as a whole. MMK 24 opens with six verses in which the opponent attacks Nāgārjuna as a nihilist who undermines the sacred Buddhist teachings. Now if Nāgārjuna had *not* been a nihilist, one would naturally expect him to respond to the critic by getting right to the point and repudiating nihilism outright. But this Nāgārjuna does not do. What he does *instead* is to accuse the critic of having misunderstood śūnyatā *and the distinction between two different kinds of truth in the Buddha's teaching.*

While the first of these two criticisms can be accounted for on the NNI, it seems to me that the second one cannot. According to the NNI, of course, the first criticism simply amounts to a denial that the Madhyamaka is nihilism. But what the NNI cannot explain, it seems to me, is why *this* criticism should have been associated with the criticism that the opponent has misunderstood or overlooked the *two truths distinction* in Buddhism.

According to the NNI, we would have to read MMK 24 as follows. According to Nāgārjuna, the doctrine that everything is void does not mean that everything is unreal or non-existent: it only means that everything is empty *in the sense that* everything arises and perishes through a process of dependent co-origination (pratītya-samutpāda); and the critic must be taken as criticizing this position. Any teaching in the Buddhist canon to the effect that some things are apratītya and anupādāya is provisional or mundane (neyārtha, vyavahārika). The highest, pāramārthika teaching is that *nothing* is exempt from causal origination (pratītya-samutpāda).

It seems to me that this interpretation of MMK 24 makes no sense. It is quite implausible to take Nāgārjuna as having attributed to his *traditionalist Buddhist opponent* the view that there is something (or at least something saṃsāric) that is exempt from the law of dependent co-origination, for the opponent, as a traditional Buddhist, *must* have accepted the universal validity of this law. What is in question for the traditionalist is precisely whether *Nāgārjuna* accepts it (at least in the final analysis, i.e., pāramārthika). The dispute between the traditionalist and Nāgārjuna was over the *meaning* of this doctrine. The opponent objects that the doctrine that everything is interdependent (pratītya) and causally originated (upādāya) makes no sense on the assumption that everything is void—i.e., that universal voidness (śūnyatā) cannot mean the same thing as dependent co-origination (pratītya-samutpāda).

Nāgārjuna's response in MMK 24.7-40 must be read as a response to *this* criticism. The NI and the NNI give very different interpretations of Nāgārjuna's response to it. According to the NNI, it seems to me, Nāgārjuna's response to this objection must be taken to mean that the view that dependent co-origination *excludes* voidness is a lower, provisional truth, whereas the view that dependent co-origination and emptiness are *identical* is the final or pāramārthika truth. But this interpretation is not only implausible a priori—it is explicitly excluded by MMK 24.18, for whatever else the term "prajñaptir upādāya" in MMK 24.18 may mean, it surely implies that the equation between dependent co-origination and emptiness cannot be taken pāramārthika. Here is where the weakness of the NNI's interpretation of MMK 24 is most apparent. According to the NNI, the equation between emptiness and dependent co-origination should represent *the absolute and final truth* (paramārtha) rather than the conventional or provisional one (saṃvṛti). This, it seems to me, is precisely what Nāgārjuna *denies* when he declares that the equation in question is an upādāya-prajñapti; and Candrakīrti's commentary on the verse bears this out. The nihilist interpretation of MMK 24, on the other hand, is perfectly straightforward. According to the NI, Nāgārjuna *sticks to his guns* as a nihilist, and maintains that ultimately there is no dependent co-origination. Since everything is entirely void (śūnyam-idaṃ sarvam), the equation between emptiness and dependent co-origination is only a provisional teaching (neyārtha, upādāya-prajñapti). Ultimately, nothing arises and nothing perishes (anirodham-anutpādam etc.).

If Nāgārjuna had meant anything else, what could he have meant by invoking the distinction between the two truths in his counter-attack against the traditionalist critic? That the critic had taken the śūnyavāda to be the provisional, lower truth, and the aśūnyavāda as the final or pāramārthika view? But this interpretation really makes no sense, because no one ever took the śūnyavāda to be a *provisional* or inferior truth. It was held to be a false, pernicious or senseless doctrine by its critics, and as the final or pāramārthika truth by its proponents; but it was never regarded by *anyone* as a candidate for the role of a provisional or inferior truth. What Nāgārjuna's reply to the critic must mean, therefore, is that the critic has taken the conventional truths of Buddhism (i.e., the four-fold noble truths, the saṃgha, the dharma, the law of dependent co-origination etc.) as final truths, whereas they are only inferior, provisional truths.

According to the NNI, Nāgārjuna's defense against the critic essentially involves taking it all back, because according to this interpretation, Nāgārjuna concedes that as he is using the term "śūnya," things are not *really* void after all. But I think it is much more likely that Nāgārjuna conceded nothing to the opponent in MMK 24. What he did, essentially, was to consign all the traditional truths of Buddhism which the critic took as the basis of his objections to the realm of conventional truth. This is the point of his criticism in MMK 24.7-11 that the teaching of the Buddhas is based on the distinction (vibhāga) between the two truths; that those who fail to grasp this distinction correctly do not understand the profundity of the Buddha's teaching; and that without relying on the mundane truth (vyavahāra) the highest truth cannot be expressed. Such truths, Nāgārjuna says, are useful and even necessary in order to wean people away from even worse errors. Deluded people have an inveterate tendency to believe that things (bhāvas) and selves (ātman) are real and even eternal. For these people, it is better than nothing to say that everything is impermanent and full of suffering, and that one should strive to liberate oneself from this real cycle of birth and death. But these are only provisional teachings. The critic has made the mistake of supposing that the *traditional* teachings of Buddhism, according to which real things arise and perish, are the ultimate teachings. This is a mistake. The final meaning or implication of the Buddha's teaching is that all things are void and non-existent.

Read in this way, the argument in MMK 24 presents no difficulties. It simply goes as follows:

> You, the non-nihilist critic (aśūnyavādin), allege that the doctrine of śūnyatā is incompatible with the treasured truths of the Buddhist dharma. On the contrary: the truths of Buddhism would be rendered nugatory if the dharmas were *real,* not if they are unreal, for if the dharmas were real, then saṃsāra would be real. If saṃsāra were real, then nirvāṇa could never be attained, for if the dharmas were real, they could not change, thereby rendering escape from saṃsāra an impossibility.[24] It follows that on your view things are devoid of causes and conditions, and you thereby undermine cause, effect, the doer, the means, the act of doing etc. Thus, you are subject to some of the same kinds of errors that you level at us—and then some, because on your view escape from saṃsāra (which you take to be real) is impossible.
>
> It is true that the Buddha sometimes spoke of the dharmas *as if* they were real, but this was only from the point of view of relative truth (MMK 24.7-11). The teaching of the Buddha was based entirely on the distinction between the two truths. You have failed to understand this, and have taken the traditional teachings

(which imply that things are aśūnya or real) to be the ultimate teaching, whereas they are only provisional.

The exoteric doctrine of real (aśūnya) causation (pratītya-samutpāda) is taught to people who have embraced the pernicious view that there are real, enduring, self-existent selves and entities. This exoteric doctrine is not ultimately valid (cf. MMK 1). Nevertheless, the causal doctrine does have one advantage over the teachings it is designed to replace. *It* leads eventually to the highest truth, according to which all things *are* void (śūnyam idaṃ sarvam; anirodham anutpādam etc). If you will only think things through to their logical conclusion, you will see that this is so.

In dealing with ordinary, deluded people, the Buddha had no choice but to refer to things on the basis of everyday, common practices (vyavahāra). Those who infer from this that the Buddha repudiated the view that everything is entirely unreal (asat, mṛṣā) are very dull-witted people who are incapable of understanding the profound nature of the Buddha's teaching (MMK 24.9). They are like those who cannot seize a snake properly or who pronounce a mantra incorrectly (MMK 24.11). They only harm themselves through their failure to understand śūnyatā.

24. Nāgārjuna concludes MMK 24 with two verses which are at first sight very puzzling, for in these verses Nāgārjuna seems to maintain that it is possible to uphold the view that all things are void in the strict sense (śūnyam idaṃ sarvam) and *also* uphold the traditional Buddhist teachings (at least at the phenomenal level).

In the first of these two verses, Nāgārjuna argues against the opponent as follows:

> If everything is non-empty (aśūnya), then there is no abandonment of the defilements, no action to abolish suffering, and no attainment of that which is not already attained.
>
> asaṃprāptasya ca prāptir duḥkha-paryanta-karma ca /
> sarva-kleśa-prahāṇaṃ ca yady aśūnyaṃ na vidyate //24.39//

In the next verse, this view is contrasted with the doctrine of dependent co-origination, which Nāgārjuna seems to identify with the śūnyatāvāda:

> Whoever sees dependent co-origination sees suffering, the origin of suffering, the extinction of suffering and the path leading to the extinction of suffering.
>
> yaḥ pratītya-samutpādaṃ paśyatīdaṃ sa paśyati /
> duḥkhaṃ samudayaṃ caiva nirodhaṃ mārgam eva ca //24.40//

MMK 26 (dvādaśāṅga-parīkṣā) provides another example of Nāgārjuna's penchant for defending traditional Buddhist teachings on the basis of the śūnyatāvāda. This chapter is devoted to an exposition of the Buddhist teaching of the twelve-fold chain of causation and suffering. Nāgārjuna handles it in a very traditional—one might almost say, conventional—way. He begins the cyle with ignorance (avidyā), which leads in turn to the tendencies (saṃskāras), which in turn lead to consciousness (vijñāna), name and form (nāma-rūpa), the six sense fields (āyatanas), feeling (vedanā), clinging (upādāna) and becoming (bhava). The ignorant are trapped in this cycle of suffering, Nāgārjuna says, because they create mental impressions and tendencies (saṃskāras), whereas the wise are freed because they do not do so (MMK 26.10). When ignorance (avidyā) is abolished, each of the succeeding links of the chain of causation is broken. In this way, all suffering is rightly extinguished (MMK 26.12: duḥkha-skandhaḥ kevalo 'yam evaṃ samyag nirudhyate).

Here, Nāgārjuna asserts a number of things that seem, prima facie, to be inconsistent with things that he says elsewhere. For example, he says elsewhere that nirvāṇa is not a mere cessation (cf. MMK 25.7-8); that there is no difference between saṃsāra and nirvāṇa (cf. MMK 25.19-20); and that everything is entirely void; yet in MMK 26 (and other, similar passages), he seems to speak, like a conventional Buddhist, of the twelve-fold cycle of causation and of its cessation.

There may, however, be a consistent reading of all these teachings, along the lines of what S. N. Dasgupta called nihilistic idealism or pure phenomenalism. According to this interpretation, Nāgārjuna holds that what is extinguished in nirvāṇa is the *appearance* of suffering—although even these appearances are not things, because, according to the Mādhyamikas, even mind is unreal. Consequently, one can speak of cessation, but only in a highly qualified sense. There is cessation (nirodha), but only of illusions—and even these illusions, qua illusions, do not exist! That is to say, it isn't that when saṃsāra ceases the phenomena that were previously existent become non-existent, for according to Nāgārjuna they are *always* non-existent—it is simply that the appearances, qua appearances, stop, cease, come to an end. Thus, what is essential on this view is simply that the phantasmagoria should stop *appearing,* for the phantasmagoria can torment us even though they are *not* real, just as an hallucinatory snake or tiger can be just as frightening as a real one. Ultimately, everything is non-existent and void. Saṃsāra is that voidness when it is obscured with the apparent defilements of the unreal, phantasmagoric movie. Nirvāṇa is the same voidness when these pictures no longer appear.

Whereas this way of looking at the matter does provide an accommodation of sorts between the traditional Buddhist teachings about the origination and cessation of suffering and the doctrine that everything is completely void, the attempts by Stcherbatsky (CBN 53-56, 70) and others to impose theistic, pantheistic or cosmotheistic views on the Madhyamaka seem to me quite fantastic. The absurdity of the latter interpretation does not lie in the suggestion that the Buddhists believed in supernatural or divine beings, for of course at the level of conventional truth (saṃvṛti) they certainly did believe in these. The mistake lies in equating any or all of these deities, Buddhas etc. with *emptiness.* To say that Amitābha, Vairocana and the Goddess Tārā (cf. CBN 55) are śūnya is true, because they are in fact only appearances, and as such really non-existent. But the relation is not a symmetrical one, for it makes no sense to say that non-existence is something. Even now, Vairocana, Amitābha, the Goddess Tārā etc. are only unreal appearances; and when nirvāṇa is finally attained, and all appearances come to an end, the unreal appearances of Vairocana, Amitābha, the Goddess Tārā etc. will come to an end as well.

1. A number of different though related questions are involved in the controversy between the proponents of the NI and the NNI. One question is whether the Mādhyamikas believed in an Absolute (tathatā, nirvāṇa); another is whether they believed in the reality of the phenomenal world (saṃsāra, vyavahāra). Any interpretation of the Madhyamaka must also give an account of the role that the two truths distinction plays in the Madhyamaka, and one must therefore consider the question whether the Mādhyamikas asserted or denied the reality of the Absolute and the reality of the phenomenal in a qualified or unqualified sense.

The following four positions are examples of possible views on these questions:

(1) The Mādhyamikas believed in the unqualified reality of an Absolute, and denied without qualification the reality of the phenomenal world.

(2) The Mādhyamikas believed in the reality of the phenomenal world in a *qualified* sense, and did not believe in the reality of an Absolute at all.

(3) The Mādhyamikas believed in the reality of the phenomenal world in a *qualified* sense, and also believed in an Absolute in an unqualified sense.

(4) The Mādhyamikas believed in the reality of both an Absolute and the phenomenal world in an unqualified sense.

Prof. Matilal's interpretation of the Madhyamaka fell into the third category, as can be seen from the following passage (LI 27-28):

> In fact, it is a common mistake—a mistake that is unfortunately being perpetuated by many today—to describe the saṃvṛti, i.e. the everyday world, as an illusion or even an appearance. It is, I think, improper to assume that the so-called appearance-reality

distinction, so well-known in Western philosophy, will also hold for Nāgārjuna and Śaṅkara. Of course, it is said that the everyday world is not real. But an object can be said to be *not real* in two very different senses. The so-called object may be non-existent, and hence deserves to be called 'not real.' On the other hand, a toy gun, for example, can be said to be 'not real' because it is a toy gun. A toy elephant (to use an image of the Laṅkāvatāra-sūtra) does not possess the own-nature or *svabhāva* that it is supposed to possess or that it professes to possess.

Similarly the everyday world, it is argued, does not embody the svabhāva or essence it professes to embody. It falls short of the ideal of the svabhāva, and in this sense it is unreal. Thus saṃsāra or saṃvṛti is not a mere appearance, still less an illusion—it is something that is not quite successful in embodying an own-nature, svabhāva. It seems to be a misrepresentation to call the everyday world an illusion, or identical with the Red King's dream in Alice's adventures.

Proper understanding of the distinction between saṃvṛti and paramārtha, between the everyday reality and the ultimate reality is, as has already been emphasized, the key to the understanding of the nature of Indian mysticism. Saṃvṛti is not identical with illusion although it may be inclusive of that which we call illusion. Thus, some philosophers (cf. Bhāvaviveka, Prajñākaramati, etc.) try to distinguish between the true saṃvṛti and the false saṃvṛti (tathya and mithya). False saṃvṛti refers to the illusory appearance of things (mirage, etc.). But true saṃvṛti is the everyday world... This is called saṃvṛti only because it covers and conceals the ultimate nature of the objects we see. This is justifiable since saṃvṛti etymologically means covering and concealing. In fact, each thing is said by the mystic to have two natures or aspects, one that is grasped by our ordinary perception and intellect, and the other that lies concealed or hidden by the first but is revealed only to the perfect wisdom or prajñā-pāramitā. Our worldly behavior operates with the first nature or the first aspect, while the second is operative only in nirvāṇa. But the Indian mystic warns at the same time that it is the first alone that can lead us to the second. And when one penetrates the second, the previous duality of nature merges into one. That is what is called the mystic "unity" or oneness of reality.[1]

2. I have cited the foregoing passage at some length because it raises a number of issues that I shall be discussing in this chapter. Here I wish to begin by examining the claim that the Mādhyamikas did not believe that the world was imaginary, dream-like or illusory, at least in any literal sense. This is now the prevailing scholarly view about the Mādhyamikas, despite the fact that there are many passages from the Mādhyamika texts that can be cited against it. The passages that I cited from the MMK(V) and the Prajñā-pāramitā in the previous chapter provide evidence that the Mādhyamikas and the early Mahāyānists who wrote the Prajñā-pāramitā sūtras did in fact believe that the world was unreal, imaginary, dreamlike and illusory. It is particularly interesting to note, however, that this interpretation of the Prajñā-pāramitā and the Madhyamaka is also supported by the very passage that Matilal cited in defense of his own interpretation.

Prof. Matilal did not specify the passage or passages from the Laṅkāvatāra that he had in mind in this connection, but I believe that he must have had in mind Laṅk. 2 kār. 147 and Laṅk.-sagāthakam kār. 54.[2] These passages will repay close examination, for when they are placed in context, they seem to me to imply the very opposite of what Matilal seems to have taken them to mean.

Laṅk. 2 kār. 147, and the passage in which it occurs, are as follows:

All things lack a self-nature (svabhāva). As a result, all words are also devoid of reality (asat). The ignorant wander about, failing to understand that the meaning of emptiness is simply emptiness.

sarva-bhāvo 'svabhāvo hi san-vacanaṃ tathāpy-asat /
śūnyatā-śūnyatārthaṃ vā bālo 'paśyan-vidhāvati //145//

All things lack a self-nature; the same is true of all the words of people. They are mere imagination (kalpanā), and even that imagination does not exist (nāsti). Even nirvāṇa is similar to a dream. On examination, one is not in saṃsāra, nor does one transmigrate.

sarva-bhāva-svabhāvā ca vacanam-api nṛṇām /[3]
kalpanā sāpi nāsti nirvāṇaṃ svapna-tulyam /
bhavaṃ parīkṣeta na saṃsāre nāpi nirvāyāt //146//

Just as a king or wealthy householder, having given his children various animals made out of clay and has them play with them, and later gives them real (bhūta) animals,

rājā śreṣṭhī yathā putrān-vicitrair-mṛnmayair-mṛgaiḥ /
pralobhya krīḍayitvā ca bhūtān-dadyāt-tato mṛgān //147//

So, too, I speak to my children about the reality limit (bhūta-koṭi) which can only be realized within oneself (mavedya) in terms of the various images and characteristics of things.

tathāhaṃ lakṣaṇaiś-citrair-dharmāṇāṃ pratibimbakaiḥ/
pratyān-mavedyāṃ putrebhyo bhūta-koṭiṃ vadāmy-aham //148 //

Note, first of all, that the toy-animal analogy in this passage is not used to describe the nature of things, but rather the nature of the Buddha's *words* or teaching about reality. In the

Mahāyāna, the true nature of things is ineffable; and all words describing reality are provisional. To realize the highest truth one has to go beyond words. This is the point of the analogy of giving a toy-animal (krīḍā-mṛgaḥ, mṛnmayair-mṛgaḥ) to a young child before the child is old enough to play with a real one (bhūta).

In LI 27-28, Matilal took the toy animal in the Laṅkāvatāra to be a description of the nature of reality, but as we have seen, this is not the case. It is used there as a description of the necessarily inadequate nature of the Buddha's *teachings* about reality. Furthermore, when the passage is placed in its proper context, the Laṅkāvatāra's description of *ultimate* reality seems to be the opposite of what Matilal took it to be. According to Matilal, since Nāgārjuna (and the Indian mystics generally) took "unreal" (asat) to mean "lacking in self-nature" (niḥsvabhāva), they must have believed in at least the qualified reality of the world. But this is the very thing that Laṅk. 2 kār. 146 explicitly denies, for it says that things lack self nature, and that they are *for this very reason* mere imagination (kalpanā) and dreamlike. Indeed, it goes further than this and asserts that even this imagination does not exist (kalpanā sāpi nāsti).[4]

The illusionistic interpretation of Laṅk. 2 kār. 147 is confirmed by Laṅk.-Sagāthakam 54, which repeats Laṅk. 2 kār. 147 with very minor modifications. Sagāthakam 54, and the passage in which it occurs, are as follows:

> What are called the various mind-seeds are seen as it were externally as the domain of the objects of the mind (citta-gocara). The ignorant imagine origination (utpatti) therein and take delight in the imagined duality.
>
> cittaṃ vicitraṃ bījākhyaṃ khyāyate citta-gocaram /
> khyātau kalpanti utpattiṃ bālāḥ kalpa-dvaye ratāḥ //49//
>
> Ignorance, desire, karma and mind and its associates (citta-caittāḥ) are not real agents (kāraka). Since mind evolves in this way, I [the Buddha] say that all this

belongs merely to what is called the "dependent nature" of things (pāratantrya).

ajñāna-tṛṣṇā-karmaṃ ca citta-caittā na kārakam /
pravartati tato yasmāt-pāratantryaṃ hitaṃ mayā //50 //[5]

The ignorant take this fundamental error—this domain of the objects of the mind—to be a reality (vastu). This imagination of theirs does not belong to the true nature of things [aniṣpanna = a-pariniṣpanna]. It is a false, confused imagination.

te ca kalpanti yad-vastu citta-gocara-vibhramam /
kalpanāyām-aniṣpannaṃ mithyā-bhrānti-vikalpitam //51//

When it is bound to causes and conditions, mind evolves in all the various beings. I do not see or speak of mind when it is free from these causes and conditions.

cittaṃ pratyaya-saṃbaddhaṃ pravartati śarīriṇām /
pratyayebhyo vinirmuktaṃ na paśyāmi vadāmy-aham //52//

When the mind no longer abides in the body, it is devoid of all self-characteristics and free from all causes and conditions. Therefore I say that the mind is in reality devoid of any objects (agocara).

pratyayebhyo vinirmuktaṃ svalakṣaṇa-vivarjitam /
na tiṣṭhati yadā dehe tena mahyam-agocaram //53//

Just as a king or a wealthy householder gives his children various fake-animals (mṛga-sādṛśāḥ), who play with them in the house like the real ones in the forest;

rājā śreṣṭhī yathā putrān-vicitrair-mṛga-sādṛśaiḥ /
pralobhya krīḍati gṛhe vane mṛga-samāgamam //54//

Just so I speak to my children about the reality limit, which can only be realized within oneself, in terms of the various characteristics and images of things.

tathāhaṃ lakṣaṇaiś-citrair-dharmāṇāṃ pratibimbakaiḥ/
pratyān-mavedyāṃ hi sutāṃ bhūta-koṭiṃ vadāmy-aham //55//

Just like waves that rise and dance uninterruptedly on water that is stirred by the wind,

taraṃgā hy-udadher-yadvat-pavana-pratyayoditāḥ /
nṛtyamānāḥ pravartante vyucchedaś-ca na vidyate //56//

The ālaya-current evolves in the same way. Constantly disturbed by the wind of the imagined objects, it dances with the thoughts of the waves of the mind.

ālayaughas-tathā nityaṃ viṣaya-pavaneritaḥ /
cittais-taraṃga-vijñānair-nṛtyamānaḥ pravartate //57//

If anything, it is clearer from this passage than it is from Laṅk. 2. kār. 145-148 that the Laṅkāvatāra's toy-animal analogy has a rather different meaning from the one that Matilal took it to have. In fact, it would be hard to find a passage that is more unequivocally committed to the view that the world is imaginary, dreamlike and illusory than this one. For example, the passage says that duality and origination are unreal (k. 49); that the domain of the objects of the mind is unreal, and therefore a false imagination (k. 51); that there are no objects to be perceived by the mind (k. 53); and that the thought of objects is merely an illusory disturbance of the mind, like waves on the surface of a body of water (ks. 56-57). As in Laṅk. 2. kār. 145-148, even the words of the Buddha are consigned to this purely imaginary reality (cf. Laṅk. 2. kār. 145). The point of the toy-animal analogy, thefore, is that even the Buddha's words are provisional and ultimately illusory. This, of course, only confirms the māyāvic interpretation of the Laṅkāvatāra.

3. The suggestion that lies behind LI 27-28 is that the claim that the world is unreal does not really mean what it seems to mean. The claim that things are actually unreal, according to Matilal, is only a very dramatic or hyperbolic way of making the point that things are impermanent. However, I do not think that the Mahāyānist doctrine that things are unreal can be dismissed as a mere rhetorical device. The doctrine of māyā (illusion) in a very strict sense is there in the Mahāyāna, deeply embedded in the philosophy and doctrines. Whereas the Hīnayāna held that things do arise (utpatti-vāda), the Mahāyāna held that things do not arise (anutpatti-vāda). Furthermore, the doctrine that things do not arise is connected in the Mahāyāna with the view that the world is *unreal* (māyā, asat), and not with the view that it is real—even in a qualified sense.

Unless these points are clearly understood, one will be at a loss to understand the dispute that took place between the Hīnayānists and the Mahāyānists, and the later history of the evolution of Buddhist doctrine and philosophy will start to look enigmatic. Take a particular example of a putative entity, e.g., a plant or an electron. To take the line that a plant or an electron is unreal merely in the sense that it is dependent on its causal conditions (niḥsvabhāva) would be to endorse the *Hīnayānist* view. That view simply amounts to this: that a plant (or electron, or dharma) would not have come into existence had it not been for the causal conditions that preceded it, and that it will cease to exist after the causal conditions that sustain its existence disappear. (Cf. seed, soil, temperature, water etc., in the case of the plant; a certain magnetic field etc. in the case of the electron.) A plant or electron or dharma comes into being (utpatti) when the requisite causal conditions are present, and ceases to exist when the requisite causal conditions fail to obtain. On this view, things really do arise. It is just that they arise in a particular *way*—i.e., concomitantly with, or subsequent to, certain kinds of other things or causal conditions. Seeing things the way they really are (yathā-bhūtam) is a matter of seeing that this is the case.

The fundamental problem with the suggestion in LI 27-28—according to which "unreal" and "empty" simply mean lacking self nature (niḥsvabhāva), in the sense of being causally originated (utpatti)—is that it is incompatible with the view that things are devoid of self-nature or self-existence (niḥsvabhāva) *in the sense that they do not arise at all* (anutpāda). If the Mahāyānist doctrine that things lack a self-nature (niḥsvabhāvatā) had only meant that things exist in dependence on other things, there would be no difference between it and the view of the Hīnayāna. But we know that there was a dispute between the Hīnayānists and the Mahāyānists over this very point. The historical and textual evidence tells us quite unmistakably that the doctrine of non-origination (anutpatti-vāda) of the Mahāyāna involves the much stronger claim that *there are no things* (sarvaṃ sarveṇa nāsti; sarva-dharma-śūnyatā), i.e., that there are no plants, electrons, dharmas etc. that arise in a real causal process. And this doctrine—at least when it is interpreted very strictly, as it was in the Madhyamaka—is the *nihilist* position.[6, 7]

4. Pace Prof. Matilal, therefore, the Mahāyānists *did* maintain that the world was unreal in the strict sense—i.e., they held that it was non-existent, illusory and imaginary. The disagreement *within* the Mahāyāna was over the question whether the *mind* was also unreal. The Vijñānavādins held that the external world (bāhyārtha) was unreal, whereas the appearance of the world (i.e., the world as a purely mental phenomenon) was real. The Mādhyamika position was that *both* mind and matter were unreal and non-existent. The Vijñānavāda, therefore, was an *ontological* idealism, whereas the Madhyamaka was a *non-ontological* idealism or nihilism, or as S. N. Dasgupta has put it, a nihilistic idealism or pure phenomenalism.

Though the parallels are not exact, there are some striking similarities between the Vijñānavāda and some Western philosophies. In the West, the whole Cartesian tradition of epistemology and the idealist philosophies that derive from it are based on the claim that it is nonsensical to assert that *mind* is unreal and non-existent. On this point, there is agreement between the idealist tradition of the West and the Vijñānavāda. On another point, however, the Vijñānavāda is diametrically opposed to the Cartesian one. In Descartes, the assertion that the mind is known with absolute certainty is bound together with the claim that the self (ego) is indubitable as well (at least as long as one is thinking). On this point the Vijñānavāda departs from the Cartesian philosophy, for as orthodox Buddhists the Vijñānavādins denied the existence of a self or ego (ātman).

For this reason, the Vijñānavāda seems to be closer to Hume's position than Descartes'. Like Descartes, Hume held that mental phenomena (thoughts, impressions, percepts, sense data, etc.) are known with absolute certainty, but Hume denied that these mental phenomena require us to suppose that there is a thinker or percipient of these impressions etc., just as, when it is true to say "It is raining," it does not follow that there is some entity or thing that is raining. What we call "raining" is not like a leaking hose. In the latter case, we can identify the source of the water and say, sensibly, that the hose is leaking water. But when the meteorological conditions justify one's saying "It is raining," there is no thing or entity that can be identified as the source of the rain in the same way. Strictly speaking, one cannot even say that a *cloud* is *raining*. This way of speaking would imply a distinction between an entity and its process or activity that in this case could not be sustained. What we call a cloud is just a mass of water vapor or water droplets, and what we call rain is just a matter of these droplets falling to earth under certain atmospheric conditions. The Humean and Vijñānavādin critique of the Cartesian doctrine of a self or ego can be understood quite well, I think, in terms of this metaphor. What the Vijñānavādins and other Buddhists argued, essentially, was that saying "René is thinking" or "Devadatta is thinking" is like saying "It is raining" rather than "The hose is leaking." Strictly speaking, there is nothing that thinks, just as there is nothing that literally rains.

Although Hume insisted that the mind was egoless, he never questioned the reality of mind itself. In this respect, even Hume remained a traditionalist. In this respect, too, his position was very similar to that of the Vijñānavādins. However, Hume's philosophical and historical background was very different from that of the Vijñānavādins. When Hume was writing, no one in the West had seriously questioned the existence of *mental phenomena*. As we shall see, this did get questioned eventually in Western philosophy, but only much later; whereas in India the Madhyamaka, which denied the reality of mind, arose even earlier than the Vijñānavāda. Indeed, the emergence of the Vijñānavāda as a distinct school of thought within the Mahāyāna was principally due to growing opposition within the Mahāyāna to the then prevailing view that even *mind* is unreal. The Mahāyānists who rejected this view came to be known as Yogācārins or Vijñānavādins. The Mahāyānists who continued to adhere to the earlier view of the Mahāyāna came to be known as Mādhyamikas.

The Vijñānavādins contended, as against the Mādhyamikas, that the *literal* reading of the Mahāyānist doctrines of non-origination (anutpatti-vāda) and non-existence of the dharmas (sarva-dharma-śūnyatā) was untenable. In any case, they argued, the literal reading of this doctrine cannot be applied to mental phenomena like thoughts, impressions, percepts etc. To read the doctrine literally and without exception in this way, they argued, would be absurd, because then the teachings would be contradicted by our own immediate experience (anubhava). If one stares at the yellow flame of a candle or an electric light and then closes one's eyes, one will often see a more or less distinct after-image of the light in one's mind's eye. According to the Vijñānavādins, it is undeniable in these cases that one is is seeing *something,* even if it is only mental (i.e., even if the image is *hallucinatory*). This became the principal line of defense within the Mahāyāna against the Mādhyamika dialectic, whereby everything tended to vanish into complete nothingness.[8]

The Mādhyamikas, for their part, seem to have regarded the Vijñānavādins as backsliders or slackers, who compromised the strict doctrine of śūnyatā with their mind-only doctrine (vijñaptimātratā). The Vijñānavādin interpretation of the Mahāyānist doctrine of emptiness is based on the contention that the physical (rūpa) dharmas are empty and unreal in a way that the mental dharmas are not. The Mādhyamikas denounced this "other emptiness" interpretation of the doctrine of śūnyatā, and, I think, for good reason, for what the doctrine of universal emptiness says, simply, is that all dharmas are void, and there is no reason to think that the *mental* dharmas are any exception. If the doctrine had meant what the Vijñānavādins claimed it meant, then one would have to suppose that things are void in two very different senses, and the Mādhyamikas were in a good position to argue that there is nothing in the texts to support this interpretation.[9]

It is true that the Vijñānavādins could cite a relatively large number of sūtra passages in defense of their mind-only doctrine. [Cf. the Daśa-bhūmika-sūtra, p. 49: "The whole universe is nothing but mind" (cittamātram idaṃ yad idaṃ traidhātukam).] But the Mādhyamikas argued that such passages do not represent the direct (nītārtha) or ultimate (pāramārthika) aspect of the Buddha's teaching. According to them, such passages are only provisional (neyārtha). Ultimately, even the view that things are mind only is false, for in the final analysis mind is no more real than matter. This is not to say that the mind-only teachings are completely useless. They are useful—indeed indispensable—for purely exegetical and didactic purposes. People of the ordinary type will always insist on asking: If the world is unreal, what is it that we *seem* to see? To people of this type it is sometimes helpful to say: "What you are seeing is an appearance in your own mind." Even this is not true, however, for the truth is that there is nothing to see—not even anything mental. There are, in the final analysis, only the words "mind" (citta, vijñāna), "ābhāsa" (appearance) etc. In actuality, there is nothing whatever corresponding to them.[10]

5. While the Mādhyamikas appear to have been on solid ground textually and doctrinally, their interpretation of the Mahāyāna was subject to strong philosophical objections, for it is hard to see how it could possibly make any sense to say that nothing exists, when our own experience seems to tell us that there is something going on in the world, even if it is only mental. So how could it possibly make any sense to say that both matter *and* mind are unreal?

It is tempting to try to meet this difficulty by invoking the distinction between two different kinds of truth (dve satye), i.e., the absolute truth or paramārtha-satya, and the phenomenal truth or saṃvṛti-satya. This distinction has a long history in India, and as we have seen, Prof. Matilal appealed to it; indeed, he regarded this distinction as the key to the understanding of the nature of Indian mysticism (LI 28). In Matilal's case, however, the distinction was not invoked in its purest form, for in his interpretation the distinction is merely between a phenomenal world which has a *qualified* reality and an Absolute (nirvāṇa, brahman) which has an unqualified reality.

Here I wish to consider the two truths distinction in its purest form. Can the distinction between two different kinds of truth be used to justify the claim that both mind and matter are unreal, on the grounds that they are real at the phenomenal level but unreal at the absolute level? I do not think that it can. Nor do I think that the *Mādhyamikas* thought so, because in the Madhyamaka, and in Buddhism generally, the distinction in question is really a distinction between two different kinds of *teaching* rather than a distinction between two different kinds of *truth*.

The distinction between a relative and an absolute truth seems to have evolved in Buddhism from an earlier distinction between the indirect and direct teachings of the Buddha. The latter distinction was introduced in order to impose some system and order on the sometimes conflicting mass of teachings and doctrines that had been handed down within the tradition. One example of this conflict within the Mahāyāna (i.e., within a *later* tradition) is provided by the doctrine of non-origination (anutpatti-vāda). This doctrine is in conflict with numerous passages in the older texts that assert categorically that things do arise (utpatti-vāda, pratītya-samutpāda). The Mahāyānists dealt with this problem by asserting that the doctrine that things do originate was an indirect teaching of the Buddha, whereas the doctrine of non-origination was the direct teaching.

Frequently, the Mahāyānists also expressed this distinction between direct and indirect teachings in terms of a distinction between two different kinds of *truth*. Caution is in order in connection with the latter terminology, however, for the latter distinction cannot be taken literally—nor, I think, is there any reason to believe that the Mādhyamikas or any other Buddhist school took it literally. According to the Mādhyamikas, the Buddha taught dependent co-origination to some people at some times, and the doctrine that things do not exist and that they do not arise to other people at other times. The former teachings were said to constitute a provisional truth, and they were given to people who adhered to even worse views. To call the doctrine of origination a provisional or lower truth in *this* sense is harmless, provided that one knows what one is doing. But since this lower or provisional truth *contradicts* the absolute (pāramārthika) truth, it must be, from a logical point of view, simply false. And this, I think, is exactly how the Mādhyamikas viewed the matter.

From the logical point of view, truth is a univocal concept, for the claim of univocality is logically equivalent to the assertion that it cannot be the case that P and also the case that not-P at one and the same time. This assertion is fundamental to all logic. Any statement that violates this logical law of non-contradiction is meaningless or at least analytically false. The distinction between two different kinds of truth cannot be used to evade or circumvent this law of non-contradiction. Saying, for example, that it is the case that x is ϕ from *one* point of view and that it is not the case that x is ϕ from *another* point of view really does nothing to mitigate a contradiction. This point—which is, I think, obvious enough—can be illustrated by the very kind of example that is often used to illustrate the doctrine of the two truths.

Consider first the case of a person walking along in the dusk who mistakes a rope lying in the path for a snake. It would be incorrect to describe this situation by saying that there is a snake in the path that is both real and unreal. Nor would it be correct to say that the snake is real from one point of view and false from another point of view. The snake is simply non-existent. There is not one thing—a snake that is both real and unreal—but two different things, or rather *three* different things. There is 1) the rope (which is real); 2) the snake which is *thought* to exist as an external object (which is totally unreal); and 3) the snake as a mental appearance in the person's mind (which is real, though of course this mental appearance is not a snake). If one considers this case carefully, in other words, there is nothing in the picture that can be said to be both real and unreal (or neither real nor unreal) at all—not even from the point of view of different levels of truth.[11]

Consider another example, slightly different from the preceding one but logically related to it. In ordinary speech we say things like "The sun rises in the East and sets in the West" even after we have learned that it is the earth that revolves around the sun rather than vice versa. But it does not follow from this that the statement that the sun rises in the East and sets in the West is true from the point of view of relative truth and false from the point of view of absolute truth. There *is* no sense in which it is true that the sun rises in the East and sets in the West. What is true is that it *appears* to someone who is standing on the surface of the earth and looking at the horizon etc. as if the sun were rising. But the statement "It appears as if it were the case that P" is a *different* statement from P itself. What we have here, then, is not a case of one statement being both true and false (or neither true nor false)—not even from different points of view or levels of truth—but two entirely different statements. Once again, then, what might appear at first sight to be an example of two different kinds of truth turns out to reduce to only one truth.[12]

There is a considerable amount of evidence that the Buddhists themselves did not believe in two different kinds of truth in any literal sense. All they maintained was a distinction between two different kinds of *teaching*, one of which was held to be true, and the other of which was held to be (in the final analysis) false. Thus, the Sutta-nipāta (884) says: "Truth is one and not two" (ekaṃ hi saccaṃ na dutīyam atthi). The same commitment to the univocality of truth was also frequently held in the Abhidharma (cf. Poussin 1936-37). Finally, the evidence is that the *Mādhyamikas* remained orthodox on this point. Consider, for example, the following passage from Candrakīrti's Madhyamakāvatāra (119, commentary on vi, 34):

> [Opponent]: All right, we will agree with you that there is not, in actuality, origination: there is no origination by self or by others. But colors, sensations etc. which are perceived either by direct perception or by reasoning, originate without any doubt from others. If

> you deny it, how can you speak of two truths? Otherwise, there would be only one truth.
>
> [Candrakīrti]: Quite so. In reality, there is only one truth, i.e., nirvāṇa. As Bhagavat has said: 'Monks, there is only one truth, nirvāṇa. All things of the causal order (saṃskāra) are false, deceptive.' But the truth of experience is the means for entering into the real truth: therefore we admit it, in conformity with the world, without examining if things are produced by self or by others.[13]

Since a lower "truth" that actually *contradicts* a higher truth cannot be a truth at all, one cannot argue, as many proponents of the NNI have argued, that the phenomenal world of cause and effect can be real according to a "lower" truth (saṃvṛti) and also unreal according to a higher truth. Things are either real or they aren't; they either exist or they don't; and they either arise or they don't—nor do the Mādhyamikas appear to have denied it. We should not be misled by the fact that they occasionally appealed to something that they *called* a distinction between two truths. For the Mādhyamikas, this was an exegetical distinction, not a logical one. The Mādhyamikas themselves appear to have believed that it is simply *false* that things originate. The ultimate truth—and therefore the only truth—is that things do not originate at all, i.e., they are completely void (śūnya) and non-existent (asat).

6. I said earlier (v. supra, p. 219) that "the doctrine of non-origination (anutpatti-vāda) of the Mahāyāna involves [the claim] that *there are no things* ... i.e., that there *are* no plants, electrons, dharmas etc. that arise in a real causal process. And this is the *nihilist* position." Many proponents of the NNI might be inclined to deny that the claim that there are no entities or dharmas amounts to a doctrine of nihilism. This particular issue, therefore, needs to be examined in more detail.

A critical juncture in the argument for the NI is the claim that emptiness cannot be equated with dependent origination. A proponent of the NNI might wish to attack the reasoning at this point. The argument might go as follows:

> The claim that no things or entities arise in the causal process does not leave us with the very limited choices that you, the proponent of the NI, wish to present to us. It is perfectly possible to affirm that no entities or dharmas exist or arise *and* affirm that everything is relative and dependent (pratītya) *and* reject the nihilist view.
>
> In Buddhism, relativity is *itself* an Absolute. There is a reality in Buddhism, but it is a reality in which there are no entities. This absolute reality can only be grasped when you give up your inveterate tendency to distinguish this from that. The true nature of things is a continuum of pure energy or pure relatedness devoid of the lumps or singularities (i.e., things or entities) that we tend to imagine there.
>
> If Buddhism looks like nihilism to you, it is probably because you are unable to grasp the fact that things are so interdependent and so interwoven that we cannot really speak of things or entities at all. Of course, the statement that things actually *arise* dependently (pratītya-sam*utpāda*) is an oxymoron. If things really did arise, then they would exist, and the Hīnayānist account of the Buddhist teaching would be the correct one. But there are two different aspects to the doctrine of dependent co-origination. The Hīnayānists have fastened on the part of it that claims that things *arise* (utpāda), but this is not the real point of the doctrine. So far as *origination* is concerned, the doctrine of dependent co-origination is merely a conventional designation (upādāya-prajñapti). As such, it relies on everyday speech in order to point to nirvāṇa and the absolute truth.[14]

> The wise person will ignore this rind of the Buddhist doctrine, and go directly to the kernel. The kernel of the teaching is that the true nature of things consists in a pure relatedness devoid of any relata. Thus, emptiness (śūnyatā), lack of self-nature (niḥsvabhāvatā) and dependent co-origination (pratītya-samutpāda) are, when properly understood, convergent doctrines. Furthermore, the doctrine on which they converge is not a nihilistic one.

The elements of the foregoing formulation of the NNI have been taken from the writings of Th. Stcherbatksy (CBN 47-58), D. Seyfort Ruegg (FPC 51; 1983: 29), et al. Although I am responsible for the way these elements have been *combined* in the foregoing formulation, I believe the formulation does capture a very important line of contemporary thought about the Madhyamaka. There are, however, a number of problems with it.

One obvious problem—a philosophical one which I shall not go into here—is that it is not at all clear that it makes any sense to speak of a pure relatedness devoid of any relata, for relations and things related by the relations would appear to be complementary notions. In other words, one cannot have relations if there are no entities that are related by them.

There are also doctrinal and textual objections to the foregoing interpretation of the Madhyamaka. First, the claim that reality consists of nothing but pure relatedness would appear to be incompatible with the traditional dharma doctrine of Buddhism, according to which there is a world of saṃsāric suffering consisting of a flow of impermanent, impersonal dharmas. Furthermore, even a realm of pure relatedness would presumably have to be a realm of dependency and relativity, and as such, would be saṃsāric and doomed to extinction, and hence could not be regarded as any kind of Absolute. To maintain that there is a domain of pure relatedness which is *beyond* relativity, dependence, impermanence and change would be quite unorthodox, for it is a fundamental teaching of Buddhism that whatever lacks self-nature is impermanent and saṃsāric.[15]

7. This last point is so important that it deserves special attention. I shall approach it by returning once again to Matilal's interpretation of Nāgārjuna in LI 27-28, where the issue emerges in a particularly clear form.

According to LI 27-28, things that arise and perish depending on causes and conditions are unreal, but only in a weak sense, i.e., they are only *less* real than what exists at the pāramārthika level. Phenomenal things lack self-nature (svabhāva), whereas nirvāṇa or ultimate truth is characterized by self-nature. We might paraphrase LI 27-28, then, as follows:

> According to the Mahāyāna, it is actually true that things (dharmas) arise. It is, however, not the whole truth. This way of viewing things is only the truth of the everyday or concealed truth.
>
> There is another truth, which only the enlightened see. This is the truth of nirvāṇa, which is self-existent and free from change. Furthermore, nirvāṇa is the phenomenal world viewed as it really is (yathā-bhūtam), i.e., as devoid of causal conditions and plurality (cf. NMD 156).
>
> Reality, therefore, has two very different aspects. The world of saṃsāra is the domain of relativity, of dependence, of change. This saṃsāric world is true in its own way, but this truth needs to be seen in the light of the absolute truth (nirvāṇa), according to which things do not arise at all.

One of the principal problems with this view is that Nāgārjuna does not seem to qualify the claim that all things lack self-nature in the way that the interpretation requires. Furthermore, if this *had* been Nāgārjuna's view, his philosophy would have been identical, at least on this point, with the philosophy of the Advaita Vedānta. But Nāgārjuna's philosophy is quite incompatible with the Vedānta precisely because he does *not* draw this distinction. For Nāgārjuna there is no exception to the rule that there is *no* self-nature (svabhāva). The Mādhyamika and the Advaitin were in agreement that anything that changes is unreal (or in Buddhist terminology, that anything that is niḥsvabhāva is unreal), but the difference between the two systems is that the Advaitin believed that there *is* something beyond change, and therefore something that *does* have svabhāva. In the Madhyamaka, the claim that all things lack self-nature was a universal, unqualified truth.

8. Much of the prevailing confusion on this point can be traced to a Vedāntist work called the Āgama-śāstra, also known as the Gauḍapādīya-kārikās. (See Wood 1990.) The author (or authors) of the last chapter (prakaraṇa) of this work did attribute to the Buddha an eternalist belief in an unchanging Absolute. Furthermore, the argumentation in support of a non-dual, unchanging Absolute in this chapter is very reminiscent of the argumentation that Nāgārjuna used in the MMK to show that all things are śūnya or niḥsvabhāva. Nevertheless, the Āgama-śāstra's position on this point is not Nāgārjuna's.

One passage in the Āgama-śāstra where misrepresentation of the Madhyamaka occurs is Alāta-śānti-prakaraṇa (AŚP) 7-9, which says:

> The deathless does not become mortal, and the mortal does not become deathless. There can be no change (literally, no 'becoming other') in nature in any way whatever.
>
> na bhavaty-amṛtaṃ martyaṃ na martyam-amṛtaṃ tathā /
> prakṛter-anyathābhāvo na kathaṃcid-bhaviṣyati // AŚP 7 //
>
> He for whom an entity (dharma), deathless by nature, undergoes death, how will his deathless entity, since it is a product (kṛtaka), remain changeless (niścala)?
>
> svabhāvenāmṛto yasya dharmo gacchati martyatām /
> kṛta-kenāmṛtas-tasya kathaṃ sthāsyati niścalaḥ // AŚP 8 //

Nature (prakṛti) is to be known as that which is self-established (sāṃsiddhikī), self-existent (svābhāvikī), innate (sahajā), not artifical (akṛtā), and as something which does not give up its self-nature.

sāṃsiddhikī svābhāvikī sahajāpy akṛtā ca yā /
prakṛtiḥ seti vijñeyā svabhāvaṃ na jahāti yā // AŚP 9 //

As V. Bhattacharya (1943: 109, 140) seems to have been the first to point out, these verses irresistibly call to mind passages in the Mādhyamika writings. For example, the second sentence of AŚP 7 has exactly the same meaning as MMK 15.8 (prakṛter anyathābhāvo na hi jātūpapadyate). But this does not mean, as Bhattacharya seems to have thought, that the author of the AŚP was teaching *Nāgārjunian* doctrines. On the contrary: he was advocating a view that directly *contradicts* the one held by Nāgārjuna.

As a follower of the Prajñā-pāramitā, Nāgārjuna believed that nothing *could* exist that was not impermanent (anitya). According to Nāgārjuna, in fact, it is precisely this characteristic of all dharmas which explains (at least at the phenomenal level) 1) why everything is suffering and how the cycle of suffering can arise, and 2) how it is possible to put an end to the cycle of suffering. Nāgārjuna intends the statement that there can be no change in nature (prakṛter-anyathābhāvo na hi jātūpapadyate) to be a refutation of the view of the opponent, who holds that things have a self-nature (svabhāva, prakṛti). Against this eternalist doctrine, Nāgārjuna upholds the view that all dharmas lack a self-nature and have no real, independent existence apart from their causes and conditions (sarva-dharma-śūnyatā).

In the Alāta-śānti-prakaraṇa (AŚP), on the other hand, the view that Nāgārjuna *attacks* is taken as the *correct* view (siddhānta). It is easy to miss this point because the AŚP fully accepts the validity of Nāgārjuna's destructive arguments as long as they are directed against the independent, self-existent reality of things or dharmas. However, the AŚP, unlike Nāgārjuna, maintains that there is a *non*-dharmic reality which is unborn, unchanging and eternal. According to the AŚP, this underlying reality is mind or consciousness (vijñāna, citta). It is the *only* thing that exists. All the dharmas (as Nāgārjuna has shown) are illusory. But mind or consciousness is real, and it is deathless, immutable, self-established, self-existent, innate, and never gives up its self-nature.

According to Buddhism, this is an eternalist (śāśvata) view—i.e., the very kind of view that Nāgārjuna was arguing *against*. Nāgārjuna does so throughout the MMK, and it is the special target of his attack in the svabhāva-parīkṣā ("investigation into self-nature") where the statement *prakṛter-anyathābhāvo* etc. is found. Nāgārjuna uses it there as an essential part of a reductio ad absurdum argument, which goes as follows: (1) If things were real and had a self-nature, they could not change; (2) But there are no unchanging entities; (3) Hence, one must either give up the view that things are real or give up the view that they have a self-nature.[16, 17]

These considerations provide strong evidence that the author of the AŚP was not a Buddhist or crypto-Buddhist, as he is frequently said to have been. No alert, orthodox Buddhist would have been taken in by the AŚP's interpretation of the statement *prakṛter-anyathābhāvo na hi jātūpapadyate* from MMK 15.8, for AŚP 7-9 actually turns Nāgārjuna's whole philosophy on its head. It seems to me that many contemporary non-nihilist interpretations of the Madhyamaka are simply perpetuating this kind of mistake.

9. The Mādhyamika view runs counter to our belief that there is *being*—i.e., that something exists—which is perhaps our deepest and most instinctive conviction. The Mādhyamikas never denied that we have this deeply rooted conviction; but they did claim that this conviction was *erroneous*. According to the Mādhyamikas, the belief in being or existence is a mistake, a false conviction, an obstinate and ignorant attachment (abhiniveśa), and nothing more.

This was the nature of the long-lasting dispute between the Mādhyamikas and the Vedāntists at its most fundamental level. The Vedāntists believed that there was something real—something unnegatable and unsublatable, which they called pure being (sat). According to the Vedāntists, this being is known in all of our experience with an absolutely certain knowledge. In fact, according to them all knowledge and all awareness is eo ipso a knowledge and awareness of *being*. According to the Vedāntists, it would be absurd for someone to assert that nothing exists (sarvaṃ sarveṇa nāsti; sarva-dharmāḥ śūnyāḥ), for being, according to the Vedānta, is revealed in every moment of experience. Even this way of putting the matter is misleading for the Vedāntin, for to say that being is revealed in experience is to suggest that being is one thing and experience is another. But being is not an object of experience, according to the Vedānta, nor is it something that is revealed in experience. Being just *is* this experience, or alternatively we might say that experience just is this being. To look for this being as an object or as an element or constituent of experience is therefore a sign of confusion. This would be as mistaken as trying to find the *self* as an object or constituent of experience. In fact, in the Vedānta "self" and "being" also have the same meaning.[18]

The Vedāntists held that being (sat) is eternal (śāśvata, nitya). Since being is a necessary thing, it cannot cease to be, although the particular forms or transformations (pariṇāma) that it manifests do appear and disappear. Similarly, there could not have been, according to the Vedānta, an *earlier* time when being was not. This was the prevailing Vedic view from very early times. It is true that the author of the Nāsadīya hymn of the Ṛg-veda (X.129), which probably dates from about 1000 BCE, asks whether it might be possible that this whole world of being came from non-being (asat). This verse is even echoed in some passages of the very early Upaniṣads, e.g., Chānd. 3.19.1 and Tait. 2.7. However, these passages are so rare as to be virtually anomalous. The overwhelming majority of the passages in even the earliest Upaniṣads favor the view that the world is an evolution or transformation (pariṇāma) of *being*. Chānd. 6.2.1 (a very early passage) explicitly repudiates the view that being could have come from non-being:

> In the beginning, my dear, this world was just being (sat), one only, without a second. To be sure, some people say: 'In the beginning this world was just

> non-being (asat), one only, without a second; from that non-being being was produced.'
>
> But verily, my dear, how could this be? ... How could being come from non-being? On the contrary, my dear, in the beginning this world was just being, one only, without a second (advaita).

The later Vedāntic tradition unequivocally follows Chānd. 6.2.1 on this point, rather than Ṛg-veda X.129 (Nāsadīya-sūkta), Tait. 2.7 or Chānd. 3.19.1. According to the classical Vedānta, since there is being now, it must always have existed, because being cannot come from non-being, and something cannot come from nothing. Being, therefore, is not a merely contingent fact: it is a necessary one.

The Mādhyamikas repudiated all the foregoing intuitions of the Vedānta, ruthlessly and remorselessly, root and branch. According to the Madhyamaka, there is no pith, no underlying being, to anything. On examination, things turn out to be nothing at all. As such, the Mādhyamika view was even more radical than the one which was considered by the unknown author of Ṛg-veda X.129. The Mādhyamikas agreed that nothing real can come from pure non-existence, but they did not conclude from this, as the Vedāntins did, that being is eternal. On the Mādhyamika view, there can be no question of something coming from nothing, *because there is nothing now.* According to the Mādhyamikas, the void (śūnyam) gives birth to the void; the daughter of a barren woman gives birth to a man with horns on his head. This is not a philosophy of being (sat, svabhāva): it is a philosophy of non-being (asat). The Prajñā-pāramitā sūtras are perfectly explicit about this. The Aṣṭa-sāhasrikā, for example, says that all dharmas without exception are signless, wishless, unaffected, unproduced, unoriginated and *non-existent* (abhāva). This, it was said, is the true nature of even the highest wisdom (prajñā-pāramitā), for the same sūtra says (p. 205), The "The perfection of wisdom (prajñā-pāramitā) is a perfection of what is not (asat-pāramiteyam)...it is the perfection of a dream, an echo, a reflected image, a mirage or an illusion." And the Sapta-śatikā says, "For what is non-existence, that is perfect wisdom (yaś cābhāvaḥ sā prajñāpāramitā)."

The differences between the Vedānta and the Madhyamaka on this point are deep, and in fact irreconcilable. The Mādhyamika view runs counter to some of our deepest and most instinctive convictions, and this is undoubtedly at least part of the reason why many interpreters in the West, at least in comparatively recent times, have assumed that the Mādhyamikas could not have meant what they said, and have therefore assumed that they must have been Vedāntists under the guise of an idiosyncratic terminology. But the evidence is overwhelming that the Mādhyamikas were not crypto-Vedāntists. The Mādhyamikas categorically denied that there was any irreducible datum as the Vedāntists claimed, i.e., some first philosophy or something undeniably real. According to them, the view that there is such a thing is merely a thought. If, therefore, one wants to see more clearly what the nature of things really is, one must carefully examine thought itself. When one does so, one will inevitably find that there is no such basis even for thought itself, which is also non-existent. The Cartesian or Vedāntist conviction of an indubitable reality is therefore just as void as everything else. It is itself an illusion—perhaps the primary illusion.

There is a great deal of evidence from the *extant* texts that this was the Mādhyamika position, so we can be certain that the other philosophers of India did not misrepresent them on this point. That is why the dispute between the Mādhyamikas and their opponents—including the Vedāntists—was so acrimonious, and why the fairly widespread confusion prevailing today about these two schools of thought represents such a serious—and indeed rather mysterious—misunderstanding. One school held that there is a reality, conceived either as the basis (āspada) of all appearances or as that of which the appearances are the modifications (pariṇāma, vikāra). The other held that there is nothing real, however it is conceived. One school believed in the void (śūnyam), another in the non-void (aśūnyam). It would be hard to imagine two more irreconcilable world views than these.

10. The evidence in favor of the NI that can be found in abundance in the writings of the other Indian schools of philosophy cannot simply be dismissed. India has had the longest as well as the richest history of religious and philosophical thinking about an Absolute (i.e., brahman) of any country in the world. Indian thinking about this concept is as old as the Bṛhad-āraṇyaka Upaniṣad (c. 800 BCE), and may be even older. As a result, Indian philosophers of all persuasions were well-acquainted with absolutist lines of thought from a very early date. If the Mādhyamikas *had* represented an absolutist line of thought, this fact would undoubtedly have been noted by the other Indian philosophers, who would not have been likely to misinterpret the Mādhyamikas on this point. It is, therefore, highly significant that the other philosophers of India, with hardly a single exception, took the Mādhyamikas to be nihilists (atyantābhāva-vādins, śūnyatā-vādins, vaināśika-vādins) rather than as philosophers of any kind of Absolute. To simply dismiss this fact is to suppose either that the other philosophers of India willfully and maliciously distorted the Mādhyamikas on this point, or that they were simply incapable of understanding what the Mādhyamikas actually said.

Prima facie, neither of these two possibilities is very plausible, but of the two, the first is perhaps slightly less fantastic than the second. In any case, when proponents of the NNI have addressed this historical issue at all, they seem to have preferred to explain the available historical data away along the first of the two lines. Prof. Matilal was fairly typical in this respect. Like most of the proponents of the NNI, Matilal rarely referred to the opposing interpretation of the Madhyamaka, but one place where he did refer to it is CMP 55:

> The doctrine of 'emptiness,' śūnyatā, is usually presented as the critique of all views, all philosophical systems. But the implication of this proposition can be misconstrued in two ways: one by the opponent and the other by the so-called proponent. *An opponent might think that the Mādhyamika position amounts to nihilism* [emphasis mine]. But this would be wrong. ...

The statement that "an opponent might think that the Mādhyamika position amounts to nihilism" seems to me to be misleading for two reasons. First, the statement that someone *might* interpret the Mādhyamikas to be nihilists fails to do justice to the fact that the overwhelming majority of philosophers for the last fifteen hundred years have in fact attributed this position to them. Second, the implication of the quoted statement is that only an *opponent* would attribute such a view to the Mādhyamikas. This also seems misleading. It is true that the other philosophers of India were critics of the Madhyamaka—even vehement ones—but it would not be fair, I think, to regard the *modern-day* scholars who have regarded the Mādhyamikas as nihilists as having been their opponents. Modern scholars who have interpreted the Madhyamaka as nihilism—and many of these have been very great scholars indeed—seem to me to have simply been doing their very best as scholars to interpret the body of texts and historical data which they had before them.

The non-Buddhist philosophers of India are not the only ones to have been accused of distorting the views of the Mādhyamikas. Indeed, proponents of the NNI have not shrunk from accusing even the *Vijñānavādins* of having misrepresented the Mādhyamikas—even though the Vijñānavādins were fellow-Mahāyānists who lived and worked in the same monasteries with them for centuries. For example, towards the end of his life Th. Stcherbatsky said (1971-1936: 158-159):

> The Mādhyamikas were accused of nihilism by the polemical fervour of the Yogācāras who imputed to them the principle *sarvaṃ sarveṇa nāsti* [nothing at all exists]. They however emphatically protested against that accusation. Relativism is not Nihilism ...

There are several aspects of Stcherbatsky's claim that need to be examined. One is the contention that the Mādhyamikas emphatically protested against the accusation of nihilism. I do not believe that there is any evidence to support this contention, and significantly, no such evidence is cited by Stcherbatsky in this passage.[19]

I am not entirely sure what Stcherbatsky meant by the phrase "polemical fervour." The implication is, perhaps, that there was at least *some* basis for this charge, which, however, the Yogācārins exaggerated and distorted. But when one looks more closely at how Stcherbatsky himself represents the Mādhyamika view in the passage that immediately precedes the one just quoted, it is hard to say why he thinks that the charge of nihilism was a distortion or exaggeration at all. Stcherbatsky described the view which the opponents distorted and misrepresented out of "polemical fervour" as follows (ibid., pp. 158-159):

> [The Mādhyamikas] neither admit the reality of the *paratantra* nor of the *pariniṣpanna* = *śūnyatā*. For them these two Absolutes are as relative as all the rest. They admit no exception from their principle of Universal Relativity, no *paramārtha-sat,* no Thing-in-Itself. They, of course, have a *paramārtha-satya,* or Highest Principle, of their own, but it consists just in the denial of the Thing-in-Itself, the denial of every ultimately real Element in existence. Tsoṅ-kha-pa, a good judge, says in his Legs-bśad sñin-po that among all systems of philosophy, Buddhist as well as non-Buddhist, there is only one which denies every kind of ultimately Real; and this is the system of the Mādhyamikas. According to the German expression, it represents "eine Verabsolutierung des Relativen." From this universal Relativity there can be no exceptions. Neither the Buddha, nor the Bodhisattva, nor Salvation and Nirvāṇa are excepted. They are dialectical Ideas, not realities. As concepts they are constructions of our productive imagination, hence ultimately unreal, *bden-par med* as the Tibetan emphatically states... [For the Yogācāra] Relativity has a subjacent Absolute Reality: for the Mādhyamikas it has none, for them it is mere *advaya* without any *eka-dravya* at the bottom.

Note that Stcherbatsky himself attributes to the Mādhyamikas the following propositions: 1) there is neither a relative reality (paratantra) nor an absolute reality (parinişpanna, śūnyatā); 2) there is an absolute truth (paramārtha-satya), but nothing which is itself absolutely true (paramārtha-sat); 3) according to so great an authority as Tsoṅ-kha-pa himself, the Mādhyamikas alone, of all the systems of philosophy, denied that there is anything that is absolutely real; 4) all conceptions, of either the relative or the absolute, are constructions of our productive imagination, and hence ultimately unreal. If these are accurate statements of the Mādhyamika position (and I believe that they are), then it is very hard to see how the Vijñānavādins and the other philosophers of India can be accused of polemical fervor for having interpreted the Mādhyamikas as nihilists. It seems to me that anyone who holds such positions is almost by *definition* a nihilist. Noting that the Mādhyamikas believed in an absolute truth hardly settles the matter in favor of the NNI, for everything then comes to depend on what the Mādhyamikas thought that absolute truth actually was. According to the NI, the absolute and final truth in the Madhyamaka is that *nothing exists*—and this is exactly the view that, towards the end of his life, even Stcherbatsky was forced to attribute to them, i.e., that they denied "every ultimately real Element in existence"—including, let it be noted, the reality of the paratantra, or realm of dependent co-origination.

The interpretation of the historical facts by the proponents of the NNI is also rendered implausible by everything we know about the conditions under which the philosophers of India debated one another. India had a very vigorous and carefully codified tradition of philosophical debate well before the time of Nāgārjuna and his critics. The rules for these debates were themselves a subject of discussion amongst the philosophers of India, and precise rules were laid down for judging who had won and who had lost a debate. In an honest or fair debate, a participant could not *misrepresent* the opponent's position. This makes it unlikely that the opponents of the Mādhyamikas would have misrepresented them—whether out of polemical fervor or any other reason—for this would have violated the spirit of the debate, and been grounds for censure. The risk was all the greater in this particular case because the point at issue was such a fundamental one. It is, of course, always possible to misrepresent a philosopher or a school on points of detail, but I think one would be hard put to name one other instance in the history of Indian philosophy where a school of philosophers was as misrepresented by their philosophical opponents as the Mādhyamikas must have been if in fact they had not been nihilists.

11. The strongest evidence against the NNI, however, is found in the Mādhyamika writings themselves. Here the passages in the Mādhyamika writings which deny that there is an Absolute are particularly important, given the overwhelming evidence that the Mahāyānists denied the reality of the *phenomenal* world. Consider, for example, the following passage from Bhāvaviveka's *Jewel in the Hand* (Kara-tala-ratna). This passage is directed against the Vijñānavādin views about suchness (tathatā) or intrinsic nature (dharmatā), which the Vijñānavādins frequently described as a kind of Absolute:

> If it be contended that the Tathatā, although it is foreign to words (abhilāpa, vyavahāravivikta), is nevertheless a reality (tattva): in that case, the expression Tathatā refers only to the ātman of the Tīrtihikas under another name. Just as the Tathatā, although it is a reality, is nevertheless, from the point of view of exact truth, beyond the concepts of being and not-being, it is the same with the ātman. The Tīrtihikas think that the ātman, which is real, omnipresent, eternal, agent, enjoyer, is nevertheless foreign to every concept (beyond the pale of conceptions). As it transcends the domain of words, and as it is not the object of the dealing-with-ideas-intellect (vikalpabuddhi), it is said to be foreign to concepts. The doctrines of the Tīrtihikas say: "The words do not go there, the thought does not realise it; therefore it is named ātman."
>
> The ātman being such, is it reasonable to assert that the knowledge (jñāna) which takes the Tathatā as its object,

> leads to deliverance, while the knowledge which takes the ātman as its object, does not? But what is the difference between the Tathatā and the ātman, since both are ineffable and real? It is only by *esprit de parti* (pakṣagrahaṇa) that it is so said.[20]

The assertion that in the Vedānta the self was regarded as neither existent nor non-existent actually seems to me to be incorrect, but this is not an important point so far as Bhāvaviveka's views as a Mādhyamika are concerned. The much more important point for our present purposes is that the Kara-tala-ratna clearly precludes reading any notion of an Absolute into Bhāvaviveka's interpretation of the Madhyamaka, including the kind advocated in many contemporary versions of the NNI. According to these interpretations, none of the Mādhyamikas' numerous negations mean that they were nihilists, any more than negations in the Upaniṣads (e.g., "neti," "neti") mean that the Vedāntists were nihilists. The sole purpose of the Mādhyamikas' negations, according to the NNI, is to negate all thinking, words and concepts *about* reality, rather than to deny reality altogether. But this Vedāntist or quasi-Vedāntist reading of the Madhyamaka is clearly contradicted by passages like the Kara-tala-ratna, which explicitly *repudiates* this kind of doctrine. It is clear from this passage that Bhāvaviveka was quite opposed to the notion of an Absolute *however it might be described.* If Bhāvaviveka was representative in this respect (and it seems he was), then it is surely quite untenable to hold that the opponents of the Mādhyamikas misrepresented them when they described them as nihilists.

12. The above passage from the Kara-tala-ratna has been cited from a paper that de la Vallée Poussin published in 1933 called "The Mādhyamikas and the Tathatā." Poussin cited the passage there to score a point against proponents of the NNI like Th. Stcherbatsky and St. Schayer, who had argued that the Madhyamaka was a kind of monism.

As it turns out, in 1933 Poussin himself was in the process of revising his views about the Mādhyamikas. Until that time, Poussin had regarded the Mādhyamikas as extreme nihilists. He had inherited this view of the Madhyamaka from one of his own teachers, S. Lévi, who in turn had received it from E. Burnouf, who at the very outset of Mādhyamika studies had declared the Madhyamaka to be a "nihilisme scholastique." Poussin devoted much of his career as a Buddhologist to expanding and deepening this nihilist interpretation of the Madhyamaka, to the extent that his own earlier writings on the subject (e.g. Poussin 1917 ff.) are now the locus classicus of the NI.

About the same time that he wrote "The Mādhyamikas and the Tathatā," Poussin wrote a much longer paper called "Réflexions sur le madhyamaka" (1932-33). This paper marked a watershed in Poussin's thinking on the subject. According to "Réflexions," the Mādhyamikas held that things do not exist at the absolute level of truth, but that they do exist at the phenomenal level, and that there is therefore a sense in which the Mādhyamikas adhered neither to existence nor to non-existence. However, at this point in his career Poussin had not yet come to the conclusion that the Mādhyamikas believed that it followed from this that there was *something that neither existed nor did not exist;* nor had he yet come to the conclusion that the Mādhyamikas believed in an *Absolute* that neither existed nor did not exist. Even as late as 1932-33, he continued to hold that it would be a grave error to reify the Mādhyamikas' views as implying a belief in an Absolute.

The distinction between the two truths (dve satye) was one of the cornerstones of Poussin's interpretation of the Madhyamaka in "Réflexions." It was this, I think, that led to a kind of crisis in Poussin's thinking about the Mādhyamikas a few years later (1936-37), when, on the basis of a careful study of an important Ābhidhārmika text, he seems to have developed doubts that the Buddhist tradition ever believed in the distinction between two different kinds of truth in any literal sense. It is not surprising that Poussin came to doubt this, for the view that a given statement can literally have two different truth values (i.e., from two different points of view) is logically equivalent to a denial of the law of non-contradiction (v. supra, pp. 222-226). These growing doubts about the validity of this distinction seem to have had the effect of moving Poussin away from his interpretation of the Madhyamaka in "Réflexions."

Abandoning the two truths distinction tends to reveal the NI in its starkest form, but giving it up does not *require* the abandonment of the NI. All that the NI claims is that the Mādhyamikas believed that all things (including mind and its experiences) *seem* to exist, but do not. Attributing this view to the Mādhyamikas does not require us to supppose that the Mādhyamikas believed literally in the doctrine of the two truths, since the proposition "It seems to me that P" is a *different* proposition from P itself.

Poussin, therefore, could have continued to hold the NI, even *after* he had abandoned the two truths distinction in any literal sense. However, when Poussin came to the conclusion that the two truths distinction could not be used to blunt the harder edges of the NI, he abandoned it. And, strange to say, when he did abandon it (in the posthumously published "Buddhica" paper of 1938), he concluded that the Mādhyamikas believed in an Absolute which had the very peculiar property of neither existing nor not existing—i.e., the very view that Bhāvaviveka explicitly *denies* in the passage I have cited from the Kara-tala-ratna.

The following passage is typical of Poussin's interpretation of the Madhyamaka in the "Buddhica" paper (p. 156-157):

> ...*The doctrine of the two truths leads to a contradiction which is unsatisfying* [emphasis mine]. To affirm at the level of vulgar opinion (saṃvṛti) and to deny at the level of ultimate truth (paramārtha) is to oppose existence and non-existence. Such is not the middle way. "Superficial knowledge," says Ki-tsang, "sees the dharmas as existing or not existing. Such a person is incapable of seeing the dharma of calm and peacefulness which destroys all views." The problem will be resolved if one rejects both the saṃvṛti and the paramārtha, existence and non-existence. ... Negation (śūnyatā, non-existence) destroys affirmation (saṃvṛti, existence), and then negation itself, its previously affirmed object having been destroyed, lacking any

> object, disappears from the liberated mind, being in effect a mere conceptual appearance. The two extremities (anta) are avoided and suppressed. This is the middle way; it leads to the right contemplation which, by the "non-perception" (anupalabdhi) of falsity, leads to the ineffable and unthinkable principle. This principle is alien to the notion of dharmas which, once posited, can only be either existent or non-existent.

At the time that he wrote this paper, Poussin seems to have thought of this ineffable and unthinkable principle as an Absolute, for he says (p. 149-150):

> One wonders if Th. Stcherbatsky did not see things more clearly in his *Conception of Buddhist Nirvāṇa* when he defined the universe of the Mādhyamikas as "monistic"; translated Nirvāṇa by "Absolute"; interpreted Candrakīrti: *saṃsāranirvāṇayor aviśeṣaḥ pratipāditaḥ*, by: "we have established that there is no difference between the phenomenal world and the Absolute (underlying it)," with the note: "This identity (of existence, Saṃsāra, and of Nirvāṇa) must evidently be understood in the sense that the Unity of the Absolute is the reality underlying the mirage of plurality."

And on the following page (151) he said:

> The Madhyamaka condemns the *tattva* of the other schools, but only to propound (préconiser) an ineffable that is even more subtle (un inéffable plus subtil).

At the same time, Poussin could not simply ignore the passage from Bhāvaviveka's Kara-tala-ratna, which states that the Mādhyamikas could in no way countenance even an *ineffable* Absolute, including one that neither existed nor did not exist. What Poussin concluded from the Kara-tala-ratna in his 1938 paper, however, was that the Mādhyamikas did not always agree in their views about the Absolute, or as he put it, "il y a Mādhyamikas et Mādhyamikas" (ibid., p. 150). Even at this point, in other words, Poussin could not help suspecting that Bhāvaviveka, at least, might have been a nihilist. About Bhāvaviveka he said (p. 150): "It seems—I say, it seems—that Bhāvaviveka (or Bhāviveka), the author of *The Jewel in the Hand*, was a partisan of negation." Poussin conceded that in the previously cited passage from the Kara-tala-ratna Bhāvaviveka "refutes the tathatā in due and proper form." But he then added, as if to deepen the mystery: "But one reads several passages also where Bhāvaviveka appears, like Ki-tsang, to want something even more ineffable (indicible) than the tathatā."

Ét. Lamotte—probably Poussin's most distinguished pupil—found this apparent volte-face in Poussin's interpretation of the Madhyamaka in the "Buddhica" paper so bizarre that he chose to regard it as a capitulation to Stcherbatsky rather than a genuine change of views. Twenty-seven years after Poussin's death, Lamotte wrote (1965: 162):

> The best introduction to Nāgārjunian doctrines is found in his [Poussin's] *Réflexions sur le Madhyamaka*, which appeared in 1932. The Madhyamaka, according to this work, admits things according to the relative truth, but denies them according to the real truth: therefore it neither affirms nor denies them. The "nature of things," the Reality, is neither existent nor non-existent: it is the absence of the nature of appearance; even its emptiness is void; even its non-existence is non-existent. It is a grave error to reify it as an Absolute. The Russian scholar [savant] Th. Stcherbatksy, who interpreted the Madhyamaka as a pantheistic monism, showed no restraint in attacking this article of Louis de La Vallée Poussin [attaqua sans ménagement]. The latter, tired of being misread and misunderstood, and already undermined by illness, seemed to make an about-face [sembla faire machine arrière] in his article Buddhica, which appeared in 1938. But I continue to believe that his *Réflexions sur*

le Madhyamaka, of 1932, remains the most accurate interpretation of Nāgārjunian thought.

13. Few would question the claim that the summum bonum of the Madhyamaka presupposes the extinction or quiescence of all thought. But how are we to understand this state? Is it merely a state of annihiliation? From the point of view of Buddhist dogma and philosophy, the answer would appear to be Yes. Canonical Buddhism had divided everything that could exist (i.e., dharmas) into two different categories, the conditioned (saṃskṛta) and unconditioned (asaṃskṛta). Nirvāṇa, one of the asaṃskṛta dharmas, was regarded as a state in which thoughts and consciousness (vijñāna, citta) are totally extinct. Is nirvāṇa, therefore, simply a state of extinction? It certainly will be if nirvāṇa is described *merely* as the extinction or cessation of the conditioned dharmas (including mind), which is exactly how the Sautrāntikas defined it.[21] Of course, other Buddhist schools did not agree with the Sautrāntikas on this point, but the Mādhyamikas *did*. The only point that differentiates the Madhyamaka from the Sautrāntika is that the Mādhyamikas believed that the *conditioned* (saṃskṛta) dharmas were no more real than the *unconditioned* (asaṃskṛta) dharmas. The Mādhyamikas, therefore, thought of nirvāṇa as something that is the true state of things even now, i.e., the absolute non-existence (atyanta-śūnyatā, atyantābhāva) of everything. What is misleadingly called attaining nirvāṇa is, on this view, just a matter of realizing and recognizing that this is the true nature of things *even now*. But neither the Sautrāntika nor the Mādhyamika view requires us to suppose—or even *allows* us to suppose—that the state where thoughts are extinguished is itself something that exists. It is surely a mistake, therefore, to regard the Mādhyamikas as believing (as the Vedāntists did) in the reality of a transcendent, absolute state of consciousness which is beyond thoughts.

It is possible, of course, to find passages in the Mādhyamika writings where it is said that the true nature of things is such that they are neither existent nor non-existent, and this may have had something to do with Poussin's claim (ibid.) that in the

Madhyamaka "right contemplation ... leads to the ineffable and unthinkable principle" which is "alien to the notion of dharmas which, once posited, can only be either existent or non-existent." But such passages do not settle the matter, either, for the claim that things are not non-existent (na *abhāvaḥ) simply seems to mean that non-existence (abhāva) is not itself a thing (padārtha), as the Mādhyamikas' philosophical opponents, the Naiyāyikas, maintained. The NI probably *would* be rendered untenable if one could find passages in the Mādhyamika writings where the assertion that things are not non-existent (abhāva) amounts unequivocally to *more* than the denial that non-existence is itself a reality (padārtha), or (more generally) where the assertion that things are not non-existent (na *abhāvaḥ) is to be taken as the contradictory rather than the contrary of the assertion that things do not exist (na bhāvaḥ). But if there were such passages, of course, one would have to conclude that the Mādhyamikas had simply *contradicted* themselves.

14. As we have seen, Poussin argued at the very end of his life that the Mādhyamikas believed in an Absolute that neither exists nor does not exist. He did so (at least in part) on the grounds that the Mādhyamikas advocated the extinction or quiescence of all *thoughts* of existence and non-existence. It is illuminating to examine this claim in the light of Bodhicaryāvatāra (BCA) 9.30-9.35.

This passage is directed against the Vijñānavādin mind only (citta-mātra) doctrine. Śāntideva criticizes this doctrine on the grounds that mind itself must be seen as void and non-existent:

> If it were just that thought is devoid of objects, then all would be Buddhas. Moreover, if things were mind only, how could merit be obtained?
>
> grāhya-muktaṃ yadā cittaṃ tadā sarve tathāgataḥ /
> evaṃ ca ko guṇo labdhaś-cittamātre 'pi kalpite //9.30//
>
> If it is merely that thought is similar to an illusion, how is passion turned aside? Even as she comes into being,

the magician falls in love with the māyā-woman that he has himself created.

māyopamatve 'pi jñāte kathaṃ kleśo nivartate /
yadā māyā-striyāṃ rāgas-tat-kartur-api jāyate //9.31//

It is essential to see that in this case the magician's impure mental tendencies (saṃkleśa-vāsanā) have not yet been removed. If he so much as sees her [i.e., the māyā-woman], his impression of the void (śūnya-vāsanā) is weak.

aprahīṇā hi tat-kartur-jñeya-saṃkleśa-vāsanā /
tad-dṛṣṭi-kāle tasyāto durbalā śūnya-vāsanā //9.32//

Through adhering to the idea (vāsanā) of emptiness, the idea of existence (bhāva) is destroyed (hīyate). Eventually, through the practice of the thought: "Nothing exists" (kiṃcin-nāstīti), even the idea that nothing exists is eliminated.[22]

śūnyatā-vāsanādhānād-dhīyate bhāva-vāsanā /
kiṃcin-nāstīti cābhyāsāt-sāpi paścāt-prahīyate //9.33//

When one does not perceive an existence (bhāva) which can be imagined as non-existing, how can non-existence (abhāva), thus deprived of any foundation, stand forth before the mind?

yadā na labhyate bhāvo yo nāstīti prakalpyate /
tadā nirāśrayo 'bhāvaḥ kathaṃ tiṣṭhen-mateḥ puraḥ //9.34//

When neither the thought of existence nor the thought of non-existence stands forth before the mind, then, being deprived of support due to the absence of any place of resort, the mind becomes still (praśāmyati).

yadā na bhāvo nābhāvo mateḥ saṃtiṣṭhate puraḥ /
tadānyagaty-abhāvena nirālambā praśāmyati //9.35//[23]

According to these verses, the state of non-thought can only be attained by those who have realized that even thoughts are unreal (kiṃcin-nāstīti), i.e., that they have no existence even as illusions or as a purely mental reality. To say that everything is mind only will not lead to the desired cessation of thoughts, Śāntideva says, and he offers as proof the fact that the magician becomes enamored of the woman he creates through his magic even though he knows that she is only thought, i.e., is unreal. He asserts categorically that if one sees anything at all—even so much as a mind-produced illusion—one has not attained the state of emptiness (BCA 9.32). Contemplation of the emptiness of all things (including mind) is enjoined as a means of counteracting the illusion that things exist. By adhering to the thought that nothing exists, one adheres to emptiness (BCA 9.33). Eventually, even the thought that nothing exists will disappear, for when the thought of existence vanishes, there is no basis for the thought of non-existence either, and the mind becomes quiet and extinguished (BCA 9.34-35).

So far as I can tell, there is nothing in BCA 9.30-35 to support either Ruegg's claim that Śāntideva bases his whole thought on the law of the excluded middle, *or* Poussin's claim that the Mādhyamikas believed in an Absolute with the very peculiar property of neither existing nor non-existing. The passage simply asserts that one must give up thoughts of both existence and non-existence—and even this is a mere corollary of the more fundamental claim that one must give up all thoughts completely.

Everything that Śāntideva says in this passage, therefore, is quite consistent with—in fact, is *only* consistent with—the NI. The only difference between Śāntideva's view and the view of the Vijñānavādins, it seems to me, is that the latter philosophers held that the incessant flow of ever-changing mental phenomena which is extinguished in nirvāṇa is real, whereas the Mādhyamikas denied this. The Mādhyamika view, unlike the Vijñānavādin view, is therefore a philosophy of absolute nothingness or voidness.

In interpreting the Madhyamaka on this point, it is important to distinguish between the concepts of illogicality and ineffability. Some proponents of the NNI (e.g., E. Conze 1980), have regarded illogicality as simply one of a number of possible kinds of *ineffability*. This lends an aura of respectability and plausibility to anti-rationalist interpretations of the Madhyamaka which such interpretations simply do not have, for while it makes perfectly good sense to speak of the ineffability of mystical experiences, the smell of a rose or the itch of a mosquito bite, it does not make any sense to speak of the ineffability of a round square or of something that neither exists nor does not exist. The assertion that one should give up all thoughts of existence or non-existence is probably compatible with a large number of philosophical views, e.g., absolute idealism, theistic mysticism, nature mysticism, pantheism, nihilism, the view that reality is logically indeterminable, etc. But I fail to see how one could make any sense of the assertion that something neither exists nor does not exist—much less of something even more "indicible" than this.[24]

Even Poussin seems to have succumbed to confusion on this point. In his 1938 paper (p. 150, n. 15) he suggested that Bhāvaviveka rejected the notion of an Absolute (tathatā) that neither exists nor does not exist because he wanted to clear the way for the assertion of something even more "indicible" (ineffable) than this. But, pace Poussin, there couldn't *be* anything more "indicible" than an ineffable reality that exists—not even an ineffable reality that *neither* exists nor does not exist; and the suggestion that there might be something that is even more "indicible" than something that *neither* exists nor does not exist makes even less sense. Saying that something neither exists nor does not exist, or that there is something even more ineffable than this, is not a matter of saying that there is something ineffable, though in the highest possible degree. Poussin writes as if an ineffable reality that neither exists nor does not exist (or something even more remote from logic and sense than this) might simply be a less crude and tangible version of an Absolute which is said to *exist*. But to speak of anything, either phenomenal or absolute, as neither existent nor non-existent (or even more ineffable than this) is to utter a mere sound-blast (flatus voci, śabda-mātra), i.e., to say nothing at all.

I find it very hard to believe that Nāgārjuna and the Mādhyamikas could have maintained anything so patently illogical. If, in the final analysis, interpreting the Mādhyamikas comes down (as it surely does) to choosing between the fundamental laws of logic, on the one hand, and nihilism on the other, I would like to suggest that one gives the Mādhyamikas a good deal more credit by attributing the nihilist position to them than the patently illogical one that holds that there is a kind of negation which has no implication to any other statement, or which holds that reality can be both existent and non-existent at the same time, or neither, etc. Nihilism, or what I have called non-ontological idealism, may not, in the final analysis, be a philosophically tenable doctrine, but it is an interesting doctrine, and one for which a case of sorts can be given (v. infra, pp. 260-280). On the other hand, I cannot see how any philosophical interest could be attached to the assertion that there is something that neither exists nor does not exist (or something beyond even this), for *that* assertion seems to me to be quite obviously meaningless and senseless.[25]

If an Absolute is anything at all, then of course it exists. Consequently, if one wants to assert that there is an *ineffable* Absolute, one has no choice but to say: "I believe in an Absolute which is ineffable," where it is understood that this Absolute *exists*. If it is philosophically tenable to maintain that there is an Absolute, one has thereby expressed one's belief in an Absolute clearly and unequivocally, and in the only way that one can express it. One does not do a better job of making this point by saying: "I believe in an Absolute which neither exists nor does not exist," nor even by denying all possible formulations or alternatives in such a way that one's interlocutor is forced to conclude that what one must *mean* is that there is an Absolute which neither exists nor does not exist (or something beyond even this). To do either of these things is not at all the same thing as making the first point, but doing it more forcefully, more elegantly, more subtly, more clearly, or more unassailably—for there could not be anything that neither exists nor does not exist.

Consequently, Poussin's suggestion that the Mādhyamikas may have believed in an Absolute even more *indicible* than one that neither exists nor does not exist cannot be taken seriously. That the Mādhyamikas themselves would have rejected this interpretation is shown by the fact that in the Mādhyamika texts violations of the law of the excluded middle are associated with examples (dṛṣtānta) of non-existent and even impossible entities like the sons of barren women. Passages where such analogies are used are an important part of the armamentarium of the NI, for of course nothing could be more clearly non-existent than the son of a barren woman or a round square. In view of such passages, one can only say that if the Mādhyamikas were not nihilists, they could not have chosen more misleading or unfortunate analogies to illustrate the main point of their philosophy than the ones they did use.

15. In the first part of this chapter, I began by pointing out that there are two different (though related) questions that are involved in the dispute between the proponents of the NI and the NNI. One is whether the Mādhyamikas believed in the reality of the phenomenal world; the other is whether the Mādhyamikas believed in an Absolute. The view that they believed in the reality of the phenomenal world was rejected on the basis of the textual evidence. It was also argued that this rejection could not be qualified by the appeal to the two truths distinction. More recently, it has been argued that the Mādhyamikas did not believe in an Absolute either—not even one that was ineffable to the point of neither existing nor not existing.

At this point, one comes up against a question that has emerged in our deliberations from time to time but which has never been confronted directly. If one cannot appeal to the two truths distinction to moderate the negativism of the Madhyamaka, how is one to make sense of its negativism? How could it be that, without any qualification at all, *nothing exists*? If saṃsāra is like the son of a barren woman or a round square, what is it that we *think* that we see?

The nature of the difficulty is seen more clearly when the Madhyamaka is contrasted with the Vijñānavāda. If one takes the line that the world is unreal in the sense in which an hallucination is unreal, then one has a way out: one can say, as the Vijñānavādins did, that the external world (bāhyārtha) is unreal, whereas the mind is real. But this was not the Mādhyamika view, as the analogy of the sons of barren women (vandhyā-putrāḥ) shows very clearly, for if the world is compared to the son of a barren woman, then one cannot even say that the world is unreal in the sense that it is nothing but mind. According to the Vijñānavāda, one can have a perception (i.e., sense datum, vijñapti) of a pink elephant even if there is no pink elephant in the physical world to be seen. But we never see, and never could see, the son of a barren woman, in any sense of the word "see."

The Vijñānavādin theory of perception was called the ātma-khyāti-vāda, which means, literally, the doctrine that the self appears as something external. The Vijñānavādins, of course, did not believe in a self, but they did believe in the existence of mind (citta, vijñāna, vijñapti), and they held that it was this that appeared as something external.[26] The Mādhyamikas agreed with the Vijñānavādins that there is no external world (at least pāramārthika), but they did not believe in the reality of mind, either. Consequently, they could not accept the Vijñānavādin account of illusory perceptions. What is it, then, that people see when they see (or think they see) mirages, dreams, hallucinations, stars when they are hit on the head, etc.? The Mādhyamika answer was: absolutely nothing at all. This theory of perception was called the asat-khyāti-vāda, which means, literally, that that which is non-existent appears. According to this doctrine, what is *said* or *thought* to appear is *entirely* non-existent (asat). As such, it cannot be mental either, just as the son of a barren woman isn't even a *mental* appearance.

16. The asat-khyāti-vāda is a very radical view—so radical, in fact, that it is not entirely clear that sense can be made of it. Nevertheless, there can be little doubt that the Mādhyamikas did hold this view. It is important to emphasize this point because proponents of the NNI have tended—on this point as on other ones—to simply deny that the Mādhyamikas could have meant what they actually said.

An example of this can be found in Prof. Matilal's writings (Perc. 188). In the context of an interesting discussion of Indian theories of perception, Matilal said:

> [The asat-khyāti theory of sensory illusion] is stated in non-Buddhist texts rather poorly and in an unconvincing manner. The object ... that is grasped in our sensory awareness is asat, unreal or non-existent. The 'correcting awareness' in which the piece appears as non-silver to the perceiver and he says 'this is *not* silver' exposes this fact ... Commentators of the non-Buddhist tradition ascribe this view to the Mādhyamika

or *śūnyavāda* school. However, this ascription need not be taken to be strictly correct.

Prof. Matilal did not say why he thought that the traditional (and literal) interpretation of the asat-khyāti-vāda "need not be taken as strictly correct." Nor did he say—either here or elsewhere, so far as I know—how the traditional interpretation of the asat-khyāti-vāda could be avoided. He did give what appears to have been his own interpretation of the doctrine on the preceding two pages of Perc. (i.e., pp. 186-188), but the account given there seems to me to be indistinguishable from the traditional account of the asat-khyāti-vāda that is called into question in the passage I have just cited.

It would be a little rash, perhaps, to claim that no intepretation of the asat-khyāti-vāda besides the one that has prevailed in India for fifteen hundred years will ever be found, but since Matilal called this interpretation into question, it may be appropriate to give reasons for thinking that no such interpretation *will* be found. To this end, I have collected the following passages from Mādhyamika, Prajñā-pāramitā, Vijñānavādin and Vaidika texts. All of them go to show that, according to the Mādhyamikas, we never see *anything*, either mental or physical, any more than one could be said to see the son of a barren woman.

a) Poussin (1932-33: 22) has cited from Candrakīrti's MABh (vi, 48 and 96) the following striking passage, which is directed against the Vijñānavāda. Candrakīrti first represents the idealist opponent as holding the following view: "Someone asleep in a small room, through the ignorance of sleep, sees in this small room a furious troop of large elephants. Therefore thought exists without an exterior object." To this Candrakīrti replies: "The example is not proved, because according to us the mind in dream is no more real than the elephants."

Note that according to Candrakīrti it is not just the *appearances*, qua appearances, of the elephants etc. that are non-existent and unreal, but the mind itself. This is exactly what one would expect. According to fundamental Buddhist principles (e.g., the anātman doctrine) the non-existence of mind follows from the non-existence of all of its putative intentional objects, since the mind was regarded in Buddhism as nothing more than the flow of percepts (vijñapti). If there are no percepts (vijñapti), then it follows directly that there is no cognizer or mind either—not even in the highly attenuated form of cognitions which are self-shining or self-illuminated. According to principles accepted by both the Vijñānavādins and the Mādhyamikas, therefore, *if* there are no cognitions, then there is no mind.

b) In adopting this position, Candrakīrti and the other Mādhyamikas were simply following the line of thought that had been laid down quite unequivocally in the Prajñā-pāramitā sūtras. I cite below two typical passages from this literature:

> Subhūti, what is meant by the Bodhisattva Mahāsattva knowing in accordance with truth about the marks of consciousness? It means that a Bodhisattva Mahāsattva knows in accordance with truth that consciousness is like things of magic. Conditions are brought together which create the supposition that something exists. But actually there is nothing that can be laid hand upon. It is as when a master of magic or his disciple at a crossroads magically creates the four kinds of army—that is to say, an elephant-army, a cavalry-army, a chariot-army and an army of foot-soldiers, or again magically creates other kinds of form, complete with their various characteristics. Such things seem to exist, but have no reality. Consciousness is also like this, and cannot really by laid hand upon.[27]

*

> The Tathāgata knows reacting thoughts for what they really are. For he knows that those thoughts represent what is not really there, that they are empty, devoid of objective support. ... The Tathāgata knows non-reacting thoughts for what they really are. For he knows that those thoughts are non-dual, and that, ultimately unreal, they only seem to arrive at some reality. ... The

> Tathāgata knows unemancipated thoughts for what they really are. For he knows that those thoughts are, in their own-being, already now emancipated, for they have non-existence for own-being (abhāva-svabhāva). The Tathāgata knows emancipated thoughts for what they really are. For the Tathāgata has not apprehended any thought as past, as future, or as present, because thought is not really there (asattvāt). The Tathāgata knows imperceptible thoughts for what they really are. For he knows that with regard to that thought that, because it is not really there, it cannot be perceived (adṛśya); that, because it has no reality (abhūtatvāt, asattvāt), it cannot be discerned; that, because it falls short of the perfect reality, it cannot be grasped,—not by the eye of wisdom, not by the heavenly eye, and how much less by the fleshly eye, since it does not come within the range of any of them. (Aṣṭa. 265-268)

These passages from the Prajñā-pāramitā assert that mind is non-existent because it cannot be apprehended, grasped or found. This amounts to a repudiation of one of the fundamental principles of all ontological versions of idealism. According to ontological idealism, it does not follow from the fact that the mind cannot be found (na vidyate) that mind does not exist, for according to these versions of idealism, the *reason* why mind cannot be found is that we *are* mind. Furthermore, finding something external to oneself implies the possibility of not finding that thing. According to traditional idealist doctrine, it is a fundamental and very serious error to think of mind in this way, for everything that we see is nothing but mind. In fact, according to ontological versions of idealism, once the true nature of mind is understood, the fact that mind is never seen or apprehended provides *indubitable* and *incorrigible* evidence that the mind *does* exist. But this fundamental principle of ontological idealism is rejected by the Mādhyamika and Prajñā-pāramitā texts.

c) The Mādhyamikas are represented as having denied the reality of the mind in the Vijñānavādin texts as well. One example of this is Kui Ji's sub-commentary on Xuan Zang's Cheng wei shilun, a commentary on the Triṃśikā of Vasubandhu. There Kui Ji describes the Mādhyamika Bhāvaviveka as a "nihilist who denies the existence of mind (vijñāna) and all the dharmas" (Poussin 1928-48: 56).

Xuan Zang, who had travelled and studied widely in India over a period of many years, and who had established his reputation there as a great Buddhist scholar, was Kui Ji's own teacher in China. Since Kui Ji was a very close disciple of Xuan Zang's, his testimony on this point is a valuable one.

d) It might be objected that one cannot take Kui Ji's account of Bhāvaviveka's thought as an objective and impartial one, since Kui Ji and Xuan Zang belonged to the Vijñānavāda. However, Kui Ji's testimony on this point is corroborated by that of Yi Jing, an adherent of the Hīnayānist school of the Sarvāstivāda, who made his journey to India about fifty years after Xuan Zang went there. Yi Jing (Takakusu 1966: 14-15) described the two schools of the Mahāyāna as follows:

> Those who worship the Bodhisattvas and read the Mahâyâna Sûtras are called the Mahâyânists (the Great), while those who do not perform these are called the Hînayânists (the Small). There are but two kinds of the so-called Mahâyâna. First, the Mâdhyamika; second, the Yoga. The former profess that what is commonly called existence is in reality non-existence, and every object is but an empty show, like an illusion, whereas the latter affirm that there exist no outer things *in reality*, but only inward thoughts, and all things exist only in the mind (lit. 'all things are but our mind').

It is unlikely that Yi Jing got this completely wrong, for he seems to have been an intelligent and responsible observer about the *other* things on which he reported. Furthermore, Yi Jing can hardly be accused of partisanship, or of having *willfully* misrepresented or distorted the views of the Mādhyamikas out of polemical fervor, for he seems to have been prepared to bend over backwards, if necessary, in order to see the merits in the views of all the Buddhist schools, as the immediately succeeding passage shows:

> [The Hīnayāna and the Mahāyāna] are perfectly in accordance with the noble doctrine. Can we then say which of the two is right? Both equally conform to truth and lead us to Nirvâ*n*a. Nor can we find out which is true or false. Both aim at the destruction of passion (kle*s*a) and the salvation of all beings. We must not, in trying to settle the comparative merits of these two, create great confusion and fall further into perplexity.

e) The non-Buddhist philosophers of India, who seem to have followed the controversy between the Vijñānavādins and the Mādhyamikas on this point with particular interest, refer to it as the principal issue that divided the two schools. Most of the compendia or catechisms of the doctrines of the Indian philosophical schools mention the asat-khyāti-vāda as perhaps the most distinctive feature of Mādhyamika thought. In this respect the following passage from the Sarva-siddhānta-saṅgraha is typical:

> The Yogācāras say that everything is mind only (buddhi-mātram), and that there is nothing else. The Mādhyamikas, however, say that the mind does not exist either (nāsti buddhir-apīti).
>
> buddhi-mātraṃ vadaty-atra yogācāro na cāparam /
> nāsti buddhir-apīty-āha vādī mādhyamikaḥ kila //[28, 29]

In view of the fact that the *Buddhist* texts attribute the asat-khayti-vāda to the Mādhyamikas, it would be very hard to argue that the non-Buddhist philosophers attributed this view to the Mādhyamikas out of polemical fervor. What the Buddhist evidence shows is that the authors of these primers or catechisms were simply reporting—truthfully and objectively—on what they (or their predecessors) knew about the views of the Mādhyamikas at first hand.

In view of all the evidence of the foregoing kind, I do not think that it would be prudent or fair to dismiss the prevailing interpretation of the asat-khyāti-vāda without offering some *other* interpretation of that doctrine in its place. It is true, of course, that one must apply the principle of charity when one is interpreting a philosophical system—or at any rate, one must begin by *trying* to apply this principle to it. I suspect that some such principle of charity may have been behind Prof. Matilal's suggestion that the literal and traditional interpretation of the Mādhyamikas' asat-khyāti doctrine "need not be taken to be strictly correct." Prof. Matilal may have felt that defending philosophically what is both the literal and the traditional interpretation of this doctrine would be impossible. Even if this were the case, however, either the traditional and obvious interpretation of that doctrine would have to be accepted as the Mādhyamika view, *or* it would have to be replaced with a better interpretation.

It seems to me that we must resist the temptation of rejecting the prima facie and traditional interpretation of texts even when those views seem to us to be absurd. The greatest possible lack of respect that can be shown to any school of philosophers is to simply refuse to believe that they meant what they said, or said what they meant, on the grounds that we are unable to make any sense of what they did say. Such a procedure would be quite arbitrary and unhistorical. As Poussin (1910: 133) warned long ago in a related connection: "The claim of the Buddhists to be śūnyatāvādins, 'doctors of the voidness,' not brahmavādins, cannot be set aside: philosophers must be credited with the opinions that they profess to cherish."

17. Having made this point, I should also add that I am not absolutely certain that the asat-khyāti-vāda *is* indefensible philosophically. It is *hard* to defend philosophically, because it is extremely counter-intuitive to deny the existence of matter unless one also accepts (as the ontological idealist does) the independent reality of mind. According to the Mādhyamikas, however, a purely non-ontological or nihilistic idealism is a consistent position. Indeed, according to the Mādhyamikas, a thorough-going, absolutely consistent idealism *entails* nihilism, for in its purest form, idealism is *nothing but* a pure phenomenalism, and as such is non-ontological—even *anti*-ontological.[30]

Thus, the Mādhyamika argued against his Vijñānavādin opponent as follows:

> You are slightly less deluded than most people. *Really* deluded people think that there is a real, external world, even though a moment's reflection should convince them that they cannot prove that the things they think they see in the waking state are any more real than the things they dream about at night. For example, you may have dreamed of a tiger last night which seemed just as real to you as I no doubt seem to you right now. You and I are in agreement on this point. Nevertheless, you continue to maintain—quite inconsistently, it seems to me—that although there was no real tiger in your dream, the *perception* or *hallucination* of the tiger was real as a *mental* phenomenon. But this won't do at all. Stop and think for a moment: where do we get our idea of existence? If the notion of existence is examined with some care, it will be seen that it is bound up with the notion of enduring, solid, tangible material objects. Yet you continue to go on speaking of real minds even after you have abandoned (or at least claim to have abandoned) this notion.

I am not sure that this criticism of the standard—i.e., ontological—version of idealism can simply be dismissed. Ontological idealists have thought, as Descartes did, that it makes sense to assert "I exist" even in the process of doubting whether one has a body or whether there is an external world at all. But if my body is no more real than the tiger in my nightmare, what is this I? A similar problem arises even if, having abandoned the notion of a self, one thinks of the mind as nothing more than an incessant, ever-changing flow of mental phenomena, as Hume and the Vijñānavādins did. Indeed, in the latter case the same difficulty appears in even sharper focus. On the Vijñānavādin view, for example, the mind is not even an entity. It is only a process, an uninterrupted succession of events which are in no way physical—nor is there anything physical for them to be related to. Philosophically, this *might* look all right, but on closer examination one cannot help wondering if the claim that this flow of percepts is *real* is not based on an unconscious and illegitimate transfer of the notion of existence from a domain where it is appropriate to one where it has no place at all.

According to the ontological idealists, the true nature of the self or mind can be seen clearly only when scepticism about the reality of the body and the external world are in full force. But the Mādhyamikas seem to me to have had a very different view of the matter. They seem to have felt that serious doubt about the reality of the body and the external world would actually *diminish*, rather than enhance, one's more or less instinctive belief in the reality of the mental. And it seems to me that the Mādhyamikas might very well have been right on this point.

18. There are some interesting similarities between the Mādhyamika view that the mind is unreal and the contemporary Western school of eliminative materialism.[31] I think that the view of these modern-day materialists provides a useful point of entry to the Madhyamaka, for this school also denies the reality of mind. The Mādhyamikas, of course, were not materialists (far from it), but since the view of eliminative materialism denies only the existence of mind, it is clearly the less radical of the two doctrines, and it is therefore appropriate to begin with it. Furthermore, once one has seen just how radical the position of eliminative materialism is, one is in a better position to appreciate the nihilist position. So far as I know, no one has ever suspected that the eliminativist is vulnerable to attack from the nihilist, but I think that this may actually be the case.

Although eliminativists concede that their view is counter-intuitive, they insist that it *must* be the correct view, because all the other possible alternatives turn out to be quite counter-intuitive as well, and in fact less defensible than the eliminativist view. As materialists, the eliminativists reject idealism and dualism from the outset. They are somewhat more sympathetic to epiphenomenalism, but they maintain that this view turns out to be untenable as well. According to at least one version of epiphenomenalism, mind is just matter in the sense that mind is a *property* of matter. That is, mind is not a substance, nor even a stream of mental phenomena or events existing independently of matter. It is just that, besides the expected material properties, some physical organisms (and possibly some physical artifacts, like robots) have mental properties as well, which are held to be essentially different from physical properties.

According to the epiphenomenalist, there is no particular harm in saying that people have minds; however, one must understand that all this claim means is that those physical organisms that we call people behave in a certain way and have certain kinds of internal or subjective properties that other kinds of physical entities, like rocks, do not have. For example, besides having physical properties like weight, color of hair and eyes, chemical constitution etc., people also manifest intelligent behavior in a way that rocks do not. People also have awareness, consciousness, volitions, sensations, perceptions, thoughts etc., whereas rocks do not. The epiphenomenalist is not willing to conclude from these kinds of properties and behavior-patterns either that people are not physical at all or that people are *both* mental and physical. What the epiphenomenalist or *non*-eliminative materialist concludes is that there are some purely physical things that have certain kinds of properties that other physical things do not have. There was a time when the universe contained only physical things and physical properties, but in the fullness of time some very complicated physical and biological entities arose that had mental properties as well. These mental properties the epiphenomenalist calls emergent properties.

The eliminative materialists have not been satisfied with this position. Perhaps their principal objection to it has been that the same kinds of problems that arise when one tries to understand the connection between the mind and the body on the dualist view tend to present themselves in a very similar form in epiphenomenalism. One naturally wants to know, for example, how a material thing *can* have mental properties like consciousness, and this question seems almost as perplexing as the related one that arises in the case of dualism. The most radical of the contemporary materialists, therefore, have done what the idealists did long before them, but in the opposite direction: they have simply denied that there is any such thing as mind. Just as the idealist has argued that there is no matter, but only mind, the modern-day radical materialist argues that there is no mind, but only matter. There is, in fact, nothing in the whole world but material substances and *material* properties.

According to the eliminativists, the claim that *mind* exists is no different in principle from any other scientific or empirical claim. Consequently, the claim that mind does *not* exist is no more absurd—though it may be more counter-intuitive—than the claim that phlogiston or demons do not exist. It used to be believed, and in some societies still is believed, that diseases are caused by demons. What we now believe, however, is that diseases have purely physical causes, e.g., viruses, bacteria, chemical imbalances in the body etc. We have concluded, on the basis of such discoveries, that demons do not exist. According to the eliminativists, mind is unreal in exactly the same way that demons are unreal. Headaches, for example, are not some strange kind of mental entity, process or property with which we are indubitably acquainted through some mysterious kind of interior perception or introspection. What we call a headache may very well be just a certain pattern of neural activity in the brain. (We need not know, for philosophical purposes, what this pattern of neural activity is. For the purposes of the present discussion let us simply agree to call it "the firing of H-fibers.")

According to the eliminativists, it is not absurd to suppose that at some point in time, when the neurosciences are sufficiently developed, people will say: "So there really is no such thing as a headache: headaches are just the firing of H-fibers in the brain." What this claim would amount to, the eliminativist argues, is simply a) that it is not the case that there is some entity (i.e., a headache) that is separate from the firing of H-fibers in the brain, and b) that it is not the case that there is a mental *property* that the firing of H-fibers has (i.e., the property of being a headache). According to the eliminativist, maintaining a) and b) would be no more absurd than claiming a′) that there are no demons, but only germs, chemical imbalances etc., and b′) claiming that chemical imbalances, germs etc. do not possess demonic properties. Just as there are no demons, so there is no mind. What we call mind is simply a brain state, and a brain state is *just* a state of matter, i.e., a *purely* physical state.

19. Like the eliminativists, the Mādhyamikas claimed that mind is entirely unreal and non-existent. The other philosophers of India seem to have found this claim totally absurd, just as many contemporary philosophers have found eliminative materialism absurd. But both the Mādhyamikas and the eliminativists have had an answer to such criticisms, and interestingly, it was the same *kind* of answer.

Both the nihilist and the eliminativist will admit that one one can assign *some* kind of meaning to the assertion that one has dreamt or hallucinated a tiger, i.e., they are prepared to admit that the expressions "an appearance" and "x saw something that was nothing but an appearance" have a legitimate role in the language. But, they have argued, this so-called appearance is not really a thing, nor even a property: it is, in the final analysis, just a locution, a figure of speech (prajñapti). The logic of it is very much like the logic of the term "non-existence" (nāsti, abhāva). Take the sentence: "The non-existence of his clothes was embarrassing to the Emperor once it had been pointed out to him." Here it would clearly be absurd to go on to ask: "Where and what is this *non-existence* of the Emperor's clothes?" Similarly, it is absurd to ask: "What is an appearance?" It makes sense to ask questions like "What is a fovea?" or "What is a dendrite?" for one can give a description of a fovea and dendrite from which it can be known or understood what it would be like to find one. But what would it be like to find an appearance? Taken literally, the expression "finding an appearance" makes no sense, for if an appearance could be found, it wouldn't *be* an appearance. Since appearances cannot be found by their very nature, the eliminativists and the nihilists hold that appearances are *unreal*, i.e., that they do not exist.[32]

The Mādhyamikas, however, went even further than the eliminativists, for according to the Mādhyamikas, *matter* is no more real than appearances are. S. N. Dasgupta, therefore, seems to me to have summarized the Mādhyamika position very well as a nihilistic idealism or pure phenomenalism. On this view, *everything* is reduced to mere appearances—or to be more exact, to nothing but a sequence of "It seems that ..." statements. Thus, to say "There is an appearance of a tiger" is just a somewhat misleading way of saying: "It seems to me that there is an orange-colored object, with such-and-such a shape, with stripes of a certain color etc. standing before me" etc. The Mādhyamika and the eliminativist are in agreement on this point, but the eliminativist believes that what we *call* mind is actually matter, whereas the Mādhyamikas believed that *nothing* is real. The position of nihilistic idealism or pure phenomenalism is, of course, a very radical view, for we naturally think that there must be something real—something existent—at the bottom of everything. According to the Mādhyamikas, this is a mistake. *Nothing* is real—not even what we call mind. Everything is just smoke and mirrors, all the way down—and ultimately, even the smoke and the mirrors are non-existent!

20. Advocates of the sense data doctrine in India and in the West have appealed to certain kinds of experiences in an attempt to establish that even non-veridical perceptions have intentional (i.e., purely mental) objects. The following are three typical examples of such alleged non-veridical percepts:

(a) The stick in water. If a perfectly straight stick is partially immersed in water, the stick is likely to look bent to an observer.

(b) Double images. If one presses one's eyeballs in a certain way while staring at a single candle flame, one can can produce for oneself the experience of seeing two flames rather than one.

(c) Hallucinations. Even when one's physical senses are not being manipulated or interfered with in any way, as in the immediately preceding example, it is still possible to see things that are not there, i.e., to have hallucinations.

Philosophers of very different persuasions in both India and the West have appealed to cases like (a) - (c) above in order to show that all perception—even non-veridical perception—is perception of *something*. If it *seems* that we are seeing something, it is said, then there is certainly something that we are seeing—if not something physical, then at the very least something mental.

Take the bent stick, for example. According to the proponents of the sense data doctrine, if it *seems* to me that I am seeing something bent, then it must be the case that I *am* seeing something that is bent, even if the thing that I see that is bent is not the same thing as the physical stick itself.[33] Similarly, it is argued, what we must conclude from the fact that one can see two candle flames when there is only one physical candle flame in one's field of vision is that at least one of the images is mental rather than physical. Hallucinations, too, have been subjected to this line of analysis. According to the advocates of the sense data doctrine, a person who is having an hallucination is seeing *something* even when the person is sitting in a bare room or has his eyes closed—it is just that *what* he is seeing is mental, rather than physical. All of this has seemed quite self-evident to many philosophers; nevertheless, the eliminative materialists and the Mādhyamikas have denied it. (The Mādhyamikas, in fact, may have been the *first* philosophers to deny it.)

One of the first philosophers to challenge the sense data doctrine in the Western tradition was W. H. F. Barnes (1976-1944), in a paper entitled "The Myth of Sense-data." Since the issues that Barnes discusses in this paper are fundamental to the controversy that took place between the Mādhyamikas and the Yogācāras over the question of the reality of the mind, it will be useful to consider Barnes' arguments in some detail.

At one point in his paper Barnes says (1976: 153):

> No one will deny, I think, that a situation may exist in which the following three propositions are true:
>
> (i) I see the rose.
> (ii) The rose appears pink to me.

> (iii) The rose is red.
>
> The belief in sensa is reached by arguing, not unplausibly, that since what I am seeing appears pink, there exists something which *is* pink; and since the rose is red, not pink, it cannot be the rose which is pink; therefore what I am seeing is something other than the rose. Whereupon the term sensum is invented and given as a name to this existent and others like it. And so we reach the conclusion:
>
> (iv) I see a pink sensum.

At this point Barnes says:

> The argument is fallacious. *That something appears pink to me is not a valid reason for concluding either that that thing is pink or that there is some other thing which is pink.* From the fact that a thing *looks* pink I can sometimes with the help of certain other propositions infer that it *is* pink or that it *is* red; I may also, with the help of certain other propositions, be able to infer that something in some other place is pink, e.g., the eletric light bulb which is illuminating the rose. But I cannot infer, as is proposed, *merely from the three facts that I am seeing something, that it looks pink and that it is red, that there is a pink something where the thing appears pink to me.*

He also says (ibid., p. 155):

> Modes of appearance are clues to the nature of what exists, not existents. I submit that it is improper to ask whether the pink mode of appearing, which is how the rose appears to me, exists.

And in the context of a reference to Lady Macbeth's hallucinatory dagger, he says (p. 163):

> It is misleading also in some degree to say that there exists "a dagger like appearance," though we need not be misled by such a use of the word *appearance* if we are careful. Strictly speaking, however, there are no such things as appearances.

It seems to me that this is exactly what the Mādhyamikas argued against the Vijñānavādins. The Mādhyamikas did not deny that it is true in some sense to *say* that things appear to be such-and-such; they simply denied that one could infer from this that there are such things as appearances (vijñapti). Expressions like "sense datum," "appearance," "vijñapti" etc. are like the expression "the rising of the sun." Such expressions are useful and harmless if understood for what they are. Just as the sun doesn't really rise and set, so the appearance of an illusory, pink elephant has no more reality than the supposed physical pink elephant that the hallucinator imputes to the *external* world.[34]

There is one important difference between the Mādhyamika position and Barnes', however, and I think it is to the advantage of the Mādhyamikas. Barnes denied that (i)-(iii) above forced one to accept (iv). According to Barnes, all we have to do, and all that we in fact do, is to recognize that things *can appear to be what they are not*. There is therefore no need to suppose that there are real entities called appearances, for appearances are just the *modes* in which things appear. Since there is no reason to be surprised that something can appear to have some quality which it does not have, there is no reason to suppose that in such cases there is something *else* (i.e., a mental something) that really does have that property.

As Barnes was aware, however, it is not obvious how this approach can be made to apply to all cases, and especially to pure hallucinations. In connection with Lady Macbeth's dagger, for example, he acknowledges that there are "certainly problems concerning exactly what it is in such circumstances appears to be possessed of qualities which it does not possess." And later (p. 167) he says:

> I do not wish to suggest that no problems beset the theory of appearing. For example the two cases of a thing's appearing double and of something appearing to be where there is no such thing, present the problem: Is the apparent expanse in these cases the actual surface of any object?

Barnes' doubt on this point is significant. According to his theory, there must always be some object which the appearance is an appearance *of*. This means, in turn, that Barnes never questioned one of the fundamental principles of the sense data doctrine, i.e., that when people report seeing *something*, there is necessarily something that they are seeing. The disagreement between Barnes and the proponents of the sense data doctrine was over what it is that we *do* see. According to the proponents of the sense data doctrine, what we see—or at any rate, what we "directly" or "immediately" see—is always a mental entity. According to Barnes, what we see, presumably, is *always* something physical (e.g., the actual surface of a real object) which can, however, appear to have some property which it does not have.

This is the great weakness—probably the fatal weakness—of Barnes' theory. The answer to the question: "Is the apparent expanse in hallucinations the actual surface of any object?" is surely No. There is by now an enormous amount of psychological evidence to support this negative answer. As it turns out, many hallucinations do have a physical trigger or basis; and as a result, it is sometimes hard to draw the line between an hallucination and a perceptual illusion. For example, if my imagination has been made vivid enough for neurophysiological or psychological reasons, or the circumstances are right, I can mistake a rope lying in the path before me as a snake. But the rope (or any other physical object) is quite unnecessary. It is possible to have a perfectly vivid hallucination or perception of a snake if one is in a room lying on a table looking up at some totally shapeless fluorescent lighting with sawed-off ping-pong balls entirely covering one's eyeballs—and it would be hard to argue, on anything but a strict eliminativist view, that what one was actually seeing when one saw a snake in these circumstances was a *ping-pong ball.*

If the answer to Barnes' own question is in fact No, what alternatives are left? It may be that there are only two alternatives. One is to fall back on some version of the sense data doctrine. The other is to simply *deny* one of the fundamental principles of that doctrine, i.e., that whenever one seems to see something, there is (necessarily) something that is seen. This is precisely what the Mādhyamikas and the contemporary eliminative materialists—for very different reasons—have denied. According to the Mādhyamikas, we never see anything under any circumstances. The position of the eliminativists is less extreme, but it, too, denies the fundamental principle that even Barnes accepted. According to the eliminativist, if there is a real dagger (i.e., a bona-fide physical dagger in the external world), then one can certainly see *it*, but if there isn't, there can be no such thing as seeing a dagger at all—not even seeing the appearance of a dagger. In short, one either sees real daggers and real things, or nothing at all.

21. Non-eliminative materialism does not deny that there are appearances. On that view, appearances like bent-sticks, double-imaged candle flames and pink elephants are real enough, but they are only modes or properties of brain processes. This view of the matter is rejected in eliminative materialism. According to the latter view, there is no such thing as seeing a pink elephant which is in fact identical with a brain state, because unless there is a real elephant in the physical world, there is no such thing as seeing an elephant at all. When people report that they are seeing such a thing and there are no pink elephants about, they are not seeing anything. All that exists empirically is a correlation between peoples' descriptions of their experiences and the pattern of the firing of neurons in the brain. Once these correlations have finally been determined, we will be in a position to say, for example, that when someone reports having a headache what is actually going on is the firing of H-fibers in the brain. But according to the eliminative materialist we cannot say, as the non-eliminativist does, that headaches are identical with the firing of H-fibers. In fact, on the strict eliminativist view, there would appear to be no way of saving the headaches that we think we experience at all.

In case this is not clear, consider the analogy of demons and viruses.[35] Let us imagine a tribe that still believes that diseases are caused by demons. We might even imagine that this tribe has an elaborate taxonomy of demons. For example, we might suppose them to believe that a demon with a blue nose causes cholera, that a demon with a red nose causes cancer, etc. What will the tribespeople conclude about demons when they are converted to the tenets of modern medicine? To accept the viewpoint of modern medicine entails the *rejection* of the demon theory (at least so far as illnesses are concerned). Since the view that diseases are caused by demons and the view that they are caused only by viruses, chemical imbalances etc. cannot *both* be true, the tribespeople cannot hold on to demons qua demons by saying: "Oh well, what we have learned, after all, is not that there are no demons, but only that demons are in fact viruses." There are no demons if only viruses cause diseases, because viruses do not have any of the other characteristic features of demons. (There are, for example, no viruses with blue noses.) Similarly, on the eliminativist view there are no appearances, because there are nothing but dendrites, axons, electrical fields, neural discharges etc. in the picture. These things lack the property of being conscious, the property of being painful etc., and have only physical properties (e.g., mass, charge, chemical properties etc.).

Eliminative materialists concede that their theory is counter-intuitive, but they are not willing to concede to their critics that this counter-intuitiveness is a *decisive* objection to it. It may very well be that most people are inclined to think that one cannot hallucinate a pink elephant without seeing *something*, even if it is not a physical elephant that anyone else can see. If philosophical questions could be decided by counting noses, the decision might very well go against the eliminativists. According to the eliminativist, however, the issue cannot be settled this way, because people are not the absolute, unquestionable authorities about what they experience. In fact, they are not even the absolute, unquestionable authorities on the question whether they have experiences at all. According to the eliminativists, the fact that people claim that they are having experiences does not entail that they are having experiences, any more that the fact that a person claims that he sees a pink elephant entails that there really is a pink elephant that he is seeing.

22. I have my doubts that the eliminativist position is a tenable one. However, it does seem to me that if one is prepared to take this position seriously, there may be no stopping a nihilist who argues against an eliminativist as follows:

> I agree with you that there are no minds and no experiences, but I don't believe in matter either. Your arguments against the existence of mind are sound, but you have failed to note that in arguing against the existence of mind you have simply cut the ground out from under your own feet. You want to construct a philosophy and science of materialism, but what will you take as your evidence for all this? If you were to pursue this question of evidence to its logical conclusion, you would see that there is no evidence for anything at all.[36] Even if there *were* such evidence, however, it could only consist in the very thing whose existence you deny, i.e., appearances or sense data, for as your idealist opponents have clearly shown, the matter which you believe in can be neither seen nor inferred. Remove the belief in sense data or appearances, and you remove the possibility of believing in anything at all, since the arguments against matter are just as irrefutable as your arguments against the existence of mind. The only logical and honest thing, therefore, is to do as we do and assert that nothing exists at all. Everything is completely void (śūnya).
>
> You materialists are fond of pointing out that when one trepan's the skull of even a living person, all we ever *seem* to see is a physical brain consisting of nerve fibers, blood vessels etc. We do not see headaches,

patches of living color, anything that looks like what might be a sound etc. In short, we do not perceive the sense data (vijñapti) that the dualists speak about at all. We quite agree with you that the obvious conclusion to be drawn from this significant fact is that there are in fact no headaches, no sensations of color and sound, no sense data, no experiences, no mind etc.

But if there are no headaches, no sensations of color and sound, no sense data, no experiences and no mind etc., what is your basis for asserting that there *are* brains, axons, dendrites, blood vessels, chemical molecules etc? The only way we could know of such things is if we *did* have minds, perceptions, experiences etc., and these things you have already categorically denied. You have apparently failed to see that if there is no mind, no sensations, no mental images etc., then there can be no perception and no cognition either. Hence *brains* are as much a figure of speech (prajñapti) as the sense data that you are so concerned to exorcise from our ontology. You can go on saying "It seems to me that so-and-so," "It seems to me that such and such" as much as you like, ad infinitum. No matter how many true statements of this form you utter, you will never be able to *justify* the inference that there is something that is actually appearing to you to be so-and-so. This is as true of physical things, which you say you are prepared to countenance, as it is of mental things (sense data, vijñapti), which you are not prepared to countenance.

Furthermore, there is no point in constructing the world view that you wish to defend. In actuality, there is nothing, either physical or mental, corresponding to what we call appearances, but even if there were, the one thing that one could say about it with absolute certainty is that it involves suffering (duḥkha). As Buddhists, we are less concerned with constructing a theory about what is called suffering than we are in eliminating it. If suffering were real, one could never free oneself from it. Fortunately, however, it is not real, even as a dream.

Consider the phenomenon called lucid dreaming. Some people (called "lucid dreamers" by the psychologists who study this phenomenon) can have the experience of waking up, getting out of bed, getting dressed, going out the door, walking down the street etc., just as in the waking state, but with two important differences. The first difference is that this experience turns out to be a dream. The second significant difference is that at some point in the dream the lucid dreamer *realizes* that he or she is dreaming, yet this does not dispel the dream. Perhaps this sort of thing happens to many people in their sleep without their ever knowing it, i.e., they simply wake up in the morning without any memory that this has happened to them while they were asleep in their beds at night. But some people realize that they are dreaming when this is happening to them, and remember this experience. If this happens to them frequently enough, lucid dreamers can even start looking for certain tell-tale features of their dream-experience—e.g., the fact that buildings are tilted ever so slightly out of the perpindicular, or tiny but ubiquitous cracks in the plaster of the walls—that can serve as clues to whether they are dreaming or not.

Now you, the materialist, and our mutual opponent, the idealist, are *both* dreaming. Even the idealist is dreaming, because there is in fact nothing that has the ontological status of even a dream. How do we know this? Because no one has ever seen, or ever will see, the percepts (vijñapti) on which the idealist bases his entire philosophy. To be fair, however, the idealist is no worse off in this respect that anyone else, for the simple truth is that there are decisive objections to *any* philosophical view, not just the idealist one. One might compare this well-known fact to the tilted buildings of the lucid dreamer's dream. A lucid dreamer might take the non-perpindicularity of the buildings in his dream as the tell-tale sign that the buildings he seems to be seeing are non-existent. In just the same way, all the philosophical problems are insoluble. The view that there is nothing but mind, the view that there is nothing but matter, the view that mind is matter and matter is mind; the view that things arise from self, that they arise from others, that they arise from both self and others, etc.: all such views are untenable. Philosophers of all persuasions will have to accept this simple fact in order to realize that everything is completely void.

One thing that you must *not* conclude from these considerations is that things *neither* exist nor do not exist, or to put this another way, that reality is in some sense logically indeterminable. This is the view of the Māyāvāda school of the Vedānta, which holds that the things we seem to see (in both the waking state and the dreaming state) are neither real (sat) nor unreal (asat). Things are not real, the Māyāvādins argue, because they do not withstand logical and philosophical investigation. On the other hand, such things cannot be totally unreal either, for we experience them (anubhava). This sad-asad-anirvacanīya-khyāti-vāda makes no sense at all. If all things are completely unthinkable in the sense that nothing you can say about them withstands investigation, then what one must conclude is that nothing exists (sarvaṃ sarveṇa nāsti), not that things are logically indeterminable. Take a specific example: the son of a barren woman (vandhyā-putra). A moment's reflection will show you that the expression "vandhyā-putra" is nothing but mere sound (śabda-mātra) without any meaning. To say that a barren woman gave birth to a son is *meaningless*. Anything, like the son of a barren woman, that is logically or semantically contradictory or logically indeterminable could not possibly exist (na vipratiṣiddhaṃ saṃbhavati), so the Māyāvādin view that the phenomenal world is logically indeterminable actually amounts to the nihilist view anyway. On investigation, all things turn out to be exactly like the sons of barren women: there couldn't be *any* reality (bhāva, sattā) corresponding to these expressions. "Neither exists nor does not exist" could not be true even of a *dream* object. Anyone who fails to realize this is not just dreaming—he is *totally* confused, i.e, asserting something that has no meaning at all.

There is one more point to be made in connection with lucid dreaming. It is not enough to *realize* that one is dreaming. To think this may or may not be a step on the way to liberation from the nightmare that is tormenting us. If it leads to the cessation of the dream altogether, the thought that things are mind only is good, but as the example of lucid dreaming shows very clearly, thinking or knowing that one is dreaming does not necessarily lead to the cessation of a dream. As Śāntideva has said (BCA 9.31-32):

> If it were merely that thought is similar to an illusion [as the Vijñānavādin maintains], how would passion be turned aside? Even as she comes into being, the magician falls in love with the māyā-woman that he has himself created.
>
> Such a magician still has impure mental tendencies (saṃkleśa-vāsanā). If he so much as sees the māyā-woman, his impression of the void (śūnya-vāsanā) is weak.

The Vijñānavāda is therefore incomplete at best. It must be seen that mind, experiences, perceptions,

> thoughts etc. are themelves unreal and non-existent. Nothing short of this realization will enable us to perceive the true nature of saṃsāra, which is nothing but a pure illusion, i.e., a sheer non-entity.
>
> Finally, you believe, as a materialist, that your involvement in the world-appearance will automatically come to an end when your physical body dies, but this is also a mistake. Physical death is also a dream. After we dream our physical death, we can, like the lucid dreamer, go on to dream all kinds of things: heavenly experiences in the deva-realms, hellish things in the piśāca-realms etc. But none of these are real, even as appearances. It is all completely void. Realizing that it has no existence *even as an appearance* is the only way to realize the voidness of all things.

23. The nihilist view is a radical one, but I am not quite sure that it is philosophically untenable, i.e., that it is actually refutable as being *incoherent*.[37] The view does not seem to involve any logical inconsistencies, and it may be possible to defend it against epistemological criticism as well. According to the nihilist, what we call knowledge consists (or *seems* to consist) of a large number of purely phenomenalistic "It seems as if" statements, and one cannot logically infer from any such statement (or the totality of them) that anything exists that is either an appearance or the thing that is doing the appearing. If the nihilist cannot be refuted on this point, then nihilism may be a defensible position philosophically.

Whereas the philosophical objections to the NI are epistemological, the philosophical objections to the NNI are primarily logical. According to most proponents of the NNI, it is possible to violate laws of logic and still utter meaningful propositions, for the laws of logic are not universally valid. This position appears in a number of different forms in the writings of the proponents of the NNI. For example, it is said that there is a kind of negation from which one cannot infer anything about any other statement; or it is said that reality is logically indeterminable; or that, although the Mādhyamikas contradicted themselves, they did so knowingly and deliberately, and that their doing so was harmless because logical laws have only psychological validity as laws of thought, whereas reality—or at least ultimate reality—is beyond logic. One of the most attractive features of the NI is that it does not require us to impute such views to the Mādhyamikas. According to the NI, there *is* no negation that has no implications to the truth or falsity of any other statement, nothing can be logically indeterminate, and no contradiction could be true.

As I have also argued, the NI is the preferable interpretation of the Madhyamaka for exegetical and textual reasons. This seems to me to be true even of those passages which have been adduced as evidence *against* the NI. The passages which might seem, prima facie, to assert that things are not entirely non-existent (e.g., MMK 25.7-8) and the passages that might seem, prima facie, to assert that things are not entirely empty (e.g., MMK 13.7), turn out, on closer examination, to actually support the NI rather than the NNI. The point that such passages seem to make is simply that non-existence (abhāvatva) and emptiness (śūnyatā) are not themselves things or existents (dravya, padārtha). This, of course, is exactly what one would expect a consistent nihilist to maintain.

The textual evidence shows that the Mādhyamikas did not *really* believe in the existence of the phenomenal world. Nor do they appear to have believed in a non-phenomenal, absolute reality. On the contrary: the Mādhyamikas devoted much of their energy and considerable abilities towards combatting this very reading of the Buddha's teachings. For the Mādhyamikas, emptiness (śūnyatā) was not a thing, process or property—not even a transcendent thing, process or property. It was exactly what the Sanskrit words "śūnya" and "śūnyatā" suggest that it was. Like empty space, like the self or soul of the ordinary man and the non-Buddhist philosopher, like an illusion, a dream or an illusory city in the sky, like a magical creation, like a mirage, like an hallucination which does not exist even as a mental phenomenon, like a clenched fist with which a child is teased, like the son of a barren woman or the horn of a hare, it was simply sheer, unqualified, absolute nothingness.

APPENDIX

MMK 1: The Examination of Causes and Conditions

pratyaya-parīkṣā

No cessation, no origination, no destruction, no permanence, no identity, no difference, no coming and no going:

anirodham-anutpādam anucchedam-aśāśvatam /
anekārtham-anānārtham anāgamam-anirgamam //1//

I pay homage to the Fully Awakened One, the best of teachers, who has taught dependent co-origination, the quiescence of all phenomena, the auspicious.

yaḥ pratītya-samutpādaṃ prapañcopaśamamaṃ śivam /
deśayāmāsa saṃbuddhas taṃ vande vadatāṃ varam //2//

***

Entities never originate, at any time or at any place, either from self, from others, from both, or from no cause.

na svato nāpi parato na dvābhyāṃ nāpy ahetutaḥ /
utpannā jātu vidyante bhāvāḥ kvacana kecana //3//

There are only four causal conditions: the primary, the objective/supporting, the proximate and the superordinate. There is no fifth.

catvāraḥ pratyayā hetur ārambaṇam anantaram /
tathaivādhipateyaṃ ca pratyayo nāsti pañcamaḥ //4//

There is no self-nature (svabhāva) of entities to be found in any of these causal conditions. Since there is no self-nature, there is no other-nature, either.

na hi svabhāvo bhāvānāṃ pratyayādiṣu vidyate /
avidyamāne svabhāve parabhāvo na vidyate //5//

Force does not have the causal conditions as a basis, nor does it have non-causal conditions as a basis. Conversely, the causal conditions do not have force as a basis, nor do they have lack of force as a basis.

> kriyā na pratyayavatī nāpratyayavatī kriyā /
> pratyayā nākriyāvantaḥ kriyāvantaś ca santy uta //6//

Indeed, it is only when things have originated that there are causal conditions. As long as these have not originated, how could the causal conditions be anything but non-causal conditions?

> utpadyate pratītyemān itīme pratyayāḥ kila /
> yāvan notpadyata ime tāvan nāpratyayāḥ katham //7//

There cannot be a causal condition for an object that exists or for one that does not exist. If the object is non-existent, what is it a causal condition of? And if the object already exists, in what respect is it a causal condition?

> naivāsato naiva sataḥ pratyayo 'rthasya yujyate /
> asataḥ pratyayaḥ kasya sataś ca pratyayena kim //8//

As there are no real, unreal or real-and-unreal dharmas which ever come about (nivartate), how could there be a cause (hetu) that brings things about?

> na san nāsan na sad asan dharmo nirvartate yadā /
> kathaṃ nirvartako hetur evaṃ sati hi yujyate //9//

A real dharma is said to be devoid of an objective/supportive causal condition. When the dharma itself is devoid of an objective/supportive causal condition, how could there be such a condition?

> anārambaṇa evāyaṃ san dharma upadiśyate /
> athānārambaṇe dharme kuta ārambaṇaṃ punaḥ //10//

The extinction of things which have never originated is logically impossible. Therefore, what is called the immediately preceding condition is logically impossible. How can something which has ceased to exist be a causal condition?

> anutpanneṣu dharmeṣu nirodho nopapadyate /
> nānantaram ato yuktaṃ niruddhe pratyayaś ca kaḥ //11//

As there is no being (sattā) of things which lack self-nature, the traditional formula for causation: "From the existence of this thing that thing comes to be" (satīdam asmin bhavatīti) makes no sense.

> bhāvānāṃ niḥsvabhāvānāṃ na sattā vidyate yataḥ /
> satīdam asmin bhavatīty etan naivopapadyate //12//

The effect does not exist in the causal conditions, either singly or collectively. How could that which is not in the causal conditions originate from them?

> na ca vyasta-samasteṣu pratyayeṣv asti tat phalam /
> pratyayebhyaḥ kathaṃ tac ca bhaven na pratyayeṣu yat //13//

If a non-existent (asat) effect can come about from the causal conditions, why couldn't an effect come about from non-causal conditions as well?

> athāsad api tat tebhyaḥ pratyayebhyaḥ pravartate /
> apratyayebhyo 'pi kasmān nābhipravartate phalam //14//

The effect, you might say, is a transformation of its causal conditions, but that cannot be so, because the causal conditions have no self-nature. How can the effect be the transformation of causal conditions which lack self-nature?

> phalaṃ ca pratyayamayaṃ pratyayāś cāsvayaṃmayāḥ /
> phalam asvamayebhyo yat tat pratyayamayaṃ katham //15//

Therefore, there is no effect, either as the transformation of causal coditions or not. Since there is no effect, how can there be causal or non-causal conditions?

> tasmān na pratyayamayaṃ nāpratyayamayaṃ phalam /
> saṃvidyate phalābhāvāt pratyayāpratyayāḥ kutaḥ //16//

MMK 13: The Examination of Mental Formations

saṃskāra-parīkṣā

The Blessed One has said that all dharmas that are delusive (moṣa) are unreal (mṛṣā). All the mental formations (saṃskāras) are delusive. Therefore, they are unreal.

> tan mṛṣā moṣa-dharma yad bhagavān ity abhāṣata /
> sarve ca moṣa-dharmāṇaḥ saṃskāras tena te mṛṣā //1//

If every dharma that is delusive is unreal, what then is it that deludes? With this point, the Blessed One fully illuminated emptiness (śūnyatā).

> tan mṛṣā moṣa-dharma yad yadi kim tatra muṣyate /
> etat tūktaṃ bhagavatā śūnyatā-paridīpakam //2//

All things lack self-nature, because they are subject to change. No entity can exist which lacks self-nature, and hence all entities (bhāvas) are empty (śūnyatā).

> bhāvānāṃ niḥsvabhāvatvam anyathābhāva-darśanāt /
> nāsvabhāvaś ca bhāvo 'sti bhāvānāṃ śūnyatā yataḥ //3//

If there is no self-nature, what is it that changes? What is it that changes if there is self-nature?

> kasya syād anyathābhāvaḥ svabhāvaś cen na vidyate /
> kasya syād anyathābhāvaḥ svabhāvo yadi vidyate //4//

It is not possible for the same thing or for another thing to change. Hence neither the youth nor the old man grows old.

> tasyaiva nānyathābhāvo nāpy anyasyaiva yujyate /
> yuvā na jīryate yasmād yasmāj jīrṇo na jīryate //5//

If something did have a changing nature, then milk itself would be the same thing as curds. Nor can the being of curds arise from something other than milk.

tasya ced anyathābhāvaḥ kṣīram eva bhaved dadhi /
kṣīrād anyasya kasyacid dadhi-bhāvo bhaviṣyati //6//

If non-emptiness (aśūnyam) were anything at all (kiṃcit syāt), then emptiness (śūnyam) could also be something (api kiṃcana). But since non-emptiness (aśūnyam) is nothing at all (na kiṃcid asti), how could emptiness be something?

yady aśūnyaṃ bhavet kiṃcit syāc chūnyam api kiṃcana /
na kiṃcid asty aśūnyaṃ ca kutaḥ śūnyaṃ bhaviṣyati //7//

The Conquerors have declared emptiness to be the cessation of all speculative views (dṛṣṭi). Those who hold a speculative view of emptiness are declared to be incorrigible.

śūnyatā sarva-dṛṣṭīnāṃ proktā niḥsaraṇaṃ jinaiḥ /
yeṣāṃ tu śūnyatā-dṛṣṭis tān asādhyān babhāṣire //8//

MMK 15: The Examination of Self-nature

svabhāva-parīkṣā

Self-nature cannot originate from causes (hetu) and conditions (pratyaya), for a self-nature which originated from causes and conditions would be something created (kṛtaka).

> na saṃbhavaḥ svabhāvasya yuktaḥ pratyaya-hetubhiḥ /
> hetu-pratyaya-saṃbhūtaḥ svabhāvaḥ kṛtako bhavet //1//

How can self-nature be created? For indeed self-nature is uncreated and not dependent on anything else.

> svabhāvaḥ kṛtako nāma bhaviṣyati punaḥ katham /
> akṛtrimaḥ svabhāvo hi nirapekṣaḥ paratra ca //2//

Since there is no self-nature (svabhāvasyābhāve), how could other-nature (parabhāva) be? For the self-nature of other-nature is that other-nature.

> kutaḥ svabhāvasyābhāve parabhāvo bhaviṣyati /
> svabhāvaḥ parabhāvasya parabhāvo hi kathyate //3//

Again, how could there be existence (bhāva) apart from self-nature and other-nature? For indeed it is only when there is self-nature and other-nature that existence is established.

> svabhāva-parabhāvābhyām ṛte bhāvaḥ kutaḥ punaḥ /
> svabhāve parabhāve ca sati bhāvo hi sidhyati //4//

If existence (bhāva) cannot be established, then non-existence (abhāva) cannot be established either. For people declare non-existence to be the becoming-other (anyathā-bhāva) of existence.

> bhāvasya ced aprasiddhir abhāvo naiva sidhyati /
> bhāvasya hy anyathābhāvam abhāvaṃ bruvate janāḥ //5//

Those who see self-nature, other-nature, existence (bhāva) and non-existence (abhāva) do not see the fundamental principle of the Buddha's teaching.

> svabhāvaṃ parabhāvaṃ ca bhāvaṃ cābhāvam eva ca /
> ye paśyanti na paśyanti te tattvaṃ buddha-śāsane //6//

"Is" and "is not": the Buddha has discussed both of these speculative views in the Kātyāyanāva-vāda-sūtra, where he has shown that things are free from the distinctions of existence (bhāva) and non-existence (abhāva).

> kātyāyanāvavāde cāstīti nāstīti cobhayam /
> pratiṣiddhaṃ bhagavatā bhāvābhāva-vibhāvinā //7//

If things were to exist in virtue of their own nature (prakṛtyā), then they could not become non-existent (nāstitā), for indeed nothing can change its own-nature.

> yady astitvaṃ prakṛtyā syān na bhaved asya nāstitā /
> prakṛter anyathābhāvo na hi jātūpapadyate //8//

How can something change which has no self-nature (prakṛti)? How can something change which does have self-nature (prakṛti)?

> prakṛtau kasya vāsatyām anyathātvaṃ bhaviṣyati /
> prakṛtau kasya vā satyām anyathātvaṃ bhaviṣyati //9//

The assertion of existence (astīti) is the grasping of permanency (śāśvata), and the assertion of non-existence (nāstīti) is the viewpoint of annihilationism (uccheda). Therefore the wise do not base themselves on existence and non-existence.

> astīti śāśvata-grāho nāstīty uccheda-darśanam /
> tasmād astitva-nāstitve nāśrīyeta vicakṣaṇaḥ //10//

According to permanency (śāśvata), that which exists of its own self-nature (svabhāvena) never becomes non-existent. It follows from this that annihilation (uccheda) is the non-existence of that which was previously existent.

asti yad dhi svabhāvena na tan nāstīti śāśvatam /
nāstīdānīm abhūt pūrvam ity ucchedaḥ prasajyate //11//

MMK 24: The Examination of the Noble Truths

ārya-satya-parīkṣā

[The opponent]:

If all this (idaṃ sarvam) is empty (śūnya), there can be neither origination nor destruction. It follows that for you the four-fold Āryan truths are non-existent (abhāva).

> yadi śūnyam idaṃ sarvam udayo nāsti na vyayaḥ /
> caturṇām ārya-satyānām abhāvas te prasajyate //1//

Since the four-fold Āryan truths are non-existent, full knowledge, the relinquishing of false views, right practice and final realization will not be possible.

> parijñā ca prahāṇaṃ ca bhāvanā sākṣi-karma ca /
> caturṇām ārya-satyānām abhāvān nopapadyate //2//

Since these are non-existent, the four-fold Āryan attainments (phala) are also non-existent (na vidyante). Since the attainments are non-existent (abhāve), there is neither attainment nor who who strives for it.

> tad-abhāvān na vidyante catvāry ārya-phalāni ca /
> phalābhāve phala-sthā no na santi pratipannakāḥ //3//

If the eight great personages [mahā-puruṣa-pudgala] do not exist, then it follows that for you the Buddhist order (saṃgha) does not exist (nāsti). Since the four Āryan truths do not exist, the Buddhist truth does not exist either (api na vidyate).

> saṃgho nāsti na cet santi te 'ṣṭau puruṣa-pudgalāḥ /
> abhāvāc cārya-satyānāṃ sad-dharmo 'pi na vidyate //4//

If neither the Buddhist truth (dharma) nor the Buddhist order (saṃgha) exists, how can there be a Buddha? Thus your assertion negates the Three Jewels.

dharme cāsati saṃghe ca kathaṃ buddho bhaviṣyati /
evaṃ trīṇy api ratnāni bruvāṇaḥ pratibādhase //5//

Your doctrine of emptiness (śūnyatā) thereby undermines the reality and existence (sad-bhāva) of the attainments, the distinction between right acts and wrong acts (dharma and adharma), and all the things and practices of the ordinary world.

śūnyatāṃ phala-sad-bhāvam adharmaṃ dharmam eva ca /
sarva-saṃvyavahārāṃś ca laukikān pratibādhase //6//

***

[Nāgārjuna]:

In reply we have to say that you do not understand the purpose of the doctrine of emptiness (śūnyatā), śūnyatā itself or the meaning of śūnyatā. You thereby bring harm to yourself.

atra brūmaḥ śūnyatāyāṃ na tvaṃ vetsi prayojanam /
śūnyatāṃ śūnyatārthaṃ ca tata evaṃ vihanyase //7//

The teaching of the dharma by the Buddhas is based on the two truths (dve satye): i.e., the concealed truth (saṃvṛti-satya) of the everyday, and the truth as it really is (paramārthataḥ).

dve satye samupāśritya buddhānāṃ dharma-deśanā /
loka-saṃvṛtisatyaṃ ca satyaṃ ca paramārthataḥ //8//

Those who do not know how to distinguish between the two truths do not know the profound nature (tattva) of the Buddha's teaching.

ye 'nayor na vijānanti vibhāgaṃ satyayor dvayoḥ /
te tattvaṃ na vijānanti gambhīraṃ buddha-śāsane //9//

Without relying on the concealed truth of the everyday, the absolute truth (paramārtha) cannot be pointed out. Without resorting to the absolute truth, nirvāṇa cannot be attained.

> vyavahāram anāśritya paramārtho na deśyate /
> paramārtham anāgamya nirvāṇaṃ nādhigamyate //10//

Emptiness (śūnyatā), when it is misconceived, will destroy a dull-witted person, like a snake that has been seized improperly or magic (vidyā) that has been employed incorrectly.

> vināśayati durdṛṣṭā śūnyatā manda-medhasam /
> sarpo yathā durgṛhīto vidyā vā duṣprasādhitā //11//

For this reason the mind of the Great Silent One (muni) was averse to teaching the Dharma, thinking that the dull-witted would be incapable of understanding it.

> ataś ca pratyudāvṛttaṃ cittaṃ deśayituṃ muneḥ /
> dharmaṃ matvāsya dharmasya mandair duravagāhatām //12//

You repeatedly make a travesty of emptiness (śūnyatā). The absurd consequences you attribute to this doctrine do not apply to our conception of it.

> śūnyatāyām adhilayaṃ yaṃ punaḥ kurute bhavān /
> doṣa-prasaṅgo nāsmākaṃ sa śūnye nopapadyate //13//

Everything makes sense if one accepts the doctrine of emptiness. Nothing makes sense if one does not.

> sarvaṃ ca yujyate tasya śūnyatā yasya yujyate /
> sarvaṃ na yujyate tasya śūnyaṃ yasya na yujyate //14//

You accuse us of your own errors (doṣa). It is as if you had forgotten the very horse that you are riding, which is right under you.

sa tvaṃ doṣān ātmanīyān asmāsu paripātayan /
aśvam evābhirūḍhaḥ sann aśvam evāsi vismṛtaḥ //15//

If you perceive things (bhāvas) as real and existent (sad-bhāva) in virtue of some self-nature, then you will have to see them as devoid of causes and conditions.

svabhāvād yadi bhāvānāṃ sad-bhāvam anupaśyasi /
ahetu-pratyayān bhāvāṃś tvam evaṃ sati paśyasi //16//

You will thereby undermine cause, effect, the doer, the means, the act of doing, origination, destruction, and the attainments.

kāryaṃ ca kāraṇaṃ caiva kartāraṃ karaṇaṃ kriyām /
utpādaṃ ca nirodhaṃ ca phalaṃ ca pratibādhase //17//

We say that dependent co-origination (pratītya-samutpāda) is emptiness (śūnyatā). That (sā) is a conventional, dependent designation. That (sā) alone is the middle path.

yaḥ pratītya-samutpādaḥ śūnyatāṃ tāṃ pracakṣmahe /
sā prajñaptir upādāya pratipat saiva madhyamā //18//

Since there can be no entity (dharma) that originates independently of its causes and conditions (apratītya), there is no entity whatever that is non-empty (aśūnya).

apratītya samutpanno dharmaḥ kaścin na vidyate /
yasmāt tasmād aśūnyo hi dharmaḥ kaścin na vidyate //19//

If all this were non-empty (aśūnya), there could be no (nāsti) origination or destruction. It follows that for you the four-fold Āryan truths are non-existent (abhāva).

yady aśūnyam idaṃ sarvam udayo nāsti na vyayaḥ /
caturṇām ārya-satyānām abhāvas te prasajyate //20//

If things originated independently of causes and conditions, how could there be suffering? For impermanence is said to be suffering, and impermanence does not exist (na vidyate) in what has self-nature.

> apratītya samutpannaṃ kuto duḥkhaṃ bhaviṣyati /
> anityam uktaṃ duḥkhaṃ hi tat svābhāvye na vidyate //21//

How could that which exists with respect to self-nature originate again? Therefore there is no origination for anything that is contrary to emptiness (śūnyatā).

> svabhāvāto vidyamānaṃ kiṃ punaḥ samudeṣyate /
> tasmāt samudayo nāsti śūnyatāṃ pratibādhataḥ //22//

There is no destruction for a suffering that exists by self-nature. Therefore, by adhering to self-nature you deny destruction.

> na nirodhaḥ svabhāvena sato duḥkhasya vidyate /
> svabhāva-paryavasthānān nirodhaṃ pratibādhase //23//

It is impossible to practice a path (mārga) that exists by possessing self-nature. Conversely, if that path is practised, it cannot possess self-nature.

> svābhāvye sati mārgasya bhāvanā nopapadyate /
> athāsau bhāvyate mārgaḥ svābhāvyaṃ te na vidyate //24//

When suffering, origination and destruction do not exist, how can one maintain that there is a path that leads to the extinction of suffering?

> yadā duḥkhaṃ samudayo nirodhaś ca na vidyate /
> mārgo duḥkha-nirodhatvāt katamaḥ prāpayiṣyati //25//

How could an imperfect knowledge of self-nature become perfect knowledge? For indeed self-nature is unchanging.

svabhāvenāparijñānaṃ yadi tasya punaḥ katham /
parijñānaṃ nanu kila svabhāvaḥ samavasthitaḥ //26//

On your view, relinquishing, realization, right practice, full knowledge and the four fruits make no sense.

prahāṇa-sākṣāt-karaṇe bhāvanā caivam eva te /
parijñāvan na yujyante catvāry api phalāni ca //27//

How could an adherent of the idea of self-nature, who has failed to grasp an object in its self-nature, attain it later?

svabhāvenānadhigataṃ yat phalaṃ tat punaḥ katham /
śakyaṃ samadhigantuṃ syāt svabhāvaṃ parigṛhṇataḥ //28//

Since attainment is non-existent (abhāve), there is neither one who abides in attainment nor one who strives for it. If the eight great personages do not exist, then the saṃgha does not exist either.

phalābhāve phala-sthā no na santi pratipannakāḥ /
saṃgho nāsti na cet santi te 'ṣṭau puruṣa-pudgalāḥ //29//

Since the four Āryan truths do not exist (abhāvāt), the Buddhist truth (Dharma) does not exist either (api na vidyate). If neither the Buddhist truth (Dharma) nor the Buddhist order (saṃgha) exists, how can there be a Buddha?

abhāvāc cārya-satyānāṃ sad-dharmo 'pi na vidyate /
dharme cāsati saṃghe ca kathaṃ buddho bhaviṣyati //30//

For you, the unacceptable result follows that the one who is enlightened (Buddha) is unrelated to enlightenment (bodhi). Likewise, it follows that for you enlightenment is unrelated to the one who is enlightened.

apratītyāpi bodhiṃ ca tava buddhaḥ prasajyate /
apratītyāpi buddhaṃ ca tava bodhiḥ prasajyate //31//

For you, anyone who is a non-Buddha by self-nature could never attain enlightenment (bodhi), even if he were to strive for it by following the path of the Bodhisattva.

> yaś cābuddhaḥ svabhāvena sa bodhāya ghaṭann api /
> na bodhisattva-caryāyāṃ bodhiṃ te 'dhigamiṣyati //32//

No one could do anything that was good (dharma) or bad (adharma). What can be done if things are non-empty? For indeed self-nature cannot be an object of activity.

> na ca dharmam adharmaṃ vā kaścij jātu kariṣyati /
> kim aśūnyasya kartavyaṃ svabhāvaḥ kriyate na hi //33//

According to you, the consequences of an action (phala) exist independently of good and bad acts. And for you, the consequences that are caused by good and bad actions do not exist (na vidyate).

> vinā dharmam adharmaṃ ca phalaṃ hi tava vidyate /
> dharmādharma-nimittaṃ ca phalaṃ tava na vidyate //34//

If for you the consequences of action based on good and bad actions do exist (vidyate), how could those consequences, arising as they do from good and bad actions, be non-empty (aśūnya)?

> dharmādharma-nimittaṃ vā yadi te vidyate phalam /
> dharmādharma-samutpannam aśūnyaṃ te kathaṃ phalam //35//

In nullifying the empiness (śūnyatā) of dependent co-origination, you nullify all the things and practices of the ordinary world.

> sarva-saṃvyavahārāṃś ca laukikān pratibādhase /
> yat pratītya-samutpāda-śūnyatāṃ pratibādhase //36//

For the one who denies emptiness (śūnyatā), there will be no object of activity and no commencement of action; and those who do nothing will be turned into agents.

> na kartavyaṃ bhavet kiṃcid anārabdhā bhavet kriyā /
> kārakaḥ syād akurvāṇaḥ śūnyatāṃ pratibādhataḥ //37//

If there were self-nature, the world (jagat) would be unoriginated, undestroyed, immutable and devoid (rahita) of the varied conditions of things.

> ajātam-aniruddhaṃ ca kūṭasthaṃ ca bhaviṣyati /
> vicitrābhir-avasthābhiḥ svabhāve rahitaṃ jagat //38//

If everything is non-empty (aśūnya), then there is no abandonment of the defilements, no action to abolish suffering, and no attainment of that which is not already attained.

> asaṃprāptasya ca prāptir duḥkha-paryanta-karma ca /
> sarva-kleśa-prahāṇaṃ ca yady aśūnyaṃ na vidyate //39//

Whoever sees dependent co-origination sees suffering, the origin of suffering, the extinction of suffering and the path leading to the extinction of suffering.

> yaḥ pratītya-samutpādaṃ paśyatīdaṃ sa paśyati /
> duḥkhaṃ samudayaṃ caiva nirodhaṃ mārgam eva ca //40//

MMK 25: The Examination of Nirvāṇa

nirvāṇa-parīkṣā

[The opponent]:

If everything were empty (śūnya), there would be neither origination nor destruction. What then, could one relinquish or destroy in order to seek nirvāṇa?

> yadi śūnyam idaṃ sarvam udayo nāsti na vyayaḥ /
> prahāṇād vā nirodhād vā kasya nirvāṇam iṣyate //1//

***

[Nāgārjuna]:

If everything were non-empty (aśūnya), there would be neither origination nor destruction. What then, could one relinquish or destroy in order to seek nirvāṇa?

> yady aśūnyam idaṃ sarvam udayo nāsti na vyayaḥ /
> prahāṇād vā nirodhād vā kasya nirvāṇam iṣyate //2//

What is not abandoned, not attained, not cut off, not eternal, not destroyed, not originated: this is called nirvāṇa.

> aprahīṇam asaṃprāptam anucchinnam aśāśvatam /
> aniruddham anutpannam etan nirvāṇam ucyate //3//

Nirvāṇa is not an existent thing (bhāva), because if it were it would be subject to old age and death. For indeed there is no existent thing that is free from old age and death.

> bhāvas tāvan na nirvāṇam jarā-maraṇa-lakṣaṇam /
> prasajyetāsti bhāvo hi na jarā-maraṇāṃ vinā //4//

If nirvāṇa were an existent thing it would be conditioned (saṃskṛta). For there is no existent at any place or at any time that is unconditioned.

bhāvaś ca yadi nirvāṇaṃ nirvāṇaṃ saṃskṛtaṃ bhavet /
nāsaṃskṛto hi vidyate bhāvaḥ kvacana kaścana // 5//

If nirvāṇa were an existent, how could it be non-dependent (anupādāya)? For there is no existent whatsoever that is not dependent.

bhāvaś ca yadi nirvāṇam anupādāya tat katham /
nirvāṇaṃ nānupādāya kaścid bhāvo hi vidyate //6//

If nirvāṇa is not an existent thing (bhāva), how could it be a non-existent thing (abhāva)? Wherever there is no existence (bhāva), there is no non-existence (abhāva) either.

bhāvo yadi na nirvāṇam abhāvaḥ kiṃ bhaviṣyati /
nirvāṇaṃ yatra bhāvo na nābhāvas tatra vidyate //7//

If nirvāṇa were a non-existent (abhāva), how could it be non-dependent? For indeed there is no non-existent thing that is not dependent.

yady abhāvaś ca nirvāṇam anupādāya tat katham /
nirvāṇaṃ na hy abhāvo 'sti yo 'nupādāya vidyate //8//

The cycle of birth and death (ājavaṃjavībhāva) is dependent (upādāya) and relative (pratītya). That which is non-dependent and non-relative is said to be nirvāṇa.

ya ājavaṃjavībhāva upādāya pratītya vā /
so 'pratītyānupādāya nirvāṇam upadiśyate //9//

The Buddha has taught the abandonment of being (bhāva) and non-being (abhāva). Thus it makes sense to say: "Nirvāṇa is not being, not non-being."

prahāṇaṃ cābravīc chāstā bhavasya vibhavasya ca /
tasmān na bhāvo nābhāvo nirvāṇam iti yujyate //10//

If nirvāṇa were both being (bhāva) and non-being (abhāva), then liberation would be both. And that does not make any sense (na yujyate).

> bhaved abhāvo bhāvaś ca nirvāṇam ubhayaṃ yadi /
> bhaved abhāvo bhāvaś ca mokṣas tac ca na yujyate //11//

If nirvāṇa were both being and non-being, then nirvāṇa would not be non-dependent. For both being and non-being are dependent.

> bhaved abhāvo bhāvaś ca nirvāṇam ubhayaṃ yadi /
> nānupādāya nirvāṇam upādāyobhayaṃ hi tat //12//

How could nirvāṇa be both being and non-being? Nirvāṇa is unconditioned (asaṃskṛta), whereas being and non-being are both conditioned.

> bhaved abhāvo bhāvaś ca nirvāṇam ubhayaṃ katham /
> asaṃskṛtaṃ ca nirvāṇaṃ bhāvābhāvau ca saṃskṛtau //13//

How could nirvāṇa be both being and non-being? Both cannot be in the same place, just as light and darkness cannot be in the same place.

> bhaved abhāvo bhāvaś ca nirvāṇa ubhayaṃ katham /
> tayor abhāvo hy ekatra prakāśa-tamasor iva //14//

The proposition: "Nirvāṇa is neither being nor non-being" would only be established if being and non-being could be established.

> naivābhāvo naiva bhāvo nirvāṇam iti yā 'ñjanā /
> abhāve caiva bhāve ca sā siddhe sati sidhyati //15//

If nirvāṇa were neither being nor non-being, who could declare it to be so?

naivābhāvo naiva bhāvo nirvāṇaṃ yadi vidyate /
naivābhāvo naiva bhāva iti kena tad ajyate //16//

Of the Blessed One it cannot be said (nājyate) that he exists after his final cessation (nirodha); that he doesn't; that he both does and doesn't; that he neither does nor doesn't.

paraṃ nirodhād bhagavān bhavatīty eva nājyate /
na bhavaty ubhayaṃ ceti nobhayaṃ ceti nājyate //17//

Likewise, of the Blessed One while he is living it cannot be said (nājyate) that he exists; that he does not exist; that he both exists and does not exist; that he neither exists nor does not exist.

tiṣṭhamāno 'pi bhagavān bhavatīty eva nājyate /
na bhavaty ubhayaṃ ceti nobhayaṃ ceti nājyate //18//

Saṃsāra is not different at all from nirvāṇa. Nirvāṇa is not different at all from saṃsāra.

na saṃsārasya nirvāṇāt kiṃcid asti viśeṣaṇam /
na nirvāṇasya saṃsārāt kiṃcid asti viśeṣaṇam //19//

The limit (koṭi) of nirvāṇa is the limit of saṃsāra also. Between them there is not the slightest difference whatever.

nirvāṇasya ca yā koṭiḥ koṭiḥ saṃsāraṇasya ca /
na tayor antaraṃ kiṃcit susūkṣmam api vidyate //20//

The speculative views (dṛṣṭi) that hold that after the final cessation (nirodha) things come to an end etc., as well as the views that hold that after the final cessation things continue eternally, are based on thinking of nirvāṇa in terms of posterior and anterior states.

paraṃ nirodhād antādyāḥ śāśvatādyāś ca dṛṣṭayaḥ /
nirvāṇam aparāntaṃ ca pūrvāntaṃ ca samāśritāḥ //21//

Since all dharmas are void (śūnya), what could be infinite? what could be finite? what could be both finite and infinite? what could be neither finite nor infinite?

> śūnyeṣu sarva-dharmeṣu kim anantaṃ kim antavat /
> kim anantam antavac ca nānantaṃ nāntavac ca kim //22//

What could be identical? what could be different? what could be permanent? what could be impermanent? what could be both permanent and impermanent? what could be neither permanent nor impermanent?

> kiṃ tad eva kim anyat kiṃ śāśvataṃ kim aśāśvatam /
> aśāśvataṃ śāśvataṃ ca kiṃ vā nobhayam apy atha //23//

All perceptions (upalambha) and all thoughts and words (prapañca) are quiescent (upaśama) and tranquil (śiva). No dharma whatever was taught at any time to anyone by the Buddha.

> sarvopalambhopaśamaḥ prapañcopaśamaḥ śivaḥ /
> na kvacit kasyacit kaścid dharmo buddhena deśitaḥ //24//

Overturning the Objections

Vigraha-vyāvartanī

Kārikās 1-20 present the opponent's objections to the statement (found in VV 1ab) that things entirely lack a self nature. Kārikās 21-70 contain the reply to the opponent.

[The opponent]:

If the self-nature (svabhāva) of all things is not to be found anywhere, your statement (vacana), which is without self-nature (asvabhāva), is unable to negate self-nature.

sarveṣāṃ bhāvānāṃ sarvatra na vidyate svabhāvaś-cet /
tvad-vacanam-asvabhāvaṃ na nivartayituṃ svabhāvam-alam //1//

Now if your statement (vākya) possesses a self-nature, then your previous proposition (pūrvā pratijñā) is destroyed. There is a logical defect here, unless you can state the difference between the two cases.

atha sasvabhāvam-etad-vākyaṃ pūrvā hatā pratijñā te /
vaiṣamikatvaṃ tasmin viśeṣa-hetuś-ca vaktavyaḥ //2//

If you say that your negation would be like saying "Do not make a sound," this would not be tenable, for in the case of saying "Do not make a sound" an existing sound now is used to prevent a sound in the future.

mā śabdavad-ity-etat-syāt-te buddhir-na caitad-upapannam /
śabdena hy-atra satā bhaviṣyato vāraṇaṃ tasya //3//

If you were to say that my negation of your negation is subject to the same fault, that also would be incorrect (asat). It is your proposition (pratijñā) which is subject to error with respect to this characteristic, not mine.

pratiṣedha-pratiṣedho 'py evam-iti mataṃ bhavet-tad-asad-
eva /
evaṃ tava pratijñā lakṣaṇato dūṣyate na mama //4//

Now if you say that you deny real things after having perceived them, we reply that according to you there is no perception (pratyakṣa) by which real things (bhāva) are apprehended.

pratyakṣeṇa hi tāvad-yady-upalabhya vinivartayasi bhāvān /
tan-nāsti pratyakṣaṃ bhāvā yenopalabhyante //5//

Furthermore, for you inference, verbal testimony and analogical reasoning, as well as the objects to be established by them, are in exactly the same position as perception.

anumānaṃ pratyuktaṃ pratyakṣeṇāgamopamāne ca /
anumānāgama-sādhyā ye 'rthā dṛṣṭānta-sādhyāś-ca //6//

Those who know the modes (avasthā) of things maintain that good things have a good self-nature, and the same distinction holds for everything else.

kuśalānāṃ dharmāṇāṃ dharmāvasthā-vidaś-ca manyante /
kuśalaṃ janāḥ svabhāvaṃ śeṣeṣv-apy-eṣa viniyogaḥ //7//

Things that lead to liberation (nairyāṇika) have the self-nature of leading to liberation. Similarly, things which do not lead to liberation, and things which have been spoken of in connection with the various states of things, have the self-nature of not leading to liberation.

nairyāṇika-svabhāvo dharmā nairyāṇikāś-ca ye teṣām /
dharmāvasthoktānām-evam-anairyāṇikādīnām //8//

If there were no self-nature of things (dharmas), then even the name "non-self-nature" (niḥsvabhāva) would not exist, for indeed there is no name without an object.

yadi ca na bhavet-svabhāvo dharmāṇāṃ niḥsvabhāva ity-
eva /
nāmāpi bhaven-naivaṃ nāma hi nirvastukaṃ nāsti //9//

Now you might say: there is a self-nature but it is not found in the dharmas. But if there is a self-nature apart from the dharmas, then the thing with which self-nature is connected needs to be specified.

atha vidyate svabhāvaḥ sa ca dharmāṇāṃ na vidyate tasmāt/
dharmair-vinā svabhāvaḥ sa yasya tad-yuktam-upadeṣṭum
//10//

There can be a negation (pratiṣedha) only of something that exists (sat), as in "There is no pot in the house." Thus, your negation must the negation of an existent self-nature.

sata eva pratiṣedho nāsti ghaṭo geha ity-ayaṃ yasmāt /
dṛṣṭaḥ pratiṣedho 'yam sataḥ svabhāvasya te tasmāt //11//

If that self-nature does not exist, what then do you negate by your statement that there is no self-nature? The negation of a non-existent entity (asataḥ) is established without words.

atha nāsti sa svabhāvaḥ kiṃ nu pratiṣidhyate tvayānena /
vacanenarte vacanāt-pratiṣedhaḥ sidhyate hy-asataḥ //12//

Perhaps you will say: "Just as a ignorant people mistake a mirage to be water, so it is when I negate a false perception of a non-entity."

bālānām-iva mithyā mṛga-tṛṣṇāyāṃ yathā-jala-grāhaḥ /
evaṃ mithyā-grāhaḥ syāt-te pratiṣedhyato hy-asataḥ //13//

But if this were the case, then there would be an aggregate of the following six things: perception (grāha), the object that is perceived (grāhya), and the perceiver (grahītṛ) of that object; also the negation (pratiṣedha), the thing that is negated, and the one who negates (pratiṣeddhṛ).

> nanv-evaṃ saty-asti grāho grāhyaṃ ca tad-grahītā ca /
> pratiṣedhaḥ pratiṣedhyaṃ pratiṣeddhā ceti ṣaṭkaṃ tat //14//

Now if there is no perception, no perceived object and no perceiver, there can be no negation, no thing that is negated, and no one to negate.

> atha naivāsti grāho naiva grāhyaṃ na ca grahītāraḥ /
> pratiṣedhaḥ pratiṣedhyaṃ pratiṣed-dhāro nanu na santi //15//

If there is no negation, nothing that is negated, and no negator, then all things are established, as well as their self-nature.

> pratiṣedhaḥ pratiṣedhyaṃ pratiṣed-dhāraś-ca yady-uta na santi /
> siddhā hi sarva-bhāvās-teṣām-eva svabhāvaś-ca //16//

You have not established a reason (hetu) for your statement. How, indeed, could you provide a reason, since according to you everything is devoid of self-nature (naiḥsvabhāvyāt)? And since it has no reason, there can be no proof (siddhi) of your statement (artha).

> hetoś-ca te na siddhir-naiḥsvabhāvyāt kuto hi te hetuḥ /
> nirhetukasya siddhir-na copapannāsya te 'rthasya //17//

If your statement negating self-nature can be established in the absence of a reason, then my assertion that there is a self-nature can be established in the same way.

> yadi cāhetoḥ siddhiḥ svabhāva-vinivartanasya te bhavati /
> svabhāvyasyāstitvaṃ mamāpi nirhetukaṃ siddham //18//

Nor would it be tenable for you to say that the very absence of the self-nature of things (bhāvāsvābhāvya) is the existence of the reason, for there is nothing (na bhāvaḥ) in the world that is devoid of self-nature (niḥsvabhāvaḥ).

> atha hetor-astitvaṃ bhāvāsvābhāvyam-ity-anupapannam /
> lokeṣu niḥsvabhāvo na hi kaścana vidyate bhāvaḥ //19//

Nor would it be possible for you to hold that the negation comes first and that the thing that is negated comes later. Nor is it possible that the negation comes after the thing that is negated, nor can it be simultaneous with it. Self-nature, therefore, does exist (sat).

> pūrvaṃ cet-pratiṣedhaḥ paścāt-pratiṣedhyam-ity-anupapannam /
> pascāc-cānupapanno yugapac-ca yataḥ svabhāvaḥ san //20//

***

[Nāgārjuna]:

If my statement (vacas) exists neither within nor without the combination of causes and conditions, then the emptiness (śūnyatva) of things is established, because in that case things would lack a self-nature (bhāvānām-asvabhāvatvāt).

> hetu-pratyaya-sāmagryāṃ ca pṛthak cāpi mad-vaco na yadi/
> nanu śūnyatvaṃ siddhaṃ bhāvānām-asvabhāvatvāt //21//

The dependent existence (pratītya-bhāva) of things is what is called emptiness (śūnyatā). This dependent existence (pratītya-bhāva) is, indeed, the same thing as its lack of self-nature (asvabhāva).

> yaś-ca pratītya-bhāvo bhāvānāṃ śūnyateti sā proktā /
> yaś-ca pratītya-bhāvo bhavati hi tasyāsvabhāvatvam //22//

Just as an artificially created person (nirmitaka) might negate (pratiṣedhayeta) another artificially created person, or a magical person might negate another magical person created by his own magic, so it is in the case of my negation (pratiṣedha).

> nirmitako nirmitakaṃ māyā-puruṣaḥ svamāyayā sṛṣṭam /
> pratiṣedhayeta yadvat pratiṣedho 'yaṃ tathaiva syāt //23//

This statement (vākya) has no self-nature; therefore, there is no harm to my statement (vāda), nor any defect, nor any special difference which needs to be accounted for.

> na svābhāvikam-etad-vākyaṃ tasmān-na vāda-hānir-me /
> nāsti ca vaiṣamikatvaṃ viśeṣa-hetuś-ca na nigadyaḥ //24//

The example (dṛṣṭānta) given by you: "It is like 'Do not make a sound'," is not appropriate. In that example a sound is prevented by another sound, but with my statement the matter is otherwise (naivam-evaitat).

> mā śabdavad-iti nāyaṃ dṛṣṭānto yas-tvayā samārabdhaḥ /
> śabdena tac-ca śabdasya vāraṇaṃ naivam-evaitat //25//

If things devoid of a self-nature were prevented by other things devoid of a self-nature, then self-nature could be established by the cessation (nivṛtti) of the lack of self-nature.

> naiḥsvābhāvyānāṃ cen-naiḥsvābhāvyena vāraṇam yadi hi /
> naiḥsvābhāvya-nivṛttau svābhāvyaṃ hi prasiddhaṃ syāt //26//

My statement could be compared to a phantom (nirmitaka) which destroys a man's false apprehension (asad-grāha) of a phantom woman that: "This is a woman."

> atha-vā nirmitakāyāṃ yathā striyāṃ strīyam-ity-asad-grāham /
> nirmitakaḥ pratihanyāt kasyacid-evaṃ bhaved-etat //27//

Now this reason (hetu) is similar to the thing that is to be proved (sādhya), for indeed sound does not exist (na hi vidyate sattā). But we do not speak without accepting the conventional truth (saṃvyavahāra).

> atha-vā sādhya-samo 'yaṃ hetur-na hi vidyate dhvaneḥ sattā /
> saṃvyavahāraṃ ca vayaṃ nānabhyupagamya kathayāmaḥ //28//

If I had any proposition (pratijñā), this defect (doṣa) would attach to me. But I have no proposition. Therefore I am not at fault (naivāsti me doṣaḥ).

> yadi kācana pratijñā syān-me tata eṣa me bhaved-doṣaḥ /
> nāsti ca mama pratijñā tasmān-naivāsti me doṣaḥ //29//

If I apprehended anything through perception (pratyakṣa), then I would either affirm or deny. But there is no such thing. Hence there is no fault (upālambha).

> yadi kiṃcid-upalabheyaṃ pravartayeyaṃ nivartayeyaṃ vā /
> pratyakṣādibhir-arthais-tad-abhāvān-me'nupālambhaḥ//30//

If, according to you, objects (artha) are established (prasiddhi) through the means of knowledge (pramāṇas), then tell me: How are the pramāṇas established?

> yadi ca pramāṇatas-te teṣāṃ teṣāṃ prasiddhir-arthānām /
> teṣāṃ punaḥ prasiddhiṃ brūhi kathaṃ te pramāṇānām //31//

If you say that the pramāṇas are established through other pramāṇas, there would result an infinite regress (anavasthā). In that case neither the beginning nor the middle nor the end could be established.

anyair-yadi pramāṇaiḥ pramāṇa-siddhir-bhavet-tad-anavasthā/
nādeḥ siddhis-tatrāsti naiva madhyasya nāntasya //32//

Now if you say that the pramāṇas are established without pramāṇas, you abandon your position. This is a fault, and you need to explain the reason for the difference, i.e., why objects are established by pramāṇas but the pramāṇas themselves are not.

teṣām-atha pramāṇair-vinā prasiddhir-vihīyate vādaḥ /
vaiṣamikatvaṃ tasmin-viśeṣa-hetuś-ca vaktavayaḥ //33//

If you were to say that the pramāṇas themselves are self-established, just as fire illuminates itself as well as other things, this assertion (upanyāsa) would be defective, because fire does not illumine itself. For the non-perception of a fire is not like the non-perception of a pot shrouded in darkness.

viṣamopanyāso 'yaṃ na hy-ātmānaṃ prakāśayaty-agniḥ /
na hi tasyānupalabdhir-dṛṣṭā tamasīva kumbhasya //34//

If, as you say, fire illumines itself as well as other things, then it should be the case that fire burns itself as well as other things.

yadi ca svātmānam-ayaṃ tvad-vacanena prakāśayaty-agniḥ/
param-iva nanv-ātmānaṃ paridhakṣyaty-api hutāśaḥ //35//

If, as you say, fire illumines itself and another self, then it should be the case that darkness (tamas) darkens itself and another self, and this is not the case.

yadi ca svaparātmānau tvad-vacanena prakāśayaty-agniḥ /
pracchādayiṣyati tamaḥ svaparātmānau hutāśa iva //36//

Darkness does not exist in fire nor does it reside in some other thing (parātmani) where there is fire. How, then, can there be illumination (prakāśa)? For illumination is the destruction of darkness.

nāsti tamaś-ca jvalane yatra ca tiṣṭhati parātmani jvalanaḥ /
kurute katham prakāśam sa hi prakāśo 'ndhakāra-vadhaḥ //37//

To say that fire illumines as it comes into existence would be incorrect. For when it is coming into existence fire does not come into contact with darkness.

utpadyamāna eva prakāśayaty-agnir-ity-asad-vādaḥ /
utpadyamāna eva prāpnoti tamo na hi hutāśaḥ //38//

And if fire destroyed darkness without coming into contact with it, then a fire here would destroy darkness everywhere, in all the worlds and all the dhātus.

aprāpto 'pi jvalano yadi vā punar-andhakāram-upahanyāt /
sarveṣu loka-dhātuṣu tamo 'yam-iha saṃsthito hānyat //39//

If the pramāṇas were self-established (svataḥ), then according to you the pramāṇas would be established independently (anapekṣya) of the objects of cognition (prameya), for self-establishment (svataḥ siddhiḥ) is not dependent on anything else.

yadi svataś-ca pramāṇa-siddhir-anapekṣya tava prameyāṇi /
bhavati pramāṇa-siddhir-na parāpekṣā svataḥ siddhiḥ //40//

If, as you say, the pramāṇas are established independently of the objects to be known, then something would be a pramāṇa without being a pramāṇa of anything.

anapekṣya hi prameyān-arthān yadi te pramāṇa-siddhir-iti /
na bhavanti kasyacid-evam-imāni tāni pramāṇāni //41//

And if you were to say: What is the fault in saying that the pramāṇas are established in dependence on something else? the answer is that in that case there would be the establishing (sādhana) of that which has already been established (siddha).

For indeed it is only something that is not already established that stands in need of something else.

atha matam-apekṣya siddhis-teṣām-ity-atra bhavati ko doṣaḥ/
siddhasya sādhanaṃ syān-nāsiddho 'pekṣate hy-anyat //42//

If the pramāṇas were established solely on the basis of the objects to be known, the establishment of the thing to be known would not be dependent (apekṣya) on the pramāṇas.

sidhyanti hi prameyāṇy-apekṣya yadi sarvathā pramāṇāni /
bhavati prameya-siddhir-nāpekṣyaiva pramāṇāni //43//

And if the things to be known are established independently of the pramāṇas, what would be gained by establishing the pramāṇas? For their purpose would already have been established.

yadi ca prameya-siddhir-nāpekṣyaiva bhavati pramāṇāni /
kiṃ te pramāṇa-siddhyā tāni yad-arthaṃ prasiddhaṃ tat //44//

Besides, if you establish the pramāṇas on the basis of the things to be known (prameyas), then the proper order of the pramāṇas and the prameyas would certainly be inverted.

atha tu pramāṇa-siddhir-bhavaty-apekṣyaiva te prameyāṇi /
vyatyaya evaṃ sati te dhruvaṃ pramāṇa-prameyāṇām //45//

But if you say that the prameyas are established through the establishment of the pramāṇas, and also that the pramāṇas are established through the establishment of the prameyas, then for you there would be the establishment of neither.

atha te pramāṇa-siddhyā prameya-siddhiḥ prameya-siddhyā ca /
bhavati pramāṇa-siddhir-nāsty-ubhayasyāpi te siddhiḥ //46//

For if the prameyas are established by the pramāṇas, and if those pramāṇas in turn are to be established by those prameyas, how will the pramāṇas be able to establish anything?

sidhyanti hi pramāṇair-yadi prameyāṇi tāni tair-eva /
sādhyāni ca prameyais-tāni kathaṃ sādhayiṣyanti //47//

And if the pramāṇas are established by the prameyas, and the those prameyas in turn are to be established by those pramāṇas, how will the prameyas be able to establish anything?

sidhyanti ca prameyair-yadi pramāṇāni tāni tair-eva /
sādhyāni ca pramāṇais-tāni kathaṃ sādhayiṣyanti //48//

If the son is to be produced by the father, and if the father in turn is to be produced by the son, tell me: who, then, produces whom?

pitrā yady-utpādyaḥ putro yadi tena caiva putreṇa /
utpādyaḥ sa yadi pitā vada tatrotpādayati kaḥ kam //49//

Tell me: who is then the father, and who the son? for in that case each would bear the marks of both father and son. This produces perplexity (saṃdeha) in us.

kaś-ca pitā kaḥ putras-tatra tvaṃ brūhi tāv-ubhāv-api ca /
pitṛ-putra-lakṣaṇa-dharau yato bhavati no 'tra saṃdehaḥ //50//

The pramāṇas are not established by themselves alone, nor by each other, nor by other pramāṇas [i.e., other perceptions, other inferences, other analogical reasonings etc.], nor by the prameyas, nor are they established even though they have no basis (akasmāt).

naiva svataḥ prasiddhir-na paras-parataḥ para-pramāṇair-vā/
na bhavati na ca prameyair-na cāpy-akasmāt pramāṇānām //51//

If those who know the modes (avasthās) of things say that good things have a good self-nature, then that should be explained for each case.

> kuśalānāṃ dharmānāṃ dharmāvasthāvido bruvanti yadi /
> kuśalaṃ svabhāvam-evaṃ pravibhāgenābhidheyaḥ syāt //52//

Furthermore, if that good self-nature of things originated dependently (pratītya utpadyate), it would be an "other nature" (para-bhāva) of the good things. How, then, could it be a self-nature?

> yadi ca pratītya kuśalaḥ svabhāva utpadyate sa kuśalānām /
> dharmāṇāṃ para-bhāvaḥ svabhāva evaṃ kathaṃ bhavati //53//

Now if you were to say that that the good self-nature of good things originates without depending on anything (na pratītya kiṃcit), then there would be no dwelling in the religious way of life (brahma-carya).

> atha na pratītya kiṃcit-svabhāva utpadyate sa kuśalānām /
> dharmāṇām-evaṃ syād-vāso na brahma-caryasya //54//

There would be neither merit (dharma) nor demerit (adharma), nor the mundane, worldly practices. All things, being endowed with self-nature (sasvabhāva), would be permanent (nitya), and being permanent they would be causeless (ahetu).

> nādharmo dharmo vā saṃvyavahārāś-ca laukikā na syuḥ /
> nityāś-ca sasvabhāvāḥ syur-nityatvād-ahetu-mataḥ //55//

The same defect would apply to bad things, indeterminate things, those things that lead to liberation, etc. Thus for you all the conditioned things would be unconditioned.

evam-akuśaleṣv-avyākṛteṣu nairyāṇikādiṣu ca doṣaḥ /
tasmāt-sarvaṃ saṃskṛtam-asaṃskṛtaṃ te bhavaty-eva //56//

Anyone who holds that names are real (sad-bhūta) is subject to the rejoinder that in that case there is self-nature (sasvabhāva). But that is not our position.

yaḥ sad-bhūtaṃ nāmātra brūyāt-sasvabhāva ity-evam /
bhavatā prativaktavyo nāma brūmaś-ca na vayaṃ tat //57//

Does the name "non-existent" (nāmāsad-iti) designate something existent (sat) or non-existent (asat)? In either case your statement is abandoned.

nāmāsad-iti ca yad-idaṃ tat-kiṃ nu sato bhavaty-utāpy-asataḥ /
yadi hi sato yady-asato dvidhāpi te hīyate vādaḥ //58//

We have already declared the emptiness (śūnyatva) of all things. Hence your criticism is directed against a non-proposition (apratijñā).

sarveṣāṃ bhāvānāṃ śūnyatvaṃ copapāditaṃ pūrvam /
sa upālambhas-tasmād-bhavaty-ayaṃ cāpratijñāyāḥ //59//

As for the statement: "There is a self-nature, but not one that belongs to things" (dharmāṇāṃ na vidyate); that doubt raised by you can be dismissed as it does not apply to us.

atha vidyate svabhāvaḥ sa ca dharmāṇāṃ na vidyata itīdam/
āśaṅkitaṃ yad-uktaṃ bhavaty-anāśaṅkitaṃ tac-ca //60//

As a matter of fact (nanu), emptiness (śūnyatva) would be established if it were the case that negation only applies to an existent thing (sataḥ), for you deny the lack of self-nature (niḥsvabhāvatva) of things.

> sata eva pratiṣedho yadi śūnyatvaṃ nanu prasiddham idam/
> pratiṣedhayate hi bhavān bhāvānāṃ niḥsvabhāvatvam //61//

On the other hand, if you negate (pratiṣedhayase) emptiness (śūnyatva) and that emptiness does not exist, then you abandon the proposition that negation is only of an existent (sataḥ).

> pratiṣedhayase 'tha tvaṃ śūnyatvaṃ tac-ca nāsti śūnyatvam/
> pratiṣedhaḥ sata iti te nanv-eṣa vihīyate vādaḥ //62//

I do not negate anything (kiṃcit), nor is there anything (kiṃcit) to be negated. Hence you malign me and misrepresent me when you say that I negate anything.

> pratiṣedhayāmi nāhaṃ kiṃcit pratiṣedhyam-asti na ca kiṃcit/
> tasmāt-pratiṣedhayasīty-adhilaya eṣa tvayā kriyate //63//

Regarding your assertion that a statement of the negation of a non-existent entity (asataḥ) is established without words, we observe: There the statement (vāk) makes it known (jñāpayate) as non-existent, it does not deny it (pratinihanti).

> yac-cāharte vacanād-asataḥ pratiṣedha-vacana-siddhir-iti /
> atra jñāpayate vāg-asad-iti tan-na pratinihanti //64//

As for the momentous inquiry (mahāṃś-carcaḥ) you have raised in connection with the example of the mirage: listen to the verdict (nirṇaya) on that matter and observe in what way that example is appropriate.

> mṛga-tṛṣṇā-dṛṣṭānte yaḥ punar-uktas tvayā mahāṃś-carcaḥ/
> tatrāpi nirṇayam śṛṇu yathā sa dṛṣṭānta upapannaḥ //65//

If perception (grāha) of the mirage were by its self-nature, then it would not exist dependently. But that perception which does exist dependently is nothing but emptiness (śūnyatā).

sa yadi svabhāvataḥ syād grāho na syāt-pratītya saṃbhūtaḥ/
yaś-ca pratītya bhavati grāho nanu śūnyatā saiva //66//

If that perception of the mirage were by its self-nature, who would be able to remove it (nivartayet)? The same rule (vidhi) would apply to the rest of the cases as well. Hence the point you raised is no criticism at all.

yadi ca svabhāvataḥ syād grāhaḥ kas-taṃ nivartayed grāham/
śeṣeṣv-apy-eṣa vidhis-tasmād-eṣo 'nupālambhaḥ //67//

Because the two cases are the same, the assertion we have just made about the rule rejecting the example of the mirage disposes of your previous objection about the absence of a reason (hetv-abhāva).

etena hetv-abhāvaḥ pratyuktaḥ pūrvam-eva sa samatvāt /
mṛga-tṛṣṇā-dṛṣṭānta-vyāvṛtti-vidhau ya uktaḥ prāk //68//

In virtue of the fact that the two cases are the same, we have also answered your previous objection about the reason for negation in the three times [cf. VV 20]. And a counter-reason (pratihetu) is thereby obtained for the adherents of emptiness (śūnyatā-vādinaḥ).

yas-traikālye hetuḥ pratyuktaḥ pūrvam-eva sa samatvāt /
traikālya-pratihetuś-ca śūnyatā-vādināṃ prāptaḥ //69//

All things prevail for the one for whom this śūnyatā prevails. Nothing prevails for the one for whom śūnyatā does not prevail.

prabhavati ca śūnyateyaṃ yasya prabhavanti tasya sarvārthāḥ /
prabhavati na tasya kiṃcin-na prabhavati śūnyatā yasya //70//

I adore that incomparable Buddha who taught the equivalence (ekārtha) of emptiness (śūnyatā), dependent co-origination (pratītya-samutpāda) and the middle path (madhyamāṃ pratipadam).

yaḥ śūnyatāṃ pratītya-samutpādaṃ madhyamāṃ pratipadaṃ ca /
ekārthāṃ nijagāda praṇamāmi tam-apratima-buddham//

iti kṛtir-iyam-ācārya-nāgārjuna-pādānām //

NOTES

EPIGRAPH

P. Heath, *The Philosopher's Alice*, pp. 200-201.

NOTES TO CHAPTER I: INTRODUCTION

1. For references to some of the Indian sources on this question, see H. Narain (1963: 312-313, ns. 8-13). I am, incidentally, greatly indebted to Narain's paper, which so far as I know was the first work to criticize what was at that time the newly fashionable non-nihilist interpretation of the Madhyamaka. The present work is essentially an extension of Narain's paper, adding new arguments and new textual evidence to it.

According to de Jong (1972a: 7), Burnouf's interpretation of the Madhyamaka as a nihilistic scholasticism was accepted by most scholars in the West in the second half of the nineteenth century and in the beginning of the twentieth century. On this point, see also de Jong (1987).

For the references to Burnouf, Jacobi, Walleser, Wach and Keith, see Stcherbatsky (CBN 42-43). Poussin's views have been cited from his early articles in the ERE. At the very end of his life, Poussin abandoned the non-nihilist interpretation. His reasons for doing so are examined critically below (v. infra, pp. 241-252).

Toward the end of his life (1934, 1936), Stcherbatsky criticized Schayer and repudiated his own previous contention that the Mādhyamikas believed in an Absolute. On this point, ironically, he seems to have switched positions with his arch-rival in Buddhology, L. de La Vallée Poussin (cf. Poussin 1938: 148).

2. Dasgupta (1962: xiii-xiv, 76-78; 152-154; 188; 191; 197).

3. Cf. PVBh III.327ab (Prajñākaragupta): "Perceptions are of themselves alone and not of some other thing" (ātmā sa tasyānubhavaḥ sa ca nānyasya kasya cit).

4. Cf. Stcherbatsky (CBN 44).

NOTES TO CHAPTER II: THE ORIGINS OF MĀDHYAMIKA THOUGHT

1. The following are some of the more important passages in the Pāli canon where the "catuṣkoṭi" appears (references are to the PTS editions): DN i.191, MN i.426, MN i.484-5, SN iii.257, SN v.437 and AN ii.41.

2. "§" refers to the subsection rather than the page number of EBThK.

3. According to Jayatilleke (EBThK §481), the questions which were set aside were distinguished by the formula "mā h'evam," whereas other kinds of rejected questions were distinguished by the formula "no h'idam." It turns out, however, that on Jayatilleke's view this is still a distinction between two different kinds of negation, rather than a distinction between negation and some other way of responding to a given proposition.

According to Jayatilleke, negating a thesis or question by setting it aside is different from other kinds of negations, because it implies that the proposition in question is of a very special kind. What this is will be explained shortly.

4. Cf. EBThK §469: "The next kind of question mentioned, the ṭhapanīya-, is interesting in so far as it seems to have a modern parallel in the kind of question which the Positivist dismisses as meaningless and unanswerable."

5. Note that the interlocutors of the Buddha do not ask him to *describe* the state of the Tathāgata after his physical death: they simply ask him whether or not he *exists* then. Had they been given an affirmative answer to the question that they *did* ask, they might well have been inclined to go on to ask the Buddha to *describe* the Tathāgata's post-mortem state, but in any case they were precluded from doing so by what the Buddha said in reply to questions about the *existence* of the Tathāgata after his parinibbāna.

6. Here, as in most other places in the text, I have used the PTS translations—in this case, by I. B. Horner (§72, p. 162-167).

In a footnote to this passage, Horner says: "Since the Tathāgata knows and comprehends, he does not hold any speculative view ... In this paragraph I have mostly translated *diṭṭhi* as view, but speculative view is meant." This seems right, not only (as Horner says) because the Buddha knows and comprehends, but also because in the suttas—including this one—a teaching is actually given, i.e., the anattā/dhamma theory.

7. The Buddha says that his is a superior and subtle teaching that cannot be attained by mere cleverness of intelligence or logic or dialectic. Nevertheless, it is still a *teaching*. Furthermore, it is clear that the teaching in question is the anattā/dhamma theory, for this part of the reply to Vacchagotta comes immediately after the passage that refers to this theory. Moreover, the passage is *followed* by an analogy (dṛṣṭānta) which unmistakably refers to the same teaching, i.e., the comparison of a person to a fire (P. aggi, Skr. agni).

8. E. Frauwallner (1973: 178-194) interpreted the fire analogy in the AVGS to mean that the fire "...does not pass away when it is extinguished but only becomes imperceptible" (p. 179). According to this interpretation, "the flaming up and extinction of fire means for the Indian of ancient times, not the origination and destruction of fire, but that the already existing fire becomes alternately visible and invisible" (p. 178).

One of the passages Frauwallner cited in support of this interpretation (pp. 375-376, n. 131) was Mahābhārata XII 187, v 2, 5-6, Kumbhakonam edition:

> The Soul which has entered the body does not pass away when the body passes away, just as the fire does not pass away or perish when the fuel is burnt out. When no fuel is brought to feed the fire, the fire is not to be seen although the fire exists because it has entered the ether (ākāśa), has no fixed place or locality and is difficult therefore to be comprehended. So also the soul, when it has departed from the body, has entered the ether and is, therefore, not to be perceived on account of its fineness or subtlety, like the fire without fuel.

I do not think that Frauwallner's interpretation is a tenable one, since the whole purport of the *Buddha's* treatment of the fire analogy, as opposed to the Mahābhārata's, is that the fire is *dependent* on the existence of the fuel, and cannot exist without it. Hence, while the passage from the Mahābhārata does show that fire was understood differently by those who wrote the epics (and no doubt others as well), it is doubtful that the passage can be taken as a reliable guide to the Buddhist teachings. That it cannot be so taken is clearly shown by the fact that the passage from the epic refers to a soul (ātman), the existence of which the AVGS denies, and by the fact that the passage from the epic refers to the concept of an ether or subtle space (ākāśa), which for the most part the Buddhists regarded as a mere absence, rather than a real entity. (For a brief note on ākāśa in Buddhism, see n. 4, p. 355.)

There are, incidentally, numerous passages from the Mahāyānist literature which are clearly incompatible with the kind of interpretation that Frauwallner recommended for the AVGS. One of these is MMK 10.1-1.7, from the agnīndhana-parīkṣā, or investigation of fire and fuel, where Nāgārjuna argues explicitly that fire cannot exist independently of fuel. Cf. MMK 10.1cd:

> If fire were different from fuel then it would exist without fuel

> anyaś ced indhanād agnir indhanād apy ṛte bhavet

where the suggestion that fire could exist without fuel is clearly taken to be *false*. Furthermore, Nāgārjuna's teachings on this point seem to me to have been fully orthodox.

It is true that the AVGS speaks of the Tathāgata as becoming, after his parinirvāṇa, "deep, immeasurable, unfathomable, like the mighty ocean." But even this statement must be understood in the light of the anātman doctrine, according to which the notion of a person or self is an illusion. This illusion persists from lifetime to lifetime in the cycle of saṃsāra, and is only terminated when the Arhat or Buddha "attains" nirvāṇa. Since there never was a self or person, no one is annihilated at this event, and what remains behind is only what there always was, anytime or anywhere, i.e., the true nature of things, the wholly impersonal, universal and all-pervading law of dependent co-origination, which is unfathomable to all but the Buddhas.

If the anātman doctrine is to be taken seriously, the expression "he becomes," as used in the AVGS's description of the Buddha's parinirvāṇa, must be taken as a metaphor, for the true nature of things leaves no room for a self or Buddha either before or after the parinirvāṇa: the Buddha simply "goes out," like an extinguished fire. Provided that it is clearly understood that there is no self or Buddha that can "become" anything, one can say that what remains after the parinirvāṇa—which is nothing more than the total annihilation of an illusion—is the true nature of things (dharmatā).

This is, incidentally, exactly the way that Nāgārjuna will describe the matter some six or seven centuries after the death of the Buddha. Cf. MMK 22.16ab (tathāgata-parīkṣā):

> The self-nature (svabhāva) of the tathāgata [whether before or after the parinirvāṇa] is simply the self-nature of the world (jagat).
>
> tathāgato yat-svabhāvas tat-svabhāvam idaṃ jagat

The only difference between the AVGS and the MMK in this respect is that the latter work expresses the Mādhyamika view that even the dharmas lack self-nature and are illusory. Hence in his commentary on MMK 22.16, Candrakīrti appeals to the Prajñāpāramitā, according to which beings, dharmas, the Buddha, and even nirvāṇa itself, are illusory (māyopama) and dreamlike (svapnopama).

For Udāna VIII.iii, which Frauwallner also cites, see Wood (1991: 3-4).

9. One must not confuse the question "In what direction did the fire go when it was quenched?" with the question "In what direction did the fire *spread*?", as Jayatilleke himself points

out (EBThK §476, n. 2). The latter question has perfectly *straightforward* answers.

Incidentally, EBThK §476 is one of the places where Jayatilleke refers to Wittgenstein, though here the reference is to the *Blue and Brown Books* rather than the *Tractatus*.

10. In §810 (p. 472), Jayatilleke gives a tree diagram of the various possibilities for interpreting the avyākata/ṭhapanīya questions. Four possibilities are considered, two under "Answerable" and two under "Unanswerable." Under "Answerable" the two possibilities he mentions are: (1) "Did not know the answer (Scepticism, Naive Agnosticism)" and (2) "Knew the answers but they were irrelevant for gaining spiritual knowledge (Pragmatism)." Under "Unanswerable" the two possibilities he mentions are (3) "Beyond the grasp of the intellect; transcends the limits of knowledge (Rational Agnosticism)" and (4) "Logically meaningless." (Jayatilleke believed that the fourth alternative was the correct one, though with some qualifications.)

The most serious objection to the diagram and to Jayatilleke's whole approach to the avyākata questions is that he has not considered the possibility that the questions are answerable, *but not in terms of the conceptual or philosophical framework in which the questions are asked*. One of the principal sources of error in philosophical argumentation is the false dichotomy, and Jayatilleke seems to have succumbed to it. In his case the false dichotomy is: "Answerable or unanswerable?" Here, surely, we need to ask: "Answerable or unanswerable *in what sense*?"

Take the question "Have you stopped smoking?" For someone who has never smoked, this question is unanswerable either affirmatively or negatively in the form in which it is phrased; yet in spite of this, no one would ever suppose that questions about smoking are logically meaningless. In fact, in cases like these it is a trivial task to reframe the question. In respect to its triviality, "Have you stopped smoking?" is like the vibhajja and patipuccha questions of the Pāli canon, and *unlike* the avyākata/ṭhapanīya questions, which according to Buddhism require for their clarification a far-reaching *conceptual* revision.

11. There is reason to believe that the Buddha rejected positions (1)-(2) and (3)-(4) for the same kinds of reasons that he rejected (5)-(10)—i.e., his general rejection of a substance view, whether this substance was conceived as a material substance, a soul or self, or even a world or universe—and not because of philosophical qualms concerning propositions about the finitude or infinitude of space and time. (On this point, see EBThK §65.) The philosophical debates of the Vedic period (brahmodya, brahmavadya) were probably concerned with competing theories about the nature of the all (sarvam) or the world (loka), conceived in some fashion as an entity or world soul. [Jayatilleke argued (ibid.) that the word "lokāyata" must originally have meant "cosmologist" rather than "materialist" or "naturalist."] In the Vedic period, loka (world) is often used synonymously with brahman, as in the Vedic formula "You are brahman, you are the yajña, you are the world (loka)," and BĀU 5.3.1: "This is brahman, this is the All" (etad brahma etat sarvam). The Buddha did not accept this way of thinking about the world, any more than he accepted the soul-theorists' way of thinking about a person or self.

12. For a discussion of the charge of eel-wriggling and other kinds of sceptical evasions of philosophical questions, and for references to some of the relevant texts in the Pāli canon, see EBThK §143-194. For a discussion of and references to casuists and sophists (vitaṇḍā-vādinaḥ), see EBThK §313-349. For materialism and the related charge that the Buddha was an uccheda-vādin, see EBThK, ch. 2 and the discussion below on the Yamaka-sutta (v. infra, p. 38-40).

13. Here I have used the H. C. Warren translation (1972: 138-145).

Sāriputta seems to have held that, even though there is nothing to what we *call* a self but the skandhas, the self cannot actually be identified with them; and he did so, presumably, on the grounds that the skandhas lacked some of the essential properties that we erroneously attribute to a self. That is, he seems to have held that X's can be nothing but Y's even though the X's have (or rather *seem* to have) properties that Y's do not have. This is the typical reductivist or eliminativist move (v. infra, pp. 260-278).

14. English translation in S. Z. Aung and C. A. F. Rhys Davids, *Points of Controversy* (1960: 62).

15. The Laṅkāvatāra (Nanjio, p. 177), a much later text, mentions the view that the world does not exist (nāsty ayaṃ loko) as one of thirty-one Lokāyata doctrines. On the Lokāyatas, see n. 10 above and the reference there to EBThK §65.

NOTES TO CHAPTER III: A CRITIQUE OF THE NNI (I)

1. Cf. NMD 164.

2. The view that there are eternal entities—i.e., things which never originate and never perish—was of course explicitly denied. Cf. the first of the two introductory verses of MMK 1, where the view that things are eternal (śāśvata) is explicitly repudiated.

3. Bhāvaviveka objected to the unqualified prāsaṅgika negation of production or origination on the grounds that it conflicted with the doctrine of dependent co-origination (Ruegg 1981: 77). In an attempt to reconcile MMK 1.3 with the pratītya-samutpāda-vāda, Bhāvaviveka proposed adding the qualification "at the level of absolute truth" (paramārthataḥ) to the prasajya negation that things do not arise in any of the stated ways. But this attempt to save the doctrine of dependent co-origination at the *phenomenal* level (saṃvṛti) will be tenable only if the two truths distinction is tenable. For an argument that this is not a tenable distinction, v. infra, pp. 222-226. (Incidentally, even Bhāvaviveka's qualification "paramārthataḥ" was criticized by Candrakīrti.)

4. Ruegg remarks (FPC 59, n. 10) that the Tibetan translations of MMK 1.3 have "ma yin" rather than "med." According to Ruegg, the former is used in the Tibetan translations for the paryudāsa negation, the latter for the prasajya.

The fact that the commentaries insist that MMK 1.3 is to be taken prasajyavat rather than paryudāsavat seems to cast doubt on the claim that "ma yin" is always reserved for the paryudāsa negation, although as a non-Tibetanist I am not in a position to pursue this question. If the Tibetan translators did preserve this distinction, then perhaps the distinction reflects what might be thought of as the difference between the surface structure (paryudāsa) and the deep structure (prasajya) of MMK 1.3.

5. Kajiyama's suggested rendering into Sanskrit of "It is false that things are produced from themselves" is: bhāvāḥ svata utpannā naiva vidyante.

6. Kajiyama's suggested Sanskrit rendering of "Things are produced not from themselves" is: "naiva svata utpannā bhāvā vidyante."

7. Kajiyama's suggested Sanskrit rendering of "Things are not produced from themselves alone" is: svata eva utpannā bhāvā na vidyante.

8. Cf. ibid., p. 26, n. 4, where Galloway says that Bhāvaviveka objects to "Things (do not arise) [from themselves or anything else]" on the grounds that it is annihilationist.

Galloway's claim that Bhāvaviveka objects to the prasajya negation of *Things arise* seems misleading. Bhāvaviveka does seem to have felt uncomfortable about the apparent contradiction between the unqualified, prāsaṅgika negation of origination and the doctrine of dependent co-origination; and he attempted to deal with the difficulty by invoking the distinction between two different kinds of truth (see Ruegg 1981: 77). But so far as I know, there is no evidence that Bhāvaviveka associated this *latter* distinction with the distinction between two different kinds of negation. Indeed, the philosophical and exegetical problem arises for Bhāvaviveka precisely *because* Nāgārjuna intended the negations in MMK 1.3 to be taken as prasajya negations.

9. According to the rules of Sanskrit grammar (see esp. Cardona: 1967) paryudāsa negation can be expressed in a single sentence (ekavākya), whereas the prasajya negation negates a sentence which has previously been tentatively or hypothetically asserted, and therefore requires the full statement of the previous sentence. (Cf. the sentence "svata utpannā jātu na vidantye bhāvāḥ," meaning "Things do not arise from self," which negates the sentence "svata utpannā jātu vidyante bhāvāḥ.") When only one idea is being negated, this is not a problem, but

when several ideas are being negated (as in MMK 1.3) the prasajya in its most explicit form cannot be employed without undue prolixity.

10. Further evidence that Bhāvaviveka regarded MMK 1 as demonstrating *non-production* can be found in chapter 25 of his Prajñāpradīpa (cf. Eckel 1980: 176, 327-328). In this passage Bhāvaviveka criticizes the Yogācārin notion of the dependent nature (paratantra) as follows:

> [The Yogācārins say:] It is the nature of dependently produced (pratītyasamutpanna) dharmas, which is the basis (āśraya) of defilement (saṃkleśa) and purification (vyavadāna).
>
>> Because imagination has a cause (nimitta), because otherwise both [defilement and purification] would not exist, and because defilements are cognized, dependent nature is thought to exist.
>
> To this we [Mādhyamikas] reply: it would be fine if dependent nature were considered part of conventional reality, but that would be pointless [since it would simply repeat the Mādhyamika position]. If it were considered ultimately [real], then it could not be dependently produced, *since production is [ultimately] negated by the method given in our chapter on non-production* [emphasis mine].

About this passage, Eckel says (1980: 176):

> Bhāvaviveka's reference here is to the opening chapter of the Madhyamakakārikās where Nāgārjuna argues that no real entity can come into existence through any imaginable variety of causal agency. The only reality that Bhāvaviveka is willing to attribute to the Yogācārin's dependent nature is the conventional reality that we attribute to certain shared illusions.

The notion that there are two different kinds or levels of truth, and that "conventional" truth (vyāvahārika satya) can actually be true, was fundamental to Bhāvaviveka's analysis of causality. Bhāvaviveka's views on the doctrine of the two truths will be criticized later (v. infra, pp. 222-226).

Relevant logic and negation

11. It might be claimed that N1/N2 are true, at the very least, for sentences that suffer radical reference failure. In the discussion of relevant logic I shall simply disregard such cases, and assume that all the propositions in question either contain no referring expressions (as for example in the case of existential and universal generalizations), or if they do, that the referential presuppositions are always fulfilled. This seems justified in the present context since we are specifically concerned here with comparing the NI and the NNI. Any reservations about N1/N2 that are based on radical reference failure would actually support the NI, since such reservations are based on the objection that in the cases in question the referents of the putative referential terms do not exist.

One could, I suppose, imagine an adherent of the NNI suggesting that the referents of the singular terms figuring in the catuṣkoṭi *neither* exist nor do not exist. However, this linguistic and logical possibility has never been considered in modern Western discussions of this issue (e.g., P. F. Strawson 1950; B. C. van Fraassen 1966; Bencivenga 1986), and in any case taking this line would appear to seriously undermine the claim that the sentences in question really do suffer radical reference failure.

12. One might say that in the case of a formal system the axioms and rules of inference make a purely *syntactic* contribution to determining the meaning of logical constants like "$\supset$" and "$\neg$"—at least in the sense that the axioms and rules of inference place constraints on the meanings that can be assigned to these expressions.

13. There are, in fact, two different versions of RL. One is the Australian (Canberra) school of R. and V. Routley and R. K. Meyer; the other is the American (Pittsburgh) school of N. D.

Belnap, Jr. and J. M. Dunn. I shall occasionally refer to these two schools as AuRL and AmRL, respectively.

The American school, which has rejected the Routley-Meyer semantics for RL that I am about to describe, tends to favor a semantics based on the *four* truth-values **True, False, Both** and **Neither**. I shall not be discussing the views of AmRL here, however, since it is R. Routley in particular who was cited by B. K. Matilal in defense of the NNI. It should be noted, however, that the four-valued semantics advocated by the American school has been criticized by some of the Australians. Meyer, for example, has argued (M78, MM86: 309-310) that a four-valued semantics is adequate only for first-degree entailments; and that for nested entailments, a *-semantics is required. [On this point, see also Dunn (1986: 208).] Routley, however, who sees no reason why a system cannot have several semantics, uses a four-valued semantics as well (personal communication).

14. R. Routley does not agree with some of what Meyer and Martin say in MM86. In particular, he holds that the notion of a proposition to which one is committed when one does not deny A is not strictly well-defined (personal communication).

15. To assert a statement A in a deductive system **S** is either to prove it or to assert it as an axiom. I shall omit the turnstile symbol "$\vdash$" in the sequel wherever it can be assumed that the context is that of a deductive system.

16. It might be thought that this objection could be circumvented by claiming that the proposition to which one is committed when one does not deny A is simply the proposition "A *or* not-A." But this will not do, either, for when $\bar{A}$ is taken in this way it fails to satisfy the relevantist condition that A, not-A can both be true. (Note: AuRL accepts bivalence.)

17. The principle invoked here, or one very much like it, was questioned by Matilal (LI 12). He claimed, on the strength of J. Buridan and A. N. Prior, that the sentence NP, "No proposition is negative," can be meaningful, and that what it asserts could actually be the case, even though NP is unassertable and could not possibly be *true*. However, I do not believe that this contention is tenable; nor do I believe that Buridan and Prior

held it, at least in the form in which it was endorsed by Mr. Matilal. (V. infra, pp. 99-103).

18. At one point in time, even Meyer (1974: 80) conceded that the semantics for negation in RL was a little "screwy." But in a more recent paper (MM86: 306-307), he has returned to a (qualified) defense of DN(RL′), as follows:

> The intuitive content of a* is that it is the proposition to which one is committed if one does not deny a. One critic (Copeland, 1979) purports to find this unintelligible. For babes in arms (and, we presume, mental defectives, truth-functional logicians, rocks, and other unfortunates) seem then committed to a great many propositions a*. Leaving aside the more controversial examples, what does a rock deny? No sentences that we can think of. More succinctly, the rock's theory is the *null* theory. Is it so strange, then, to say that, whenever A is a formal sentence and a is the corresponding proposition, to hold the null theory is to be committed to a*? All that it means is that $\sim$A isn't in the null theory. Of course it isn't. Nothing is. What would make the process strange would be if our rock were actually required to *do* something, to signify its commitment to a*. But all that is required is *failure* to do something; a rock, a babe in arms, and so forth can certainly meet this requirement.

I have to say that I *do* find attributing the null theory to a rock or a chair strange (not to mention ad hoc). Furthermore, as I have just argued, unless A is used in "not-A," "not-A" cannot be regarded as a negation. Thus, putting A (or the non-denial of A) into the null theory removes the possibility of providing a significant or meaningful definition for "not-A" altogether.

It seems likely to me that the claim that negation can be defined in terms of non-denial confuses asserting not-P (i.e., true denial or negation) with *not asserting that p*, which is a quite different thing. I shall return to the importance of this distinction shortly (v. infra, pp. 81-91).

19. The preceding discussion has a direct bearing—and, I believe, a negative one—on Jayatilleke's interpretation of the catuṣkoṭi.

According to EBThK, there is an important distinction to be drawn between rejection and negation, for when P is rejected, it is held to be meaningless, whereas this is not the case with ordinary denials or negations. This was the key to Jayatilleke's defense of the consistency of the catuṣkoṭi, for while it is not logically possible to jointly deny or negate propositions that are in fact contradictory, it is perfectly possible to reject propositions that have the *syntactic form* of contradictions but which are in fact meaningless.

The preceding discussion should help to clarify just how radical Jayatilleke's concept of rejection is, and how very different it would have to be from ordinary denial or negation. It is true that some philosophers and linguists have wanted to argue that there are syntactically well-formed sentences of a language which are actually meaningless (as opposed to analytically false)—which is what Jayatilleke's interpretation requires. But even if there were such sentences, one would still be left with the difficulty of applying Jayatilleke's notion of rejection to the catuṣkoṭi itself. The problem here, as I have already pointed out, is that none of the propositions figuring in the catuṣkoṭi or avyākata/ṭhapanīya questions seems to be *meaningless* in this way—nor is there any reason to think that the Buddha or his followers thought that they were.

20. The quodlibet, which goes back at least to Duns Scotus (or to the pseudo-Scotus), can be set out as follows:

(1)	$p \wedge \neg p$	contradiction
(2)	p	1, simplification
(3)	$\neg p$	1, simplification
(4)	$p \vee q$	2, v-introduction
(5)	q	3, 4 disjunctive syllogism.

Note that one of the crucial steps in the derivation is (5), which uses the disjunctive syllogism (D.S.). D.S. is accepted in classical logic, but rejected in RL. In classical logic, where p cannot be both true and false (nor neither true nor false), ¬p in some sense cancels or erases the p of *p* ∨ *q*, giving q. But if p, ¬p can both be true, as in relevant logic, p is not cancelled or erased by ¬p, and hence q cannot be derived.

21. On this point, see D. K. Lewis (1988).

If it is true that the quodlibet is irrelevant (in *some* sense of the word "irrelevant"), whereas the D.S. is not, then the irrelevance of the quodlibet must arise in steps (1)-(4) of the derivation given in n. 19 above. It seems to me that if there is irrelevance in (1)-(5), it must be lie in v-introduction—i.e., step (4)—rather than in step (5).

22. Cf. Belnap and Dunn (1981). G. Priest (1990), who advocates what he calls dialetheism, and who is allied with the relevantists on many issues, has recently taken the same line.

23. The inferential or deductive-theoretic nature of relevant logic may also explain why algebraic methods of investigation have proved so useful for RL (and other non-classical logics generally), whereas classical logic is still investigated primarily by model-theoretic ones.

Lattice theory, a branch of algebra, investigates what might be called the accessibility relations between points in a logical or mathematical space. This field has proved to be particularly useful for the study of non-classical logics like RL, since this kind of investigation translates rather easily and naturally into the study of whether a proposition or statement is derivable (either directly or indirectly through a series of intermediate steps) from another one. Algebraic investigations have shown that relevant negation—often symbolized as ($^-$)—can be understood as a composition of a quasi-Boolean inversion on an algebraic structure called a De Morgan monoid.

In any case, it is important to note the distinction between soft paraconsistent (or inconsistency tolerant) logics, and dialethic (or inconsistent) logics. According to the advocates of dialethic logic (e.g., R. Routley), some contradictions—such as those of the logical paradoxes—are true, and classical logic is incorrect; but other relevants do not accept these claims, and advocate only inconsistency tolerant logics. For a more recent treatment of negation from the more radical, dialethic point of view, see Routley and Routley (1985).

Speech act theory and the catuṣkoṭi

24. Cf. Perc. 66.

25. Actually, Nāgārjuna tends to be treated in Perc. as only one of a number of Indian sceptics to whom the speech act analysis can be applied. Other philosophers that are mentioned in this connection are Śrīharṣa and Jayarāśī.

26. Here Matilal referred to NMD 162-5.

27. See the brief discussion of this passage, supra, p. 19.

28. Cf. MMK 25.5-6 (na hi vidyate: it is not the case), MMK 25.10-11 (na yujyate: it is not possible), MMK 25:15 ([na] sidhyati: cannot be established), and MMK 25: 17-18 (nājyate: it cannot be said).

29. One problem with the rules just mentioned (ad FIL 169 and FIL 161) is that they would appear to preclude at least one version of scepticism, according to which it is always possible to give good reasons for both P and not-P. (A related but even more general objection to the rules would be that they exclude the obvious possibility that for any proposition P, one can suggest that P *and* suggest that not-P.) This counter-example shows, I think, that the rules in question need refinement, but I shall not pursue this problem here. I shall, however, argue in the next subsection that scepticism offers no solution to the consistency problem either.

30. A similar point about the role of scepticism in the Madhyamaka was made some years ago by P. T. Raju (1954: 703, 709).

Obviously, scepticism about the fundamental doctrines of common sense does play a crucial role in Mādhyamika thought, but this scepticism is not an end in itself. For the Mādhyamika, the role of scepticism has been exhausted once it has served the purpose of undermining common sense claims about perception etc., and has thereby dispensed with common sense objections to the claim that self and dharmas are equally non-existent.

In other words, scepticism in the Madhyamaka is the handmaiden of what E. Burnouf (1844: 560) called a nihilistic scholasticism. There is no scepticism in the Madhyamaka about the anātman doctrine or the doctrine that all dharmas are void.

The Mādhyamikas' use of the catuṣkoṭi and the Liar Paradox

31. Cf. LI 7: "Nāgārjuna wrote the MMK primarily to show the essentially conditional and provisional nature of the dharma theory of the Abhidharma school, and along with this he wanted to expose the necessarily provisional nature of any philosophical theory of reality."

32. At this point Matilal referred in a footnote to Prior's papers, "Epimenides the Cretan" and "Some Problems of Self-reference in John Buridan."

33. For a discussion of Udayana's theory, which seems to be remarkably similar to Russell's theory of types, see NMD 159-60.

34. Cf. LI 11, where Matilal argues that one cannot interpret Nāgārjuna to mean by NS that no statement *except NS* is true.

35. Recall that Prior was interested in outlining an alternative to the hierarchical theories of Russell and Tarski, according to whom C, as a *self-referring* sentence, is *always* meaningless.

According to Prior, a self-referring expression is not necessarily meaningless, although he did hold (as we shall see) that there are *some* circumstances in which C, taken as self-referring, becomes meaningless.

36. One point to note in this connection is that Prior, like Buridan, was a nominalist—though I think Buridan's nominalism may have been seriously compromised by his speaking of sentences as *expressing* propositions. But I shall not pursue this point.

37. I cannot help feeling, incidentally, that Buridan as a theologian may have gotten too subtle on these points for his own good, for some of his views appear to lead to questionable—even odious—theological opinions. The Buridan-Prior view, for

example, seems to me to imply that there could be some facts that even God does not know, and even more strangely, that there could be some facts that God could *bring it about* that He does not know.

Either NP exists or it does not. According to Buridan, presumably, if NP does not exist, then even God could not know it to be true or even think it, for God cannot do what is logically impossible, and according to Buridan, one cannot *know* or even think a proposition that does not exist. But according to Prior and Buridan, if NP *exists* God cannot know it to be true either, for one cannot know NP (or any other proposition) to be true unless it is true, and according to Buridan a proposition must exist in order to be true, and when NP exists it is necessarily false. And all this despite the fact that, according to Prior, things are as NP says they are in the case where God annihilates all negative propositions. From this it would appear to follow that there could be some fact or state of affairs of which God was ignorant.

To speak of God, as Buridan and Prior do, as creating and annihilating propositions only adds to the perplexities. This way of speaking suggests that God could think NP in a world where it exists as a proposition (and is therefore false), and could then annihilate all negative propositions. The result would appear to be that God could intentionally *bring about* a state of affairs which as a matter of logic He could not possibly know.

It might be objected that the theory could avoid this difficulty by simply maintaining that God's knowledge is not propositional, i.e., that God is in the favored position of being able to know facts or states of affairs directly, without the intermediation of propositions. However, this proposed solution can also be seen to be problematic, for if we are forced to drop propositions as the objects of God's *knowledge*, then presumably we should also drop them as the objects of God's *thought*. But facts cannot be made the objects of God's *thoughts*, for then God could only think what was true (i.e., what exists). This conclusion would, among other things, be theologically objectionable, for if God creates the world, then He must be able to *think* it or conceive it in His mind before it comes to be.

Finally, it might be suggested that "There are no negative propositions" is *thought* as a proposition by God when it is false, and *known* as a fact by Him when it is true. But this way out of the difficulty would seem to be arbitrary; and in any case the suggestion would seem to imply that what God knows when NP is true is not the same thing as what He thinks when NP is false, and this implication, even if it is not unacceptable, seems peculiar.

38. Some philosophers have maintained that what people assert, deny, believe etc. are sentences rather than propositions. But on this view Matilal's claim seems even more clearly untenable, for then his claim that Nāgārjuna can consistently hold that no statement is true without asserting NS must be interpreted to mean that Nāgārjuna can utter NS (with the relevant intentions etc.) without uttering NS.

I have similar problems with another remark of Matilal's in this passage (LI 13). "Only a proposition can be true or false," he said. "But since NS is not claimed as a proposition, we cannot even begin to think of its contradictory, viz., 'some statement is true.'"

I am not sure how to interpret this statement. Surely we *can* think of the contradictory of "No statement is true," for the contradictory of this statement is "*Some* statement is true," and this is in fact what we *do* think. If anything, it is the statement "No statement is true" which (taken as self-referring) may be meaningless and therefore unthinkable.

The Vigraha-vyāvartanī on the emptiness of statements

39. The text and a translation of the VV (without the vṛtti) is given in the Appendix.

40. Corroboration for this point can be found in VV 2, where the opponent refers to Nāgārjuna's previous proposition (pūrvā pratijñā), which seems to refer to the general proposition "All things are empty" (cf. VV 1a); while what might be called the later or present proposition is the special case, "All statements are empty." (cf. VV 1c).

41. If nothing exists, then the negation of P must be just as unreal and non-existent as P itself. But Nāgārjuna probably understood this as an ontological or metaphysical point, and not as a syntactic or semantic one about the nature of negation.

According to Nāgārjuna, the statement that all things are void (SDŚ) is true, even though there are no dharmas or bhāvas, nor any propositions. That is, Nāgārjuna holds that SDŚ is true even though—and even because—a) there is nothing that makes it true and b) even though (and even because) SDŚ cannot itself be said to exist as an entity, either as a sentence or abstract proposition. Furthermore, since SDŚ is true, it is false that Nāgārjuna asserts it (for even Nāgārjuna is unreal). Among other things, all of this involves a very radical abandonment of the correspondence theory of truth. As radical as it is, however, I am not sure that it can be dismissed on the grounds of *logical* inconsistency.

42. In VV 22 Nāgārjuna explicitly equates lack of self-nature (asvabhāvatva) with emptiness (śūnyatā). Cf. also VVV 57, where it is said that all names are non-existent (asad-bhūta) because all names are void (śūnya), and that all names are void because names have no self-nature (niḥsvabhāva), i.e., bhāva-svabhāvasyābhāvān-nāma niḥsvabhāvam, tasmāc-chūnyam, śūnyatvād-asadbhūtam.

43. In my exposition of Nāgārjuna's views I have of course referred to the *statement* or *proposition* that all things lack self-nature, and even abbreviated this statement as SDN (or alternatively, as SDŚ). It must be understood, however, that for Nāgārjuna the expression "the statement that ..." can only be a term of convenience—a mere façon de parler—for Nāgārjuna does not believe in the existence of propositions or sentences any more than he believes in anything else.

As Nāgārjuna says in VV 28cd, he himself feels free to resort to conventional modes of expression (saṃvyavahāra) when it suits his purpose. Ordinary language locutions—even misleading ones—can be employed if it is convenient to do so, provided that one is not taken in by them. Thus, there is nothing wrong with using phrases like "the rising of the sun," provided that one does not take this to mean that the sun really rises.

(Personalist language—i.e., all the ordinary language locutions that seem to involve commitment to a self or person—are to be regarded in the same way.) Similarly, expressions like "the proposition that...", "the sentence that...", "the expression that...", can be used, provided that one does not infer from these locutions that there really are such things as sentences, propositions, expressions etc.

44. Perhaps the most interesting of these arguments is this: that the opponent's requirement that a proposition must be established (siddha) by a pramāṇa leads to an infinite regress (anavasthā), and that this regress involves the opponent in the very scepticism that he wishes to avoid.

This criticism of Nāgārjuna's is reminiscent of the claim that has been made in Western philosophy that one must know that one knows that p in order to know that p ($Kp \rightarrow KKp$). This question has frequently been discussed in Western philosophy in connection with the problem of scepticism, for it is often claimed that one can never know that one knows something, and this generates the sceptical problem, for from 1) $\neg KKp$ and 2) $Kp \rightarrow KKp$, one immediately derives $\neg Kp$—i.e., one can never know anything.

For an interesting discussion of the pramāṇa-anavasthā objection and its Western counterpart, see Matilal (Perc. 141-179).

45. Cf. MMK 24.14:

> Everything makes sense if one accepts the doctrine of emptiness. Nothing makes sense if one does not.
>
> sarvaṃ ca yujyate tasya śūnyatā yasya yujyate /
> sarvaṃ na yujyate tasya śūnyaṃ yasya na yujyate //24.14//

46. Cf. VV 57-58, where Nāgārjuna denies that SDŚ could be true only if there were a niḥsvabhāvatā of things, as the opponent claims in VV 9.

47. According to Nāgārjuna, everything is false (mṛṣā), though things may appear to be true (tathya). Nāgārjuna might, therefore, have admitted the validity of the correspondence theory

of truth at the conventional level. It is also possible, however, that he would have preferred, even at that level, the semantic conception of truth, which simply holds, for example, that the sentence "Snow is white" is true if, and only if, snow is white.

The semantic conception of truth has the advantage of capturing many of our intuitions about truth, while at the same time avoiding the formal difficulties with which the notion of "correspondence with reality" is connected. For the difference between the semantic theory of truth and the correspondence theory of truth, with which it is frequently confused, see Tarski (1952: 343 et seq.).

48. It might be useful here to list the differences between the Buridan-Prior view, B. K. Matilal's view, and the nihilist view of the emptiness of statements.

(a) Buridan and Prior, as nominalists, regarded statements as sentences. On their view, the statement that Nāgārjuna asserted NS means (roughly) that $\exists x$(x is a sentence & (x="No statement is true") & Nāgārjuna asserted x).

Buridan and Prior did *not* believe that statements were empty, nor did they believe that someone could *hold* a proposition like NP without *asserting* the proposition (i.e., sentence) NP. It was, in fact, precisely for this reason that Buridan and Prior held that it could not be the case that things actually are as NP says they are.

(b) According to Matilal, Nāgārjuna could *hold* that no statement is true even though he could not *assert* the sentence NS which means that no statement is true. On the basis of this claim, Matilal argued that it can actually *be* the case that no statement is true.

(Note, incidentally, that Matilal seems to have been committed to the view that, according to Nāgārjuna, the proposition NS does not exist, for he was committed to the view that Nāgārjuna could hold that no statement is true only if there is no proposition that asserts this!)

(c) According to the NI, "x is non-existent" is what "x is śūnya" means for *any* x, including the statement "The *proposition* x is śūnya." The NI interprets Nāgārjuna's assertion that he has no proposition (nāsti ca mama pratijñā) accordingly.

If SDŚ does mean that nothing exists, then the only way that SDŚ could be true is if nothing existed (including itself as a proposition or sentence). This means (if one wants to hold that SDŚ could be true) that one must abandon the correspondence theory of truth.

Note also that on this view one must distinguish between what might be called the syntax and meaning of statements involving SDŚ/SDN and the ontology that is implied by these propositions. From the viewpoint of grammar and meaning, the assertion that one can hold SDŚ/SDN (or any other proposition) to be true without asserting the proposition SDŚ or SDN is untenable, for this is just what "holding true" means. But according to Nāgārjuna, it does not follow from this that there actually is a sentence or proposition that is asserted, just as it does not follow from the truth of *John noticed the non-existence of the Emperor's clothes* that $\exists x$ (x = the non-existence of the Emperor's clothes). Like the term "non-existence," the expressions "proposition" or "statement" are nothing more than terms of convenience (façon de parler).

As I shall point out subsequently, the Mādhyamikas held that statements about appearances are also prajñaptisat. At the level of ultimate truth, therefore, even statements about how things *seem* cannot be true or false, for there is nothing for even appearance statements to be true or false *about*.

NOTES TO CHAPTER III: A CRITIQUE OF THE NNI (II)

D. Seyfort Ruegg's interpretation of the Madhyamaka

49. Cf. de Jong (1987: 113).

50. Cf. Ruegg (1983: 209): "The doctrine of Emptiness (śūnyatāvāda) [does not have] the sense ... of negativism or nihilism (abhāva) but of origination in dependence (pratītyasamutpāda)."

51. Whether (4) implies a doctrine of annihilation depends on whether there is anything that is not subject to the law of dependent co-origination. Notoriously, the Sautrāntikas thought

that all things were subject to this law, since they denied the reality of the so-called unconditioned (asaṃskṛta) dharmas, i.e., space (ākāśa) and the two extinctions (prati- and aprati-saṃkhyā-nirodhas). On the Sautrāntika view, therefore, one cannot say that there is an Absolute (or any other non-phenomenal existence) that remains when the phenomenal, saṃsāric world of dependent co-origination comes to an end.

Since the Mādhyamikas did not believe in an Absolute either (v. infra, pp. 235-252), there was a close doctrinal affiliation between the Mādhyamikas and the Sautrāntikas. The main difference between the Sautrāntika and the Mādhyamika seems to have been over the reality of the *phenomenal* or *conditioned* (saṃskṛta) dharmas. The Sautrāntikas believed in the reality of these; the Mādhyamikas did not.

52. The same kind of problem arises in connection with the related Mādhyamika equation between pratītya-samutpādaḥ and śāntaḥ (peace, quiescence, stilling, cessation, tranquilization). As Ruegg notes (1981: 2, n.5), this identification seems to be an *oxymoron*, as indeed it must be in the context of principles that were accepted by all of the Buddhist schools.

53. For passages that express what I have called the Hīnayānist view, cf. the following passages which are cited by Ruegg (1981: 17, n. 39): MMK 24.36c (pratītya-samutpāda-śūnyatā); MMKV 24.13 (śūnyatārtha=pratītyasamutpādārtha); MMKV 24.40 (sarva-dharma-pratītya-samutpāda-lakṣaṇā svabhāva-śūnyatā); VV 22; and the Vṛtti's concluding laudatory verse on the VV.

54. Cf. FPC 61, n. 34: "The Buddha sometimes teaches an ātman to exclude nihilism, and sometimes he teaches the anātman to exclude eternalism, the two philosophical extreme positions."

55. As we shall see later (v. infra, p. 147-150), the concepts of imaginability and thinkability play an important role in Ruegg's interpretation of the Madhyamaka.

56. More precisely, the Naiyāyikas thought of abhāvas in terms of the absence of something in a locus. For an extensive discussion of the Naiyāyikas' views about abhāvas, see Matilal (1968).

57. The fact that there are passages where one finds the Mahāyānists asserting that things are non-existent (abhāva, asat) *simpliciter* supports this claim. Cf. the Aṣṭa-sāhasrikā, where the statement that all dharmas are signless, wishless, unaffected, unproduced, unoriginated and *non-existent (abhāva)* appears as a leitmotif at least six different times. (Rajendralal Mitra ed., pp. 273, 298, 341, 379-380, 424, 482.)

58. In a later work (1981: 37-38), Ruegg says that the prasajya-pratiṣedha, unlike the paryudāsa-pratiṣedha, does not commit the Mādhyamika to the *contradictory* of the proposition that he has negated. One example he gives in this connection is the prasajya-negation of the proposition that an entity is produced in a certain way, which, he says, does not commit the Mādhyamika to the assertion of the contradictory proposition that an entity is produced in the "opposite" way. But the proposition that an entity is produced in *another* way is not the contradictory of the statement that it is produced in a certain way; it is a *contrary* of the latter statement. I shall argue later (v. infra, pp. 179-183) that the same is true of Ruegg's example of the propositions that nirvāṇa is not a positive entity (bhāva) and that it is not a negative entity.

59. Matilal's position on this point can, I think, be interpreted in two ways. On the one hand, he might have been arguing that the catuṣkoṭi is meaningful *despite* the fact that it is inconsistent. On the other hand, he might have held that the catuṣkoṭi is not inconsistent at all, on the grounds that the kind of negation that is involved in the catuṣkoṭi is a non-standard or non-classical kind of negation.

There are some passages in his writings (e.g., NMD 158; NMD 164, ls. 23-28) where even the law of non-contradiction seems to be in question. But it seems to me that the prevailing view in his writings is that the catuṣkoṭi is meaningful because it is *not* inconsistent. This is particularly true of those passages where negation in the catuṣkoṭi is analyzed in terms of speech act theory and the concept of illocutionary force.

60. Although Staal criticized Matilal for claiming that the prasajya negation of the Indian grammarians does not involve the possibility of logical contradiction, at another place he has

appealed to Kajiyama (and also Stcherbatsky and de la Vallée Poussin) as having shown that when the Mādhyamikas negated a proposition P they did not necessarily accept the *negation* of that proposition (i.e., *not*-P). [Cf. BI: 44.] This does not seem to me to be consistent with the criticism of Matilal that I have just mentioned.

Staal's position on the matter, therefore, is ambiguous. What I have attributed to Staal in the passage to which this is an endnote is the position that seems to me to be the prevailing one in his writings on the subject, and also the clearest.

I shall have occasion to return to Staal's treatment of the catuṣkoṭi again (v. infra, p. 353, n. 73).

61. E.g., FPC 49-50, where Ruegg insists that the propositions (pratijñā) uttered by the Mādhyamikas are meaningful ones.

62. The principal difference between Ruegg's position and the one I am arguing for seems to me to be this. According to Ruegg, P & not-P, not-P & not-not-P etc. can be meaningful even when P is an unanalyzable proposition. The position that I am advocating is that P & not-P, not-P & not-not-P etc. are meaningless unless there is an analysis of P according to which P & not-P, not-P & not-not-P etc. do not exhaust all the possible logical alternatives. One kind of case where this can occur is when P is a subject-predicate proposition and the subject term of P is held to be non-referring.

63. keṣāṃ cit-tv-aticirābhyasta-tattva-darśanānāṃ kiṃcin-mātrānutkhātāvaraṇa-taru-mūlānāṃ naivātathyaṃ naiva tathyaṃ tad-iti deśitam / tasyāpi kiṃcin-mātrasyāvaraṇasya prahānārthaṃ vandhyā-sutasyāvadāta-śyāmatā-pratiṣedhavad-ubhayam-etat-pratiṣiddhaṃ.

64. Cf. FPC 20-21, where Ruegg says: "It is noteworthy also that Bhāvaviveka regards the Mādhyamika propositions (pratijñā) consisting in the negation of the four positions as belonging, despite their verbalized form and consequent discursivity (prapañca), not to the level of surface convention (saṃvṛti) to which the prapañca is normally assigned, but rather to a special form of paramārtha that entails construction (abhisaṃskāra). This level is termed pure worldly knowledge

(śuddhalaukikajñāna) in order to distinguish it from the supramundane (lokottara) nature of the supreme paramārtha, which is quite free from prapañca and cannot therefore be verbalized."

65. For a different, and more extensive, philosophical defense of the LEM against *Strawsonian* kinds of criticisms, see Dummett (1978: xiii-xxiii; 1-24; 25-28). Dummett does not regard non-referring expressions as counter-examples to the LEM, though he does reject the LEM on other grounds. He also favors demoting the concept of truth in favor of the notion of a "designated value."

66. The notion of the significance of statements may also be useful in dealing with problems of vagueness. One possibility is to regard vagueness as a property of our concepts rather than of reality, which is always either this or that. According to this view, concepts like "is bald" or "is green" are meaningful only when the law of the excluded middle applies to them. In the fuzzy or vague regions where it does not, statements using such concepts are strictly speaking not *significant* (i.e., are meaningless in the Russellian sense). This approach to the question implies a rather strong version of metaphysical realism. A perfectly rigorous and precise language which fully reflected the nature of reality according to this metaphysical view would have no vague or fuzzy terms at all.

67. On the Vatsīputrīyas or Pudgalavādins, who held that the person (pudgala) is inexpressible (avācya), see Conze (1967a: 122-134, and especially the references given there in endnote 4, pp. 280-281).

68. I supppose it is possible, in view of the fact that Ruegg tends to equate emptiness and the true nature of things with dependent origination, that his position is that the notion of a non-conceptualizable reality is unobjectionable provided that it is not interpreted to mean that there are any entities or non-entities.

But there would be at least two problems with this suggestion. One is that it would have to be shown that dependent origination is in fact non-conceptualizable. (This may have been the Mādhyamika view, but it was not, I think, the view of the majority of the Buddhist schools.) The much more serious objection is that there are doctrinal reasons why dependent origination cannot literally be identified with the Mādhyamikas' *paramārtha*. (V. supra, pp. 124-129; v. infra, pp. 192-199.)

69. It might be worth noting at this point that the null/not-null distinction distinction is not the same thing as the conceptually imaginable/conceptually unimaginable distinction. For example, there are things that do not exist that are conceptualizable, such as a snake in the path that appears as a rope, the present king of France in 1994, or the winged horse Pegasus. Conversely, it could be argued that there are things that are not conceptualizable (or at least not imaginable) that *do* exist, such as quarks and leptons, curved space, God according to most theologies, and the Kantian Ding an sich. Thus, nothing but confusion will arise from treating "null" and "conceptually imaginable\unimaginable" as synonymous, logically equivalent, or even loosely connected with each other.

70. Note in this connection that the claim that the mind can become quiet only by being objectless is an *empirical* claim. Many philosophers in India would have denied this claim, including the Patañjali of the Yoga-sūtras. As Patañjali might well have asked: why couldn't the mind become quiet by concentrating single-mindedly on the law of the excluded middle?

Dhāraṇā was not the procedure that Śāntideva recommended in BCA 9.35, of course, but that is another matter. The point to be made here is that BCA 9.35, which is clearly a recommendation for spiritual or meditational practice, can neither be justified nor refuted by appealing to the law of the excluded middle; nor is there any reason to think that Śāntideva thought that it could be.

I shall have more to say about BCA 9.35 below (pp. 247-252).

71. For some of the relevant references, see the bibliography in Abbagnano (1972).

72. It has been suggested that a new kind of logic (and in particular one that rejects the classical law of distribution) needs to be invoked in order to account for the puzzling phenomena that are described by quantum mechanics.

If this claim could be established, it would provide a counter-example to the claim that classical logic is universally valid. I shall not pursue this question here, however, for two reasons. One is that the claims of quantum logic have *not* as yet been established. (**Q.L.** is very far from being the prevailing interpretation of even quantum mechanics.) Another reason is that the issue of quantum logic does not seem particularly relevant to the concerns that Ruegg raises in his paper.

First, the LEM remains valid in **Q.L.** (at least in the now standard von Neumann formalization of it); consequently, **Q.L.** itself has no *direct* bearing on most of the logical issues that are discussed in the FPC. Second, the quantum logician believes that the nature of quantum reality can be described by some logic or mathematics or other, even though it cannot be described by classical logic. But Ruegg seems to me to have taken the much more radical position that ultimate reality cannot be described by language or logic at all (cf. FPC 20-21). Finally, the purport of **Q.L.** is that there are *entities* (i.e. particles) that are in certain ways physically indeterminate; but according to Ruegg the Mādhyamikas did not believe in the existence of *indeterminate* entities, either.

73. J. F. Staal has argued (BI 38-40) that the example of non-standard logics like intuitionistic logic (**I.L.**) shows that at least some aspects of the catuṣkoṭi which have been *claimed* to be irrational are not irrational at all. Staal made this claim for the fourth koṭi in its *un*negated form, which apparently denies the law of the excluded middle (LEM).

It is not at all clear, however, that **I.L.** can throw any light on the unnegated fourth koṭi, since, as Staal himself notes, the denial of the LEM in **I.L.** is connected with the claim that the law is invalid for sets consisting of infinitely many objects. This particular claim of the intuitionists has no obvious bearing on the issues surrounding the catuṣkoṭi, since there is no evidence that the Buddhists ever claimed (as the intuitionists did) that it makes no sense to speak of closed or completed infinite sets. [The example of many-valued logics—or even better, truth gappy logics—which Staal also mentions in this connection (BI 39) would seem to be more apposite.]

It is also worth noting here that one cannot cite the example of intuitionistic logic in order to resolve the *consistency* problem that is presented by the catuṣkoṭi.

According to Staal, it wouldn't necessarily be irrational to reject the LEM, since some systems of logic (e.g., the intuitionistic logic of L. E. J. Brouwer) do reject it. The more serious problem, according to Staal, is the *un*negated form of the third koṭi, which denies the LNC (law of non-contradiction). According to Staal, denying the LNC *is* nonsensical. Staal argued that the only way of resolving these riddles was to insist on the primacy of the *negated* form of the catuṣkoṭi, because, when the third koṭi is negated, the principle of non-contradiction is endorsed rather than denied. (Note, however, that in the negated form of the catuṣkoṭi, the fourth koṭi *affirms* the LEM.)

Taking the negated form of the catuṣkoṭi as fundamental does resolve the inconsistency problem so far as the third koṭi is concerned, but it does not resolve all of the problems. Staal considered the problem of contradiction only as it presents itself *within* each of the koṭis, but it is equally important to avoid contradictions between and among the four positions. Here the fundamental problem lies in reconciling the first and second koṭis. Significantly, this remains a problem even in the *negated* form of the catuṣkoṭi. Given the rule of adjunction (an extremely weak rule which is accepted even in **I.L.**), $\neg P$, $\neg\neg P$ are contradictories. (Cf. Heyting 1971: 105, l. 9.)

NOTES TO CHAPTER IV: A DEFENSE OF THE NI

1. I shall be applying the nihilist interpretation to the following passages from the MMK: MMK 13, MMK 15, MMK 24 and MMK 25 (taken either in whole or in part). The Sanskrit and a complete translation of these chapters of the MMK can be found in the Appendix.

2. On the nāga legend, see K. Venkata Ramanan (1966: 26-27) and the references given there.

One passage that illustrates the role that the Prajñā-pāramitā sūtras played in Mādhyamika thought has been mentioned above

(p. 50). There it was noted that Bhāvaviveka argues against attributing to Nāgārjuna the view that there are things that are unproduced, and he does so on the grounds that this view would deviate from the prajñā-pāramitā.

In the opening passage of the MMKV, Candrakīrti also links Nāgārjuna with these sūtras: ācārya-nāgārjunasya viditāviparīta-*prajñāpāramitā*-nīteḥ karuṇāyā parāvabodhārthaṃ śāstra-praṇayanaṃ.

3. The sentence I have quoted forms a kind of leitmotif of the Aṣṭa-sāhasrikā, particularly in the last half of the sūtra. It appears also at Aṣṭa. 273, 298, 341, 379-380 and 424.

Here and elsewhere in the text I have used, usually without modification, Conze's translations of the Prajñā-pāramitā sūtras. (I have, however, added the inserts giving some of the more important Sanskrit terms.)

4. In the Hīnayāna, typically, nirvāṇa and space (ākāśa) are two of the unconditioned (asaṃskṛta) dharmas. The analysis of space was therefore a major issue in Buddhist thought, for the analysis of space had obvious implications for the analysis of nirvāṇa as well.

The prevailing view of the Buddhist schools was that "space" is a mere word or conventional designation (prajñapti), i.e., it does nothing more than describe the fact that we fail to encounter resistance to our movements in the absence of matter etc. This was also the view of the Mahāyānists. It is, therefore, significant that the Prajñā-pāramitā and Mādhyamika texts compare the self (ātman), beings, illusion (māyā), nirvāṇa, the perfection of wisdom (prajñā-pāramitā), the Buddha, and all the dharmas etc. to space. Given the analysis of space as non-existence, the plain meaning of these comparisons is that selves, beings, dharmas etc. are unreal and non-existent, just as one might say, after a visual hallucination has vanished, that one had been seeing only empty space.

5. It is true that the term "māyā" appears considerably earlier than this in some of the Upaniṣads, but there the term does not mean illusion. In the Upaniṣads, this term refers to a special power (vibhūti) by which brahman or the Vedic deities transform themselves (pari√nam) into a multiplicity of forms and

appearances. For a brief discussion of the differences between these two meanings of māyā, see Wood (1990: 152-59).

6. This is an interesting example of a philosophical play on words. The sūtra begins by suggesting that dharmas exist, but not in the way that foolish people suppose. But in the end the passage does deny that the dharmas exist (avidyamāna), and it does so on the grounds that they are simply the product of illusion or ignorance (avidyā).

7. I subjoin Ruegg's and Galloway's translations of this verse. Ruegg (FPC 55) has:

> If something not empty existed, something called 'empty' would exist; something not empty does not exist, and how will there [then] exist something empty?

Galloway (1989: 23) translates the verse as follows:

> If there were anything nonempty there would be something empty; but there is nothing nonempty, so from whence will the empty be?

The translation in Robinson (1957: 297), incidentally, is virtually the same as Ruegg's and Galloway's translations for MMK 13.a-c, but for 13.7d Robinson has: "and so nowhere does there exist a non-empty something." MMK 13.7d, however, plainly has the term "śūnyam" (empty), rather than the term "aśūnyam" (non-empty), so Robinson's translation of MMK 13.7d is surely wrong, at least so far as the Sanskrit is concerned.

8. For a cautionary note about confusing "if" with "if and only if," see Quine (1982: 54).

9. Cf. AKBh ii 55: "Nirvāṇa is the deliverance of the mind, like the extinction of a flame; consequently, nirvāṇa is non-existence; thus it is that the deliverance of the mind of the Buddha is accomplished" (pradyotasyeva nirvāṇaṃ vimokṣastasya cetasaḥ; yathā pradyotasya nirvāṇam-*abhāvaḥ*; evaṃ bhagavato 'pi cetaso vimokṣa iti).

10. The cessation (dhvaṃsa) of something that has previously existed was recognized in Indian philosophy as one of

the ways in which non-existence could be conceived. Others were prior non-existence (prāg-abhāva), mutual non-existence or difference (anyonyābhāva), and absolute non-existence (atyantābhāva).

11. Note that this line of argument simply applies to the *dharmas* what the Hīnayānist schools had already said about the self. Cf. the AVGS, the Yamaka-sutta, and the Kathā-vatthu (v. supra, pp. 40-41), which argue that it cannot be said that the Tathāgata is annihilated at his parinirvāṇa, since there is no Tathāgata *before* his parinirvāṇa. These passages from the Hīnayānist literature maintain—as Nāgārjuna did later when he adopted the way of speaking of the Sautrāntikas—that abhāvaḥ = ucchedaḥ, i.e., that something can be abhāva only if it has previously existed.

12. Nivṛtti and nirodha (esp. pratisaṃkhyā-nirodha, or "deliberate extinction") are frequently used as synonyms for nirvāṇa in both the Hīnayānist and Mahāyānist literature. For a brief description of the conception of nirvāṇa in early Buddhism, see Wood (1991: x-xi; 1-6). In this earlier work I have also discussed the attempts by the Yogācāra and Tathāgata-garbha schools to interpret the annihilationistic nirvāṇa of early Buddhism in a non-nihilistic way, i.e., as an Absolute (ibid., chs. 1-4).

13. Stcherbatsky's interpretations of MMK 25.9 and 25.19-20 have been endorsed by many later proponents of the NNI. T. R. V. Murti (1955: 233) cited Stcherbatsky's interpretation/translation of MMK 25.19-20 verbatim.

14. sarvathā yady-ayam-upādāya prajñapyate, yadi vā pratītya jāyata iti vyavasthāpyate, sarvathāsya janma-maraṇa-paraṃparā-prabandhasyāpratītya vānupādāya vā yā 'pravṛttis-tan-nirvāṇam-iti vyavasthāpyate / na ca apravṝttimātraṃ bhāvo 'bhāvo veti parikalpituṃ pāryata iti / evaṃ na bhāvo nābhāvo nirvāṇam //

15. M. Sprung's translation of the same passage from MMKV 25.9 (1979: 255) also involves some heavy editorializing:

> In any case it is certain that whether understood as dependent on something outside itself (upādāya) or as

> originating from causes (pratītya) it is the ceasing to function (apravṛtti) of this continuous round of birth and death, due to its being taken as uncaused or as beyond dependence, that is said to be nirvāṇa.

There is nothing in the Sanskrit that corresponds to the phrase "... due to its being taken as uncaused or as beyond dependence." Moreover, as I shall presently argue, this phrase cannot even be made to *fit* the text.

16. The much-debated question whether the Tathāgata does or does not exist after his parinirvāṇa is relevant to the interpretation of MMK 25.9. For some remarks on this conundrum, see note 8, pp. 327-329.

17. There is further support for my interpretation of MMK 25.9-10 in MMK 25.11-14.

If nirvāṇa and saṃsāra were simply the same thing viewed in different ways, then one would have to say that ultimate reality is, in some sense, *both* a bhāva and an abhāva, or alternatively, perhaps, one might say that ultimate reality is *neither* a bhāva nor an abhāva. But both of these alternatives are repudiated by Nāgārjuna. In MMK 25.11-14 he denies that nirvāṇa is both existent and non-existent (bhāvo bhāvaś-ca); and in MMK 25.15-16 he denies that nirvāṇa is neither existent nor non-existent (naivābhāvo naiva bhāvaḥ).

18. This has been a persistent theme of the NNI. V. supra, pp. 124-129 and the discussion there of Ruegg's interpretation of the Madhyamaka.

I shall have occasion shortly to emphasize the fact that in the Madhyamaka the equation between emptiness and dependent co-origination is a mere dependent designation (upādāya-prajñapti).

19. Cf. Ruegg (1983: 209): "The doctrine of Emptiness (śūnyatāvāda) [does not have] the sense ... of negativism or nihilism (abhāva) but of origination in dependence (pratītyasamutpāda)." Cf. also Matilal (NMD 148-151).

20. Cf. the following sentence from Candrakīrti's commentary on MMK 24.18, which seems, prima facie, to support this interpretation:

> Dependent co-origination, which consists in the manifestation of seeds, consciousness etc. in dependence on causal conditions, is the non-arising of things according to self-nature (svabhāvenānutpādaḥ), and the non-arising of things according to self-nature is emptiness.
>
> yo 'yaṃ pratītya-samutpādo hetu-pratyayānapekṣyāṅkura-vijñānādīnāṃ prādur-bhāvaḥ, sa svabhāvenānutpādaḥ / yaś-ca svabhāvenānutpādo bhāvānāṃ sā śūnyatā

21. Cf. MMK 1.1a, 1.3, 1.4 and 1.5-16, all of which imply that nothing originates (v. supra, pp. 48-49). Cf. also the following passage from the beginning of MMKV 13:

> The origination of things from self, from others or from both, or from no cause, turns out, on examination, to be unreal (nirūpyamānaṃ bhāvānām asat), nor is there (asat) any other way that they can arise. Nevertheless, to the ordinary people, whose eye of understanding is afflicted with the ophthalmia of ignorance, things *seem* (khyānti) to arise (utpanna) and have form (rūpatva). Thus, even though things are without self-nature (niḥsvabhāva) and are intrinsically deceptive and inconsistent (visaṃvādaka), like an illusory elephant or snake, ignorant people are taken in by them, but the wise are not.
>
> sva-parobhaya-kṛtam-ahetu-samutpannatvaṃ ca nirūpyamānaṃbhāvānām-asad-anyaś-cotpādakovidhir-asan, utpanna-rūpatvena caite bhāvā avidyā-timiropahata-mati-nayanānāṃ bāla-pṛthag-janānāṃ khyānti; tasmān-niḥsvabhāvā eva santo bālānāṃ visaṃvādakā māyā-kārit-uragādivat-tad-anabhijñānāṃ, na tu vijñānāṃ

Note that this passage states quite unambiguously that it is false (asat) that things originate in any of the four recognized ways—or for that matter *in any other way*.

22. Prof. Matilal (NMD 148-151) offered what seems to me to be a rather different interpretation of MMK 24.18, the purport of which is that dependent designation is to be understood as a term that refers to the nature of *reality*, which is conceived as *logical indeterminacy*. According to his interpretation, the term "prajñaptir upādāya" in MMK 24.18c is in *apposition* with the terms "śūnyatā," "pratītya-samutpāda," and "madhyamā pratipat," and all four terms are to be taken as referring to the same thing, i.e., the indeterminate nature of reality. (This interpretation, of course, is what one might almost have predicted, given that Matilal took "x is śūnya" in the Madhyamaka to mean "x is logically indeterminate.")

The main problem with the interpretation, it seems to me, is that in the Buddhist tradition "prajñaptir upādāya" was reserved for terms that were taken to refer to *un*realities (e.g., the ātman). (Cf. the preceding citations from Edgerton.) If "prajñaptir upādāya" had meant something like logically indeterminate in the Buddhist tradition, then one would have to say that the terms "pudgala" and "ātman" also referred to logically inderminate entities. *But this was not the orthodox Buddhist view.* It was the view of the *heterodox* Pudgalavādins, who maintained that there was a self which was neither the same as nor different from the skandhas.

The Pudgalavādin view was rejected with something like abhorrence by the orthodox Buddhists, who held that the term "self" (attā, ātman) was a "prajñaptir upādāya," i.e., a "désignation métaphorique." The orthodox and unorthodox were in agreement that the self could be neither identical with nor different from the skandhas, but the two parties disagreed over what was to be concluded from this fact. The Pudgalavādins concluded that there is a reality (i.e., the ātman) which is logically indeterminate or inexpressible (avācya). The orthodox, on the other hand, seem to have taken the position that since there could not possibly be anything that *is* logically indeterminate, *there is no self.*

Note also that, *in the final analysis*, it only makes sense to say that a term like "self" or "chariot" is an upādāya-prajñapti if one believes that the things that serve as the basis of these expressions (i.e., the skandha-dharmas; the axle, chassis etc.) *are* real. If absolutely everything were prajñaptisat, then everything would be unreal, and there would be no basis for any designating expression (prajñapti) whatever. This, in fact, is what the Mādhyamikas maintained—but it is the nihilist position.

23. According to Ruegg (1981: 75)—if I understand him correctly—the Mādhyamikas (or at least Candrakīrti) believed that things originate in some inexplicable, indeterminate, antinomic or inconceivable fashion. I do not believe that this is the case. It is true, of course, that there are many passages in the Mādhyamika writings that state that things are (or arise) like magic (māyā), but in the Madhyamaka (as opposed to the Vijñānavāda), this assertion must be interpreted in the light of the additional claim that even this illusion does not exist. Furthermore, Nāgārjuna says explicitly in MMK 1.4 et seq. that 1) things do not arise in the four designated ways and 2) that there is no fifth way that things can arise—and not just that there is no *determinate* or *conceivable* way that they can arise.

24. Cf. MMK 15.8:

> If things were to exist in virtue of their own nature (prakṛtyā), then they could not become non-existent (nāstitā), for indeed nothing can change its own-nature.
>
> yady astitvaṃ prakṛtyā syān na bhaved asya nāstitā /
> prakṛter anyathābhāvo na hi jātūpapadyate // MMK 15.8 //

NOTES TO CHAPTER V: THE RED KINGS' DREAM AND BEYOND (I)

1. The interpretation of the Madhyamaka that I have attributed to Matilal is that the phenomenal world is real in a qualified sense and that the Absolute (nirvāṇa) is real in an unqualified sense. LI 27-28 is, perhaps, not quite as explicit on the second point as it is on the first, but there are other passages in Matilal's writings where the second point comes through more clearly. At LI 8, for example, Matilal attributes to Nāgārjuna the

view that "everything is empty or devoid of its own-nature *because* everything is 'dependently originating.'" It would seem to follow from this definition that nirvāṇa will have self nature (svabhāva) if it is *not* subject to dependent co-origination. As it turns out, this is a property that Matilal believed that nirvāṇa does have, as the following passage shows (NMD 156):

> The Absolute and the Phenomenal are not different. This world, when it is understood with reference to causal conditions and plurality, is called the Phenomenal or the 'concealing' (saṃvṛti) one. But, when it is understood without reference to such causal conditions and plurality, it is called Nirvāṇa, the ultimate.

2. Cf. Suzuki (1934) under $\sqrt{}$krīḍ for krīḍā-mṛgaḥ (animal kept for pleasure or toy animal).

3. At this point B. Nanjio has the following footnote: "The following three lines [of the Sanskrit] are incomplete. Tib. renders as a verse and a half, as follows: 'All things have no self-nature. And on examination of man's speech, even it does not exist. Like a flower, a dream, and a vision, on full examination neither one transmigrates nor enters eternal peace.'"

4. The claim that even mind or imagination is unreal is perhaps the most distinctive feature of the Mādhyamika philosophy. Laṅk. 2 kār. 146 is somewhat anomalous for this reason, for the Laṅkāvatāra tends to support the Vijñānavāda and Tathāgata-garbha view on this point rather than the Mādhyamika view. (The Laṅkāvatāra, in fact, is generally regarded as primarily a Tathāgata-garbha text.)

I mention this point because the Laṅkāvatāra must be handled with great care if one wants to use it (as Matilal did in LI 27-28) to throw light on *Nāgārjuna's* views (much less Śaṅkara's). As it turns out, Laṅk. 2 kār. 145-148 does fit the Mādhyamika philosophy, but in this respect it is a bit anomalous.

5. I have followed Suzuki (transl. 1978: 230, n. 2) in reading "kārakam" into Sagāth. 50b, but I have read it as "citta-caittā na kārakam" rather than "citta-caittānaṃ kārakam."

6. Cf. Laṅk. 62, l. 7-12 (Nanjio):

> Furthermore, Mahāmati, the Tathāgatas of the past, present and future teach that all dharmas are unoriginated (anutpanna). Why? Because they are mind only (svacitta-dṛśya), because they do not exist (abhāvāt), because they are not born of being or of non-being. Mahāmati, all things (sarva-dharmāḥ) are like the horns of a hare, horse, donkey or camel because they are imagined by the imagination of foolish, deluded people.

7. It is true, of course, that the Buddhist and Vedāntist māyāvādins of India sometimes distinguished between a true and a false saṃvṛti (cf. LI 27). But this was simply a distinction between a consensual and coherent illusion or dream and one that was private and incoherent. *Both* were held to be illusions.

8. Dharmakīrti, a later (nyāyānusārin) Vijñānavādin, drew this line of defense in a particularly succinct fashion in NB I.12,14, which declares that the "own characteristics" of things (svalakṣaṇas) are absolutely and indubitably real (paramārthasat). [NB 1.12: tasya viṣayaḥ svalakṣaṇam; NB 1.14: tad-eva paramārthasat.] The declaration that the svalakṣaṇas are paramārthasat was like a bomb tossed into the camp of the Mādhyamikas, for the view that nothing exists is rendered untenable if one can establish that something is actually *seen*. (This will be true even if the thing that is seen is only mental.)

Dharmakīrti hoped, presumably, that there were at least two things about the putative svalakṣaṇas that made them invulnerable to the Madhyamaka onslaught against the notion of existence. One was that the svalakṣaṇas, as properties of the impermanent dharmas, were held to be instantaneous (eka-kṣaṇika). This, prima facie, exempted them from the Mādhyamikas' strictures against the notion of changing but enduring substances (dravya, svabhāva). Second, the svalakṣaṇas were said to be directly apprehended in one's own, immediate experience. As such, there was some reason to hope that the svalakṣaṇas would prove to be immune to sceptical attack, e.g., the standard argument from illusions, hallucinations etc.

9. V. infra, pp. 256-257, for two passages from the Prajñā-pāramitā, which assert that the mental dharmas are void in the very same way that the physical (rūpa) dharmas were said to be void.

10. Cf. VV 30, where Nāgārjuna asserts that there is no perception of anything at all (yadi kiṃcid-upalabheyaṃ ... pratyakṣādibhir-arthais-tad-abhāvān-me..). VV 65-67 shows that Nāgārjuna believed that this was true even of purely mental objects or appearances, like mirages or magical appearances. Cf. also the nirmitaka of VV 27.

11. In speaking of the snake as a mental appearance in the person's mind, which is real as a mental phenomenon (though of course this mental phenomenon is not a snake), I have adopted the point of view of non-nihilistic or ontological idealism. The Mādhyamikas rejected this view. For them, appearance statements are true, even though there is nothing that makes them true—and this is just as true of mental statements and so-called mental phenomena as it is of non-mental statements and non-mental phenomena. According to the Mādhyamikas, the truth of appearance statements is purely conventional.

The Mādhyamika theory of perception (asat-khyāti-vāda) is explained in more detail later (v. infra, pp. 254-280). It will be argued there that even the asat-khyāti-vāda does not require or permit a *literal* or philosophical distinction between two different truths.

12. For more discussion on this point, v. supra, pp. 64-77.

13. My translation is from Poussin's French (1932-33: 23). Besides Poussin's incomplete translation (1907-11) of the MA(Bh), there are now two English translations of the MA. See C. W. Huntington, Jr. (1989) and P. Fenner (1990).

The passage from the Madhyamakāvatāra that I have cited is in all probability based on earlier canonical sources, e.g. MN iii, 40, p. 330: "The light of a lamp burns depending on the oil and the wick; it is neither in the one or the other, nor is it anything in itself; phenomena are, likewise, nothing in themselves. All things are unreal; they are deceptions; nibbāna is the only truth."

14. Cf. MMK 24.10:

> Without relying on the concealed truth of the everyday,
> the absolute truth (paramārtha) cannot be pointed out.
> Without resorting to the absolute truth, nirvāṇa cannot
> be attained.
>
> vyavahāram anāśritya paramārtho na deśyate /
> paramārtham anāgamya nirvāṇaṃ nādhigamyate //24.10//

15. Ruegg (1981: 44-45) has argued that a distinction must be drawn between pratītya-samutpāda taken extensionally and pratītya-samutpāda taken intensionally. The former, he says, includes "all conditioned factors originating in dependence ... whose nature is to be empty." This belongs to the saṃvṛti level. The latter, he says, concerns the "ultimate reality or truth of emptiness," which belongs to the paramārtha. The distinction between these two things, he says, is the distinction between the "dependently produced conditioned factors" (pratītyasamutpannā dharmāḥ), on the one hand, and "the fact (or truth) of dependent origination" (pratītyasamutpāda), on the other, which he also links with the nature or essence of dharmas (dharmatā). He draws a similar distinction between "śūnya," which he takes to be an epithet of all dharmas; "śūnyatva," which is the state or property of emptiness of all dharmas; and "śūnyatā," which "tends to be reserved for this fact or true state of affairs."

Ruegg invokes these distinctions, it seems to me, in order to explain the ambivalence in the Mādhyamika texts on the question of dependent origination. On the one hand, the process of origination and cessation is regarded as saṃsāric, involving as it does the conditioned factors of the world. On the other hand, dependent origination is linked in the Madhyamaka texts with soteriologically *approved* things like śūnyatā and quiescence (śānta, śivam).

It is doubtful, however, that the distinctions that Ruegg draws can be used to dispel the logical problems connected with the ambivalence in the Mādhyamika texts on this question. If it is true that things are impermanent, and if it is true that it is their very nature to be so, then invoking the distinction between a thing and the nature of that thing (dharmatā) will not help one to avoid the logical problem presented by texts which sometimes associate the law of dependent co-origination (pratītya-samutpāda) with the absolute reality (paramārtha). All that one is likely to gain by making this move is the following pair of assertions, which is also inconsistent:

(1) The essence of things (dharmatā, pratītya-samutpāda-tvam) is that they arise and perish depending on causes and conditions.

(2) The essence of things (dharmatā, pratītya-samutpāda-tvam) is that they do not arise and perish depending on their causes and conditions.

See Wood (1991: 56-58), where a similar problem is discussed in connection with the Triṃśikā, a Vijñānavādin text that seems to assert, inconsistently, that the mind is by nature (vijñaptimātratā) both mutable and immutable.

16. Although Nāgārjuna and the author of the AŚP are in agreement that *things* (*dharmas*) are unreal, they draw different conclusions from this contention, because the former holds that emptiness (śūnyatā) and non-self-naturedness (niḥsvabhāvatā) hold universally, while the latter does not.

17. There are, of course, Madhyamaka and other Mahāyānist passages which assert that the paramārtha is unchanging etc. because the dharmas are *devoid* of self-nature. But these passages lend no support to the NNI, precisely because these Mahāyānist passages link unchangeability in *this* sense with unorigination (anutpatti-vāda), emptiness (śūnyatā) and non-existence (asattva, abhāvatva). These passages, therefore, actually support the NI rather than the NNI, for what they show is that the only possible kind of unchangeability that the Mādhyamikas recognized was the unchangeability of nothingness or non-existence. Thus, the Mādhyamikas seem only to have

allowed that things are unchangeable in the sense in which one might say that space (ākāśa)—a mere nothingness or non-entity (prajñaptisat)—is unchanging.

Note that the *Vedāntists* (unlike the Mādhyamikas) never declared that things are (in reality) unchanging in the sense in which unreal entities (e.g., sons of barren women) are unchanging. The obvious explanation of this, of course, is that the Vedāntists did not do so because they *did* believe in an unchanging Absolute, whereas the Mādhyamikas did not.

18. The Vedāntist texts fight constantly against the tendency of language to presuppose a distinction between language (or thought) and the thing that language or thought is *about*. To avoid this problem, the Vedāntins sometimes used pure names or pure designations—e.g. "that" (tat)—in place of conceptual terms like being (sat, sattā). Even more radically, sounds or mantric words devoid of either sense *or* reference were invoked (e.g. Aum) for the purposes of meditation. With the mantra Aum, in particular, the Vedāntists seem to have reached the philosophical extremity referred to by Russell, i.e., that of uttering meaningless noises. However, the Vedāntists had their reasons for trying to subvert discursive language and discursive thought, for on their view reality is, in the final analysis, ineffable. (As it turns out, the Mādhyamika view was also ineffable, but for a different reason, for the Mādhyamikas held that *nothing* was real.)

19. Perhaps what Stcherbatsky had in mind here are passages like MMK 25.7-8, which deny that nirvāṇa is an abhāva. But such passages can hardly be construed as emphatic protests against the charge of nihilism. All that MMK 25.7-8 means is that nirvāṇa is not an abhāva in the sense of a non-existent *entity* (abhāva-padārtha)—and all that *this* shows is that the Mādhyamikas were *consistent* nihilists.

I believe that H. Narain (1963: 313) was therefore correct in saying: "... the Mādhyamikas themselves refer to Yogācāras and others as interpreting them nihilistically, without taking the least exception to this interpretation."

20. Cited from Poussin (1933: 30-31), "The Mādhyamikas and the Tathatā."

21. On the Sautrāntika conception of nirvāṇa as an abhāva, see note 9, p. 356 above.

22. Note the equation in BCA 9.33 between emptiness (śūnyatā) and the claim that nothing exists (kiṃcin-nāstīti)—or if not that, at least between the thought of emptiness (śūnyatā-vāsanā) and the thought that nothing exists.

There are many such passages in the Madhyamaka writings, where "śūnyatā" is taken to mean simply non-existence. This is, of course, the primary and direct meaning of the term in Sanskrit. All such passages lend support to the NI.

23. V. supra, pp. 150-151 for a discussion of D. Seyfort Ruegg's interpretation of this verse.

24. If this seems unduly dogmatic, stop and think for a moment of what your reaction might be if you were asked to buy a used car or a bridge that neither existed nor did not exist.

25. The NI has struck many as an implausible interpretation, but to be fair it needs to be compared with its available alternatives. The assertion that nothing exists may be strange, but it seems to me that it isn't nearly as strange as the view that things *both* exist and do not exist, or that things *neither* exist nor do not exist.

Saying that the world both exists and does not exist raises all of the problems involved in the nihilistic assertion and more, for it includes the assertion that nothing exists as a conjunct, and then proceeds to conjoin this assertion with the claim that the world does exist, which is a contradiction.

NOTES TO CHAPTER V: THE RED KING'S DREAM AND BEYOND (II)

26. Cf.: (1) Ālambana-parīkṣā 6ab: "That which is an internal, mental form appears as something external" (yad-antarjñeya-rūpaṃ tu bahirvad-avabhāsate). (2) Pramāṇa-viniścaya I.55b: "There is no difference between the color blue and the cognition of blue, because they are always found together" (sahopalambha-niyamād abhedo nīla-tad-dhiyoḥ). (3) Prajñākaramati's Pramāṇa-vārttika-bhāṣya III.327: "Experience

grasps itself and nothing else; perception and the thing perceived are equally nothing but that" (ātmā sa tasyānubhavaḥ sa ca nānyasya kasya cit / pratyakṣa-prativedyattvam-api tasya tad-ātmatā //).

27. Mahā-prajñā-pāramitā, tr. Xuan Zang, fasc. 532, ch. 29 (I). I have used E. Conze's translation in Conze et al. (1954: 157).

28. SSS p. 9 (Mādhyamika-matam), v. 6.

For a discussion of the authorship of the SSS, see B. N. K. Sarma (1930-31).

One point which is not discussed by Sarma but which may be important is the SSS's use of the term "catuṣkoṭi" (SSS, p. 10, v. 9). According to Ruegg (FPC 3), the term "catuṣkoṭi(kā)" is not found as such in either the MMK (c. 1-2nd century CE), Āryadeva's Catuḥ-śataka (c. 1-2nd century CE), or the MMKV (c. 7th century CE). The earliest extant text to use the term, apparently, is the Bodhi-caryāvatāra-pañjikā (9.2) of Prajñākaramati (fl. 1075). Even in the BCAP this term appears in connection with a quotation (FPC 59, n. 6), and this makes it difficult to date the introduction of the term exactly, but in any case the date of its introduction seems to have been rather late.

If the Buddhist term "catuṣkoṭi" is later than the date of Ādi Śaṅkara (c. 710 to 820 CE), then the SSS could not have been written by him, unless one were to suppose that the Buddhists adopted the term from the *non*-Buddhists, which seems unlikely. This may help eventually to throw some light on the dating of other important Indian texts as well. For example, the term "koṭyaś-catasra" is found in the work known as the Gauḍapādīya-kārikās or Āgama-śāstra (AŚP 84). The appearance of the term there may mean that this verse of the ĀŚ (and possibly others as well) are quite late. This would lend additional support to a number of historical theses which I have defended elsewhere (Wood 1990).

The foregoing line of reasoning is at least complicated by Acintyastava 23 (catuṣkoṭi-vinirmuktās tena dharmās tvayoditāḥ...), which Ruegg may not have taken into account. For some brief remarks on, and references to, the authenticity and dating of the Acintyastava (which are under dispute) see

Lindtner (1982: 121-127, esp. n. 149) and de Jong (1972a: 11-12).

29. There were Mahāyānists, like Śāntarakṣita and Prajñākaragupta, who attempted to combine elements from both the Madhayamaka and Vijñānavāda. Some of these philosophers were designated as Yogācāra-Svātantrika-Mādhyamikas (i.e., as Mādhyamikas who were influenced by Vijñānavādin ideas), or as Svātantrika-Mādhyamika-Yogācāras (i.e., as Vijñānavādins who were influenced by Mādhyamika ideas). The statement that the Vijñānavādins believed in the existence of the mind applies without qualification only to those philosophers, like Vasubandhu, Diṅnāga and Dharmakīrti, who embodied the Vijñānavāda in its pure form.

30. P. Unger (personal communication) has objected to the following argument in defense of strict nihilism on the grounds that there are other possibilities that it fails to consider, e.g., neutral monism. I doubt that this is the case, however, since the argument is based on the contention that the arguments for idealism and the arguments for strict materialism are *both* valid. *If* this is the case, then the arguments for idealism, for example, will exclude the possibility of neutral monism, since if idealism is true, there is nothing that is not wholly mental, including anything that might be called "neutrally monistic."

In the late 1970s and early 1980s, incidentally, Unger was a proponent of what he then called "nihilism," although he has recently told me that he never meant by this that *nothing* exists, but had in mind something like a Parmenidean monism.

It would seem somewhat misleading to call Parmenides a nihilist, and Unger now concedes that he was not sufficiently careful in his use of the term "nihilist." Nevertheless, there are some very interesting similarities between some of Unger's arguments for what he once called nihilism and the Mādhyamika dialectic—so much so, in fact, that I believe that it would be quite natural to draw a strictly nihilistic conclusion from his arguments. Unger has argued, for example (1979b), that the term "person" is logically inconsistent, and that there are therefore no people, just as there are no round squares. At the time he wrote this paper, Unger believed that this was true of *all* of our concepts.

If one accepts this much, then there would appear to be only four remaining possibilities: 1) there is something real, and logical inconsistency is simply an unavoidable feature of it; 2) there is something real, but it is beyond the reach of all concepts, consistent or inconsistent; 3) nothing at all exists; and 4) there must be other concepts that *are* logically consistent which correctly describe reality. Unger says now that he favored the last alternative, regarding the deconstruction of all our ordinary concepts as a kind of propaedeutic to the creation of a new language and metaphysics.

Unger and the Mādhyamikas part ways on this point. The Mādhyamikas did not believe that reality could be described by *any* set of consistent concepts; nor did they believe in a non-conceptualizable Absolute like the Vedāntic ātman/brahman; nor did they believe in an ineffable, logically anomalous reality. Hence the conclusion (which is amply supported by their own statements) that they were nihilists.

31. Reductive and eliminative materialism have been the two major versions of the materialist position on the mind-body problem in recent discussions. However, R. Rorty (1979: 117-120) has argued for a version of strict materialism which, according to him, is not an identity theory in *any* sense; he has, accordingly, disavowed the eliminativist position he had previously endorsed (1965).

In the sequel, I shall usually refer to the strict materialist position as "eliminativism." As I use this term, it designates the materialist viewpoint that mind, consciousness etc. do not exist in any form, either as substance, property, events etc. So far as I can tell, this position is close enough in spirit for our present purposes to the strict materialist position that Rorty has defended in his *Philosophy and the Mirror of Nature* and later writings, despite the fact that Rorty's more recent formulation of strict materialism attempts to finesse the question of what one is referring to when one speaks of pains, headaches etc., whereas mine does not.

For references and some discussion of the issues surrounding reductive, eliminative and "non-identity theory materialism," see Rorty (1979: 117-120).

32. Cf. G. A. Paul (1936), where the example of finding a fovea is contrasted with the case of finding a sense datum. One cannot read this early and influential paper in the analytic tradition without being struck by how similar Paul's position was to the Mādhyamikas' (at least on this particular point). This is one of a number of instances where the Mādhyamika philosophy appears to have anticipated a contemporary Western philosophical position by many centuries.

33. Cf. C. D. Broad (1923), who says (in connection with the bent-stick example):

> It is very hard to understand how we could seem to ourselves to see the property of bentness exhibited in a concrete instance, if in fact nothing was present to our minds that possessed that property.

Cited in Barnes (1976: 162).

34. At one point (p. 163) Barnes says about the hallucinatory dagger: "It is easy of course to object that an illusory dagger is not just nothing." He then proceeds to argue (unsuccessfully, I think) that we do not have to accept the sense data doctrine in order to avoid the conclusion that an hallucinatory dagger is an absolute nothing.

The Mādhyamikas would surely have objected to Barnes at this point. According to the Mādhyamikas, this is precisely what an hallucinatory dagger is, i.e., *nothing*. "Hallucinatory dagger" is only a figure of speech.

35. Cf. R. Rorty (1965) for what is now the classic application of this analogy to the mind-brain identity problem.

36. Cf. VV 30-51, where Nāgārjuna argues that there is nothing that can be perceived or known through perception or through any other pramāṇa (means of knowledge).

37. In a previous work (Wood 1990: 160) I said: "The reality of the phenomenal world cannot sensibly be denied." I am now somewhat less sure of this than I was when I wrote it. The denial of the phenomenal may be tenable philosophically, provided that one is prepared to follow the logic of the argument

to the very end. In this respect, nihilism may resemble solipsism.

BIBLIOGRAPHY

This bibliography is intended to be reasonably comprehensive, at least for the topics treated in the text. It includes references which are not actually cited in the text. References which are treated in this way do not necessarily reflect the views of the author.

ABBREVIATIONS OF JOURNALS, SERIES AND INSTITUTES

ABORI = Annals of the Bhandarkar Oriental Research Institute
AL = Adyar Library
AO = Acta Orientalia
APhQ = American Philosophical Quarterly
AS = Asiatische Studien
BB = Bibliotheca Buddhica
BBh = Bauddha Bhāratī
BEFEO = Bulletin de l'École française d'Extrême-Orient
BEHE = Bibliothèque de l'École des Hautes Études
BI = Bibliotheca Indica
BSO(A)S = Bulletin of the School of Oriental (and African) Studies
BST = Buddhist Sanskrit Texts
CJPh = Canadian Journal of Philosophy
ChSS = Chowkhamba Sanskrit Series
CZPh = Conceptus. Zeitschrift für Philosophie
EPh = Encyclopedia of Philosophy
ERE = Encyclopaedia of Religions and Ethics
GOS = Gaekwad's Oriental Series
HJAS = Harvard Journal of Asiatic Studies
HOS = Harvard Oriental Series
IHQ = Indian Historical Quarterly
IIJ = Indo-Iranian Journal
IS = Indiske Studier
ISPP = Indian Studies Past and Present
JAOS = Journal of the American Oriental Society
JGIS = Journal of the Greater India Society
JIBS = Journal of Indian and Buddhist Studies (=Indobukkyogaku Kenkyu)
JIES = Journal of Indo-European Studies
JIH = Journal of Indian History
JIPh = Journal of Indian Philosophy
JNCL = Journal of Non-Classical Logic
JOR = Journal of Oriental Research
JPh = Journal of Philosophy
JPhL = Journal of Philosophical Logic

JRAS = Journal of the Royal Asiatic Society
JSL = Journal of Symbolic Logic
JTU = Journal of the Taisho University
KPJRI = K. P. Jayaswal Research Institute
LA = Logique et analyse
LM = Le Muséon
MASB = Memoirs of the Asiatic Society of Bengal
MChB = Mélanges chinois et bouddhiques
NDJFL = Notre Dame Journal of Formal Logic
OI = Oriental Institute (Baroda)
OLZ = Orientalistische Literaturzeitung. Leipzig, 1898 ff.
PAS = Proceedings of the Aristotelian Society
PEFEO = Publications de l'École française d'Extrême-Orient
PTS = Pali Text Society
PhEW = Philosophy East and West
PhPhR = Philosophy and Phenomenological Research
PhR = Philosophical Review
PhS = Philosophical Studies
RCM = Revista Colombiana de Matématicas
RM = Review of Metaphysics
RPhR = Revue philosophique et religion de la France et de l'étranger
RO = Rocznik Orientalistyczny
SACPhMS = Society for Asian and Comparative Philosophy Monograph Series
SL = Studia Logica
SOR = Serie Orientale Roma
SPh = Studia Philosophica
StII = Studien zur Indologie und Iranistik
TSWS = Tibetan Sanskrit Works Series
VBhS = Visva-Bharati Studies
WZKM = Wiener Zeitschrift für die Kunde des Morgenlandes
WZKSOA = Wiener Zeitschrift für die Kunde Süd- und Ostasiens und Archiv für indische Philosophie

SANSKRIT AND PĀLI TEXTS

Abhidharmakośa

Abhidharmakośa with Vasubandhu's Bhāṣya and Yaśomitra's Sphuṭārthā Vyākhyā. Kośasthānas 1-8, 4 vols. Dvārikādāsa Śāstrī, ed. (1970-73). BBh. Vārāṇasī.

Abhidharmakośabhāṣya of Vasubandhu. P. Pradhan, ed. (1967). KPJRI 8. Patna.

Ālambanaparīkṣā of Diṅnāga. Tola, F. and C. Dragonetti, eds./trs. (1982). "Dignāga's Ālambanaparīkṣāvṛtti." JIPh 10: 105-134.

Aṅguttara-Nikāya. R. Morris et. al., eds. (1885-1910). Vols. I-VI. PTS. London.

Aṣṭasāhasrikāprajñāpāramitāsūtra

Aṣṭasāhasrikāprajñāpāramitā with Haribhadra's commentary called Āloka. P. L. Vaidya, ed. (1960). BST 4. Darbhanga.

Aṣṭasāhasrikāprajñāpāramitāsūtra. R. L. Mitra, ed. (1888). BI 110. Calcutta.

Bodhicaryāvatāra. The Bodhicaryāvatāra of Śāntideva with the commentary Pañjikā of Prajñākaramati. P. L. Vaidya, ed. (1960). BST 12. Darbhanga.

Daśabhūmikasūtra et Bodhisattvabhūmi, chapitres Vihāra et Bhūmi. J. Rahder, ed. (1926). Paris, Louvain.

Majjhima-Nikāya. Vol. 1: V. Trenckner. Vol. 2-3: R. Chalmers. Vol. 4, Index: C. A. F. Rhys Davids (1888-1925). PTS. London.

Mūlamadhyamakakārikāḥ (and Prasannapadā)

Madhyamakaśāstram of Nāgārjuna with the commentary Prasannapadā of Candrakīrti. Dvārikādāsa Śāstrī, ed. (1983). BBh. Vārāṇasī.

"Textcritical notes on the *Prasannapadā*." J. W. de Jong (1978). IIJ 20: 25-59; 217-252.

Mūlamadhyamakakārikāḥ. J. W. de Jong, ed. (1977). AL. Madras.

Mūlamadhyamakakārikās (Mādhyamikasūtras) de Nāgārjuna, avec la Prasannapadā commentaire de Candrakīrti. L. de La Vallée Poussin, ed. (1903-13). St.-Pétersbourg: BB IV.

Nyāyabindu. Dharmottarapradīpa of Paṇḍita Durveka Miśra, being a sub-commentary on Dharmottara's Nyāyabinduṭīkā, a commentary on Dharmakīrti's Nyāyabindu. D. Malvania, ed. (1971). TSWS 2. Patna. [First edition, 1955.]

Prajñāpāramitāhṛdayasūtra. In E. Conze (1967b), *Thirty years of Buddhist studies*: 145-167.

Pramāṇavārtikabhāṣyam (Vārtikālaṅkāraḥ) of Prajñākaragupta, being a commentary on Dharmakīrti's Pramāṇavārttikam. R. Sāṅkṛtyāyana, ed. (1953). TSWS 1. Patna.

Saddharmalaṅkāvatārasūtra

Saddharmalaṅkāvatārasūtram. P. L. Vaidya, ed. (1963). BST 3. Darbhanga.

Laṅkāvatāra Sūtra. B. Nanjio, ed. (1956). Kyōto: Otani Univ. Press.

Saṃyutta-Nikāya. L. Feer, ed. (1884-1904). 6 vols. PTS. London.

Saptaśatikāprajñāpāramitāsūtra

Saptaśatikāprajñāpāramitāsūtra. J. Masuda, ed. (1930). JTU. Vols. 6-7, part 2 (European section): 185-241.

Saptaśatikāprajñāpāramitāsūtra. Tucci, G., ed. (1923). Atti della R. Accademia Nazionale dei Lincei. Memorie della classe di scienze morali, storiche e filologiche. Serie V, vol. XVII: 115-139.

Sarvasiddhāntasaṅgraha. The Sarva-Siddhānta-Saṅgraha of Śaṅkarācārya. M. Raṅgācārya, ed./tr. (1909). Madras: Government Press.

Śikṣāsamuccayaḥ of Śāntideva. P. L. Vaidya, ed. (1961). BST 11. Darbhanga.

Viṃśatikā. In Vijñaptimātratāsiddhi. Deux traités de Vasubandhu: Vimśatikā et Triṃśikā. S. Lévi, ed. (1925). BEHE. Paris.

Vigrahavyāvartanī

Vigrahavyāvartanī. Chr. Lindtner, ed., in Lindnter (1982).

Vigrahavyāvartanī of Nāgārjuna. E. Johnston and A. Kunst, eds. (1948-1951). MChB 9: 99-152.

CONTEMPORARY WORKS

Abbagnano, N. (1972). "Psychologism." EPh.

Abhyankar, K. V. (1977). *A dictionary of Sanskrit grammar.*[2r] OI. Baroda.

Anderson, A. R. and N. D. Belnap, Jr. (1975). *Entailment: the logic of relevance and necessity.* Vol. 1. Princeton: Princeton Univ. Press.

Aung, S. Z. and C. A. F. Rhys Davids, trs. (1969). *Points of controversy (Kathā-vatthu).* London: PTS.

Austin, J. L. (1962a). *How to do things with words.* Cambridge, Mass.: Harvard Univ. Press.

Austin, J. L. (1962b). *Sense and sensibilia.* Oxford: Clarendon Press.

Bahm, A. J. (1957). "Does seven-fold predication equal four-cornered negation reversed?" PhEW 7: 127-130.

Bareau, A. (1955). *Les sectes bouddhiques du Petit Véhicule.* Saigon: PEFEO.

Barnes, W. H. F. (1944-45). "The myth of sense-data." PAS 45. Also in R. J. Swartz, ed. (1976): 138-167.

Belnap Jr., N. D. (1977). "A useful four-valued logic." In J. M. Dunn and G. Epstein, eds. (1977):

Belnap Jr., N. D. (1976). "How a computer should think." In G. Ryle, ed. (1976): 30-56.

Belnap, N. D. Jr. and J. M. Dunn (1981). "Entailment and the disjunctive syllogism." In Fløistad and von Wright, eds. (1981): 337-366.

Bencivenga, E. (1986). "Free logics." In D. Gabbay and F. Guenthner, eds. (1986): 373-426.

Bhattacharya, K., tr. (1978). *The dialectical method of Nāgārjuna (Vigrahavyāvartanī).* [Includes edition of E. Johnston and A. Kunst (1948-1951).]

Bhattacharya, K. (1977). "On the relationship between the Vigrahavyāvartanī and the Nyāyasūtra-s." JIES 5: 265-273.

Bhattacharya, V., ed./tr. (1943). *The Āgamaśāstra of Gauḍapāda.* Calcutta: Univ. of Calcutta.

Berkeley, G. (1948). *Works*, ed. T. Gessup and A. Luce. London. [Includes *Three dialogues between Hylas and Philonous* and *A treatise concerning the principles of human knowledge*.]

Borst, C. V., ed. (1970). *The mind-brain identity theory.* New York: St. Martin's Press.

Broad, C. D. (1923). *Scientific thought.* London: Routledge & Kegan Paul.

Burgess, J. P. (1983). "Common sense and 'relevance.'" NDJFL 24: 41-53.

Burgess, J. P. (1981). "Relevance: a fallacy?" NDJFL 22: 97-104.

Burnouf, E. (1844). *Introduction à l'histoire du Buddhisme indien.* Paris: Imprimerie Royale.

Cardona, G. (1967). "Negations in Pāṇinian rules." Language 43 (1): 34-56.

Chari, C. T. K. (1955). "Quantum physics and East-West rapprochement." PhEW 5: 61-67.

Chari, C. T. K. (1954). "On the dialectical affinities between East and West, Part II." PhEW 3/4: 321-336.

Church, A. (1950). "On Carnap's analysis of statements of assertion and belief." Analysis 10: 97-99.

Church, A. (1946). Review of: A. Koyré, *The liar.* JSL 11: 131.

Conze, E. (1980). "Contradictions in Buddhist thought." In *Indianisme et bouddhisme: mélanges offerts à Mgr Étienne Lamotte.* Louvain: Université Catholique de Louvain.

Conze, E., tr. (1973a). *The short Prajñāpāramitā texts.* London: Luzac & Company.

Conze, E., tr. (1973b). *The perfection of wisdom in eight thousand lines & its verse summary.* San Francisco: Four Seasons.

Conze, E. (1967a). *Buddhist thought in India.* Ann Arbor: Univ. of Michigan Press.

Conze, E. (1967b). *Thirty years of Buddhist studies.*

Conze, E. et al., trs. (1954). *Buddhist texts through the ages.* New York: Harper & Row.

Conze, E. (1953). "The ontology of the Prajñāpāramitā." PhEW 3(2): 117-129.

Copeland, B. J. (1986). "What is a semantics for classical negation?" Mind 95: 478-490.

Copeland, B. J. (1979). "On when a semantics is not a semantics: some reasons for disliking the Routley-Meyer semantics for relevance logic." JPhL 8: 399-413.

Cousins, L. et. al., eds. (1974). *Buddhist studies in honour of I. B. Horner*. Dordrecht: D. Reidel.

Cowell, E. B. and A. E. Gough, trs. (1961). *The Sarva-darśana-saṃgraha, by Madhava Āchārya*. ChSS 10. Varanasi. [First published 1882.]

Curry, H. B. (1976). *Foundations of mathematical logic*. New York: Dover. [Ch. 6: "Negation."]

Van Dalen, D. (1986). "Intuitionistic logic." In D. Gabbay and F. Guenthner, eds. (1986): 225-339.

Dalla Chiara, M. L. (1986). "Quantum logic." In D. Gabbay and F. Guenthner, eds. (1986): 427-469.

Dasgupta, S. N. (1962). *Indian idealism*. Cambridge, UK: Cambridge Univ. Press. [First published, 1933.]

Dummett, M. (1978). *Truth and other enigmas*. London: Duckworth.

Dummett, M. (1977). *Elements of intuitionism*. Oxford: Clarendon.

Dummett, M. (1973a). "Philosophical basis of intuitionist logic." In Dummett (1978): 215-247.

Dummett, M. (1959). "Truth." PAS 59: 141-162. In Dummett (1978): 1-24.

Dunn, J. M. (1986). "Relevance logic and entailment." In D. Gabbay and F. Guenthner, eds. (1986): 117-224.

Dunn, J. M. (1976). "Intuitive semantics for first degree entailments and coupled trees." PhS 29: 149-168.

Dunn, J. M. and G. Epstein, eds. (1977). *Modern uses of multiple-valued logic*. Dordrecht: D. Reidel.

Eckel, M. D. (1985). "Bhāvaviveka's critique of Yogācāra philosophy in chapter XXV of the Prajñāpradīpa." In Chr. Lindtner, ed. (1985): 25-75.

Eckel, M. D. (1980). *A question of nihilism. Bhāvaviveka's response to the fundamental questions of Mādhyamika philosophy*. Unpubl. diss., Harvard Univ.

Edgerton, F. (1953). *Buddhist hybrid Sanskrit grammar and dictionary*. Vol. II: Dictionary. New Haven: Yale Univ. Press.

Edgerton, F. (1929). *The Mīmāṅsā nyāya prakāśa*. New Haven: Yale Univ. Press.

Edwards, P., ed. (1972). *Encyclopedia of philosophy*. New York: Macmillan.

Evans, R. D. and B. K. Matilal, eds. (1986). *Buddhist logic and epistemology*. Dordrecht: D. Reidel.

Fenner, P. (1990). *The ontology of the Middle Way*. Dordrecht: Kluwer.

Feyerabend, P. (1963). "Materialism and the mind-body problem." RM 17. Also in Borst (1970).

Fløistad, G. and G. H. von Wright, eds. (1981). *Contemporary philosophy: a new survey*. Vol. 1. The Hague: Nijhoff.

Van Fraassen, B. C. (1966). "Singular terms, truth-value gaps, and free logics." JPh 63 (7): 481-495.

Frauwallner, E. (1973). *History of Indian philosophy*. Delhi: Motilal Banarsidass. Vol. 1-2. Translation by V. M. Bedekar of *Geschichte der indischen Philosophie* (1953). Vol. 1-2. Salzburg: O. Müller.

Frege, G. (1919). "Negation." In P. T. Geach and M. Black, eds. (1952): 117-135.

French, P. A., T. E. Uehling, Jr., and H. K. Wettstein, eds. (1980). *Studies in epistemology*. Midwest Studies in Philosophy: Vol. 5. Minneapolis: Univ. of Minnesota Press.

French, P. A., T. E. Uehling, Jr., and H. K. Wettstein, eds. (1979). *Studies in metaphysics*. Midwest Studies in Philosophy: Vol. 4. Minneapolis: Univ. of Minnesota Press.

Gabbay, D. and J. M. Moravcsik (1978). "Negation and denial." In F. Guenthner and C. Rohrer, eds. (1978): 251-265.

Gabbay, D. and F. Guenthner, eds. (1986). *Handbook of philosophical logic*. Vol 3: *Alternatives in classical logic*. Dordrecht: Reidel.

Galloway, B. (1989). "Some logical issues in Madhyamaka thought." JIPh 17: 1-35.

Geach, P. T. and M. Black, eds. (1952). *Translations from the philosophical writings of Gottlob Frege*. Oxford: Blackwell.

Grice, H. P. (1989). *Studies in the way of words*. Cambridge, Mass.: Harvard Univ. Press.

Guenthner, F. and C. Rohrer, eds. (1978). *Studies in formal semantics: intensionality, temporality, negation.* Amsterdam: North-Holland.

Hastings, J., ed. (1909ff). *Encyclopaedia of religion and ethics.*

Hazen, A. (1987). "Contra Buridanum." CJPh 17: 875-880.

Heath, P. (1974). *The philosopher's Alice: Alice's adventures in wonderland & Through the looking-glass, by Lewis Carroll.* New York: St. Martin's Press.

Herzberger, H. G. (1975). "Double negation in Buddhist logic." JIPh 3: 3-16.

Heyting, A. (1971). *Intuitionism: an introduction.* Amsterdam: North-Holland.

Hirst, R. J. (1972). "Phenomenalism." EPh. New York: Macmillan.

Horn, L. R. (1989). *A natural history of negation.* Chicago: Univ. of Chicago Press.

Hughes, G. E., tr. (1982). *John Buridan on self-reference: chapter eight of Buridan's Sophismata.* Cambridge, UK: Cambridge Univ. Press.

Huntington, C. W., Jr. (1989). *The emptiness of emptiness.* Honolulu: Univ. of Hawaii Press.

Huntington, C. W., Jr. (1983). "The system of the two truths in the Prasannapadā and the Madhyamakāvatāra: a study in Mādhyamika soteriology." JIPh 11: 77-106.

Jayatilleke, K. N. (1967). "The logic of four alternatives." PhEW: 17: 69-83.

Jayatilleke, K. N. (1963). *Early Buddhist theory of knowledge*. London: George Allen & Unwin.

de Jong, J. W. (1987). *A brief history of Buddhist studies in Europe and America*.[2r] Indo-Buddhica 33. Delhi: Sri Satguru Publications.

de Jong, J. W. (1972a). "Emptiness." JIPh 2: 7-15.

de Jong, J. W. (1972b). "The problem of the absolute in the Madhyamaka school." JIPh 2: 1-6. [Engl. tr. of "Le problème de l'absolu dans l'école Madhyamaka," RPhR 1950, pp. 322-327.]

de Jong, J. W. (1949). *Cinq chapitres de la Prasannapadā*. Leiden: E. J. Brill.

Kalupahana, D. (1986). *Nāgārjuna: the philosophy of the Middle Way*. Albany: State Univ. of New York.

Kajiyama, Y. (1973). "Three kinds of affirmation and two kinds of negation in Buddhist philosophy." WZKSO 17: 161-175.

Kawamura, L. S. and K. Scott, eds. (1977). *Buddhist thought and Asian civilization: essays in honor of Herbert V. Guenther*. Emeryville, Cal.: Dharma.

Kristeva, J. (1969). *Σημειωτική: recherches pour une sémanalyse*. Paris: Éditions du Seuil.

Kunst, A. (1957). "The concept of the principle of the excluded middle in Buddhism." RO 21: 141-47.

Lamotte, Ét. (1965). "Notice sur Louis de La Vallée Poussin." Académie royale du Belgique—Annuaire pour 1965: 145-168.

La Vallée Poussin, L. de (1938). "Buddhica." HJAS 3: 137-160.

La Vallée Poussin, L. de (1936-37). "Documents d'Abhidharma: les deux, les quatre, les trois vérités. Extraits de la Vibhāṣā et du Kośa de Saṃghabhadra." MChB 5: 159-187.

La Vallée Poussin, L. de (1933). "The Mādhyamikas and the tathatā." IHQ 9 (1): 30-31.

La Vallée Poussin, L. de (1932-33). "Réflexions sur le madhyamaka." MChB 2: 1-146.

La Vallée Poussin, L. de (1931-32). "Le nirvāṇa d'après Āryadeva." MChB 1: 127-136.

La Vallée Poussin, L. de (1928-48). *Vijñaptimātratāsiddhi. La Siddhi de Hiuan-tsang.* 3 vols. Paris.

La Vallée Poussin, L. de (1917, ff). "Madhyamaka," "Nihilism (Buddhist)," "Nirvāṇa," "Philosophy (Buddhist)." ERE.

La Vallée Poussin, L. de (1910). "Vedanta and Buddhism." JRAS: 129-40.

La Vallée Poussin, L. de, tr. (1907-11). Madhyamakāvatāra: introduction au Traité du Milieu de l'Ācārya Candrakīrti, avec le commentaire de l'auteur. LM (1907) 8: 249-317; (1910) 11: 271-358; (1911) 12: 236-328.

Leblanc, H., ed. (1973). *Truth, syntax and modality.* Amsterdam: North-Holland.

Lewis, D. K. (1988). "Relevant implication." Theoria 54 (3): 162-174.

Lewis, D. K. (1982). "Logic for equivocators." Noûs 16: 431-441.

Lindtner, Chr. (1986). "Bhavya's critique of Yogācāra in the *Madhyamakaratnapradīpa*, chapter IV." In R. D. Evans and B. K. Matilal, eds. (1986): 239-263.

Lindtner, Chr., ed. (1985). *Miscellanea Buddhica*. IS V. Copenhagen: Akademisk Forlag.

Lindtner, Chr. (1982). *Nagarjuniana*. IS IV. Copenhagen: Akademisk Forlag.

Lindtner, Chr. (1981). "Buddhapālita on emptiness [Buddhapālita-mūlamadhyamaka-vṛtti XVIII]." IIJ 23: 187-217.

Linsky, L. (1952). *Semantics and the philosophy of language*. Urbana: Univ. of Illinois Press.

Łukasiewicz, J. (1971). "On the principle of contradiction in Aristotle." RM 24 (3): 485-509.

Macdonald, G. F., ed. (1979). *Perception and identity*. Ithaca: Cornell Univ. Press.

McGuiness, B. F. (1966). "The mysticism of the *Tractatus*." PhR 75: 305-328.

Mäll, L. (1968). "Une approche possible du Śūnyavāda." Tel Quel 32: 54-62.

Marconi, D. (1981). "Types of non-Scotian logic." LA 95-96: 407-414.

Martin, R. L., ed. (1984). *Recent essays on truth and the liar paradox*. Oxford: Clarendon.

Martin, R. L., ed. (1970). *The paradox of the liar*. New Haven: Yale Univ. Press.

Matilal, B. K. (1986). *Perception: an essay on classical Indian theories of knowledge*. Oxford: Clarendon.

Matilal, B. K. (1977). *The logical illumination of Indian mysticism*. Oxford: Clarendon.

Matilal, B. K. (1973). "A critique of the Mādhyamika position." In L. Cousins et. al., eds. (1974): 139-169.

Matilal, B. K. (1971). *Epistemology, logic and grammar in Indian philosophical analysis*. The Hague: Mouton.

Matilal, B. K. (1968). *The Navya-nyāya doctrine of negation*. HOS 46. Cambridge, Mass.: Harvard Univ. Press.

May, J., tr. (1959). *Candrakīrti Prasannapadā Madhyamakavṛtti*. Paris: Adrien-Maisonneuve.

May, J. (1958). "La philosophie bouddhique de la vacuité." SPh (Separate Vol.) 18: 123-37.

Meyer, R. K. (1979). "A Boolean-valued semantics for R." Research Paper No. 4, Research School of Social Sciences, Australian National Univ., Canberra.

Meyer, R. K. (1978). "Why I am not a relevantist." Research papers of the Logic Group No. 1, Research School of Social Sciences, Australian National Univ., Canberra.

Meyer, R. K. (1974). "New axiomatics for relevant logics I." JPhL 3: 53-86.

Meyer, R. K. (1973). "Intuitionism, entailment, negation." In H. Leblanc, ed. (1973): 168-198.

Meyer, R. K. and E. P Martin (1986). "Logic on the Australian plan." JPhL 15: 305-332.

Meyer, R. K. and R. Routley (1973). "Classical relevant logic, II." SL 33: 183-194.

Meyer, R. K. and R. Routley (1972a). "Classical relevant logic, I." SL 32: 51-68.

Meyer, R. K. and R. Routley (1972b). "Algebraic analysis of entailment." LA 15: 407-428.

Murti, T. R. V. (1973). "Saṃvṛti and paramārtha in Mādhyamika and Advaita Vedānta." In M. Sprung, ed. (1973): 9-26.

Murti, T. R. V. (1955). *The central philosophy of Buddhism*. London: George Allen and Unwin, Ltd.

Narain, H. (1963). "Śūnyavāda: a reinterpretation." PhEW 13: 311-338.

Norman, J. and R. Sylvan, eds. (1989). *Directions in relevant logic*. Dordrecht: Kluwer.

Obermiller, E. (1934). "The term śūnyatā and its different interpretations, based chiefly on Tibetan sources." JGIS I: 105-117.

Oetke, C. (1992). "Pragmatic implicatures and text-interpretation (the alleged logical error of the negation of the antecedent in the Mūlamadhyamakakārikās). StII 16/17: 185-233.

Oetke, C. (1991). "Remarks on the interpretation of Nāgārjuna's philosophy." JIP 19: 315-323.

Oetke, C. (1990). "On some non-formal aspects of the proofs of the Madhyamakakārikās." In *Earliest Buddhism and Madhyamaka* (Leiden, 1990), pp. 91-109.

Oetke, C. (1989). "Rationalismus und Mystik in der Philosophie Nāgārjunas." StII (15): 1-40.

Oetke, C. (1988). "Die metaphysische Lehre Nāgārjunas." CZPh XXII, Nr. 56: 47-64.

Oetke, C. (1988). *"Ich" und das Ich: Analytische Untersuchungen zur buddhistisch-brahmanischen Ātmankontroverse.* Wiesbaden: Franz Steiner.

Parsons, T. (1984). "Assertion, denial, and the liar paradox." JPhL: 13: 137-152.

Paul, G. A. (1936). "Is there a problem about sense-data?" PAS: 15. Also in R. J. Swartz, ed. (1976): 271-287.

Pind, O. H. (1983). "Emptiness—towards a semiotic determination of emptiness in Mādhyamika discourse, I." In E. Steinkellner and H. Tauscher, eds. (1983): 170-204.

Priest, G. (1989). "Boolean negation and all that." JPhL 19 (2): 201-215.

Priest, G. (1987). *In contradiction: a study of the transconsistent.* Dordrecht: Nijhoff.

Priest, G. (1979). "The logic of paradox." JPhL 8: 219-241.

Priest, G. and R. Routley, eds. (1988). *Paraconsistent logic.* Munich: Philosophia Verlag.

Priest, G. and R. Routley (1983). "On paraconsistency." Research Papers of the Logic Group, No. 13, Research School of Social Sciences, Australian National Univ., Canberra.

Priest, G. and R. Routley (1982). "Lessons from pseudo-Scotus." PhS 42: 189-199.

Prior, A. N. (1976). *Papers in logic and ethics*, ed. P. T. Geach & A. J. Kenny. London: Duckworth. [Contains "Epimenides the Cretan" (pp. 70-77) and "Some problems of self-reference in John Buridan" (pp. 130-146).]

Prior, A. N. (1969). "The possibly-true and the possible." Mind 78: 481-492.

Prior, A. N. (1961). "On a family of paradoxes." NDJFL 2: 16-32.

Quine, W. V. (1982). *Methods of logic.* Fourth edition. Cambridge, Mass.

Raju, P. T. (1954). "The principle of four-cornered negation in Indian philosophy." RM 7: 694-713.

Renou, L. (1942). *Terminologie grammaticale du sanskrit.* Paris: Champion.

Robinson, R. H. (1972). "Some methodological approaches to the unexplained points." PhEW 22: 309-323.

Robinson, R. H. (1969). Review of: K. N. Jayatilleke, *Early Buddhist theory of knowledge.* PhEW 19: 69-81.

Robinson, R. H. (1967). *Early Mādhyamika in India and China.* Madison: Univ. of Wisconsin Press.

Robinson, R. H. (1957). "Some logical aspects of Nāgārjuna's system." PhEW 6: 291-308.

Rorty, R. (1979). *Philosophy and the mirror of nature.* Princeton: Princeton Univ. Press.

Rorty, R. (1965). "Mind-body identity, privacy and categories." RM 19. In C. V. Borst, ed. (1970).

Routley, R. and R. K. Meyer (1973). "The semantics of entailment I." In H. Leblanc, ed. (1973): 199-243.

Routley, R., R. K. Meyer, et al. (1983). *Relevant logics and their rivals (I)*. Atascadero, Cal.: Ridgeview.

Routley, R. and V. (1985). "Negation and contradiction." RCM 19: 201-230.

Routley, R. and V. (1972). "Semantics of first degree entailment." Noûs 6: 335-359.

Routley, R., V. Routley, R. K. Meyer, and E. P. Martin (1982). "On the philosophical bases of relevant logic semantics." JNCL 1: 71-102.

Ruegg, D. Seyfort (1986). "Does the Mādhyamika have a thesis and philosophical position?" In R. D. Evans and B. K. Matilal, eds. (1986): 229-237.

Ruegg, D. Seyfort (1983). "On the thesis and assertion in the Madhyamaka / dBu ma." In E. Steinkellner and H. Tauschner, eds. (1983): 205-241.

Ruegg, D. Seyfort (1981). *The literature of the Madhyamaka school of philosophy in India*. Wiesbaden: Harrassowitz.

Ruegg, D. Seyfort (1977). "The uses of the four positions of the catuṣkoṭi and the problem of the description of reality in Mahāyāna Buddhism." JIPh 5: 1-171.

Ruegg, D. Seyfort (1971). "On the knowability and expressibility of absolute reality in Buddhism." JIBS 20 (1): 1-7.

Ruegg, D. Seyfort (1969). *La théorie du tathāgatagarbha et du gotra*. PEFEO 70. Paris: Adrien-Maisonneuve.

Russell, B. (1905). "On denoting." Mind 16: 479-493.

Ryle, G., ed. (1976). *Contemporary aspects of philosophy.* London: Oriel.

Sarma, B. N. K. (1930-31). "A note on the authorship of the Sarvasiddhānta Saṃgraha." ABORI 12: 81-83.

Schayer, St. (1935). "Das mahāyānistische Absolutum nach der Lehre der Mādhyamikas." OLZ: 401-415.

Schayer, St. (1931). *Ausgewählte Kapitel aus der Prasannapadā.* Polska Akademja Umiejetności, No. 14. Kraków.

Scott, T. K., tr. (1966). *John Buridan: Sophisms on Meaning and Truth [by] John Buridan.* New York: Appleton-Century-Crofts.

Searle, J. R. (1969). *Speech acts.* Cambridge, UK: Cambridge Univ. Press.

Searle, J. R. and D. Vanderveken (1985). *Foundations of illocutionary logic.* Cambridge, UK: Cambridge Univ. Press.

Sperber, D. and D. Wilson (1986). *Relevance: communication and cognition.* Cambridge: Harvard Univ. Press.

Sprung, M., tr. (1979). *Lucid exposition of the Middle Way: the essential chapters from the Prasannapadā of Candrakīrti.* Boulder: Prajñā Press.

Sprung, M. (1977). "Non-cognitive language in Mādhyamika Buddhism." In L. S. Kawamura and K. Scott, eds. (1977): 241-253.

Sprung, M., ed. (1973). *The problem of two truths in Buddhism and Vedānta.* Dordrecht: D. Reidel.

Staal, J. F. (1988). *Universals: studies in Indian logic and linguistics*. Chicago: Univ. of Chicago Press.

Staal, J. F. (1975). *Exploring mysticism*. Berkeley: Univ. of California Press.

Staal, J. F. (1962). "Negation and the law of contradiction in Indian thought." BSOAS 25: 52-71. [Also in Staal (1988: 109-128).]

Stcherbatsky, Th. (1977). *The conception of Buddhist nirvāṇa*.[2r] Delhi: Motilal Banarsidass. [First published, Leningrad 1927.]

Stcherbatsky, Th. (1971). *Madhyānta-vibhaṅga (I): discourse on discrimination between middle and extremes*." ISPP 12: 153-311; 345-407. [First published BB 30 (1936).]

Stcherbatksy, Th. (1934). "Die drei Richtungen in der Philosophie des Buddhismus." RO 10: 1-37.

Steinkellner, E. and H. Tauscher, eds. (1983). *Contributions on Tibetan Buddhist religion and philosophy*. Wiener Studien zur Tibetologie und Buddhismuskunde, Heft 11. Wien: Arbeitskreis für Tibetische und Buddhistische Studien, Universität Wien.

Strawson, P. F. (1950). "On referring." Mind 59: 320-344.

Streng, F. (1967). *Emptiness: a study in religious meaning*. Nashville: Abingdon Press.

Suzuki, D. T. (1934). *An index to the Lankavatara Sutra (Nanjio Edition)*.[2r] Kyōto.

Swartz, R. J., ed. (1976). *Perceiving, sensing, and knowing*. Berkeley: Univ. of California Press.

Takakusu, J., tr. (1966). *A record of the Buddhist religion as practised in India and the Malay Archipelago (A.D. 671-695), by I-Tsing*. Delhi: Munshiram Manoharlal.

Tarski, A. (1944). "The semantic conception of truth and the foundations of mathematics." PhPhR 4. In L. Linsky, ed. (1952): 13-47.

Tillemans, T. J. F. (1989). "Formal and semantic aspects of Tibetan Buddhist debate logic." JIPh 17: 265-297.

Tola, F. and C. Dragonetti (1981). "Nāgārjuna's conception of voidness (śūnyatā)." JIPh 9: 273-282.

Tuck, A. P. (1990). *Comparative philosophy and the philosophy of scholarship: on the Western interpretation of Nāgārjuna*. New York: Oxford Univ. Press.

Tuxen, P. (1937). "In what sense can we call the teachings of Nāgārjuna negativism?" JOR 11: 231-242.

Unger, P. (1980a). "The problem of the many." In P. A. French, T. E. Uehling, Jr., and H. K. Wettstein, eds. (1980): 411-468.

Unger, P. (1980b). "Skepticism and nihilism." Noûs 14: 517-545.

Unger, P. (1979a). "I do not exist." In G. F. Macdonald, ed. (1979).

Unger. P. (1979b). "Why there are no people." In P. A. French, T. E. Uehling, Jr., and H. K. Wettstein, eds. (1979): 179-222.

Unger, P. (1979c). "There are no ordinary things." Synthèse 41 (2): 117-154.

Venkata Ramanan, K. (1966). *Nāgārjuna's philosophy as presented in the Mahā-prajñāpāramitā-śāstra.* Rutland, Vermont: Charles E. Tuttle.

Warder, A. K. (1973). "Is Nāgārjuna a Mahāyānist?" In M. Sprung, ed. (1973): 78-88.

Warren, H. C. (1972). *Buddhism in translations.* New York: Atheneum.

Wayman, A. (1969). "Contributions to the Mādhyamika school of Buddhism." JAOS 89: 141-152.

Wayman, A. (1977). "Who understands the four alternatives of the Buddhist texts?" PhEW 27: 3-21.

Wood, T. E. (1991). *Mind only: a philosophical and doctrinal analysis of the Vijñānavāda.* SACPhMS 9. Honolulu: Univ. of Hawaii Press.

Wood, T. E. (1990). *The Māṇḍūkya Upaniṣad and the Āgama Śāstra: an investigation into the meaning of the Vedānta.* SACPhMS 8. Honolulu: Univ. of Hawaii Press.

Zemach, E. (1964). "Wittgenstein's philosophy of the mystical." RM 18: 38-57.

INDEX

ABOUT THE AUTHOR

Thomas Wood received his B.A. and Ph.D. in philosophy from the University of California at Berkeley. He has taught Eastern and Western philosophy at the California State University at Fresno and the State University of New York at New Paltz. He is presently an Adjunct Professor at the California Institute of Integral Studies in San Francisco, where he teaches comparative philosophy and religion. He is the author of two other books in Indian philosophy, *The Māṇḍūkya Upaniṣad and the Āgama Śāstra: An Investigation into the Meaning of the Vedānta* (1990) and *Mind Only: A Philosophical and Doctrinal Analysis of the Vijñānavāda* (1991).

SOCIETY FOR ASIAN AND COMPARATIVE PHILOSOPHY
MONOGRAPH SERIES
Henry Rosemont, Jr., Editor

No. 1 *The Sage and Society: The Life and Thought of Ho Hsin-Yin,* by Ronald Dimberg, 1974

No. 2 *Studies in Comparative Aesthetics,* by Eliot Deutsch, 1975

No. 3 *Centrality and Commonality: An Essay on* Chung-Yung, by Tu Wei-Ming, 1976 (out of print)

No. 4 *Discourse on the Natural Theology of the Chinese,* by Gottfried W. Leibniz, translated with an introduction, notes, and commentary by Henry Rosemont, Jr., and Daniel J. Cook, 1977 (out of print)

No. 5 *The Logic of Gotama,* by Kisor Kumar Chakrabarti, 1978 (out of print)

No. 6 *Commentary on the* Lao Tzu *by Wang Pi,* translated by Ariane Rump, introduction by Wing-tsit Chan, 1979

No. 7 *Han Fei Tzu's Political Theory,* by Wang Hsiao-po and Leo S. Chang, 1986

No. 8 *The Māṇḍūkya Upaniṣad and the Agama Śāstra: An Investigation into the Meaning of the Vedānta,* by Thomas E. Wood, 1990

No. 9 *Mind Only: A Philosophical and Doctrinal Analysis of the Vijñānavāda,* by Thomas E. Wood, 1991

No. 10 *Accomplishing the Accomplished: The* Vedas *as a Source of Valid Knowledge in Śaṅkara,* by Anantanand Rambachan, 1991

No. 11 *Nāgārjunian Disputations: A Philosophical Journey through an Indian Looking-Glass,* by Thomas E. Wood, 1994

Title orders should be directed to the University of Hawaii Press, 2840 Kolowalu Street, Honolulu, Hawaii, 96822. Manuscripts should be directed to Professor Henry Rosemont, Jr., Department of Philosophy, St. Mary's College, St. Mary's City, Maryland 20686.